DRIVEN BY DREAMS

*From the Mountains of Colorado to
the Mysteries of Papua New Guinea*

Bill Briton

DRIVEN BY DREAMS

*From the Mountains of Colorado to
the Mysteries of Papua New Guinea*

BILL BRUTON

Wokabaut Publishing, Westminster, Colorado 80030

DRIVEN BY DREAMS

*From the Mountains of Colorado to
the Mysteries of Papua New Guinea*

BY BILL BRUTON

FIRST EDITION
Copyright 2007 © Bill Bruton

Printed in the United States of America
ISBN -13: 978-0-9791704-0-9
ISBN-10: 0-9791704-0-0
Library of Congress Control Number: 2007922228

Wokabaut Publishing
Westminster, Colorado 80030

Driven by Dreams *is dedicated to my lady,*

Sandia, to our children, grandchildren,

and their children, to both our fathers, and

especially to both our mothers, who birthed

us, raised us, and taught us to love life.

TABLE OF CONTENTS

Acknowledgments

So great is my debt to my lady, Sandia, who accepted me as I was, and loved me for it—there is no story, or spirit, without her. To all our children, and grandchildren, they continue to fill my heart and give my life purpose—to live an example for them. To the people of Papua New Guinea, in particular, my coworkers and so many others that offered their hands in friendship, I extend my utmost gratitude for letting me immerse myself in the culture of your remarkable "Land of the Unexpected." This list has to include Jim and Mary Ann Wright, for the opportunity, the late George Hook, for getting things done, Frank Faulkner, for his insights, Ray West, for his patience and accounting procedures in life, Robert Jacobsen, for his hospitality, Rob Coleman, for his laughter, the Leahy family, for all their teachings, Laurel Appleton and Sally Wallace, our Peace Corps buddies, for being our close wontoks, Dick Himes, my friend, for sharing some of it with me, and last, but certainly not least, my men, for all their hard work, acceptance, and enlightenment. To all our many friends, throughout the world, who helped, your love and spirit will always be within us. To the publishers of <u>The Lonely Planet Travel Survival Kits</u>, I offer much gratitude for your research and guidance which made our travels in this world a whole lot easier. Sandia and Kirsten, thank you for your patient reading and useful comments, and to Nino of Pero Designs for your invaluable help with the graphic design.

We all have a place in the sun. The excitement in life is searching for it!

Foreword

James L. Wright, *Australia*

Serendipity played a large part in the events that led to my friendship with Bill Bruton.

At the end of 1983 after travelling the world for seven months with my future wife, Mary Ann, we visited Colorado. After spending a short time with friends in Grand Lake, we decided to buy a cabin there that we could visit for a long holiday each year.

Our search was intended for a small cabin, but when our realtor walked us through the larger home that Bill and Sandia had built, there could be no other choice. With some short-term vendor finance and our realtor's arrangement to assume Bill's Veteran's Administration Loan, we completed the purchase requirements in two weeks and headed back to my businesses in Papua New Guinea.

In May 1985, we had the opportunity to return and live in the house for an extended period of time. We decided to add-on a large garage/workshop, and wishing it built in a matching style, I started asking the question, "Where is this Bill guy?"

It turned out that Bill was in Las Cruces, New Mexico building a shopping plaza. We found him, persuaded him to design the garage/workshop and eventually talked him into building it. We felt an immediate rapport with Bill and Sandia. Then toward the end of our stay in Grand Lake, I had an urgent need to find a new manager for my construction business in P.N.G.

Having watched over and worked with Bill on the garage/workshop, it seemed quite a natural thing to offer Bill the position in P.N.G. I remember well popping the question late one afternoon and observing his reaction to this way out thought. The proposal "stopped him in his tracks" for a bit and then the questions started. He went off with, "Yes, it sounds interesting, but I want to talk it over with Sandia."

Next morning at 7 A.M., I was working in our beautiful heated, hand crafted garage/workshop when there came a knock on the window, Bill. His reply—Yes, to Papua New Guinea!

Thus started an adventure for me as our friendship with Bill and Sandia grew while they both worked in our businesses.

We shared many experiences often associated with flying trips in P.N.G. This book tells the stories better than I ever could. To me, the most unforgettable of all occurred during our last adventure together. The memories of sharing that flying trip through Australia's Outback and real camaraderie with two Yanks are as vivid now as they were ten years ago.

We now live on separate continents, but remain close. I have watched as Bill's book has grown. It is truly a captivating and inspirational personal story of the triumph of spirit over life's challenges.

Adolph Coors, *Colorado*

We all meet hundreds of people as we walk through this life. Some, we can scarcely remember their faces, let alone their names. Only a small handful leaves a lasting impression. Bill Bruton is one of those men. If you have ever encountered him, he is not easily forgotten; after your life has intersected with his, you are never quite the same. The adjectives, humble and brilliant, are infrequently found in the same sentence to describe a man. However, both characterize Bill. His existence has counted as he pledged it would to God, after the Creator spared his life. Bill has impacted so many on his travels along the way from Connecticut, to the mountains of Colorado, to Papua New Guinea.

The golden thread woven through <u>Driven by Dreams</u> is the author's love for his lady, as he affectionately calls Sandia. Bill encourages the reader not to live vicariously through his dreams, but to discover their own dreams and to live them passionately while there is still time. As you read through these pages, you will want to rush out and triumph in your own life.

La Casita del Rio, a result of Bill and Sandia's dream and hard work in the Colorado Mountains became our dream in 1994. We purchased the home from them, as they were embarking on their journey to Papua New Guinea. Thus, his legacy also began an adventure in our lives. Thank you, Bill, for sharing your life in Driven by Dreams. My life has been both enhanced and enriched by knowing you.

Introduction

A knock and a voice awakened me from a deep, tired sleep.

"Moning tru, Masta Bill. Emi kwik tiam nau bilong moning kai."

The now familiar foreign words came from one of my men who just wanted to make sure I was awake and knew that breakfast would soon be over. I laid there for a moment, seeing the ceiling of my small cubicled room, as my eyelids tried to close again, but the rising level of noise in the mining camp around me kept me from returning to my deep slumbered retreat.

Finally, I pushed my tired legs over the side of the narrow single bed and rubbed my eyes into a semi-visionary mode. Pulling on my old faithful sweat pants, with my legs on "autopilot," I opened the door to my bunkhouse room and headed for the "gang" bathroom and shower facilities down the corridor.

The cool gentle shower water brought me closer to full awareness as the smells from the nearby camp mess hall started my stomach juices into a slow hungry rumble. Soon I was dressed halfway presentably, and upon locking up my room, headed for the exit door to begin another day, with whatever new challenges it would bring my way.

Outside the construction camp bunkhouse, or "donga" as the Aussies called it, which my men and I had built earlier on, I crouched down to study the log tiered foundation. We built this temporary structure in deep mud and I opted to "float" the twelve man dormitory structure on three horizontal levels of logs, notched in at the corners, much like a log cabin. Bargaining with the locals for the seventy-foot long hardwood Casuarina trees had been a definite challenge. Now the mud had dried and the log foundation remained like a tabletop. The Australian camp boss remarked, "Bloody fine idea, these logs. You Yanks are thinkers."

As I rose from my crouched position and turned in the direction of breakfast, I hesitated for a moment to drink in the view as the smell of coffee wafted past my nose. The soft white morning clouds settled into the Porgera valley below me and rising from them, at the far end of the valley, stood the chalk white limestone faces of Mount Kajindi, leading up from the clouds to the abrupt, dramatic summit of that spectacular mountain. Standing there at about the 9,000 foot elevation of Top Camp, Kajindi rose several thousand feet above me. I never tired of the sight of that mountain, as it always had a way of demonstrating to me my humanness. That particular morning, when the view remained novel for me, I stared in awe, while consciously making a vow to one day write it all down—all the things that brought me from my beloved Colorado Mountains to live and work amongst those majestic peaks and the people in the highlands of Papua New Guinea.

There is some of the same fitness in a man's building his own house that there is in a bird's building its own nest. Who knows but if men constructed their dwellings with their own hands and provided food for themselves and families simply and honestly enough, the poetic faculty would be universally developed, as birds universally sing when they are so engaged? But alas! We do like cowbirds and cuckoos, which lay their eggs in nests which other birds have built, and cheer no traveller with their chattering and unmusical notes. Shall we forever resign the pleasure of construction to the carpenter? What does architecture amount to in the experience of the mass of men? I never in all my walks came across a man engaged in so simple and natural an occupation as building his house.

. . .

I went into the woods because I wished to live deliberately, to front only the essential facts of life, and see if I could not learn what it had to teach, and not, when I came to die, discover that I had not lived.

Henry David Thoreau

PART I
The Apprenticeship

chapter one

Growing Up

I was born in the summer of 1937 in San Diego, California to a career U. S. Navy enlisted father and an old fashioned full-time mom. My dad's paternal grandfather and grandmother originated from France and the U.S.A., respectively. His father, William, my namesake, disappeared into Mexico in the 1920's, never to be heard from again, as the story was handed down to us. Back at the turn of the century, he dragged my dad and siblings around Idaho and Northern California in search of his "Eldorado." I can remember my dad's stories about crossing swollen rivers in Idaho as a youngster, pulling himself by a "greasy" cable while sitting in a solitary pulley chair, and being scared the whole way across. All of this effort proved necessary to get to remote sites where his father and uncle needed even young help with the sluice boxes and mercury amalgams to separate the precious gold from its gravel carrier. When my Dad joined the Navy at the age of seventeen, the handed down stories told of my grandma supporting the family by running a boarding house in Oakland City, California. There she catered to the needs of a

when the voice of challenge calls out your name

stand square to answer, running is the shame

slew of lodgers, along with a few of her own youngsters, while my grandpa continued to follow one adventure after another.

Mom, on the other hand, came from a little more stable, farming lineage. Her ancestors emigrated from the Palatine in Prussia in 1747 to escape religious persecution. They were Dunkards (Church of the Brethren) and, although lesser known, much like the Amish and Mennonites. That first many-great grandpa Jacob Stoneking (Steinkoenig) lost his wife, Maria Barbara Schenckles, and only daughter, Maria Ursula, to sickness on the voyage across the Atlantic. After burying them on the shores of the new Pennsylvania colony, Jacob pushed inland to the eastern foothills of the Allegheny Mountains with his four sons, aged from nine years down to three. A year later, in a "blanket" ceremony, Jacob married a Seneca Indian chief's daughter, named Aliquippa (Summer Eve), near Cumberland, Pennsylvania and eventually pushed over those mountains into southwestern Pennsylvania in search of fertile farmland. They must have found it and in spite of the French-

3

Indian War raging around them, they managed to have eight more children, amongst whom was Jacob the second, or younger, my ancestor. The Dunkard codes allowed a member to make their own decisions about fighting in a war, and hence young Jacob saw fit to volunteer as a fifer in the Revolutionary War at about fourteen years of age. He went on from marching with a fife to serve in several other capacities, including guarding prisoners in Lancaster, Pennsylvania, while others shipped out to fight against the British General Cornwallis. Records show that Jacob II later petitioned the state legislature for several years of back Army pay, not an uncommon happening in those days of the young Republic!

Later, young Jacob married Mary Flowers, another Seneca, and fathered a passle of kids, seventeen in number. I found him in the 1840 U.S. census, in Dunkard, Pennsylvania, at seventy-five years of age with five of his offspring still under fifteen years of age.

One of Jacob II's grandsons, William, with wife and four young sons in tow, left Dunkard and headed west in a covered wagon in 1844 to stake out a farm in the newly opened, fertile, "black-earthed" Iowa Territory. In Iowa, just outside of Cedar Rapids, a couple of generations later, my mom came into this world. The year was 1911. Her mom, young Hazel Stoneking, worked as a live-in maid for a wealthy family. When she became pregnant, there was a quick marriage to one of the household's rich sons, followed by an even quicker annulment. Mom's grandparent's farm then served as her birthplace. Hazel left Mom at the farm in the care of her parents and headed off into the world. About ten years later, grandma Hazel, after marrying for the second time to a career Navy man, sent for Mom to come and live with her in "navy town," Pensacola, Florida. There in Pensacola, in 1930, Mom at the tender age of 19 met a sailor named

Roy, fell in love, married, and began life as a career navy wife.

Thirteen months after my birth in California, my dad transferred to Canal Zone, Panama and there we remained until the Japanese attacked Pearl Harbor. Some of my first memories include those sandbags they piled up around our living quarters with fifty caliber machine guns pointing skyward to protect us in case of attack. I believe our military leaders thought there was a possibility that the Japanese would head straight for the Canal as another strategic point after destroying our Pacific Fleet at Pearl Harbor. Many were the nights after that when I would fall asleep with my head in my mom's lap, on the cool concrete basement stairs, with the air raid sirens wailing into the empty sky. Then word came down from those in charge, that all dependents needed to be shipped back to the States, by whatever means possible. Mom proceeded to shepherd us four kids onto a banana boat headed across the Caribbean Sea for New Orleans, with one stopover in Guatemala to pick up bananas. Several things stick in my mind about that trip across. To my almost five-year old mind, it seemed a long way down to those waves from the deck railing and it took a while, along with some helpful coaxing from my older brother and sister, before I felt comfortable gripping that steel railing to just look out at the ocean. Adults near me talked of looking for things called "periscopes" and "U-boats," but all I ever saw were fish that jumped out of the water, flapped their fins, and went a long way before hitting the water again. People told me they were flying fish and I spent a lot of the trip thereafter, eating bananas and watching those fish fly over the waves.

No "U-boats" ever showed up and the five of us made the Port of New Orleans. After a few months of temporary housing, we arrived at my dad's new place of duty, U.S. Naval Air

Station, Squantum, Massachusetts, about 20 miles south of Boston. Dad was assigned to teach aircraft powerplant mechanics to personnel heading overseas. More time passed in temporary Quonset hut quarters, until my dad showed up from Panama. Soon after, my parents bought a little house near the beach about a dozen blocks outside the base. We stayed in that beautiful little semi-urban house, always filled with the smell of the ocean, while my father transferred to various other duty stations around New England. He used to show up at least two weekends a month for the next ten years until he retired after thirty-two years of service to Uncle Sam. Dad ranked as a chief petty officer, but with all those service "hash marks" on his sleeve, I always felt like he was an Admiral.

Life proved pretty normal for us kids growing up. Sure, we got into trouble, and that mostly meant me, but by today's standards, we were mellow—no guns, drugs, or stuff like that. When gangs fought back then, you used your fists and maybe the occasional two by four. A bottle of beer with the boys in the clubhouse on the weekend made up the big stuff. I got suspended from high school once for smoking in the boy's lavatory, along with another guy who owned up to taking part in the act. Four other guys denied (liars) any part in the caper and got away with it. Talk about embarrassment, I brought my mom up to see the Principal in order to be reinstated, a first for her! At least he told her that I showed honesty about what I did and that made her feel a little better. I still caught a dose of the old leather belt when my father came home the next weekend! Our discipline always manifested itself as the hurting kind, which maybe made it harder to forget. Guess that was the point of it all.

My older brother, Roy Jr., joined the Navy not long after high school and served aboard the aircraft carrier Midway for most of his four-year hitch. I remember the return address on some of his letters to me used to say, "Canoe Club." Contents of those letters used to make the military sound like fun. My older sister, Helen, became head cheerleader in high-school and taught my little sister Dottie all the moves, so of course, when the time came, she did well in tryouts and ended up on the cheering squad through junior and senior high. I really displayed no claim to fame in those days. The football coach sent me packing in short order because I was too small and might get killed! Tried a little track, but couldn't run fast enough, or jump high enough. I really think my problem centered in the lack of a thing called athletic "coordination."

As a male growing up in the late forties and early fifties, the "right of passage" took on a physical meaning more so than an intellectual one. There were always the schoolyard challenges and fights, usually more in the way of bravado, than a "fight to the death" mentality. Sort of like in the animal kingdom where a greater show of strength would back down a challenger. In grammar school and junior high, I managed to hold my own in the schoolyard. After junior high though, I stayed at the lean 135 pound level, while others grew past me.

One evening when I was about sixteen, I strolled with a few friends down the beach boulevard, a few blocks from home, when the distinct voice of challenge called out my name. I turned toward the source and saw a larger group of "macho" guys from our high school football team. The voice belonged to our star halfback, a good sized and muscular, Jimmie Fallon. I remember fighting him back in the sixth grade and whipping him pretty good while we remained similar in size. I guess he never forgot that earlier beating, in the encirclement of peers, just outside our elementary school building. Jimmie obviously saw this present moment as a great time for revenge, especially while being egged on by his large support crew.

Jimmie's supporting cast began taunting my few buddies to get involved also, but I could see in my friends eyes that they wisely wanted no part of this whole thing, outnumbered at least two or three to one. My friends began edging subtly away leaving me to face a big choice—walk with them down the boulevard to momentary safety or face up to the main perpetrator by myself. I knew if I walked away, I'd have to live with the future abuse, so for me there appeared no choice. I walked up to Jimmie Fallon, stood with hands on my hips and called his bluff. All his friends came to their feet now, shouting for him to punch me out! They seemed all pumped up for a "rumble." Jimmie had no choice then either, so I watched for his first punch and ducked it, but didn't see the counter punch coming. I found myself suddenly on the ground with bright flashes bursting inside my head. That did it for me, the anger quickly welled up inside and I was on my feet and into his face in one rapid movement. I think in the second exchange, I may have landed one good punch, but it was again the bigger and clearly stronger Jimmie Fallon. I found myself face down on the ground for the second time. I heard one of their voices say, "Stay down, stay down you jerk!" but the angry voice inside of me screamed louder, "Get up, get up!"

I kept getting up and each time I ended up going down again without inflicting much damage on my opponent. Once from the ground, I managed to tackle him and bring him down to the grass level for the first time, but ended up with a black eye for the effort. The fact is, I didn't come close to beating Jimmie, but I didn't give up either.

They all finally shrugged me off and left me standing there with my clenched fists raised defiantly in front of me. A few insults came my way over their departing shoulders and then suddenly I stood alone on my "field of honor." The anger slowly ebbed from me and I lowered my fists as my body shook through its entire being. Only then did the pain set in as my head and jaw started aching in a pulsing rhythm.

I looked down the beach sea wall in the direction my friends took in their hasty exit, but couldn't see them. I walked in that general direction, feeling with each step some other sore spot. As I walked faster and gained back my poise, I remember thinking that at least I must have hurt him a little bit, and more importantly, I didn't run from his challenging taunts.

I found my friends, heard their apologies, assured them the fight was mine, not theirs, especially with the numbers involved. From there, we went on to do our night beach hangout thing. My face brought some stares, but I just shrugged them off. The fight was over. I'd look in the mirror later. I didn't realize then that the next morning would bring the real climax to the fight.

I started out a little late in walking to school the next morning, and as a result, missed my friends and walked the distance alone. I hadn't slept well, having fought the fight a thousand times over during the night, getting in better punches in my wishful imagination than happened in reality. As I got closer to my highschool, I began to think about walking alone through the gauntlet of guys that always hung out at the school entryway until the warning bell sounded and had nothing better to do than to throw out comments at the "passers through." Maybe I'd be lucky and they wouldn't have heard about "the fight" yet.

As I walked on, deeply immersed in my thoughts, I heard my name called from behind and turned to see Jimmie Fallon running to catch up with me. He didn't say a lot, just smiled, shook my hand, and said, "Bill, I'll walk to school with you." That was to be the first and only time we ever walked together, but his gesture that morning said what a lot of fancy words couldn't say.

As we neared the school entryway, I saw immediately that my thoughts of the word maybe not having spread were totally optimistic. One loud-mouthed "jerk" from Jimmie's group of the night before gave blow by blow demonstrations to many eager listeners as we approached. Suddenly someone spotted us. They all turned to stare at the two of us walking up to school together. No one said a word; even the blabbermouth just stood there with his jaw dropped open. I'm sure the listeners saw the truth of the story in my marked up face, but more expected to see gloating from my adversary, instead of the parting handshake followed by the friendly, "Bill, I'll see you later!"

I earned my "right of passage" with that totally unexpected challenge and fight, my unwillingness to back down from the odds of it, not giving up, and finally Jimmie's public expression of respect for my effort. Nobody ever bothered me in school after that incident. In life, I have found so many times, you don't have to always win; you just have to always try.

I muddled my way through all the high-school courses and managed to barely qualify for graduation. That was really a feat as I think back on it now because I never even studied. It wasn't cool in the 50's to walk out of school with a book. If you wanted to be one of the "boys," you didn't ever carry a book. I dumbly believed it, but never got to be one of the boys anyway!

My character contained enough rebellion to break the Navy tradition in my family. In the

summer before my senior year, on the day of my seventeenth birthday, I signed on with the Marine Corps Reserve. After graduation in those days, all able-bodied males had to volunteer or be drafted for a tour of duty with the military. So the day after I walked up on that graduation stage to accept my barely earned high-school diploma, I headed for Marine boot camp as an active reservist. I worked hard at boot training and became first squad leader, first platoon. Only had one swagger stick broken over my head and still have the lump to prove it. I held that M-1 rifle out on my finger tips until the beads of sweat literally popped out of my forehead – nobody, drill instructors, included, ever broke this stubborn guy! So after another graduation, this time from boot, I headed off to a special radar school in North Carolina.

Two things became clear to me in that Cherry Point radar school. First, it proved difficult to make rank in the U.S.M.C.R. and second, regular marines did not like reservists, in fact, they detested us, constantly reminding us of their feelings. Not much I could do about the rank thing, but I vowed to become a regular marine the first chance I got. So when I finished radar school, getting my first leave, I made a mental note to stop by and see the Marine recruiter near home to join the regulars.

A funny thing happened with that "joining the regulars" intention. About half way through my leave, I stopped by the U.S.M.C. Recruiting Office. As luck would have it, the recruiting sergeant took that Friday afternoon off and wouldn't be in until Monday morning. No big deal, I'd return after the weekend. However, the person giving me the scoop on timing was the Navy chief and recruiter who shared the office with the Marine sergeant.

I remember him saying as he wrote my name down on a slip of paper to leave on the sergeant's desk, "Name sounds familiar. Was your dad ever in the Navy"?

I replied that my father just retired a few years earlier and had been "piped" ashore from the Naval Air Station at nearby Squantum. As he asked further questions regarding places I'd lived as a youngster, the recruiter mulled over, with a furrowed brow, how he knew the uncommon name. Then the light came into his eyes.

"Your father became my Leading Chief in Panama. It was my first duty assignment in the Navy. We flew PBY amphibious aircraft looking for submarines!"

He seemed really excited talking about past duties. One thing led to another and that Navy recruiter ended up at dinner that night at our house hashing over the good old days with my dad. Toward the end of the evening, they called me into the living room, laying out a proposition they had been talking about. The gist of their conversation boiled down to what the Navy could offer me if I joined the regular Navy instead of the Marines. They offered me one step-up in rank from my present basic Marine private, where I'd been ranked for thirteen months since joining the U.S.M.C.R., and guaranteed me schooling to learn a trade. The schooling part, along with my father's ever-present persuasion, finally overcame my "Espri-de-Corps" and I agreed to join the regular Navy —a four-year volunteer hitch. One catch though, I needed to head off to boot camp again, my second boot training of 1955. How bad could it be after surviving and thriving on the Marine Corps version?

It was bad! Not so much the physical part,

that proved a "piece of cake", but the mental part seemed tough. Guys always got set back, which meant you needed to go back to a new company and start all over again. If you really fouled up, they put you in a special retraining company for "misfits" and you had no choice but to shape up, or be "shipped out" of the U.S.N. Fouling up could be as small as having one dirty thread on the inside neck of your skivvy shirt during an unscheduled locker inspection!

Three months later, I graduated from Navy boot and got my first look at the outside world in a while. The Navy called this time off base, "liberty." I didn't even march with my own company at the graduation ceremonies, because earlier in the program my skipper, or C.O., noticed how well I handled that lightweight Springfield rifle (about half the weight of the Marine M-1). I ended up on the Navy Drill Team. The main upshot of that venue meant getting up one and a half-hour earlier than everyone else each morning for six weeks of practice. It proved a good way to wake up. I remember how great that breakfast always tasted when we got to the mess hall after drill team practice, just as everyone else straggled in, just out of their bunks.

All good things had to come to an end and so it followed with my career in boot camps. I moved onto two years of Navy schooling where I learned to be an aviation electrician and a specialist on certain types of aircraft guidance and navigation systems. It certainly ended up a solid trade to learn. I admitted that running into that Navy recruiter, along with my father's coercion, resulted in a fortunate piece of "networking."

chapter two

A Moment of Character Definition

Many people have an occurrence, or maybe a person, that they can look back at, knowing it, or they, profoundly influenced their life. My own character forming moment in time occurred while I served in the Navy.

Based at Naval Air Station, Norfolk, Virginia at the tender age of nineteen, I approached the fall of 1956 with a bit of reckless abandon. A "Dear John" letter from my girl friend back home was angrily thrown someplace in the bottom of my locker. It seemed fitting to spend liberties in one of the many accessible bars in nearby Norfolk. Never a really good drinker, I knew in my heart I overdid things, but it didn't seem to matter much at the time. My stomach rebelled on me many of those nights, but I kept on drinking. Bar fights seemed a good way to get rid of the pent up anger.

One night, a bar waitress, probably feeling sorry for me after I fought with some Marines, took me home to her nearby apartment. A boyfriend of hers then showed up unexpectedly. His unannounced arrival resulted in my going down two flights of stairs head over heels. I honestly

sometimes, we lose control, our choices bad

given another chance, we should be glad

don't remember who gave me a ride that night, but they dumped me out, in my very scroungy dress whites, onto the grass in front of the Naval Air Station entry gate. The Marines on duty found a way to get me to my barracks. After spending most of the night huddled with the cool porcelain of a toilet bowl against my cheek, the squadron duty chief reamed me out the next morning for not reporting to work and being "written up" by the Marine Gate detachment.

I cooled it for a while, but the friends I ran with gladly showed me the way back. The weekends became blurs again – lots of partying, but at least I kept my work on the aircraft electrical systems under control during the week.

One of my friends, Henry, dated the younger sister of another sailor stationed at Naval Air Station, Norfolk. He told me about another sister named Irene that currently remained "available." Henry took me up one weekend to where Irene's family lived, just outside of Williamsburg. It turned out I got on really well with Irene. She was a cutie approaching her seventeenth birthday and seemed to like me quite a bit. When we left,

9

I felt excited about getting back to see her again.

Henry and I both pulled weekend duty the next weekend, but the very next weekend we headed for Williamsburg. We traveled with two other navy friends in a two-car caravan as they had dates near to us also. Two cars seemed better for double dating, the way we figured it. I rode shotgun in Henry's Chrysler, Town and Country Sedan. The sum total of the trip manifested in us drinking a lot on the road and arriving at Irene's families' house very late on Friday night. No problem, we'd sleep in the car along their graveled entry road and knock on their door in the morning. Their place was situated in the country with an outhouse, chicken coops, lots of junk cars, and scads of acreage.

It ended up cold that fall night and Henry wanted to leave the car idling with the car heater on low. My reluctant protest met with his firm rebuttal, "I do it all the time. It's not a problem."

In my inebriated, tired state, I didn't argue. I opened one rear window a crack, stretched out on the back seat, found a comfortable position, and fell right to sleep. Actually, passed out would probably be the better description!

My next semi-conscious impression was the sound of a rooster's crowing. It seemed to last for hours. On and on that rooster crowed. The sound rattled around inside my head. I couldn't seem to respond to the sound of it. On and on it went. My eyes finally opened slightly. The gray dawn of early morning filtered into my consciousness. I started to reach up for the back of the front seat to pull myself into a sitting position. My arm felt numb and unresponsive. I struggled to finally sit up dizzily with my chin against the seat top in front of me. The red ignition light on the dashboard glowed brightly in the dim morning light. The gas gauge indicated the gas tank remained half-full. Henry lay passed out on the front seat.

I reached over very slowly to find my door handle. The next thing I knew, I fell to the ground outside in a heap, right through the car door whose handle I'd somehow managed to open. I laid there in a daze, shaking my dizzy, throbbing, and bursting head. Then two words struck my barely functioning brain – carbon monoxide!

Pushing up with my arms, I slowly gained my unsteady feet. I tried to walk downhill toward the house for help. It seemed as if I was running so fast. The sensations felt as if I possessed no control over my arms and legs. I slammed into the side of a junk car that somehow got into my running path. I think I yelled for help as I went down, crashing face first into the ground. I went out cold.

I awoke sometime later, on my back, still lying where I'd fallen. A ring of blurry faces peered down at me. Their lips moved, but the sounds seemed far away and weirdly amplified. Irene's face came into partial focus, along with several sisters, a brother, and both parents. I passed out again.

Finally, I came back to consciousness on sort of a chaise lounge on their verandah. Irene sat beside me with a very concerned look on her face. My lips blurted out, "Carbon monoxide, the car's exhaust!"

I heard Irene's voice telling me of Henry's vomiting and bad sickness. Our other two friends had taken him, unconscious, to a nearby hospital and would return soon to check again on me. They thought I slept okay with a smooth breathing rhythm and didn't appear as violently sick as Henry.

My head definitely cleared with every deep breath my lungs sucked in and slowly breathed out. Irene babbled about her father saying the car was parked on a slight incline, causing an exhaust leak to find its way into the interior of the car.

The gravity of the whole thing was hitting me clearer now. Too drunk to protest Henry's car heater and sleeping intentions, I'd gone to sleep with the window above my head in back slightly open. Henry, who slept in the front seat, must have breathed more of the fumes than I did. Then I remembered the red ignition light and the half-full fuel gauge. The car had stalled for some reason. Tears rolled unchecked from my eyes, streaming down my cheeks. I was alive and regaining my strength many hours after that Chrysler Town and Country stalled in the night. The result, without the stall, would have probably ended in death. The tears kept coming. It proved a compelling realization to deal with.

After a while, I slipped unsteadily away from the house and slowly made my way into the adjoining forest. Falling to my knees, with clutched hands, I looked skyward through the treetops above and the blur of my own tears. Words poured from my lips to thank an invisible God for His mercy. I gave Him my solemn pledge to make something of the life He'd chosen to spare. My body stayed slumped in that position of repentance and thankfulness until Irene, with some more of the worried family, found me later.

Henry transferred to a Naval Hospital, while I soon transferred to another duty station at Jacksonville, Florida. Henry seemed much affected by the occurrence we'd survived. His memory turned out affected and his bodily controls were diminished, but the doctors thought he would improve with time. We lost touch after I transferred, beginning my life anew, and much more responsibly. You just cannot make good decisions when you're out of control. For me it became a credo, "Stay in control. You only get one body in this life. Don't abuse it!"

chapter three

Suburbia and the American Dream

Life for the next dozen years seemed what I'd have to class as normal. In that stretch I did all the things that my father and society deemed important. I married my high-school sweetheart (the one who thought better of her "Dear John" letter), fathered two children before getting out of the Navy, followed by three more beautiful children while working my way through the university to earn a Master's Degree in physics. I gladly gave up a Doctoral fellowship when my wife got pregnant with our fifth child. It was clearly time to get my "butt" to work and out of academia! I found an excellent job in a research laboratory, just outside of Hartford, Connecticut, and bought a split-level ranch home in the suburbs. We had suddenly arrived at the American Dream. What more could we have hoped for? We had it all! We owned an acre of green lawn to mow every weekend. I built a green-clay (Har Tru) tennis court in the side yard, along with a big redwood deck attached to the house, overlooking the court. Visions of family tennis flowed through my brain. Our first four children were daughters and the youngest, a son. We perceived tennis to be an opportunity

lawns and fine houses, the American dream

but what happens within, could make you scream

for the girls to learn and participate in a sport, during an era seriously lacking in organized female sporting activities. Tennis was my favorite pastime and I welcomed the chance to teach the kids and pass on my love for the game. What could be better than having your own court in the yard?

For several years, things were fantastic. Two of the girls, Lynne and Andrea, along with Gary, took to tennis really well. Sherrie and Deborah decided other things seemed much more important and for them at that time, they were right. I did okay at first with the tennis teaching, but the emotions soon started to get in the way as we progressed beyond the fundamentals of tennis. Any parent, who has tried to be their kids' coach also, would understand what I'm talking about. So I hit on a great idea. A friend who taught tennis professionally had asked about paying me to use our court for private lessons. At first I didn't want to commercialize the court and have lessons going when one of us wanted to use it, but I made her a proposition that met all of our needs and she accepted. Whenever she gave private lessons on our court, she would schedule one of my kids for a lesson right afterwards as payment for court time. So the kids got private lessons from an excellent ranked tennis player and they didn't get angry with good old Dad for drilling them too much! It resulted in a good marriage of sorts. Lynne and Andrea went on to play on the high school boy's team (there existed no girl's team) as number one and three, respectively. Gary won the town eight-year old championships, and a couple of years later, followed it up as the ten-year old tennis champion. They all enjoyed the game, even playing it to this day as fun and exercise. Even Sherrie and Deborah, who had reluctant starts, have given the sport a try.

I have to relate a fun sidelight to my kids' tennis court capers. While we had our "family" court thing going, another family of four young girls across the street took notice. They started hitting tennis balls back and forth in the street while we played on the court. Later, when we would obviously be finishing up, they would politely ask if they could use the court for a little while. Our answer mostly ended up with the affirmative and they would never leave the court without giving it a good clean up and brooming. With that start, along with a very demanding father, two of those girls went on to be ranked tennis players on the New England tour. My own tennis playing daughters used to comment, later in life, what they could have done if only I'd pushed them. Then they would look at me and have a good laugh at the humor in it all.

All five of the kids participated on the swim and tennis teams, to varying degrees, at our local swim and tennis club. It became great summer fun in Connecticut. As I look back now, I think that's when the "virus" of suburbia began to slowly creep into our family. Summer fun meant parties, and parties meant alcohol, and in the presence of alcohol, things happen. If a big party was scheduled at one place in suburbia,

there would be a warmer upper party scheduled on the way. I know the choice remained with us. I know that no one physically twisted arms for our presence at those parties, but in a subtle way, they did. You always think you can handle it. The parties, and drinking, in general, turned into a slow creeping thing that started as arguments, drunken arguments that serve no purpose, except for tearing a relationship apart at its very fabric. I began to blame suburbia and refuse invitations, but my wife kept accepting them and sometimes it proved easier to just go, than to argue about it. My optimism began to wane. I sought counseling for our problems. I tried the minister of our church, without much success, and then a psychologist. My wife had a problem called alcoholism, but wouldn't admit it, even to herself, let alone talk about the possibility with a counselor. So we got nowhere fast. When I tried to talk to my dad about it, he told me, "You made your bed, you lie in it!" So it went on for several more years, filled with broken promises, and just getting worse. Those were the days when you told yourself that you hung in for the sake of the kids. That was all a lie. Then one night I came home late and went to each of the kids in their beds, giving them a good night hug. I remember it as plain as yesterday when Lynne looked up at me from her tear stained pillow and sobbed to me, "Dad, you always tell us how great life is, but you are wrong. It's really terrible and I wish I was dead!" I never found out what had happened to make her utter such a profound statement on the value of life, but it really made me think about the validity of what was truly best for the kids and their futures. I found out many years later that the kids didn't confide in me, regarding some of their bad experiences with their mom, because they thought it would start another one of those "donnybrooks."

In the middle of all of this, my dad, diagnosed with cancer of the rectum, needed a "Colostomy." They scheduled him for the operation right away at the Chelsea Naval Hospital near Boston. The hospital administrators told me, "Don't worry about your father. This is a routine operation."

I had earlier left my research position and enjoyed teaching mathematics at a local community college. I remember teaching a late afternoon class before driving from Connecticut to Boston, to spend some time with my father, the night before his scheduled operation. It proved a good time of reflection for both of us, but mostly for him. Dad did most of the talking and seemed in great spirits. Whenever a nurse would look in on him, he told them, "Take care of those young guys from Viet Nam. I'm doing great." I felt glad to have taken that moment in time to be with him and drove those 120 miles back that night late feeling better about life in general. A father's stories, along with expressed confidence in you, have a way of lifting you up a bit.

The next morning I played an early round men's doubles match in our club tennis championships, when a friend came running over, he thought dutifully, to tell me quietly through the chain link fence, that my father just died suddenly in the hospital recovery room after the "routine" operation. I went into a daze, just going through the tennis motions for the few remaining games, thinking stupidly about not letting my partner down, together with knowing I couldn't do anything about anything anyway. We lost the match, and I ran for a private spot to let it all burst forth from my chest, inhaled it all back in, and headed for my mom. I needed to be with her to help with so many things that needed to be done.

The military took care of many of the details. A few days later, as they lowered my father's body into the ground, a U.S. Marine Corps Honor Guard fired a rifle salute skyward, followed by Taps on the bugle. As those poignant notes sounded in our ears, a brisk wind blew off my mom's favorite hat and we all watched it swirl up into the air. All of those mourners became transfixed as the little hat, caught in a gust of wind at the seaside cemetery, did a few complete circles, and then came back down slowly, right down onto my father's coffin, which by then had come to rest at the bottom of the prepared hole. Someone volunteered to go down and fetch the hat, but my mom said "No," seeing it as a sign from God. It actually lifted her spirit a bit, even in her grief, as she kept asking me later in the day, "Billy, did you see my favorite hat go to be with your father? That was such a beautiful message."

Something happened to me after my father died. I still can't really explain it in detail, but I just made up my mind to do things the way I thought best and to hell with what other people thought or would advise me. I guess I found myself tired of living up to what society taught as correct, or what my father had preached as the right thing to do. I knew well the finiteness of life. I told my wife that there seemed no future for us except divorce and started proceedings to gain custody of my children. That study got a bit nasty in some parts, taking the better part of a year to complete. The year was 1975 and in those days, fathers didn't win custody except in extreme cases, but, as always, I remained the optimist throughout, trying to reason what appeared best for the kids. I knew for sure, the best wasn't the two of us together! The neighbors were questioned, friends were questioned, and the kids were queried. It proved hard on everyone. In the end, the judge granted custody to my wife. That night, after hours of mostly angry reflection, I set out searching for her. After making the rounds of drinking places, I found her nearly passed-out drunk in her male friend's Cadillac, parked behind a bar. I've never experienced a rage like I felt at that moment as I pulled her from the car and shouted, "You wanted those kids! You get your butt home and take care of them!" Maybe this is what happens in violent domestic crimes, but I'm thankful I saw the futility in it. With clenched fists and gritted teeth, I left her there, sprawled across the hood where I'd pushed her. The guy in the driver's seat never even woke up from his stupor. As I walked away, I swore I'd reopen the whole custody case and start all over again.

I never did reopen the case because back then you had to really show the mother to be a total derelict in order to win custody. She certainly didn't fit that bill. My wife only suffered from the disease of alcoholism. She would have to deal with it herself, which she finally did many years and another unsuccessful marriage later. I knew the research about it being a genetic, chemical, and incurable disease, but understanding the science didn't make the emotional part any easier to deal with. While sobriety constituted the only answer, alcohol remained the everyday choice. It ruined us. I came out of the emotionally draining experience needing to start a new life, with a rekindled spirit, and leave those awesome scars far behind! I wanted to show the kids, by example, that life is, after all, a great and beautiful chance.

Brown Paper Bag with a Bottle Inside

Got to have it, even with loss of pride
Night's too long, too painful, to be without
Brown paper bag with a bottle inside.

Can make it through the daylight, then I slide
When darkness comes on me, I want to shout
Got to have it, even with loss of pride.

I let it build up, if only I'd cried
This hurt in my heart, it fills me with doubt
Brown paper bag with a bottle inside.

Afraid to ask for help, I know, I've tried
Getting through the night, what it's all about
Got to have it, even with loss of pride.

Not my fault, the torment that's been applied
Abuse began, mom and her swears, her clout
Brown paper bag with a bottle inside.

The rest of my heartsickness, he supplied
Know it's a disease, need help to climb out
Got to have it, even with loss of pride
Brown paper bag with a bottle inside.

chapter four

A New Direction

I turned my focus toward work, and with the exception of getting sidetracked in one relationship that wasn't meant to be, things inside began to heal. Life took on a new excitement, with a kind of mental freedom I hadn't previously known. My work was tennis and it truly became a "labor of love." I did the work I wanted to do. I worked around the kind of people I wanted to be around. My sport "hobby" became my vocation.

The tennis life began a few years earlier as an offshoot to building the tennis court in my side yard. As a "poor" instructor of college mathematics, I needed to augment my income during the summer months and ended up installing a few courts for other tennis enthusiasts. One tennis playing friend and real estate developer, Gary Pizzitola, helped me to win a contract for two courts at a new condominium project in a nearby town. From the completion of that project, only the sky seemed to be the limit. I just did the engineering and layout, while subcontracting all the labor and big machinery. Gary and I formed a partnership called New England Tennis Systems, which was a play on initials (NETS).

> *not just any job; find the work you love*
>
> *then leave the rest, to the One up above*

We actually began to get sizable contracts. The summer job took on the potential of a full-time job centered upon tennis construction. It proved hard work, but fun also. Gary and I always initiated each newly completed court by installing the net, followed by squaring off for one of our "no holds barred, no quarters given" matches. We remained pretty even in tennis skills, about intermediates at the club level, so it always provided fun and exercise. And our tennis consistently left room for improvement!

Although the tennis work felt great, I wasn't ready to give up my teaching position at that point in time. I had been promoted to department chairman, and even at our low pay scale, there remained a lot of great benefits' along with a steady monthly check that paid the bills. And besides, the college tennis team thought my coaching was indispensable.

Then a new tennis phenomenon hit town, or actually just outside of town about 40 miles west of Hartford on the interstate. A tennis development group from New Jersey built an indoor tennis center in Southington, and our "hither to fore" summer sport in New England suddenly took on a year round aspect. Area tennis players didn't seem to mind driving the distance or playing inside a big metal building. Prior to then, you just didn't play in the winter or else you switched your game to platform tennis, which was played outdoors on an elevated smaller court, after you swept the snow out specially designed side gates. The fact is, almost immediately, the Southington Indoor Tennis Center did a bustling business.

With a few tennis buddies one night at the newly opened indoor club, we tried to book a "Saturday night" party, thinking we could get together a large group of players and rent the whole club for the night, bringing refreshments—maybe pizza, beer, or just pot luck. Anyway the manager said most Saturday nights had reserved time and he couldn't bump anyone to accommodate our party idea. I remember he appeared not very sincere in his apology and actually seemed a bit flippant, or condescending, to us. We turned away in disappointment and someone in my group said, "The hell with it, we'll build our own club, then we'll party whenever we want!" I'm sure it was uttered more to get back at the manager's attitude, than anything else.

That off-handed outburst of a statement, made in jest to their manager, took root in the fertile "soil" of my mind. My three buddies didn't see it as a serious thought at first, but my partner Gary, ever the developer, soon sided with my expressed positive thoughts on the idea, and a "tree" from that seed began to grow.

Soon after, we hit a pooled football "card" and the winnings turned out to be enough to buy the business cards and stationary for our newly conceived company, Myriad Enterprises—four friends with a dream! We then carefully selected several upscale towns just west of Hartford and I developed a demographic "least squares"

analysis of each. The analysis data was based on several successful clubs we visited in New York and New Jersey on weekends. I studied the income base and housing values within a five-mile radius of each club to come up with a demographic formula for a club location comparison. We settled on the town of Farmington, Connecticut which according to the formula showed a high success probability, along with land values that we thought we could afford in the overall project costing estimates.

The next step was "seed" capital and for that we needed a bank connection. One of the other guys, Nick Cecere, arranged a meeting with a loan officer at a bank where he had a good rapport. The meeting went well, although the loan was approved on our four signatures rather than the creditability of our one common tennis business idea.

We took the borrowed ten thousand dollars, putting part of it on a six month land option, with another part as a retainer at an architectural firm, in order to get development plans drawn, and most of the rest went to a legal fee retainer. Gary and I worked full time at the liaison required with the Farmington town "fathers", while our two partners, Bob and Nick, kept their jobs, promising to make it up later. The town planner, in charge of enforcing zoning regulations, made some kind of an early on statement like, "You'll never put up one of those ugly metal buildings in this town while I'm here, even to play tennis in!" So it proved to be a fight from the outset. We convened the Building Board of Appeals, which hadn't met for something like thirty years. In fact, two of its members had died since they last met. Gary and I got on the agenda of the Town Council and pushed them to appoint two new members to the Appeals Board, so we could appear before it to try and change the zoning law, which forbade metal buildings in Farmington.

Armed with conceptual renderings, or isometric drawings, which showed gambrel (barn-like) buildings with some portion of wood siding, we succeeded in changing that zoning law. I think the tennis concept, along with the name, Farmington Farms Racquet Club, held enough "pizzazz" to be the clincher. Soon after, we found ourselves with all the Council approvals required and owned the development rights to an indoor racquet club on our optioned piece of land. All we needed then to complete the dream was about a half million bucks and we'd be home free!

With the last dredges of our loan money, we printed club brochures and started handing them out everywhere, along with general flyer announcements. A few people even took paid memberships, as we began to accumulate a small kitty to work with, although we knew we'd have to refund it if we didn't get the club built. I felt particularly responsible because much earlier in our thinking my more conservative partners wanted to do questionnaires and mailings in the proposed club area to determine interest. I remember believing in the demographic analysis, insisting it remained full-steam ahead—the concept would prove a valid business venture. In fact, another group had a similar idea for a Farmington club in the same time period and began circulating interest questionnaires. Gary and I pushed to borrow the money to begin the approval phase of the development. If nothing else, an approved development right would become a sellable commodity. We left the questionnaire group in the dust soon thereafter.

At every tennis event or tournament, we would be in the parking lot putting club flyers optimistically under windshield wipers and, in general, talking up the future club. It was spring-time and our promised opening was scheduled for early fall of the same year. Needless to say, we had our work cut out!

Aetna Insurance Company of Hartford had just agreed to sponsor what was to be called the World Cup of tennis, pitting the dynasty of Australia players against the best of the U.S.A.. At that spring Cup in '72, we spread out over the Hartford Coliseum talking up the Racquet Club. Tennis interest was growing by leaps and bounds. The Aussies, Rod Laver, John Newcombe, John Alexander, Roy Emerson, and the likes, were good naturedly, but determinedly kicking our collective "butts" on the tennis courts, as well as everyone else in the world. Only several years later, would Jimmy Conners and company help to turn the tide in bringing the Aetna World Cup back to Hartford, and the U.S.A. I also think the "aging" of that Australian tennis dynasty helped turn the tide. But in the excitement of those '72 Cup matches, we pushed our club idea to many potential investors.

Then it happened. Through our attorney, we found the investor. I remember making the presentation in our counsel's office—all my demographic charts in full color, data from existing clubs in New York and New Jersey, a "break even" proforma analysis based on court rental costs, membership fees, and concession/pro shop incomes, versus the estimated debt service for our development costs, along with operating expenses. Not only did the investor want in, but the attorney wanted a piece of the action also. We closed a deal! It's hard to describe the elation and euphoria my partners and I felt at that point in time. We would own half the club, with them putting up all the necessary funding to own the other half.

The excitement began to wane after a few days, as the reality of the work needed to open the club in just five months became apparent. The burden fell to Gary and I again as we quickly moved a rented office trailer onto the club development site and literally took up residence. We had the general contractor lined up beforehand, the same one that did the Southington club, and immediately put them on the job. The well driller started "witching" for water, bulldozers started altering the natural lay of the land, and all the other activity showed that we were clearly underway. Everyday new faces came by our trailer to sign up. Our inaugural membership list kept on growing. With the exception of leaving the site for a regular game of tennis in Gary's and my ongoing challenge series, one of us always stayed to make decisions, push the general contractor, talk to potential members, line up potential club employees, and just be there for support in general.

Not only did we finish the Racquet Club on schedule, but even got enough ahead of the construction to allow about two weeks of free play before the beginning of the regular season's scheduled and reserved court time. Tennis players came by in large numbers to see our new facility and try out the courts. The synthetic elastic court surface appeared well received as it played a lot like clay and would be fun for all levels of play. We provided double the normal space between courts, with divider nets, so the occasional miss-hit wouldn't interfere with the game on the next court. When you are paying a fee for court time, you want to spend your time playing your game; not chasing down your neighbor's errant shots! Forty-foot peak heights of the gambrel roof design proved ample for almost any lob shot. In the clubhouse, we built lounge-viewing decks on either side looking out onto three courts in both directions, high enough above the court level so as not to be a distraction to the players. Some tennis players love to be watched and made special requests for those clubhouse adjacent courts. Besides the sauna baths in each

locker room, the women's facility had individual private shower and lavatory rooms. Coffee locker, kitchen, children's nursery, administrative offices, and pro shop made up the rest of the clubhouse. We even put in a guest office for the daytime businessman who needed a little privacy to call his office or a client. Seeing was believing. The membership rolls swelled during that open house period.

As a natural evolution of my passion for the project, I agreed at a previous board meeting to manage the club during its first year of operation. It would be a labor of pleasure for which I also received a reasonable salary. My responsibility was defined to set up the necessary systems to keep the club affairs in order for the years ahead and to hire and train staff in club procedures. Our side of the partnership, for our fifty-percent, was responsible for the working side of the club anyway. The investors, for the other fifty-percent, had the financial responsibilities for any cash shortfalls, and we all signed the long-term bank mortgage.

That first year proved hard work, but at the same time a lot of fun. I met a lot of great people and always seemed to be filling in for someone who couldn't make their game. I played my favorite sport almost every day, sometimes several times a day. My body, and mind for that matter, definitely thrived on the physical exercise. My philosophy and approach everyday was, "Run a good fun club where people want to be and the business will follow!" I remember proposing at a board meeting early in that first year that we start a junior program where kids could play free right after school let out until the prime evening time started. My argument showed that it produced more wear and tear on the court light ballasts to shut them down, than the few pennies gained in electricity savings. I felt if more kids got involved, then their parents and friends might join also.

We had a very healthy and heated debate on the proposed junior program, in which most partners thought the juniors would run rough shod over the club. In the end though, after promising to take the responsibility for any mishaps, the partners finally voted me a three-month trial period for my envisioned program.

Those first year juniors turned out to be a club asset. They got in a lot of tennis, with our club becoming the place to go right after school. Some days they would be in the clubhouse just doing homework or helping me out with maintenance. They would pick up and vacuum the locker rooms, fill the soda machine, clean up the kitchen and coffee areas, and in general look after "our" club. From that base, we formed a Farmington Farms junior team, with which the teaching tennis pros I had on staff helped, and challenged other clubs within a hundred-mile radius to play us. Those matches were played on Saturday mornings, with enough volunteer parent drivers to get us to the away locations. Most kids enjoyed the team concept, including a couple of my own, and a few participants, like Barbie Potter and Tim Mayotte, went on to play the game professionally. At the end of the three-month probationary period, my partners unanimously agreed to leave the junior program in place as a permanent effort.

Most of our court time filled in as that first season moved towards its conclusion. For what open time remained, we filled it in with challenge ladder matches and regular men's and women's doubles competition. I put together the mechanics of the first Farmington Farms Racquet Club Tennis Championships near the end of the season and from there, we had waiting lists for the next indoor season. We did it. We did it from the first idea all the way to a very suc-

cessfully operating club and business.

At the end of that first year, after the glow of the accomplishment wore off, I realized that although I enjoyed getting things going, starting from the ground up, it looked like time to move onto other things. I knew for sure that I wanted to continue working in the tennis industry. So it seemed a natural extension to keep our tennis court construction crew going, along with indoor club consulting work using the demographic analysis techniques I had developed, and also became a technical representative for several court surfaces and court lighting systems. I made a decent living and still found time to get on the tennis court most days. To say I loved my work would have been a gross understatement! I lived literally on top of the world. I moved, after my divorce, to a small suite on the top floor of the Hartford Hilton, while working out of an office on the top floor of an adjacent building. I spent time with my kids on a regular basis. Several of the girls continued to take lessons and just played tennis in general. Their old tennis teacher from the "home court" was now on the club staff at Farmington Farms. I coached little league for my son's team, so between the tennis and baseball, and also other things like homework helping, we had some good rallying points to keep our relationships on a positive note. I know it was a difficult time for the kids. Divorces are never easy for anyone involved, except maybe the legal beavers!

The only thing missing for me in those days was a meaningful relationship, but I felt a bit paranoid, and you'd probably say, scared off by anything that looked like it could become "long term." I had tried one dating sequence with an ex-math student of mine; a recently divorced young woman named Shoshanna, and ended it because things just got too serious after a while. You start out saying you can handle it, without admitting it's a testosterone driven decision, and next thing you know marriage is coming up in conversation more and more often. You're suddenly having, "Out of the frying pan—into the blazing hot fire" thoughts, when you are not even truly in love. The worst part after the realization of where you are at, comes with trying to end it, without hurting the other person—not easily done, and not done overnight for sure. You can't avoid the hurt. It had to come. I retreated to my Hilton and hid out—"gun shy." The odd date happened, just for conversation and companionship. On two occasions, I remember, even feigning sleep to avoid getting into another relationship. That is paranoia. Those were the mixed up days. I am only glad now that I had my kids and work for stability.

A couple of years later, our club partnership group decided to parlay our first club success into a second one, this time on the other, or eastern side, of Hartford and the Connecticut River. My numbers and analysis said the Town of Glastonbury would work just fine. We subdivided a piece of an old tobacco farm on Oakwood Drive and our sister club, Oakwood Farms Racquet Club, was underway. Again it evolved with my partner Gary and I as the development team while our other two "working" partners kept their regular type jobs. It seemed okay with me as I loved the work and my return proved adequate to live on.

To start the construction, we needed to tear down an old tobacco barn that our farmer Joe Oberge helped his father build back near the turn of the century. It represented an emotional experience for Joe, so we told our crew to get it down as quickly as they could. We also promised Joe to use the old weathered barnwood as

an accent throughout the new club's interior. This club was to be more elegant than the one in Farmington and we did get a little carried away with the amenities, but at the time competition was beginning to grow. We added whirlpool baths, as well as saunas, to each locker room. The appointment throughout looked beautiful, with oak tongue and groove walls, even complete with a huge circular fireplace in the center of the clubhouse. In two directions, from viewing decks, were banks of three courts each, and from a third side of the clubhouse were two more courts. All eight tennis courts were surfaced with the very popular HarTru green clay. It is a forgiving surface, which is really easy on the legs and can be played on for longer periods of time by the average club player. People, knowing our track record in Farmington, signed up early with us—a membership in one club gave the same privileges in the other. The dual membership provided a great marketing tool and we looked forward to another successful club, even though the debt service turned out to be almost three times that of Farmington. We would, however, have the additional income from two extra courts to help offset the extra costs.

This time our construction schedule got totally messed up. Maybe Gary and I pushed our general contractor too hard, maybe there existed too many extra details, anyway he had a sort of physical—mental breakdown causing us to get months behind schedule. In the end, we were finally ready to open by early spring of 1976 and again offered two weeks of free play to try out our special green clay courts and the rest of the amenities. This time I agreed only to help manage the new club until all the control systems fell into place, with all the bugs worked out. The challenge felt exciting.

chapter five

A Lady Named Sandia

In those days, I kept all my business affairs and some personal appointments in order with the help of a very efficient part-time secretary and friend, Linnea. We had met several months earlier under sort of funny circumstances. Friends set up a blind challenge tennis match for me against Linnea. That was the first time I saw her as I walked onto the court to play a singles match with her. They purposely chose a court next to the viewing deck, so invited spectators could watch. I knew during warm-ups that I was in trouble. She proved an excellent player. To make a long story short, Linnea beat me that first match and also in a later second rematch, played at my macho request. After that, I chased the old "macho" syndrome out of my head, played my game, and won quite a few times. During that match stretch, Linnea and I developed a friendship during which she agreed also to take on a part-time role with our tennis business effort.

Soon after Linnea was reminding me who I had meetings with and when, typing letters and articles for a monthly publication I started, The Greater Hartford Tennis News, and in general, keeping my created mess in decent order. One

my eyes gazed upon her, toward me she came

I knew then, life would never be the same

day just before Oakwood Farms Racquet Club, or the big Oak as we came to call it later, was scheduled to open, Linnea handed me a note that was to change my life very deeply. We were hiring staff for the new club at that time. The note read, "Sandra Yoell, seeks employment, 646-0285." Other than reflect on the different sort of surname, I just stuck the note in my pocket. Later, I recalled it, and thinking it was a friend of a friend of Linnea's, I should at least follow it up with a courtesy call. The spirited voice of Sandra on the other end of the telephone greeted me and subsequently agreed to stop by the big Oak that same night to see me for a preliminary employment chat at the finish of my regular Monday night doubles game.

I never gave the meeting with Sandra much thought after the phone call until I tiredly came off the court with my tennis buddies to slump into a chair clutching an ice-cold beer. As we started into our post game match analysis, one of the staff called out to me that there was a young lady waiting to see me. That's when I first saw her, standing at the main desk, all bright eyed, beautiful, and bubbling over with enthusiasm and spirit. Her jet-black hair and light brown skin were in beautiful contrast to her flashing white smile. We found a couple of empty club-house easy chairs and sat down to talk. I remember sitting up straight, offering her a beer, which she accepted, talking for a little while about club operations and her background for club type work. All during the conversations, my heart rate accelerated due to a keen awareness of her physical presence sitting across from me. I ended the interview by telling her that I would talk to our regular full-time manager. He would probably be in contact with her for further discussions. Two strong thoughts profoundly surfaced in my mind as I turned to watch Sandra walk out of the club-house that Monday night. First, her spirit, smile, and genuine friendliness would be needed at the new club—it would be an asset, and secondly, I felt like I should definitely keep my distance, as I was already smitten by her. I remember feeling lifted in a way I'd never experienced before just being around her those few minutes.

Sandra, or Sandia as I would come to call her in favor of her uncle's pet nickname, hailed originally from Colorado, was Mexican-American nationality, and had recently separated from her husband, an international lawyer, in Germany. Not quite ready to return to the scrutiny of the family in Colorado, Sandia stayed with her avid and ranked tennis-playing sister-in-law, Marti, in Manchester, an eastern suburb of Hartford. She just wanted a job to pay her own way, along with that of her six-year old daughter, Kirsten, while she sorted out the details of divorce.

Our full-time manager, Jack, told me late the next day that he met with Sandia and, agreeing with what I told him, hired her on the basis of the one interview. Sandia snapped right into the swing of things to immediately become an integral part of the staff. I occupied a private office on the first level of our two-story club-house, so I saw her from time to time, but still feeling a little gun shy, kept my distance. The indoor season ended in May, with Linnea, that summer of '76, unable to work with me at the downtown office. So we offered the job to Sandia and she accepted. My resolve to stay away from her, trying to maintain an employee-employer relationship, only lasted about one month until I couldn't stand it anymore. I asked her out to one of Hartford's then nightspots, the Brownstone, for a few beers and conversation.

That first Saturday night date almost turned into a disaster. I played tennis all day on some outdoor red clay courts in a brilliant sun, not realizing I had a bit of heat stroke. Several ice cold Michelobs later as I dropped Sandia at her place which she shared with a roommate, Pam, and sometimes babysitter for Sandia's daughter Kirsten, I asked my way to the bathroom. Once inside the bathroom, I passed out, clubbing my head on the edge of the sink on my way down to meet the floor. What a first impression I must have made, lying there, out cold on the bathroom floor. The only good part of the episode was I ended up on the living room couch for most of the night with my head in Sandia's lap. I remember the scent of her, the softness of her body, and the soothing sound of her voice as she nursed me back from the oblivion of heat stroke.

A week later, an old friend and suitor, Kenner, came through town to find Sandia to invite her off for an extended trip into Mexico. She refused, stayed on, and I wouldn't learn of the trip offer until much later on. For the first time, in a long time, I wanted to be involved—really involved with Sandia. My life began to focus on the next time I would see her.

My partners found out that we dated and began dictating by the textbook that Sandia had to be fired from the club staff. They thought we were sure to foul things up—an owner and an employee. I won my case by arguing that the two of us, working together for the good of the club, would be the best of all scenarios. Again, they put me on trial, but I wasn't worried. We both remained ferocious workers.

That summer of '76 turned into a dream, a woven collage of beautiful memories. We went to see the Tall Ships at Newport, Rhode Island in my old restored purple (actual color was Renegade Plum) Dodge van; slept in the van, then awakened to those magnificent sails at sunrise. We took Kirsten on that holiday, as she had to soon thereafter get on a plane to spend the summer with her dad in Germany. She seemed so grown up at seven—walked onto that big jet by herself with such poise and lack of fear.

Then Gary's little league team went all the way to the area championship game, where they lost a close one. Gary appeared very accepting of both Sandia and our relationship, and seemed excited when she came to his games to watch and cheer. Gary starred as the cleanup hitter on the team, at one time batting for a 0.823 mid-season average. It always seemed to me that he would hit best when he had two strikes called against him, then he'd rap a clean single over the infield. We saw the girls in their tennis tournaments also. They seemed less accepting of Sandia, maybe because they were daughters, I don't know. But Lynne and Sandia would end up later as a women's doubles team competing in the Greater Hartford Women's Tennis League.

We would end up sleeping at her place or at my Hilton hideaway and always seemed to be trying to figure out where we left the cars. I had two vehicles and Sandia had one. I finally sold my new Mustang, keeping just the restored purple van. Some nights we would even sleep at the big Oak after a late tennis game, Jacuzzi, and shower. We'd just curl up on one of those big comfortable red corduroy clubhouse lounges.

One night we forgot to lock the front clubhouse door and were in a deep naked sleep when some early morning summer players came bounding through the door. We woke abruptly, sitting up with a start, as they laughed and headed for their court.

The summer flew by. Soon it became mid-August. I arranged a special surprise party with the Hilton's maitre de for Sandia's 25th birthday. She seemed a bit overcome by all the attention in that exclusive restaurant, but we had a ball. Excellent wine and food, followed by a personal birthday cake, is always fun.

Not long after that, President Ford paid a visit to Hartford, staying on the floor below my little 18th floor suite. Sandia and I thought we'd be clever one day during his visit and take a stroll on the 17th floor maybe bumping into the President, with a chance to say "Hello." So instead of pressing our normal 18 on the elevator, we just pressed 17. We were alone on the elevator by the time it slowed to a stop at the 17th floor. The doors started to slide open. Standing about six inches in front of the doors, facing us, stood two seemingly huge guys dressed in dark blue suits with ties. They greeted us with, "What do you two think you are doing here?" We looked at each other anxiously, immediately realizing they were probably Secret Service, and our effort at seeing the President proved at best foolhardy.

I quickly muttered something like, "Oh, sorry. We live upstairs. Must have pushed the wrong button. Goodbye!" and reached out to mash the 18 button. Once the doors closed, and we started to rise to the sanctuary of the 18th floor, we both broke out in uncontrollable laughter and were crying with glee by the time we stepped off on our familiar floor above. What had we thought to step off on the President's floor to just stroll nonchalantly up to his room? I guess it was the shock of the suddenness of those two bodyguards appearing, followed by my quick exit that struck us so funny after it ended. I was discovering Sandia's adventuresome nature and loving it.

Soon it would be time to open the big Oak for its first full regular season (September to May), but we had time for one more adventure before that. Kenner, Sandia's old friend from Washington, D.C., sent word to her that he was sailing his boat, Seafever, north along the New England coast, and would love to have the two of us join him in Maine onboard for however long. Was there any choice? We headed for Maine and the town of Freeport to await Kenner's arrival. After a few days of lazy waiting, the 32 foot Seafever pulled into Freeport and we went aboard. Kenner already had two temporary crew people aboard which we joined to make a total of five sailors of varying skill levels. Alice had come on board for a day trip and was still tripping a week later. The other guy looked like John Denver and didn't seem to mind me calling him that, especially since he always played another folk tune on his ever-present guitar. I don't remember how long John had stayed on the Seafever at that point, but all in all, it turned out to be a great crew. Sandia and I stayed at least a week, during which we cooked and ate local lobsters until our forearms were caked with butter, swam in the cold Maine seas to fight off the atrophy, and learned some sailing from Kenner as I came to know what a beautiful person he is. My last time at the steering became alarmingly stormy with ocean swells reaching eight or nine feet. That's when the news of an approaching hurricane reached us on the shipboard radio. We quickly found a small port where we threw out double storm anchors to wait for the big blow to pass. At that point, Sandia and I decided we'd better start south to Connecticut to

get ready for the club opening, now less than a week away. After warm hugs of goodbye, Kenner rowed us to the nearest shore in a rubber dinghy. We hitched back to The Renegade Plum Van in Freeport and headed south. On the way back we reflected on the summer of spirit '76. My batteries certainly felt charged back to "overflow" on the spirit capacity level.

Our full time manager took another, bigger, tennis job down in New Jersey, with the management of the big Oak that next season falling to me, and in every respect, to Sandia. We started with the same good staff from the previous spring and soon had the club to a very high membership level. As a business, the big Oak prospered under our close personal and spirited attention. We also took in a new investor partner to help with the additional debt service. With that many partners, infighting was inevitable. As a group, we just couldn't agree on how things should be done. The simplest issues seemed to take forever to be resolved, if they got solved at all. I felt like one millionaire partner watched the pennies so carefully, that he missed the dollars. But as usually happens, those with the money, end up with the biggest say. Right or wrong, it became my opinion that we were slowly moving towards becoming ineffective as a viable business group.

As the ownership group deteriorated, Sandia and I worked hard at keeping the morale of the club going, as well as that of the staff for the '76/'77 season. We decided that maintaining two residences was crazy after I nervously asked her what she thought about getting a place together. In her always-lighthearted way, she answered, "Let's do it for as long as it's good for both of us." After looking at available rentals for a while, we settled on a summer cottage on nearby Lake Taramugus in the town of Marlborough. It remained available for the winter season only and proved perfect for us. We got Kirsten enrolled in the local elementary school, arranging for another mom to watch her after school until we could get there to pick her up. With the exception of a few lake ice skating gatherings and one Christmas party that we hosted, we didn't spend much time at our rented cottage that winter. Most of the time we spent at the club, chaperoning its affairs and filling in wherever needed. Kirsten did her homework at the club and often played in the Jacuzzi with her friend and cousin, Binky. We always went out for a quick bite or sent one of the staff out for fast food. Sometimes the cheeseburgers would show up with a single bite out of each one, or the pizzas with missing slices, but it was all in fun with long hours of work and short nights of sleep.

One night Sandia said out of the blue, "Why don't we stay home tonight and I'll cook us something?" I realized that after being together for about six months, we'd never stayed home to eat. It turned out to be a great meal of Beef Stroganoff, during which I discovered yet another talent in my lady.

Soon after, at our favorite pizza place, I asked Sandia to marry me and she accepted. We married in June of '77 beside Lake Taramugus where we had based that winter of happiness. Our minister was Kenner, by now our mutual friend, from D.C. He drove up to Connecticut to marry us. Actually, he only got as far as Princeton, New Jersey, where his old Volkswagen bug broke down. He took a train from there as he was running late. Sandia's ex-husband had sold Kenner that Volkswagen, so we started jokingly calling its breakdown, "Peter's Last Revenge." Anyway, after Kenner arrived, we planned out the lakeside ceremony late the night before we took our own scripted vows to each other, pledging, "to take it one day at a time, as it had been since our beginning of love and devotion, to keep it fresh

as the newly blooming flowers of springtime." My brother, Roy, younger sister, Dottie, and my Mom showed up for us. My four daughters, Sherrie, Lynne, Andrea, Deborah, and soon-to-be step-daughter Kirsten, as well as Sandia's nieces, Laura and Binky, were all flower girls. My son Gary was my best man. Sandia's (ex)sister-in-law, Marti, was her matron of honor. Marti's husband, Brad, gave Sandia "away." We were even treated to a very gentle rain shower during the ceremony that had a cleansing, starting over, and fulfilling effect. We closed the big Oak to membership play that day, while opening the clubhouse for our reception. Lots of tennis club members came to the celebration of our marriage, with the staff volunteering to host the affair. Our sea captain minister, Kenner, with his long red hair, open pancho, and sandals, danced my Mom across the clubhouse floor. Pablo kept the champagne fountain flowing. Bub kept his entire Beatles collection constantly playing through his amplifier and gigantic speakers. Family and friends renewed and visited. The Marlborough Tavern catered a traditional Greek buffet. The foreman of my tennis court construction crew, Gary LaRocque, a close friend, was there with his lady, Denise, as well as my investor partners. I remember reflecting that special day on the beautiful breadth of our friendships. We had a ball. It proved too good a time to leave early. We celebrated into the night. Then Sandia and I finally got away to, where else, the Honeymoon suite at the Hilton. The rooms were magnificent. They provided a fruit basket and a large bottle of champagne on ice, compliments of the house. Sandia and I looked at the champagne, then each other, and silently agreed we'd had enough of the fizzy stuff, as we dove for that huge bed to get some much needed rest in each others arms. In the morning, we could party some more!

Having totaled my old purple van, I replaced it with a newer blue Dodge van and had created pseudo living quarters inside, complete with icebox and bed—the important things. The day after the wedding, we got Kirsten to her plane for Europe to see her Dad for a few months and we took off for a short stay at a friend's cottage on Block Island. A lot of toll booth operators laughed and let us through for free noticing all the white shoe polish writing the kids had done on the van about "getting married"—"If this vans rockin, don't come knockin, finally legal, etc." Strapped up on the back of the van in special stirrups was my new, "previously owned" Yamaha 175 Enduro dirt bike. It would be a great way to explore the island, with my lady hugging me from behind.

After a week of unbelievable bliss in that beautiful island setting, we drove our van onto the ferry and headed back for the mainland. Sandia and I had one more secret mission before we would head west for a few months of honeymooning and to spend a little time with her family, I had yet to meet. My daughter Lynne was due to graduate from high school a few days hence and we wanted to surprise her at the Graduation Ceremony. She thought we had already headed west on our trip, so it would be a fun surprise! I had earlier on given her my classic '68 Mustang convertible as a senior-graduation present, so she thought we were long gone.

It turned out to be an excellent surprise and then a great excuse to get together for a party afterwards. We met

a lot of Lynne's friends and my oldest daughter Sherrie and her husband joined us also. Sandia and I left them really late that night, and having made no other plans for a place to stay, we decided to head for the "Big Oak" and our favorite

Marriage by the Lake

red couch! When we finally got to the club parking lot, we were so tired and partied out that we decided it was easier just to get undressed and crawl up into the van bed in back. Within milliseconds, we were fast asleep.

In that deep, tired sleep, someone started pounding on the side of the van and I slowly began to come out of my "comatose" state as I heard voices shouting outside. As I finally opened the side door, with a pillow clutched to my groin area to cover my nakedness, a flashlight beamed into my eyes, and I perceived the silhouettes of two town policemen. I remember the questions came rapid fire.

"What are you doing here? Who's the female in there with you? Whose van is this?"

I slowly focused on the female question and in my tiredness realized that we had just married. I blurted out something like, "That lady is my wife and this is my tennis club!"

They both laughed out loud and thought they had now heard it all. One of them said, "Sure and I am the president of the U.S.A.. too!

Let's have a look at your license and registration."

I was now more awake and feeling pretty silly with my pillow, but there wasn't much I could do about the situation except comply with their request. Fumbling around in the dark, I finally found my wallet and gave them my license and registration. They took them and headed over to their idling police cruiser to check me out. I pulled my pants on, in the meantime, and was trying to explain to my "groggy" lady what was going on. They returned and were kind of sheepish as they apologized.

"We checked ownership and everything and we are sorry we troubled you, Mr. and Mrs. Bruton. We'll be on our way now."

As they walked away, I shouted something like, "Thanks for keeping an eye on the club for us!"

Sandia and I had a good laugh in relief as we headed inside the club to our beloved red couch, where we could sleep an uninterrupted sleep. In the morning, we would head west!

6

The Honeymoon

And head west we did, but by way of Washington D.C. with Kenner's Volkswagen bug in tow behind us. We went to Princeton, New Jersey, where Kenner had left his malfunctioning car, hooked it up to the blue van via a rigid tow bar, and navigated south toward Kenner's brownstone abode in the inner city of DC. It was the least we could do for our sea captain minister friend that had just married us at that beautiful lakeside ceremony.

Sandia and I had fun and took our time going west from DC, stopping at many places to see the sights, including a river boat ride on the Mississippi in St. Louis under the evening shadows of the Gateway Arch to the West. Our riverboat turned out to be a little bit of a surprise for us, but was none the less, a very unique experience for my journals. After a long hot dusty day on the road, visions of a couple of cold beers while hanging over the boat's rail taking in the sights along the shore, was what we had in mind as we parked our van in that riverside parking lot. Walking from the van towards the demarcation dock, we noticed a boat was getting ready to pull away from the pier, so we ran easily toward

> *wherever the van headed, we couldn't miss*
>
> *on a honeymoon, there's nothing but bliss*

the gangplank and made it just in time to hop aboard as it pulled away into the river. It seemed funny that no one asked us for a ticket, or money, but we thought that maybe they would collect upon exiting the boat. We thirstily headed for the bar below decks. On finding it, we ordered a couple of cold ones from the lady behind the bar as I reached for my wallet to pay for the order.

She looked up from her work in surprise and said, "Sorry, but the bar is closed for the duration of this special church group trip."

Sandia and I looked at each other in dismay as the reality dawned on us. That's why no one had asked us for a ticket, it was a special church charter!

Since there wasn't much we could do until the boat docked again, we just joined in with the gospel singing and foot stomping and in general made it a fun time. At one point during the celebrations, an assistant minister came over to meet us and introduced us to his wife. She was curious who we were and how we got on the boat and thought our story was hilarious. We chatted with her until the boat finally docked and found her to be a really fun loving lady. As we said our good-byes, her husband returned and invited us to their house for the night. Sandia and I tried to graciously decline, but they remained firm and we finally figured "what the heck." So we followed them to their suburban home in St. Francis, just west of St. Louis. It was on our way west anyway. We'd just get up in the morning and head out for another day on the road. We both laughed at the way things happened to us—to get on a wrong boat and end up sleeping at a minister's home.

They gave us refreshments at the house and showed us the sofa bed that we could use for the night. He excused himself—something about an early meeting—and went to bed, but his wife was a real live wire and wanted to stay up and talk about life. I had the distinct impression that she was not very happy in the church life and longed for a freer type of existence. And here we came through her life, just enjoying every minute, reaching out to touch every part and person we met, at a time when she was having doubts about her own choices. At one point she asked if there was room in the van for her and if she could go west with us! That seemed to be her intent as we said goodnight and gave her a warm three-way hug. Well we felt awkward for her and after only a few hours sleep on their so-fabed, I wrote them both a "thank you" poem of spirit and left it on the kitchen counter on our way out the back door to fire up the East Coast Sunshine Van. I have often thought of those two and wondered how they got on in life after we went through; if she ever found that freedom she seemed to desire so desperately, not even realizing that it comes just from your perspective of life and can't be given by anyone on the "outside."

We pushed on toward Colorado and just had fun taking in the sights. Curious about Sandia's hometown of Fort Lupton, about 25 miles north of Denver, I would constantly ask in each small town through which we passed, "Is this the size of Ft. Lupton?"

She always answered, "No, this is bigger!"

Once she told me that there existed only three police cars in her town when she went to high school. As the miles passed, I continually pumped her for information about her town, childhood, and family. I guess I just wanted to know the circumstances that had molded this woman I had come to love so deeply. How had she come to love life so passionately? I was slowly learning from her stories about a childhood that included working in the fields and being raised by hard working parents who backed up their discipline with unconditional love. Sandia's father, Francisco (Frank) Yañez Gomez had immigrated to this country when only a small boy of about four along with siblings and his parents to escape the chaos of revolution in the Mexico of the early '20's. The blood of the proud Purepeche Indians ran in his veins. Sandia's mom on the other hand, was a direct descendent from Spain and came from early Spanish settlers to our own southwest. Blue eyed, light-haired brothers attest to her lineage. So Sandia was a true *mestiza*, or mixed race, as they are called in the Spanish language. I loved her identity and the concept of it, and was anxious to meet the parents whose love had given the seed of life to my lady. My only apprehension, as I remember it driving toward the setting sun and my upcoming meeting with her family, was my age, or I guess Sandia's youth, fourteen years my junior. It never bothered us a bit, but the impending scrutiny of parents and family members made me think about it. I was less concerned about being an anglo, or an outsider, at the time as I just didn't know much about Mexican-American life and how they viewed the anglo culture, and vice versa.

chapter seven

Family and the Mountains

I met the family at their small mountain cabin located only a few miles from the western entrance to Rocky Mountain National Park near the picturesque village of Grand Lake, Colorado. The drive up into the mountains had literally taken my breath away. Having been raised in the suburbs of Boston, basically on the shores of New England, weaving up through those Rockies to the summit of Berthoud Pass at an elevation of 11,300 feet and then gazing down upon the Western Slopes for the first time was truly an unforgettable experience!! Filled with the excitement of the journey, we pulled up to that little fishing cabin and witnessed no less than 23 family members assembled there to greet us. I remember feeling totally overwhelmed as Sandia said to me, "This is only a small part of my family. There are lots more!" The warmth of their welcome and the genuine acceptance I felt in those initial days of meeting have always remained with me.

Sandia's mom and dad insisted that first night that we take their bedroom, the only private bedroom in the cabin. The next morning, I was gently awakened and invited to join Sandia's dad and brothers for an early morning fishing

at times, bad things, can be the best cause

to look at your life, a moment to pause

trip down to a nearby lake. Dad gave me a quick tutelage in his way of fishing and soon I had hauled in a few of those Colorado Mountain trout all by my "city boy" self.

What a feeling it was there amongst those green pine trees, bright sunshine, clean, crisp mountain air, just fishing the morning away with my new family relating stories of past adventures. I learned that Sandia's mom had eight brothers and she was the only girl born right in the middle of all those boys. No wonder she was so good at taking care of large groups of family. She had met and married Sandia's dad when she was only thirteen years old. By the time mom was eighteen, she already had four children. Sandia would arrive on the scene six years later to become the true "baby" of the family. Spoiled a little, yes, but a brat, no. In Sandia's family, everyone learned to work hard. Even as the youngest, Sandia was in the fields, helping with the picking of beans when she was only six years old. The stories had it that her picked volumes weren't record breaking, but the eagerness to help and do her part was evident from the start. In poor, hard working families in those days, youngsters didn't get shipped off to "day care," they stayed with the family and did what they could to contribute.

Sandia's and my plans were to stay in Colorado for a little while, be with the family, and then head back to the Northeast to "mother" the tennis club through another season, but a letter arrived that would change all of that. Our "penny watching" investor partner stated in his letter that Sandia's vacation pay had been allocated to cover extra expenses they had incurred as a result of our not being there to take care of things! I don't know what he expected as we had always worked 10 to 14 hours a day to cover all ends of things—the extra time was gratis. Anyway, that thoughtless gesture, along with the general deterioration of the ownership group to function in a viable way together, prompted me to write them and tell them to hire another manager and we'd be back whenever we got back. They were taking a lot of the fun and spirit out of the work by focusing on the "buck" and losing sight of the membership as people trying to enjoy their leisure time while getting some great social exercise.

I have to note here that the other partners restored Sandia's vacation pay and stated that it was withheld without their knowledge. We didn't go back anyway, so they hired the new investor's son to manage and he was canned after only one season of huge losses.

I had seen enough in those years dealing with the lives of the "rich and famous" that I wanted little more to do with the priority of making money above all else. I'm not saying all money is made unscrupulously, either, although I witnessed less than honest dealings often enough. I just didn't want my main focus in life to be the acquisition of money, and thereafter, the "devoted" maintenance of that acquired personal fortune!

These beliefs, experienced in my life's apprenticeship to that point, came into Sandia's and my discussions about the future as we looked at a life together that would no longer involve the husbandry of indoor tennis clubs. We finally said our good-byes to Sandia's family, and with the tingle of parting embraces still vibrating through our beings, we headed the blue van westward towards California to explore the area for possible future residence.

Grand Lake in the Colorado Mountains

chapter eight

What's Next?

California provided beauty, but there were just too many people for our way of thinking. I took Sandia to La Jolla cove where I had done a lot of snorkel diving while stationed at Mirimar Naval Air Station on my tour in the U. S. Navy. Back in '59 and '60, there would be three or four people at most swimming in the cove at any given time. But in the summer of '77, Sandia and I had a tough time finding a place just to put down a towel to sit on. It was "wall to wall" people. I could hardly believe it. I took Sandia to see the campus of San Diego Junior College, where I had studied daytimes for a year while stationed at Mirimar and assigned to the second shift. It had been converted to a four-year college and was now called San Diego City College. There were malls everywhere and freeways and unending people. I interviewed for a research position at the University of California - Irvine Campus and was actually offered the position with the Plasma Physics group, but after several days of deep contemplation, turned it down. We had agreed that California did not need two more people at the time, at least not our two warm bodies. So after visiting friends and family,

leaving things behind, and starting anew

can be fresh for the heart, like morning dew

saying more "good-byes," Sandia and I headed south into Mexico along the Baja 1000 route.

We spent a fun few weeks kicking around the Baja, visiting the whaling museum on the West Coast, then heading for the beaches on the East Coast. It was summer time and hot, so we didn't go all the way down the Baja, just to Santa Rosalia, about 600 miles south of the border. From there we caught a car ferry across to Guaymas and headed north along the mainland coast towards Arizona and the U. S. of A. After three weeks of varying degrees of Mexican food, the first place we headed in the border town of Nogales, Arizona was to the Golden Arches and promptly wolfed down quarter pounders with cheese. How American! Shortly thereafter we were both pretty sick and enjoyed a laugh not knowing whether it was some kind of lingering Moctezuma's Revenge, but finally deciding that it was probably the cheeseburgers that did it.

The blue Dodge van, or East Coast Sunshine Van as we called it, had come through those rough roads in Mexico with nary a whimper. We treated her to a good bath to remove the caked on mud and dirt from so many unpaved roads and then a good polish job for accent. The Yamaha dirt bike that spent most of the trip strapped into her rear stirrups was the hardest to get clean. It had spent most of the trip in the dust vortices of the van. Had we run into van problems in the middle of nowhere in Mexico, that bike would have gotten us to the nearest town and repair parts, or perhaps a mechanic — the Enduro 175 insurance. We then pointed the van Northeast and headed for my niece Shellie's wedding in Lawton, Oklahoma.

We made Lawton the morning of the wedding and after showering and dressing at a public swimming pool facility, we asked directions to the military base and the wedding chapel. Most of the family seemed surprised we arrived on time. It felt great to be together again for a celebration and a party. The whole warm experience just seemed to end too quickly and soon we were waving good-byes at the airport. Then Sandia and I looked at each other and realized we were suddenly alone and hadn't made plans where to head next. What fun! What freedom!

It didn't take us long to decide to get out of the Oklahoma summer heat and head for the cool of those high Colorado Rockies and another more leisurely look at the surrounding mountainsides near the village of Grand Lake. So we stocked the van with supplies and pointed her westward once again in the cruise mode.

We stayed a glorious month at Sandia's folks cabin and built them a huge sundeck to accommodate those sometimes large family gathering groups. It proved a pleasurable project to work on. I even found that breathing at high altitude proved easy once you got used to it. I believe it is called acclimatization. The high altitude presented no hindrance to working hard at all. We met some interesting mountain people during that stint. All in all, Sandia and I fell in love with those enchanted mountains and set a new long term goal—to go back to Connecticut long enough to accomplish the sale of my club shares and return to this small mountain village to build a home, live in the clean crisp air and green trees, and leave the turmoil of the bustling Northeast behind us. With that mutual pledge between us, and the strength of our love binding us, we drove down out of the mountains and headed east.

chapter nine

The Bumpy Road Back to Colorado

Sandia and I arrived back in Connecticut, resolute in our decision to return to those Colorado Rockies as soon as possible. This goal left us with a couple of loose ends to tie up before we could pursue our mutual dream. First, my business interests had to be sold. Secondly, we had to educate ourselves on house construction—actually, construction in general, because neither Sandia nor I had ever built anything before, except a couple of "over-built" sundecks.

While learning to build seemed straightforward enough, the sale of my club shares would be anything but. The portion of the two indoor tennis clubs I had helped develop, build, and manage possessed a certain glory associated with them, but not a substantial income. The leisure time tennis industry had grown very competitive and could very well follow the pattern of the past bowling alley boom and bust, where only the well run bowling alleys survived. But even at "break even," with tax shelter benefits for owners, a piece of country club tennis could be considered prestigious. I just had to find a buyer wanting a bit of prestige, along with a lot of tennis playing time.

keeping things in balance, both bad and good

yin and yang, an art, must be understood

After putting out the word in the tennis community on the availability of my shares in our two clubs, keen interest surfaced by way of a regular female player at our Farmington Club and her doctor husband. She, no doubt, made up the driving force in their approach to me expressing a possible purchase of my partnership interests. She played a lot of tennis, while he only infrequently dabbled at the tennis game. Several meetings later, the good doctor grabbed my hand to shake it vigorously in a demonstrative way of saying, "We have a deal." His attorney had already started the paperwork. Only a few weeks and my part of the tennis business would have a new owner.

So on to the second step, that of designing and learning how to build our homestead in the mountains. A Christmas gift from a friend who was aware of our dream started us on our way. The title, _30 Energy Efficient Homes_, gave a clue to the book's contents, which contained seeds well beyond the book itself.

One of the houses in the book was owner built in 1975 at the phenomenally low price of $4,800.00—this in the age of the $60,000.00

plus home! Better yet, this particular home was heated during the cold winters in Bath, Maine using only the sun and two cords of wood as back-up. The owners pumped their water with a hand pump and used a composting toilet for the daily necessities. A solar shower cleansed their bodies. It represented a true pioneering effort by an energy conscious couple with an eye to the future. This couple, Pat and Patsy Hennin, could have been many different places and surely earning a substantial living with Pat's credentials—a Doctorate of Law from Harvard University. But they chose instead the role of showing others that our country's appetite for the unchecked consumption of non-renewable energy cannot go on forever.

With this theme, the Shelter Institute in Bath, Maine began, with the Hennins as co-founders. So around 1970, from small beginnings, the Hennins, with the help of others dedicated to this and similar themes, "Shelter" had grown to represent a respected educational purpose—the teaching of energy efficient construction to aspiring owner-builders.

After several telephone calls to Maine, Sandia and I found ourselves enrolled in a two week "crash course" in home-building at Shelter. We felt ecstatic. Having shaken hands with the doctor on the sale of my shares in the racquet clubs, all missions seemed "go." As the days ticked by, we read avidly on house design. Finally, the mid-February course time had arrived. Financially strapped, but sure of the imminent sale, we took

a small personal loan from our attorney who had become in tune with our mission. Our spirits soared high as we readied our van for the trip from Hartford, Connecticut north to Bath for the "Shelter Experience".

As we packed for the two-week stay, the telephone rang. I ran to the phone in high spirits. The caller was probably another friend wanting to say goodbye, as we had let it be known that we would be heading for Colorado as soon as the building course ended. I said a cheery "hello" into the receiver and then it became stomach-wrenching time. It was the good doctor expressing his regrets and inability to go forward with our deal as we had agreed. As I listened numbly to his apologies and his reasons why he was unable to complete the sale, I could barely hold onto the receiver. What could I do? "Handshake deals" no longer constituted binding contracts between people in our day and age. I hung up the phone and sat there stunned for a long time. I needed to gather up the strength to tell my Sandia. She took the news well, demonstrating a "toughness" we would later require very much. The next Shelter course was not scheduled until the summer, which seemed centuries away to us, so we decided to leave the next day for Bath as scheduled.

Friends gave us a going away party that night. We "faked" our way through it, not wanting to spoil their genuine good wishes. Smiling, we left the party late to grab a few hours sleep before our trek north.

chapter ten

The Shelter Experience

Sandia and I assailed Bath, Maine and the Shelter Institute with renewed spirits. I had talked to another interested buyer, who assured us that he wanted the shares from the business badly and would come up with the money somewhere, somehow. His determination made us both feel better.

We rented a room from a host family that possessed roots many generations back in Maine. The house we shared with them had been built in the 1800's. It's timber frame possessed a strength and a durability about it, as well as a certain warmth and character.

Having arrived late in the evening before our first day of classes, we hardly became acquainted with our host family before we retired to our room. Filled with anticipation and excitement, we talked late into the night about our future. Keeping us warm was a log cabin quilt that we had just finished making only days before. Feeling the silks, satins, velvets, and eyelet laces of the quilt made me remember my promise to Sandia. I told her that by the time the quilt was finished, I would have sold the business and then we could go to Colorado. She worked hard on

stitch, sew, pattern and quilt, study and dream

plan a house that fits, like coffee and cream

the quilt for three months. In the last few weeks, it had become a symbol of "going" to us. Toward that end, we worked in shifts on it. Sandia would stitch until her fingers became sore while I read a book of poetry aloud, then I would quilt until my fingers went numb, with Sandia reading. Finally, that beautiful quilt had been finished and here we lay in Shelter country, feeling secure with the warmth of each other under our quilt. We slept a smiling sleep.

Sandia and I woke at the sound of the alarm, quickly got ready and drove the ten miles to Bath. The Institute was located in a building right out of the 1920's, with a character befitting the Shelter purpose. Two of the rooms in the building made up the school; an administrative desk and a browsing library in the first room, and a large classroom in the second. Other students wandered in, asking questions, meeting others, glancing at books, and registering at the desk. Over coffee, we found out that the Institute had acquired another building, a block away. This latest facility acquisition housed a cabinet-making shop and a store with everything for sale, from books and engineering supplies

Sandia and our log cabin patterned quilt

to woodburning stoves, all at student discount prices.

Pat Hennin then ambled in with a notebook under one arm, uncombed hair hanging in his eyes, and hands buried deep in his pockets. He called our class into session. Sandia and I quickly found seats and got our pens and notebooks ready. I wanted to get every word written down!

Pat spent that first morning talking about philosophy. He lectured on the philosophies of energy, construction, and lifestyle, each of which is highly relevant to building your own "nest." We discussed our country's decision to emphasize the highway and the truck, along with air-freight, instead of railways and sea going freighters, even though the fuel consumption per pound of freight was a great deal more for the former than the latter. We looked at conventional construction techniques—"gorilla cages"—and

their relevance. We considered lifestyles depicted by large houses with energy expenditures at dishonest levels for the sake of convenience, family rooms in damp, dark basements, and our overall craving for everything at our finger tips at a moments notice.

Pat gave no philosophical dictates, only thought provoking observations of where we were headed. Pat's closing statements emphasized the Shelter purpose, which was to stimulate the owner-builder to shape and create his or her own environment. The Shelter faculty would present some alternate ways to build, but we were encouraged to go beyond these suggestions, using our own ingenuity.

The lunch bell sounded and we wandered into town, hoping to find an economical, but nourishing lunch. Sandia and I talked excitedly over lunch. This whole Shelter theme was for us. It represented our feelings, our backgrounds, and our direction. I had spent several years trying to save energy in our tennis clubs, and I had consulted experts on active solar installations, heat reclaiming, and waste conversion to energy. I learned many things in those studies, but mostly that the majority of people and corporations did not really seem to care about the reckless energy course that our society was steering.

Afternoon classes began with site selection and microclimate considerations. It is an unfortunate fact that too many houses have been built on a site without much thought given to the sun's orientation or winter storm directions; only that the front door faced the street. The criteria for most suburban developers has been to get the maximum number of houses allowed by zoning on a particular tract of land, to remove or level all trees because they get in the way of rapid building. Thought was never given to those precious root systems fighting soil erosion or the buffering of the north winds by those leafy branches. Maximizing the profits has been and continues to be the guiding theme.

Evening came and our first day of classes ended. Homework problems were assigned and all fifty or so students were off in different directions. Sandia and I found a warm pizza parlor and spent several hours there in a booth working on those problems in between bites of pizza. We discussed our impressions of the first day and came to the conclusion that it had been extremely productive and informative for both of us.

We studied the only photograph we had of our piece of land in the Rockies. Sandia had put some money into it years earlier, when her folks had bought a block of land in the same mountain subdivision, thinking of a possible summer cabin or just an investment. We looked at the land on our honeymoon trip that previous summer, initially thinking of selling it, but finally getting caught up in the idea of actually living there. Those rugged peaks had slowly but surely captivated us to the point that our main focus, or goal, now in life was just to go and live amongst their peaceful and magnificent splendor—to become mountain people. The passion of our dream was so strong; we could taste it with our hearts.

Looking at that photograph, with our lectures on microclimate fresh in our minds, we verified that the slope of the land was indeed to the south, knowing the time of day the photograph was taken and noting the shadow directions. There was a large natural berm of rock formations behind the property to buffer the northern storms and there were no tall evergreen trees to the south to block the rays of that warm old sun. We were to learn later that a forest fire seventy-five years earlier had cleared our site of ponderosa pine and blue spruce trees, the result of which, all these years later, was a new growth of lodge pole pines. There were many things we

would not know until we got there. Would there be rock formations in conflict with our foundation system? Would building officials look favorably upon us building our own place? We would just have to cope with those things and many more when the time came.

We spent the next ten days at Shelter, going step by step, from the foundation to the roof framing, including electrical, plumbing, ventilation, acoustics, lighting, and heating. In general, we followed our text, _From the Ground Up_. My notebook scribblings and sketches filled pages at a rapid pace!

At the mid-point of the course, we spent the day visiting seven student-built homes in the Bath area. Although none of the houses resembled our dream home, seeing them gave us a feeling of confidence. Others had done it. We saw the practical examples of our classroom theories, from chalkboard to reality. It was poignant in demonstration of the owner-builder's ability to succeed. We knew we could do it too. Enthusiasm and passion would build bridges over our gaps of knowledge.

The notes I took on that tour, from discussions with the owner-builders themselves, showed that the average student built home cost per square foot varied from about $9.00 to $15.00, which was about 25 % of conventional costs, the higher cost occurring with the hiring of additional carpenters.

Before we knew it, the final lecture ended. A couple from Canada had the honor of presenting our class gift to Patsy Hennin. It was a pretty special baby blanket, as Patsy was expecting a child very soon. We all expressed our thanks to the staff for giving us such a great "Shelter Experience."

Sandia and I climbed into our van after saying our good-byes to other aspiring builder friends, amid promises to write to each other with our respective progress. We then headed south to Connecticut, directly into the teeth of a late February blizzard.

We scheduled a return to the Institute in a little over a month for a weekend design seminar. At that meeting, the entire staff would go over our completed design drawings, offering alterna- tives and solutions to perceived problem areas in the plan. This gave us a bit more than five weeks to design our house and get the business deal wrapped up. Needless to say, we had plenty to chatter about as we drove slowly southward through that heavy falling snow.

11

Final Mechanics

As soon as we arrived back in Connecticut, I called potential buyer number two, Nick. Anxious and optimistic, I drove over to meet him. It turned out that what he wanted to tell me in person

after anxious waiting, not lots of fun

sign on the line, write out the check, it's done

tors. Whenever I needed to wait around, which occurred often enough, I sketched and planned ideas for later discussions with Sandia. Ever the optimist, or maybe the dreamer, I felt deep in-

was that he had searched out all of his immediate financial sources, but couldn't come up with the necessary backing "at this point in time." Nick told me that if he had another few weeks, he was sure that he would "put it together!" I wasn't so convinced myself and after much discussion, we found a compromise. We agreed that I could seek out other buyers, while at the same time, he continued to look for the necessary funding package. If he came up with the financing first, he had the first rights, but in the meantime, I was free to talk with other interested people. At least, I wouldn't be losing time if it turned out that Nick's quest represented a "wild goose money chase."

Sandia and I were both anxious to convert Shelter teachings and our own lifestyle into a practical homestead plan, but at the same time, knowing that no buyer meant no "homestead," I found myself carrying a sketchbook around to meetings and presentations with interested inves-

side that this would all come together somehow. Maybe those feelings just stemmed from wanting it to happen so badly.

And then it happened! After quite a few days of scurrying in and out of lots of "maybe, give me a while to think about it" type of meeting responses, potential buyer number three arrived on the scene. He had heard about the availability of my shares through one of my business partners. He exhibited genuine interest. In fact, his wife worked on staff at the "big Oak", so he knew of the operations and partners from the inside out. They told me to go ahead and get the papers drawn up, we had a deal! I cleared it with Nick, who still hadn't put together the money, and then drove toward my Sandia to tell her the great news. I can still remember the brightness in her smiling eyes as we danced great circles on the rug. We could virtually smell the freshness of the trees and the clean, crisp air in those Rocky Mountains!

Thus began the legal countdown as I drove documents back and forth between our respective attorneys. They would have used the U. S. Postal system for the twenty-mile trip between offices, but I preferred the legwork. Also deep in my consciousness, I thought there could be a chance for something to get fouled up, so I wanted to stay on top of things I could control like paper shuffling. Maybe it was just being "gun shy" from the first two buyer experiences, but I wanted to get it done as straightforward and quickly as possible.

Asking about the gist of all the typed sheets, our attorney told me a lot of the generated paperwork stemmed from his effort to tie together loose ends in the legalities of the original limited partnership agreement for the two tennis clubs. The buyers' attorney would not allow his clients to buy into nebulous and incomplete agreements. So the club partnership gained a "cleaned up" legal agreement as a result of my attempt to sell my portion of the two indoor racquet clubs.

What I gained in time from my legwork, I soon lost when the buyer's attorney informed me that he was leaving for a previously scheduled one week vacation in Bermuda. "Don't worry. My law partner will keep things going while I'm gone," he told me. A week later I knew that what he really meant was that his partner would stall things until he got back, because absolutely nothing happened on the buyer's end that week. But really, what is a week in the grand scheme of things?

I used the week to literally go back to the drawing board (with the telephone always within reach)! After days of discussions on how we would actually live and function in our home, I drew the final floor plan. Believe me, that is the toughest part of it—the plan has to fit your lifestyle, your family, your friends, and most of all, your spirit. With that major decision ac-

complished, I dove into the easy part for me, the structure, which included framing, beam sizing, heat loss, insulation, solar gain, heat storage, and lots of other mechanical details. The floor plan had been psychological; the rest consisted of plain old wood physics. I calculated the beam sizes for first and second floor loads followed by the ceiling rafters, using ten feet of snow as the live roof load. It is necessary to design for the worst case scenario, as those conditions can happen at some point in time.

The buyer's attorney returned and I went back to running contract drafts between their offices. I knew every bump in the road between those two offices by that time, but felt heartened because we were getting it close to done. Then, to our complete surprise, the buyer decided to treat his wife to a two-week vacation in Aruba. With the paperwork nearly complete, maybe they just wanted to be alone for a while to talk about their future. We had no idea. It must have been an absolutely wonderful time for them, however for us, it meant a couple more weeks of waiting and wondering. I'm glad I had the homestead planning to bury myself in.

Tanned and rested, our buyers returned, reviewed the final contracts and signed them. I signed them in turn and their attorney handed me the check. What a rush as that check entered my grasp, like a gentle breeze across a high mountain lake, like an eagle soaring on a warm updraft. Dreams do come true. Seven months and three buyers had passed since we left those fantastic mountains behind. Now we could head west again, this time to stay, and build, and live.

Soon after, that sale check was promptly "divvied up" by our attorney to my debtors. We would leave with very little cash, but we would head for the Rocky Mountains free and clear, with all debts paid. Our wealth lay in our spirits, which soared up in the stratosphere someplace.

We needed to make one last stop before the journey west, the Shelter Institute and the design seminar. By now, our timing seemed incredible to me. We had taken a "shot" and scheduled the design seminar for April 2nd and 3rd, and had signed over my business interests on April 1st. Somebody definitely watched over us and it wasn't an April fool.

With our plans reasonably complete, we spent those two days at Shelter with the staff going over our calculations and suggesting alternatives to some of the house structure. Most of their suggestions came from the economic standpoint, or less expensive ways to accomplish the same end without sacrificing structural integrity. Incorporating some of their alternatives, but determined to do certain aspects our own way, we expressed our farewells and thanks and excitedly headed south to pack up our trailer in Connecticut for the long awaited trip west.

12

The Trip West

The snow subsided as we drove closer to Hartford, and we arrived in the early morning, exhausted, but anxious to be on our way to Colorado. We cruised into Marti and Brad's house, which we shared, and slept soundly for several hours.

We woke to the sound of the telephone. It proved to be some more of our beautiful friends wanting to have one last farewell party. Neither Sandia nor I wanted to face the difficulty of saying goodbye again, so we just politely begged off and started to make our last minute checks and loading. The trailer lights worked, our suitcases were loaded, and sleeping arrangements had been made for Kirsten, and us. Even with minimal possessions, late morning quickly grew into evening, in spite of help from our faithful friend, Pablo, who always seemed to show up when we needed a couple of extra hands. Finally, loaded and ready, and after refusing an offer to "stay one more night", we rolled out of the driveway, waving goodbye to Pablo, Marti, and Brad. That little four by eight-foot trailer may have held all of our worldly possessions, but at that moment, the whole world was not big enough to hold

go west with spirit, but stop on the way

balance that load, else the trailer might sway

our enthusiasm and spirit! Colorado here we come.

Despite our attempt to pack the trailer neatly, we must have looked like something out of The Grapes of Wrath. My handmade headboard, made with some of that barnwood from Joe Oberge's barn, faced rearward from the trailer. Strapped onto it was Kirsten's yellow bicycle. Above the bike was a tin sunshine, which would eventually hang in our future mountain solar home. In front of the headboard were piled boxes with our few pieces of furniture interspersed, bed parts, mattress, box spring, a bookcase, even a desk.

Fatigue caught up with us after only a few hours on the road, but we were on the road! We pushed on for several more miles, mostly out of sheer determination, but then sensibly decided to stop and get some sleep. The rest area north of New Haven, Connecticut, provided a welcome sight to tired eyes. No one else parked in the area, so I had no problem jockeying the trailer into a secure position from which we could pull straight ahead upon leaving in the morning. We crawled into our sleeping spots and soon fell fast asleep.

I woke up many hours later, hearing the gentle patter of rain on the roof of the van. As I lay there with heavy sleep in my mind, it suddenly dawned on me that we had to cover our open trailer. What an oversight I'd made in all the hurry to get on the road. Our few, but precious things were being penetrated by the moisture of that gentle rain. I bolted upright, pulled on some clothes, and climbed forward to the driver's seat. The "sunshine van" started up and rolled south out of the rest area. We had to find a rain cover quickly.

Being near the Connecticut shore, we soon found a boat dealer and hoped he would have a canvas around somewhere. Sure enough, he produced a used heavy waterproofed canvas tarpaulin with grommets, which he sold to us at a reasonable price.

We threw it over the trailer and cinched it down with some rope pulled through the metal grommets and stepped back to survey our work. It looked just like a miniature covered wagon. So fitting—a covered wagon headed west, driven by a new kind of "pioneer."

We decided to head down to Washington, D.C. to see Kenner. Then we would angle a little bit north and catch the Pennsylvania turnpike due west. Kenner, our friend and minister, had come up to that beautiful lake in Marlborough to marry us a year earlier. We figured it was not too much out of the way, especially for a special friend, so the "sunshine van," with the covered wagon trailer in tow, steered a course south for D.C.

Our visit with Kenner and family seemed short, but warm. We didn't want to stay overnight as we feared the trailer would get pilfered on the inner city streets, or maybe just vandalized. Also we wanted to stop on our way out of the city for a look at the famed cherry blossoms. The date was early in April and would be a great time to view the fragrant pink flowering.

Finding a parking spot for a van and a trailer

The sunshine van and trailer headed west

near the Tidal Basin, where the cherry trees are located, proved no easy chore but we prevailed and found two parallel spaces together. I even managed to get the trailer backed in reasonably straight. Maybe I would get the backing up sequence with the trailer down pat before getting to Colorado. For now the modus operandi lay in not backing up at all, always go forward-no matter the cost.

We stopped for a snack, followed by a casual stroll through the gardens, enjoying the beauty of the cherry trees before heading back. As we approached the spot where the van was parked, we noticed barricades all around the streets that we had come in on. Since something was always going on in D.C., we mused at what it might be this time.

With the van started, we headed off in the one direction allowed to us by the barricades. Soon we found ourselves in the middle of a great mass of humanity. All around us, there must have been about 40,000 people demonstrating against unfair labor practices or something to that effect, judging from the placards they brandished. The demonstrators seemed angry; probably the reason for a large police presence for crowd control. One policeman shouted in our window, "Back this rig up and get out of here. Where do you think you're going anyway?"

"Colorado," I answered boldly. He grunted and pointed the way behind us with a fierce look on his face.

"And make it snappy!" came his parting comment.

Well, I had been having trouble backing the trailer up in calm, quiet places, so you can imagine what it felt like in this panic-stricken situation! People moving all around us. There seemed no way I was going to be able to do it without running someone over. I even, at one point, jumped out of the van and tried to physically drag the trailer around. My heart pounded like a bass drum. I could hear its lub-dub, lub-dub above the noise of the shouting around me. Another policeman shouted and motioned at us to get out of their way, but there appeared nothing I could do. I told Sandia and Kirsten to stay in the van, while I kept watch back by the trailer. Maybe the whole thing would end soon.

All of a sudden, out of the crowd came a police motorcycle escort for us and away we went—straight ahead—with sirens in front of us, our covered wagon trailer with the tin sunshine and the yellow bicycle behind us, and the yelling crowds all around us. Those D.C. cops led us through some barricades and pointed the way out. We smiled and waved to our departing escorts. They did not smile or wave back!

It certainly seemed quiet away from that demonstration. I hadn't a clue where we were, but Sandia, ever the navigator and once having lived in D.C., assured me she knew where we were going, as she pointed this way and that. The next thing I knew, we approached those unmistakable barricades again. The van pulled a quick U turn and headed for as opposite a direction as we could find, as fast as we could! Still laughing, we found our way northwest toward the Pennsylvania Turnpike. A rest area and a peaceful sleep felt earned and welcomed that night.

The next day, a Sunday, we found ourselves humming steadily westward on the turnpike. We still chuckled about the events of the previous day. What else could happen after the melee of that demonstration? At about the same time that confidence settled in, one of the trailer tires blew out and we came to a rocky stop in a pull-off area. Not having been able to find a spare tire of that small size before we left Connecticut, we figured we would just unhitch the trailer, leave it where it sat, go to the town at the next exit a few miles down the road and buy a tire. The only difficulty we might have would be tire shopping in a small town on a Sunday.

Waiting in line to pay our exit toll, I could not have anticipated what was about to happen. The elderly tollbooth operator reached for my IBM card, looked quickly at it and our van and quoted me a toll price. He then looked down at the card again. This time he came right out of his seat. He jumped out of the booth shouting, "You can't exit. You came on this turnpike with three axles and you cannot leave with only two!" He was already signaling the people behind us to back up. He then made us back into a parking area, which was still on the turnpike. No matter how much we tried to explain to him what had occurred, the rule to him remained clear and the only way we would drive off that turnpike, was with a trailer in tow! I imagine that if our little trailer had disintegrated, we would still be there on the turnpike, today. It reminded me of that old song about the Boston MTA—"I'll ride forever neath the streets of Boston, he's the man who never returned." The guy had lost his transfer coupon. His wife would throw him a lunch as the subway went by each day—what a laugh!

We could, however, walk off the turnpike, so hoof it we did. The town of Donegal, Pennsylvania lay several miles away from the turnpike exit, so we stopped at the first phone booth, and with a pocket full of dimes, "let our fingers do the walking" for us. Well, not unexpectedly, trying to get a small trailer tire in a small town on a Sunday afternoon turned out to be quite an undertaking. Luckily, we finally found a guy who just stopped by his tire store, who happened to answer his phone, and who happened to have a spare tire on his own trailer that he was willing to sell us, rim and all, if we would pay a good price. Under the circumstances, I made a deal. He even knew where we were located and drove it to us. So we paid the price, got the tire, thanked him, and walked back to the tollbooth. Smiling as we held up our new tire, they let us through.

After putting the new tire and wheel on the trailer, we decided to spend the night in Donegal, redistribute the load on the trailer, and get a new trailer spare in the morning. Too much weight on one side had probably been the cause of the blow-out and it would be foolish, at best, to go even one more mile without a proper spare tire, so off that exit we went again, this time driving with our regulation three axles.

The next morning we found a new tire and wheel at half Sunday's price and had it mounted on the other side of our covered wagon trailer. With the two new six-ply tires on the trailer and our old four-ply as a spare, we again headed west, this time with wary confidence. Leaving Donegal behind us, we decided we'd never forget that little town or that panicky toll booth worker. It was probably the greatest amount of excitement he had seen in a long time.

Happily, the rest of the trip went smoothly, except for Kirsten getting a little bit "van sick" and throwing up on my sheepskin coat someplace in Nebraska. She loved lying on that big, old, soft coat in her van spot. No worry, coats could be cleaned. Soon those Rocky Mountains came into our view and we experienced some of the elation that the "old pioneers" must have felt even though our trip wasn't nearly as long and the fact that our "beasts of burden" lay in the horsepower of a blue Dodge van. After traveling so many miles on the plains, those mountains provided a truly awesome sight! I imagine part of the awe of the "old pioneers" laid also in the fact that they needed to get over them, as well as appreciate their beauty and powerful impact, rising sometimes another 9,000+ feet above those mile high plains!

Getting Started

beginning is always the hardest part

with a wise plan, shovel in hand, just start

We made a short stop in Fort Lupton, Colorado, which is about twenty-seven miles north of Denver. I can best describe Fort Lupton as being Michener's model for Centennial, also located on the Platte River. There we dropped off our trailer and unloaded the van into temporary storage in Sandia's parent's garage, then headed for the mountains. It was April 10th, which is spring in most parts of the country, but in the mountains, it definitely remained winter.

We drove slowly over Berthoud Pass, the Continental Divide, and gazed westward at the peaceful snow covered mountains of the western slope. What a sight it proved for me, never having seen a winter in the Colorado Rockies. As so many tourists often do, we took the photo opportunity beside the summit sign, showing the pass elevation at 11,382 feet. A few minutes later, we passed the Winter Park ski area and again stopped to gaze in amazement at the magnificence of the slopes and the number of skiers on that sunny April day. I remember picturing myself cruising down those slopes, the easier ones to start with, and vowed to do it one day.

Forty miles later, we arrived in the small village of Grand Lake, the western entrance to Rocky Mountain National Park. In fact, as I was to learn later, Grand Lake is the biggest natural lake in the state and is the headwater for the Colorado River, which moves westward toward the Pacific by way of its most magnificent and famous sculpture, the Grand Canyon. Until 1923, the Colorado River was known as the Grand River, at which time it was changed, I believe, by Congress, to show point of origin.

Within a few minutes northwest of the village, up toward the Park, we walked knee-deep in the snow on our little piece of this beautiful earth. The view proved wondrous and unimpeded to the south. Hundreds of acres of recreation land along with an 18-hole golf course lay right in front of us in all its snowy splendor. Our southern land boundary was midway along the eighth fairway. The only time I had ever been there before was in the summer, and I just stood there transfixed by the winter scene. A few questions ran through my mind. "How cold are the winters here? How much snow would we get?" I knew that the summers were pure heaven, but how were the winters and what did the local people do? A little bit of uncertainty crept into my dreamy state.

Suddenly some hammering started and I turned eastward toward the source. There to our left was a new house under construction, with several pick-up trucks parked in that snowy neighbors driveway. Sandia suggested that we walk over and talk to those carpenters about local conditions. It was about 4:30 in the afternoon on a Friday, so we thought they would be calling it a day pretty soon and might be open for some talking.

I can still remember the looks on some of their faces as I, after introductions, casually remarked that Sandia and I planned to build a passive solar home on the adjacent sloping lot by ourselves. Someone immediately asked, "Have you ever built anything before?"

"Well, just a couple of sundecks, but we have studied a lot and we went to school to learn about owner-building."

That carpenter then responded, "How long was your school?"

To this Sandia answered, "Two weeks." Her answer brought snickers and sideways glances amongst the crew. I started to expound on the virtues of passive solar design and how I noticed looking over at our south facing slope, how much less snow was remaining there than on surrounding level ground. I explained that each degree of southerly pitch was like moving the land 300 miles south as far as the weather and the plants were concerned. Now I got at least some curious stares to replace the "you don't know what you're doing" looks.

Another carpenter asked, "Have you ever seen what winter is like up here?" When I told him that I had not, he told us, "We get twenty feet of snow on average. You wait and see!"

One of the group, obviously the boss, told the rest of the crew to pack it in for the weekend.

He then wandered over to us and introduced himself. Ted Burch was originally from Illinois, more lately from the Northern California Mountains in Salmon River country. He and his wife Deborah would become two of our closest friends in the years ahead.

Ted stayed, while the others left, and chatted for another hour or more about construction and local conditions of life in general. I remember at one point, Sandia asked a question which involved some carpenter "jargon" about structure. Ted looked at her and remarked, "You really have done some studying." He went on to smilingly answer our questions until a little later, when he politely excused himself from the anxious queries. He would admit to us a year or so later that he had thought we were "crazy" and would not end up doing what we had described. Ted also said at that later point that he had mostly respected the enthusiasm that we had poured out in the original conversation.

The sun was setting, the carpenters had left, and Sandia and I were back standing on our land, reflecting on the day we had had. We agreed that there was no way we could start building right away and tried to guess as to when the grass would begin to show through that snow. Two weeks, perhaps a month, judging from what we had been told, even knowing that the sun would speed things up on our south facing slope.

We drove back over the pass that night, disappointed in the respect that we could not start building right away, but at the same time, trying to exercise a little patience. This would give us some time to submit our plans to the County Building Department for a "permit to build" and maybe research some sources for construction materials and tools we needed anyway. We determined to make the time well spent.

As it turned out, Sandia's father knew that

some laborers were required for a Stapleton Airport job. Knowing we would need more funds later, I went and got into the job seekers line at his company. I suppose a combination of factors got me that job. First, not all the applicants wanted the job, and I would soon find out why. Secondly, Sandia's father had a reputation with the boss for being a super worker and being his new son-in-law didn't hurt my chances. He had been a laborer with them for 23 years and now even at 60 years of age, he gave his best to whatever they assigned him to do.

My first day on that job just about broke my back. Our job was to seal the above ground parking lots at the airport, so that they did not drip onto cars parked on the level below. This was accomplished by spreading a hot—400 degrees Fahrenheit—rubberized asphalt tar over the whole parking surface. An experienced crew of squeegee pushers spread the tar after it was heated in large gas-fired vats. All that remained was to get the hot tar from the fired vats to each point of application to the surface of the parking lots. That is where the other two newly hired guys and myself came in. Our job was to carry that smoking hot stuff in five-gallon pails. One of my cohorts was a muscular 19-year-old. The other was a 110-pound Mexican immigrant, who said this kind of work was still better than his "lot" in Mexico City. Santos had been in the United States about four years at that time. He was 28 years old with a wife and one small child. I remember we figured out that when Santos carried two full five-gallon pails at once, they weighed almost as much as he did. He never quit though. He taught me a lot about determination on that job. Toward the end of the day, when we could see that he could not carry another pail, the other carrier and I would station Santos at the vat spigot and put him in charge of pouring our buckets. Only then would he back off from

carrying and stood proudly as the spigot boss to dispense our measured loads. I should remark, for clarity, that we had to carry two five-gallon pails at once. After some experimentation with only one pail, we found that the two proved the best way to keep the hot tar away from our legs. It was a balanced load with one pail on each side, held out far enough so that they would not bump our pant legs. In spite of this effort, our pant legs turned out to be a mess by day's end because sometimes the bumping couldn't be helped.

Back and forth, for days and then weeks, we went from vat to application spots. Slowly we could see our progress toward the contract goal. I remember that whenever my forty-year-old body would get really tired and sore, I would look westward at those Rockies for strength. I'll bet half the people in Denver do that also, take spirit from those majestic peaks, while thinking about spending time up there amongst them. I was already learning the names of a few of those mountains, Long's Peak, for example, reaching in excess of 14,000 feet above sea level was the highest one we could see from the job.

Each night as the job progressed, I would literally collapse into bed, tiredly rationalizing to myself how much stronger I felt and how much easier our own timber beams would be to lift into place. I often built our house in my dreams during those deep sleeps.

One day, with the end of the contract work in sight, some union officials came onto the job. The boss knew that I did not have a union card, so he sent me scurrying into the airport terminal while the "big whigs" made their tour. After a very relaxing hour of coffee and a stray newspaper, Santos came to get me. On the way back to the job, I managed to understand enough of what he said to figure out there was some kind of strike brewing, but he did not know any of the details. It turned out that my "temporary" company walked off the job the very next day, with approximately one day's work left to finish the contract. I felt so aggravated after those weeks of hustling the hot rubber sealer around those expansive parking lots. I wanted to see it completed. One pro-union worker told me not to worry. He said the strike would be settled quickly, allowing us to finish the job.

The job supervisor, who was a non-union consultant out of Chicago, came over and offered me a job on the road with him. I told him thanks for the offer, but I had reasons to stay there. I pointed out the mountains northwest of there and told him about our little piece of land and the house that my lady Sandia and I planned to build on it. He left me standing there staring at those mountains. I thought that it was probably time to get up there and get the building started anyway.

That strike was never to be settled and the company threw the union out, finally, and became a non-union shop. My father-in-law was offered a job with a non-union status, but he was a true blue, first priority in life after family is your union dues kind of a man, so he looked for union work elsewhere. Dad, as I came to call him, because he accepted me and taught me like one of his own sons, did find union work with a concrete firm carrying those heavy concrete forms around. He never complained about hard work, lived a thrifty life, worked diligently to provide for his family, and never bought a thing on credit in his life. I still reflect often on the simple beauty of the things that he taught me about life. At four years of age, Dad had walked out of Mexico, with a mother determined to leave the revolution behind her, and another brother and sister. His father, Julio Cruz Gomez, as lead scout, had found work up North in the

state of Colorado. In those days, there was no border patrol, only an immigration station where they signed in at to get the proper papers for the journey northward. Dad had married Sandia's mom when she was only thirteen years old, not uncommon at all in those depression years. They raised a family of five children by one philosophy—hard work and proudly living and sharing within their means. Earlier in his life, Dad used to work the graveyard, or midnight, shift underground in a coal mine and upon leaving that job, would join his family in the fields planting, thinning, or picking until the sun went down. Sandia's mom told me that he used to show up a little late because of the mine shift hours, but then would commence to out work everyone by the time they quit for the day. This man was to be immeasurable help and inspiration to us during our building project.

The next day, I called the Grand County Building Department and found out that our building permit had been approved and was ready to be picked up. They had a few questions on how our design was going to work heatwise, but the structurals had checked out fine. Since I had calculated every timber size in the house from scratch myself, we both breathed a sigh of relief. Knowing that whenever a beam size was marginal in strength, I always used the next bigger size, we remained confident about the design, but it is still a good feeling when the Building Officials agree with the structural sizings from their chart comparisons, and pass your plans on the first "go-around." I took great pains to draw the plans out on clear vellum so we could make as many sets of blueprints as we needed. I studied other sets of architectural prints and tried to make ours as professional looking as possible, complete with architectural short hand symbols and title boxes.

We immediately gathered up what gear we

would need to live in those mountains, along with some tools that Sandia bargain shopped for while I carried the hot rubber. Our abode had been her sister's basement in Denver for a little over a month, so we could be near the airport job. We pulled Kirsten out of her second-grade class a few blocks away to head up into those Rockies for good. We told her the school in the mountains would be more fun anyway. She did not seem to mind, being used to moving quite a bit already in her young life. She had been born in Virginia, and subsequently lived in England, Germany, and Connecticut, where Sandia and I met and married. Kirsten's dad still lives and works in Europe and the Middle East today.

We stopped and picked up our building permit, answered the curious inspectors' questions, paid our fees and headed for the land. The inspectors told us about a rough sawn lumber mill in Kremmling, Colorado. It would be about forty miles from our project, but it was the closest mill to us and with the local prices would be well worth all our future trips there.

As we walked onto our land, the solar orientation of that south sloping land was so evident in contrast to adjacent lands not oriented toward the friendly warm sun. Grass and earth showed on our land with only a few patches of snow left, while some of the land around us remained fully snow covered. We thought we'd use those last snow mounds on our ground to get a few beers cold so we could toast our progress at the end of each day, sort of like an on site refrigerator, or cooler.

Sandia and I found a few pieces of scrap lumber and ceremoniously built a small wooden bulletin board, complete with protective overhang, for displaying our permit to build. There it was nailed up to a tree on the corner of our lot facing the cul-de-sac for anyone to inspect. We were legally ready to start building our home. As

we gazed at the permit, a voice came from our neighbor's house that was under construction, "You're really going to do it, aye?"

We literally answered in unison, "You bet we are!" and went over to see how those guys' work progressed. We took some more kidding, but I guess they saw the stubbornness in us, because this time their joking was a little kinder.

The next few days, after getting Kirsten lined out for school and the bus for her sixteen-mile journey, Sandia and I contacted the local electric company for an owner's wiring permit and temporary power at the job site. We carefully staked out the house corners and set about clearing our future "house spot" and driveway of trees.

We found the sequence of falling the trees to leave about four feet of exposed stump remaining for the best leverage, and attaching a length of chain and a come-along (hand winch), it worked really well for us. That thirty-dollar Sears come-along pulled out sixteen stumps for us. We had to sequence them so that we always had another stump to wrap the chain around for leverage, leaving the last stump near a "live" tree for its power in removing that final stump.

Once the stump holes were filled in, we ordered a truckload of road gravel, which the driver dropped in one pile at the edge of our driveway. We learned later that he would have "tail gated" it (raising his dump bed slowly as he moved down the driveway) over the whole drive if we had asked, but we did not know any better at the time. It took us a whole day to shovel, wheelbarrow, dump, rake, and tamp it in place. The blue van was used as the final compactor and besides it looked nice sitting there off the road in our own driveway. We both felt a good tired that evening, but we celebrated the driveway and tree clearing, and the power company even showed up to give us a temporary power drop on their nearest pole which was the better

Using a hand winch to pull out stumps

part of 100 feet away. Not too bad for our first few days, I thought.

Our next step would be to lay out the foundation and dig those holes. We planned to mix our own concrete; in fact, we planned to do every bit ourselves. The next order of business had to be a cement mixer and our water source.

Those carpenters next door, who were calling us the "pioneers" by now, owned a mixer and told us we were welcome to use it. It belonged to Ted, who wouldn't take any payment for its use. He said just to take care of it and that they would know where it was if they needed it, our first taste of mountain hospitality. Ted went on to ask why we had not hired a bulldozer to clear the stumps and build the driveway. I told him our feelings about heavy machinery and the destruction of vegetation and ground cover. Our plan was to raise the house on twenty-three piers of concrete on adequate footings, with two back

corners of short stem walls for racking strength, and not to disturb the soil elsewhere. We hoped that the ground squirrels would still come and go under our house as they had always done. To all of this he replied, "I still think that a bulldozer and a full basement would be a better idea."

Our water tap was located twelve feet underground on the far side of our cul-de-sac, so here was the one place we would need a big machine, a back hoe, to bring our sewer and water up either side of our new driveway. We had no choice in this rocky soil but to have a machine carefully dig, using our drive as a base, and bring those lines up to the house perimeter. We would take it from that point. At least most of their digging would be out in that circular roadway, with only maybe seventy-five feet onto our land. The water lines up here near the 9,000 foot elevation level would sometimes freeze even buried under twelve feet of soil. We heard that in the past, such frozen water lines hadn't thawed out until the following August! This of course could never happen to us!

With the back hoe lined up for Monday morning, Sandia, Kirsten and I celebrated that Friday night with a real restaurant meal. We talked throughout dinner about our plans and gave Kirsten some weekend chores so she could feel part of "*La Casa del Sol*" also, our new name for our homestead—the house of the sun. We returned after dinner to Sandia's parent's small cabin in which we would live until *La Casa* was ready to move into. Having the use of that cabin, located about one-half mile from our building site was such a fortunate benefit.

Sandia's mood changed later that night, which was remarkable in itself, because she so seldom deviated from her spirited outgoing self. She suddenly became sullen and quiet. I remember trying to get at what bothered her. We were both very tired, hence irritable, so my attempts at talking to her ended with her tearful exit from the cabin. I let her go, but after a few minutes, I felt the loss and took off to chase after her. I found her walking on the gravel road toward *La Casa*.

"We can't do it," she blurted out and cried even harder. "It's too much—we can't do it!"

It showed that the anticipated magnitude of the entire project was getting to her after we'd only coped with the first few details. It must have seemed enormous to her at the time.

"Let's just go down to Denver, get normal jobs and rent a place. This is going to be too much for us," she then shouted at me.

I started to talk slowly and gently to let her know that I thought we could do it and that I didn't plan to "pack it in now." I'm sure the sequences and structural details which seemed reasonably clear in my mind, but not in hers, gave vent to Sandia's explosive declaration of doubt.

We soon reached a crisis point when Sandia told me that I would have to do it myself as she was going back down to Denver and that was that! I guess I fought back stubbornly trying to convince her that we could do it, others had. At one point then, we walked away from each other, both resolute to our respective cause. I think it happened then, being parted in purpose, that we both realized what we meant to each other. We found each other in the dark, under that spectacular starry sky, and held on. There was no way that this house, or anything else for that matter, would split us apart.

Sandia, yielding to my stubborn resolve and probably the fact that she really wanted our own place in those mountains, made me promise that night that if it ever got to be too much for our relationship, that I would leave it. I easily made the promise, knowing that she meant more to me than any rock, concrete, wood, or glass ever could. It was only doing it and creating it together that possessed any meaning. Otherwise it would simply be a shelter. We could live anywhere as long as we lived there together. That night of soul searching made us stronger for facing some of the demands and the strains that lay before us. Believe me though, looking back now, the beauty and the rewards as the project progressed, far exceeded any setbacks we ever experienced.

chapter fourteen 14

"The Base of it All"—The Foundation

The backhoe never arrived on Monday morning, so we chased them down on another job. The operator told us, "We can't really say when we'll be there. It will be as soon as we finish this work, maybe one more day, maybe two." Without any apparent alternative but to wait, we went back to hand digging our foundation holes, just a wee bit wiser from the event. This was our first encounter with a phenomenon we dubbed, "mountain mentality." It is best described as, "Don't really count on when I say I'll be there to do the subcontract work, but it'll be as soon afterward as I'm able."

Four days later, the backhoe showed up, with a cohort plumber right behind. The equipment operator dug the trenches and the plumber followed laying out the pipe. When the dust cleared late in the day, we had a capped sewer line at the edge of our house and a copper water line just inside the house perimeter so it would come up under the house in the "crawl space." The water line was complete with a hose bib to give us a shutoff and spigot in the foundation area. Under our careful gaze, that big machine had only gouged the bark on one tree and caused another

sturdy houses, worthy lives, need a strong base

something to be fastened to, just in case

tree to tilt sideways at a slight angle—not too bad for a big machine. We enjoyed relief when they loaded up and left. A good chunk poorer, but we felt thankful for what had been accomplished and what had not been damaged. We also felt lucky to be near a small community water supply and sewer collection system instead of having to deal with the uncertainties involved in a well, leach field, and septic tank system.

The hand digging of the foundation holes progressed well. Only in the last four or five holes did we run into sizable rocks that we needed to lever out with a heavy steel bar. One of those rocks turned out to be so large that we decided to leave it and just pin the footing to it. When we finished, the house site looked very complicated with twenty- three holes on that slope and string lines running all around. The layout, however, hadn't been that difficult with the aid of our trusty builder's transit. I can't imagine building a foundation without one.

An experienced builder had advised me, "If your foundation is off, the error will follow you all the way to the roof." I thought of his words

55

A white mountain surprise in May

many times as we checked and rechecked the layout of those piers.

Finally satisfied with the alignment, we began to build the footing forms out of inexpensive roughsawn boards from the Kremmling sawmill. The work progressed well. I liked cutting and nailing boards together a lot better than digging holes and rocks out of the good, but unpredictable earth. We set up our radial arm saw in a small shed that we built from downed trees on the site and bark slabs from the sawmill. At night we could leave all our tools in the shed and not have to carry them back and forth to the van each day. The shed also kept our tools dry during bad weather. In fact, we experienced a late May snowstorm which dumped six inches of snow on us, but it melted away the next day under the onslaught of our friend—that bright, clear, and unpolluted Colorado Mountain sunshine.

Footing forms completed and in place, we measured and began to cut the deformed steel bar required to give the tensile strength to the footing concrete. I guess we did that the hard way too, but Sandia cut every piece with a hacksaw and quite a few blades. We wired the steel into its proper place within each footing form and promptly telephoned the Building Department for out first inspection. We were actually ready to pour our first concrete, provided we passed the footing inspection!

The inspector showed up early the next morning and walked amongst our forms. He then looked at our set of required on-the-job blueprints for a moment, then walked over and initialed his approval for the footing inspection.

He remarked as he left, "You know you'll be able to build a hotel on top of this thing when you're done."

We laughed, said goodbye, and turned back to the building site, anxious to get to work. Maybe it would be a bit overdone, but this was to be our place in the sun and we figured it's better to overbuild than to try and cheat and underbuild. I'm sure that's the attitude for most people who build their own homes.

As the inspector drove off, Sandia and I literally jumped up and down with joy. We ran to drag the concrete mixer into place and get set up. Now we felt like we were really getting started with the actual building.

We began a rhythm of Sandia shoveling the sand, stone, and cement into the mixer, one scoop at a time, and me "grunting" the wheelbarrows full of that wet gray stuff to each form. An old friend of Sandia's, Linda, her closest friend throughout school, stopped up that day to visit and ended up helping. I can still remember her smile as she smoothed off the surface of the southwest corner footing and we promptly reached down and wrote her name in the wet concrete. Sandia reflected out loud, "Now this gives the concrete a little character."

We went on to inscribe each of the twenty-three footings with peoples' names that were of special inspiration to us, and some other special thoughts. Sandia was right. Concrete is cold and gray and without much character, so we injected a little love into the surface of it.

"They'll all be covered with dirt," I told her.

"Yes, but we'll know they're there—our friends and all of our hopes. They'll be holding us up, nice and strong!"

Her thinking seemed so true. Those things in our concrete affirm the foundation and substance of life anywhere—Our Maker, family, friends, and dreams! Even the spider's web, in all of it's intricate woven beauty, needs to be anchored somewhere to something solid.

Though we needed twenty-three piers on top of our footings, we built only four collapsible sets of plywood forms as tall as the tallest of the piers. We would then mix and pour four in one day, knock the forms off the next morning, set them up for the next four piers and pour those. We saw gray concrete in our sleep those days.

Then Pablo and two other young tennis friends, and ex-workers from the Big Oak, Carlos and Tomas, flew in for their vacations from Connecticut, to help us build. What a pleasant surprise that turned out to be. Pablo always helped us before, why not now? In fact, he flew back to Colorado at least four more times in the next few years to help us out. Is that a friend or what?

Pablo assigned Carlos and Tomas to wood-cutting and they spent days cutting a good portion of our next winter's wood supply. He had been their boss previously at the Big Oak, so it

still came naturally to him now. Pablo had been a great supervisor on our staff. One of those guys who could see what needed to be done and was not at all shy at jumping in and getting it done. Pablo took turns with the wheelbarrow, while we both helped Sandia mix.

About that same time, another good friend and his lady stopped to see us on their move from Key West to San Francisco. Gary LaRocque just pitched in and started helping us also. All of a sudden, we had a lot of muscle on the job. After a few days, Gary and Denise, captivated by the sunshine and enticing mountain environment, talked about staying the entire summer to help us. The two of them engaged in quite a debate, before finally succumbing to the pressures of the practical world, and deciding to push on, as planned, to Frisco, and getting started with their new life. After they left, Sandia and I remarked on the fun spirit they brought us as we etched their names into our concrete "memory book" along with Pablo, Carlos, and Tomas.

Part of our deal with Pablo was that their work would allow us all a little extra time for play. We managed to work in several rounds of golf and some evening fun in our little village also—"party time!"

The foundation of it all

The beer store owner would remark to us weeks later, "Where are your friends? I miss them."

Those guys helped us celebrate our first wedding anniversary together—they would return for the next one too—as we all remembered the lake wedding and the tennis club reception afterward. As only can happen in a small town, the featured guitarist and folk singer, Christy, at the restaurant-lounge, where we celebrated our anniversary gave us a special rendition of our song, Elton John's "Your Song."

She sang the words as, "I'll build a big solar house in which we both can live." Great memories!

The boys, as we called them, left for Connecticut the day after our anniversary party. We sorely missed their jokes and youthful spirit. We buried ourselves into the building, still reflecting on their recent presence. Their names remained etched in the finished gray, for as long as concrete lasts, certainly well beyond us.

The concrete now done, we moved happily into building with warm wonderful wood. Besides, my kids were arriving in two weeks, and that Colorado sunshine beamed down on us each day. We lived in a dream world!

Setting the forms for the final piers

Myself, Pablo. Tomas, and Carlos (l to r) with the last pier finished

the first aside
Bikini on the Eighth Fairway

A rather humorous aside developed while Pablo and the boys helped us out on the concrete part of La Casa that first summer. It came from the direction of our neighbor, the Grand Lake Golf Course, which bordered our land on two sides—the eighth fairway, down in front of us, and the maintenance area, off to our west, nestled into the pine trees.

It occurred that summer; the young lady hired to run the fairway mowing machine happened to be nineteenish, a little over six foot tall, with long slender legs, and, frankly, very beautiful. Her name was Kendra. She worshipped the sun and this devotion led to her habit, more often then not, of running that big mower rig up and down those fairways dressed only in her bikini!

Kendra's sun worship did not go unnoticed by the boys and their raging college hormones. One day they asked my permission to use the K&E Builder's Transit as a telescope to get them closer to their object of fantasy as she drove by. They took turns watching our lady of the bikini on sunny days as she passed back and forth in front of our building site. Maybe there appeared

the mower sound, on the fairway below

run for the transit, ready for the show

a little bit of exhibitionism on display? Sandia, Pablo, and I got a kick out of it, when Carlos and Tomas would push the other out of the way for their respective turn at the eyepiece of our trusty transit.

I remember a lunch time when Kendra ate her meal in the adjacent maintenance area still dressed in her favorite mowing attire. One of boys peered through the transit, following her every bite and chew. Suddenly, he jumped back from the eyepiece, quickly and guiltily turning his head away.

We heard his voice, in a bit of panic, exclaim, "She looked straight at me!"

We rolled in laughter as we finished our own lunch break.

That eye contact turned out to be as close as either of our shy college boys came to actually knowing Kendra. The whole scene proved a fantasy and something to talk about as they headed back east.

After the boys left with Pablo, returning to their homes, Sandia and I got to know most of the Golf Course maintenance crew as they followed the progress of our owner-builder project

59

and would stop by to chat sometimes after work. They even pitched in a few times later when we needed extra muscle. One day, I ran into Kendra at the maintenance area after work and, in the course of our conversation, I mentioned the boys notice and telescoping of her mowing attire. Kendra laughed good naturedly about the revelation, then voiced a thought to me.

"It might be fun," she said, "if I posed on the mower in my bikini and you took a couple of photos. You could send them to the guys, sort of like a souvenir." Kendra's eyes had a mischievous teasing twinkle as she spoke and awaited my response.

"An awesome fun idea!"

We agreed on a time for a later photo shoot and got it done in the best "cheese cake" tradition. Playboy, eat your heart out. I, of course, took my time to get the lighting and background just right. Then it became developing and double print ordering time. Off they went in the mail with Kendra's autograph as an extended touch in the fun plot. Sandia and I remarked that we would love to be a "fly on wall" when those two letters were opened. We knew our friends would love the spoof.

The story didn't end there as Pablo and the boys would return the following summer. Of course a little romance with Kendra blossomed and continued off and on over the next year or so, with Kendra traveling to the East Coast and one of the boy's university for a bit of a tryst. I never learned the details, they remain personal stuff, but it finally petered out kinda like two different planets that collided, exploded into a bright fantasy of splendor, then all the sparks subsided and the dust settled back into the realistic residuals of their two different worlds. Oh, the power and beauty of being young!

End of that aside.

chapter fifteen

Onward and Upward—The Wooden Structure

Working with that warm and wonderful wood helped to compensate for the leaving of our friends. In fact, Kirsten flew back with them as the first leg of her journey to be with her father in Germany on her summer vacation. In a phone conversation with Kirsten before she boarded her Lufthansa flight to cross the Atlantic, she told us the flight back east went well except that she had to take care of Pablo. When questioned further, we learned that Pablo became airsick and spent some amount of time "with his face in a bag," as Kirsten put it. Poor beautiful Pablo, he was always so afraid of aircraft. But, what a friend. He flew so many times to help us out in spite of his fears!

Things went smoothly now. Maybe it had something to do with the fact that we worked with wood. Sandia joked and sang as we labored. We didn't feel rushed, so I kept checking and rechecking our alignment, or squareness. I think that process helped make things fit together smoothly later on.

Then came word that another crew needed the precious concrete mixer. We had one concrete job remaining that we had been putting

framework of lives, like structure of a house

must be planned and built, by you and your spouse

off—the foundation for the 30,000 pound rock mass we would mortar up later inside the house. The rock mass would serve as the aesthetic heat storage for our passive solar design. No choice but to drop the wood and get humping on that foundation as we couldn't count on when the mixer would become available to us again. It proved good incentive to get the job over with.

Early the next morning found us back into our previous rhythm of mixing, wheelbarrowing, and bucketing the "mud" into our homemade foundation forms. Twenty-two batches later, when the two workers, whose job needed the mixer, showed up, we were not quite finished. Those guys, seeing how tired we appeared, just pitched in for an hour to help us finish the foundation wall. When they finally left, towing that "putsy-putsy," we felt mixed emotions. How could someone miss a concrete mixer! I could remember Kirsten in the swing that I built her on trees near the mixer, just swing back and forth while imitating the rhythmic noise it made. But truthfully, we turned happily back to working with our roughsawn wood, with all of its unique character, breathing a small sigh of relief.

With the sub-floor finished and squared, it became a huge work platform that provided a level surface to work on, in comparison to our sloping ground. Sandia started work on our first exterior door. She planned on making all four of our outside doors. This was our first decision after, what some would call a "heated" argument. Sometimes with two people working on the same item all the time, especially when the man "knows" how to do it best (ha!), arguments can result. We talked it out and agreed that working on different projects, all with a common goal, according to our respective talents, would be best for our relationship. Looking back now, we know that our union became stronger from the decision that day, giving each freedom to express their own particular talents. Sandia, an Art History major in college, took over the artistic creation of *La Casa*, while the science of the building fell to me. And together, we could keep the spirit of it all foremost.

I built our first post and beam, or timber-framed, wall. It measured seventeen and one-half foot tall by sixteen foot wide with seven large window openings and one door in it. It was my first wall ever, so it took two full days to build. Finally it sat there on the sub-floor, squared up, braced and ready to raise. All we required was manpower to lift the wall frame into place, as no trees grew on the south side large enough to pulley it from.

Like in most small towns, the post office is always a hub of transitional activity, so I headed there first to ask for help. I picked the biggest guy in the lobby, introduced myself, and asked if he would help. He folded up the letter he was reading and tucked it away in his shirt pocket as he responded, "I'd be glad to help, but you've got to tell me the size of the wall we'll be raising."

After describing the wall and telling him

First it's on the subfloor, then it's in the air

where our building site was, Steve Hardy took off in his pickup to grab what he described as a couple more "willing volunteers." I headed back to the job to double check everything in preparation for our first "wall raising." Sandia put some beer and soda on ice and got her camera ready. I fussed over the raising gear, not wanting anything to go wrong or anybody to get hurt. We had flattened beer can hinges nailed at the base pivot, or swivel point, vertical lumber stoppers nailed to the rim joist, in the event the hinges failed, to keep the wall base from sliding off the front of the sub-floor, and a long carefully measured length of safety rope attached from the top of the wall to a tree in back to prevent the top of the wall from pitching past the upright vertical position and crashing off the front of the floor. This was a tall wall.

Steve showed up with three other guys and they all soon stood over and reflected on the "wall." All were carpenters and used to lifting eight-foot high wall sections into place. They hadn't seen a timber framed wall section before and mused the height of it as they asked questions. We explained the design and how it was all going to fit together. They chuckled at some of our precautionary raising apparatus, but went along with it, commenting, "I hope you calculated the length of that safety rope correctly and not too short!" I told them I used the Pythagorean theorem for right triangles and was sure of the length and had allowed a couple feet of "slop." Big Steve really laughed then and said, "Oh well, if you used whatever you said his name was, it must be right. Let's get this hummer in the air!"

The five of us took holds on the top of the wall and grunted it up. Up to the forty-five degree point, its all muscle as you lift and walk toward the wall base at the same time. After that more of the weight comes down on the wall base and sub-floor making it easier to lift. That's what we meant the safety rope for, to prevent all that exuberance from pitching the top of the wall right over and down to a nasty crash. We plumbed it vertically and nailed temporary angle braces in place to hold it until the side wall and roof framing would lock it into place. Then those super guys headed for their truck, refusing any

cold drinks, and humbly accepted our thanks. They just waved while driving away.

Sandia and I stood looking up at that wall. That's when she realized that she'd been so emotionally caught up in the raising that she'd forgotten to take any pictures on its way up. We both laughed. I climbed that beautiful wall and sat in each of the window openings to test out our future views. I never knew how spiritual a simple wood wall frame could be. We both stayed there until sunset that evening, looking at and toasting our magnificent first wall.

The next two walls were back, or north, walls, with only two small window openings and two exit doors. They were shorter, easier, and quicker for me to build.

It occurred during my building of those two walls that Sandia's door construction got to her. Without any carpentry experience to speak of, her artistic diagonal design would not quite fit together, no matter what she tried. I only became aware of it when she threw down her tools and stomped off with tears rolling down her face. I dropped what I worked on and went over to her door, while her figure retreated from my view. As I gazed down at the door I could see the angled pieces that frustrated her.

I wondered if I should chase after her and try to talk to her or if I should stay here and finish the door for her. I decided neither of those alternatives was the right one and walked back to work on the wall. I felt that she would come back, but I have to admit, two and one half hours later when she returned, I was getting a little bit worried. Sandia just quietly picked up her tools and started in again. My heart got so big at that moment, it almost took my breath away! I knew right then that we would finish *La Casa del Sol*, and that we would finish it together! Any doubts I had about our capacity to prevail were put to rest that moment by the demonstration of Sandia's grit. She finished that first door, by herself and ultimately built four more before we finished, each more creative than the previous one.

Because we had some stout trees on the back, or north, side of the house, we were able to use them with big pulleys and our new (but really old and beat up) four wheel drive pickup, to raise our back walls. I should note here that big Steve had advised me that the order of a mountain man's priorities had to be first, a good chain saw, then a good four-wheel pickup, and lastly, a good warm woman! Mountain lore—back to the walls! Sandia and I arranged the pulleys to give us proper change of leverage angle and we just ran the rope from the top of the wall to be raised, through the pulleys, and looped the rope's end over the trailer hitch of the pickup. Down the driveway, I drove the pickup and up went the walls—one at a time. They were splendid walls too, but not quite as poignant as that first wall.

My kids arrived and became so excited about living in the Colorado Mountains. Lynne, Andrea, Deborah and Pedro, Lynne's beau, all found part-time jobs in the busy economy of a tourist summer in beautiful and scenic downtown Grand Lake. Lynne and Pedro waited tables, Andrea cleaned motel rooms and Deborah sold T-shirts. My son Gary helped us a little around the job, trapped ground squirrels with homemade traps and let them go, and played golf by himself on our neighboring golf course. Our house lay about even with a good drive off the eighth tee, so he could always yell up his score as he went by a little below us to hit his second, or sometimes third shot. He always looked so small down there with my big bag over his shoulder, but we figured he got stronger with each nine holes he played. We bought a family membership so he could play as often as he wanted. Sometimes, at the clubhouse, they

would put him in a twosome or a foursome and he proudly pointed up to our construction project as he went by, waving up at us.

Sandia's mom and dad came up on weekends to relax and do some fishing. Dad taught Gary to fish for those great tasting rainbow trout in a nearby small lake. Mom always cooked my favorite Mexican food when she came up. She always said, "Your Dad brings you construction supplies and tools when he can, the least I can do when I'm up is cook for you both, so you can keep working." If you have ever tasted homemade tortillas, green chile, and chicken enchiladas, served with rice and beans, you know what I'm talking about. When she wasn't cooking, Mom was always bringing friends by for a tour of the house on those weekends. Sometimes I thought she seemed prouder of our effort than we were ourselves.

The biggest wall—the main house solar wall—went up in two sections, as it measured twenty foot tall by thirty-two feet wide with sixteen big solar window openings and one sliding glass door. It was just too big and heavy to physically lift into place as one frame. The first half, Ted Burch came with his whole crew of guys. It took seven of us and all of our strength to walk it up into place. Those guys were becoming very supportive of our project. Helpful suggestions now replaced their earlier joking. We were all fast becoming friends.

The golf course maintenance crew had been watching our project from their various vantage points and became so intrigued with it all, that they approached us while I built that last half wall section, and asked if they could help with the raising. We were flabbergasted, but realized that the little community around us, the neighborhood, rallied to our spirited efforts.

There were nine of us under that last wall when it went up. It was the only one that scared me, though. Those guys, God bless them, just did not have the same strengths as our previous carpenters. Most were college students on a summer job. When we finally got it struggled up to stand in place, I looked over at Lynne's beau Pedro, who helped me that day, and we both breathed a real sigh. About one third of the way up, we both had started yelling loud encouragement. I am sure that helped. I have only been under one wall since that we didn't get up. A guy yelled, "We'll never make it," out loud, part way up and it really weakened everyone. You have to believe!

Those golf course guys thanked us for letting them help and went back happily to their jobs. After that, I could always see them look up at *La Casa* as they drove their maintenance equipment by below us on the eighth fairway. They had a little piece of spirit in that place up there too!

All the walls were up now so we started fitting in the second floor loft timbers, one at a time. I chiseled each horizontal beam into its respective post and cut a scrolled corbel, or gunstocking, to shore up the joint directly underneath. Sandia followed me with her electric engraving tool and paint to add designs, unique to each corbel. She carved flowers, birds, stars, and other thoughtful things of our world. The roof didn't even exist yet, but our wood was carved and painted. Sandia had vases attached to selected posts and kept fresh wildflowers in them each day. People might have thought we enjoyed the whole process of building our home.

Second floor support timbers into place, I moved to the heavy roof rafters. Gary helped me a little, but he used to scare me walking around up there. He felt unafraid and found walking around on a four inch wide rafter, eighteen feet above the sub-floor, not too big a deal. My heart skipped many a beat as he jumped from rafter to rafter. When he wanted to play golf, I totally en-

Ted and crew helping to raise one of our front walls

The golf course crew helped raise one too

couraged him. We could watch the whole course from the roof vantage point.

The roof decking, and secondary rafters were in place, and ready to be insulated prior to closing up the roof. The morning I started to insulate, Sandia came up with a great idea, which I totally rejected at first, then after some reflection, really got into it. At six locations in our cathedral ceilings, I (being a decent artist) drew things out of the sky, like a crescent moon, stars, an eagle, and we even traced our old tin sunshine. We then cut these out with an electric jigsaw and inset stained glass of the appropriate colors. It took the whole day to do the cut outs and glass, but we were never sorry for the extra time spent. How many people can lie on their living room floor to look up at stained glass eagles and sunshines in their knotty pine ceilings?

Several times one of Sandia's uncles would show up, grab a hammer, and ask for instructions to help. Ted and Deborah came one Saturday afternoon and helped me put that pink fuzzy itchy stuff in the roof. Once a guy showed up that I had never seen before, with his own hammer, and nailed beside me for three hours. He said that he had a little cabin down the road, heard about our project, and just wanted to help! Sandia's brothers showed up once to play golf and instead ended up banging nails. We may not have hired anyone, but we did not do it all. All those that helped, friends, family, and stranger, will be in the spirit of *La Casa del Sol* forever and inside of us, too!

We were getting closed in. Plywood sheathing and pine shiplap siding went smoothly. Sandia always had the last say on the different angles of those pine boards. She would say, "We need them going up like rays of sunshine," or "They have to be opposite to the roof pitch." She did her thing; I did mine, and our home grew artistically because of it.

Chiseling a beam pocket

A touch of corbeled artwork

Stained glass ceiling cutouts

That Breakable Glass—The Windows

The coolness of fall touched us as our work on *La Casa* continued to the point that it was completely roofed and sided, the exterior doors were in place, and only the window openings needed to be glazed and trimmed to close us in entirely. In addition to the six small operable window units we needed for ventilation and fire egress, our design called for thirty seven double glazed fixed windows (thermal panes) of various sizes. Most of these were of one large size to be installed in our high south wall. They would serve to let the warm radiant sunshine into the house during the cold of the winter when the sun was at its lowest inclination angle in the southern sky. The much higher summer sun would be blocked from entering by a four-foot roof overhang above these same windows—the passive solar design.

Buying that many factory-made thermal pane units would have "broken our bank", so to speak, so we had earlier decided to make those thermal panes ourselves, according to training received at the Shelter Institute. We ordered only the operable windows, ready to install. The smaller thermal panes were designed to be either one-half or one-third the size of the larger repeti-

to let in the sun, and the mountain view

frame lots of south glass, and night shutters too

tive units. This gave us real efficiency and economy in our glass use. Forty four large sheets of glass now awaited us in Denver, divided into two cases, each weighing about 1,000 pounds—a ton of glass! Buying glass by the full crate in one size is relatively inexpensive compared to buying finished windows.

So there we were at the glass company in Denver picking up our two cases. They put the wooden crates of glass onto our trailer with a forklift. I watched the leaf springs flatten out and asked about the weight, to which the foreman answered, "No sweat." I remember remarking that we would make the 200 mile round trip twice if he thought we needed to. Again, his response was, "No sweat, the trailer will hold this load easily." They braced those two crates in an upright, on the long edge, position. When they finished banging nails into the braces, trailer floor, and crates, the foreman handed me the bill. I checked over the load and asked about adding a few more braces. He told me how many times they'd done this sort of thing before in such a way that I felt a little foolish for even asking. So we paid the bill and drove slowly away.

Well, like concrete, I had never been especially comfortable working with glass, let alone pulling our little four by eight trailer with one ton of the stuff aboard. I crawled along. We got plenty of dirty looks and gestures that day from other drivers, but we just tried to be patient. The priority was to get the load safely to the mountains.

Two hours later, we'd covered only forty miles, but at least we were at the approach to Berthoud Pass. The pass consists of six horseshoe curves, or switchbacks, on the east side and four more on the west slope side—our home side. We made the first eight of those curves in fine, slow methodical style. Swinging around the ninth one, though, I happened to glance in the rear view mirror just as one of the angled braces popped out. We were only going about seven or eight miles per hour, but before I could stop, both crates of glass tumbled over and lay in the middle of the road.

The guy in the car right behind us pulled over, jumped out, and told me that he would help me put the crates back on the trailer. I can still visualize his reaction when I told him that each case of glass weighed 1,000 pounds.

"Whoa ho, we need help," he said flat out. Next thing I knew, he was flagging down cars and volunteering the occupants to help. I backed the trailer up as close as I could to that fallen glass and got out to help. By that time, our self appointed foreman had assembled about a dozen "volunteers."

We all lifted the closest case onto the trailer and just laid it there flat. It was too heavy to try and stand it on end, especially on the roadway of that switchback. We also didn't want anyone to get hurt in all the confusion. The second crate followed and we laid it carefully on top of the first. I gave all my thanks to our helpers as they went back to their cars and their journeys, prob-

ably remarking how glad they felt that it didn't happen to them.

Sandia and I pulled off the roadway and got out for a closer inspection of the glass. Any hopes we had for the intactness of the glass died when my knife cut through a small place in the Styrofoam packing. Every sheet we could see in that top case was broken. Tears welled up in both our eyes as we numbly secured the "broken" load with ropes and headed for La Casa. We did not talk as we drove over nine miles of bumpy road repair through Winter Park. Nothing seemed to matter much at that point. I blamed myself in my own thoughts, because I had not insisted on more bracing. Your head goes through all sorts of miseries in situations like that. What a setback! We'd waited six weeks for that glass to arrive after ordering, and needed it now. Even our tight budget seemed less troublesome than the possibility of a stormy fall or an early winter.

We pulled up at our building site and I used the pickup to drag the top case of broken glass off. Then I cut into the bottom case. When we pulled the Styrofoam packing away, to our amazement only one sheet had broken in that bottom case. It fell off the trailer too and then rode flat, with the other case's weight on top of it for about forty-five miles, some of which crossed bumpy road repairs. Someone watched out for us! It was bad, but we felt thankful that it wasn't worse.

Ted and a few other friends came over that night to cheer us up. That really helped us pull it all back together. The next day was Saturday and the glass company was closed, but we would call them on Monday and see what we were going to be up against to get another case of glass quickly. A check with our friendly insurance agent revealed that the broken glass was not covered. Only "on site" damage was covered. Monday came and the glass suppliers said that they felt sorry for us, but could not cover the damage. The loss belonged to us. Upon further conversations with their boss, however, he offered to get us a new case of glass at their cost only. He would get the order in progress "as soon as he hung up." This seemed to be the best way to handle things, so I told him, "Do it!"

Since we needed fourteen full size windows, or twenty-eight full sheets, we could make all of our smaller sized thermal pane units, which required cutting the glass sheets we had on hand. Then when the new case of glass arrived, we could just construct the large thermal panes, without any cutting at all.

We set up in our future workshop to cut the glass for the twenty-three smaller windows. If you have ever cut glass, especially 3/16-inch thick float glass, you know there is a real technique and psyche to it. The first window we decided to build required a straight six- foot scribe and a "snap." We made the scribe using a new sharp glass cutter and straight edge and then poised that large sheet (72"x 44") on the table edge and brought it down too gently. It broke with a curve instead of on our beautiful scribe line. Sandia and I both stared down at the bad break and wondered what kind of a night it was going to be!

We finally figured that we just had to take authority over the glass and treat it very deliberately as we had seen them do at both the glass factory and the Shelter Institute. We spent a few minutes huffing and puffing ourselves up, including shouting at the glass. We then made a bold scribe, followed by a commanding strike on the table edge. "*Voilá*," a perfect break. Then we really got into it, yell-

ing, scribing, shouting, snapping, and strutting around. I am sure that if anyone heard us that night, they thought we had really bought the "funny farm." Another bad break did not occur and we cut all of our smaller windows that night. We even managed to make one of the smaller units out of the first piece that broke off the line.

The replacement case of glass arrived in only two weeks. Sandia and Deborah, Ted's wife, took the pickup down this time to get it—no van, no trailer! This time those glass company workers braced the crate onto the pickup bed so strongly it took me half a day to get it loose. The new foreman, who was in charge of the bracing, felt sorry for our trouble and told the ladies to help themselves to whatever they wanted from broken sheets of stained glass in their warehouse, while he got the crate of glass loaded. They came back with lots of stained glass that we would put to

All windows now in place

creative use later on.

The last of our windows were made and put in place. Let the wind howl or the snows come; we were ready. It was inside work from there on out with a warm wood stove and the sun to heat up our approaching winter workdays!

chapter seventeen

Employment—Nails, Boards, and Burritos

Our first summer of building in those remarkable mountains drew to a close. Gary and Andrea returned to school and their mother in Connecticut. Lynne and Pedro found jobs and a place to live down the mountain, in Denver. My daughter, Deborah, stayed on with us and began the tenth grade in our local high school, sixteen miles away. Kirsten returned from Germany and anxiously began the third grade. Autumn set in with beautiful sunny days and crisp, cold nights. It was good for snuggling and sleeping. Sandia's parents little uninsulated cabin seemed to get a little colder each night. At the same time, Sandia showed me that our budget was getting colder, and a little scary, at the same time. We both looked up from the cold hard numbers and knew that the luxury of working full time on *La Casa* had run its course. The time had come to find gainful employment! No regrets, we felt pretty lucky to be where we were.

I took a job with Ted and his new partner, Dick, as an apprentice carpenter. Along with two other carpenters, and the two bosses, we could really hum along those fall days in the warm sunshine. Grand Lake Construction, as they called

at times, you do what you must; for us

selling "hot" food, built a budget surplus

their company, lined up enough work to last all of us through the winter. That was a feat those days in Grand Lake, when a lot of people left the area to find winter work and would return in the late spring. Maybe just the thought of twenty feet of snow drove them off.

Secure in a reasonable paying job, and anxious to learn more of the art of carpentry, Sandia and I settled into a routine of sorts. I got my eight hours in on the job each day and then would meet Sandia at *La Casa* and usually work until midnight. Sandia worked along with me, in support, in spirit, and made the long hours a true pleasure. No one had us on a schedule, so it was all self-motivation and we maintained plenty of that between the two of us. We mutually agreed that if one of us was down, the other had to pick him up. It worked most of the time! Kirsten and Deborah always joined us for supper on the job, along with any homework questions that needed discussion.

Soon we progressed at *La Casa* to the point where we had an operating woodstove, albeit with a temporary chimney. That wonderful woodstove made the chilly nighttime work go a

72

lot smoother. Things are just easier when you are warm. We concentrated on the rough-in of electrical wiring and plumbing. Sandia managed our finances well, which enabled us to continue buying the construction materials we needed. Our little effort and partnership we named Rocky Mountain Homesteaders and had a checkbook to prove it. The name and checkbook got us contractor discount prices from suppliers and made the budget last a little longer. Every bit saved paid for another board or two!

Sometimes, on my day time carpentry job, the guys asked me how it felt to leave work each afternoon and then go to work for another shift at *La Casa*. I tried to explain to them the feelings of eagerness and excitement that I felt about my own house—it wasn't work, it wasn't energy draining at all, it supplied energy to me. In fact, on the job with them, my mind delighted in applying what I learned there, to how I could use it on our own house. On breaks, and on routine labors, during the day, my mind always worked on the plan for that night's work. Sandia and I pretty much gave up any social activities. We were called kiddingly, "social bores." It proved the only way to get it done; the house was not going to build itself!

The phone company was nice enough to install a construction telephone at *La Casa*. Communications and coordination suddenly got a little easier. We were linked to the outside world. Pablo, as if with psychic powers, got our number from information and called to offer his help again. Thanksgiving was coming up and he had a few days off. Did we need any help? Was there anything he could do? What a friend! We told him, "For sure," and out he flew, fortified with Dramamine for the flight, just to help for a couple of days.

Our electric and plumbing passed rough-in inspection, so when Pablo arrived, we were put-

ting the pink fuzzy itchy stuff in the walls. Pablo was a great help, and with the three of us working, the job went quickly. During the day, while I made hammering noises like an employed carpenter, Sandia and Pablo began the task of collecting native stone and moss rock for our future chimney and thermal mass. They did it one pickup load at a time and accumulated quite a stack of rock beside our house. The mountains around us were loaded with rock and it was free for the taking. One only had to pick and choose, exert the effort to load, drive the pickup, and then unload the rock.

I remember it was late on Thanksgiving eve and we were on ladders finishing the wall insulation, when winter started. Moving by one of the windows, I happened to look out to spy that first big white snowflake falling. The snow had begun and would not stop for three weeks.

Ted and Deborah, along with their two children, Elijah and Rachel, shared their Thanksgiving with us at their home. Pablo joined us in the sharing and it became one of those remarkable times when you just felt so lucky to be alive. There was nowhere else we wanted to be, except right where we all were, and for that we gave thanks!

Pablo flew back to Connecticut and Sandia and I went back to our work routine. My carpenter mates and I got more and more days off because of the snow and cold temperatures on the job. One day we framed walls on a new house at twenty-three degrees below zero. My bare fingers stuck to a saw blade I tried to change. Just getting nails out of your nail bags became a feat. You could only last so long without gloves, then had to put them on for a while, which made everything harder to handle. We finally packed it in about 2:30 in the afternoon that December day. The joy of those "lost" days at work is that they became "found" days at *La Casa*. The inside walls, installed with lots of different diagonal patterns, proceeded at a rapid, but careful, pace.

Finally, the week before Christmas, we moved into our new, partially built home. Sandia's parent's cabin was freezing, in spite of the electric heat running on maximum. The $150 electric bill wasn't even keeping us warm, so we winterized their cabin and shut it down until springtime. At *La Casa*, we made the plumbing operable and temporarily wired our construction power to our electric service box. It gave us lights and some receptacles, but no 220 voltage for cooking. No drama, we could do that on our trusty woodstove. It would take some planning, but we had to keep the living out of the way of the construction, which can be difficult. Nobody likes sawdust in their mashed potatoes, even if they do blend in!

My daughter Deborah and her boyfriend, Steve, surprised us with a freshly cut spruce tree to decorate for Christmas. We all pitched in with the decorations, mostly of our own making, and even managed to slip a few presents under that beautifully scented tree. It looked like a mountain Christmas house, bathed in sunshine, with three feet of snow piled up outside, but really toasty and warm on the inside. A memorable holiday.

After Christmas, the weather got even colder, our "baptism" of frost, I guess you could call it. One morning we awoke to fifty-five degrees below zero. Neither of our vehicles would start, but with the sun and our woodstove, our house maintained a steady fifty-five degrees (above zero) that day, a difference of 110 degrees above outside air temperatures. Needless to say, I didn't work on the job that day or the whole next week, as temperatures hovered around forty degrees below zero every morning. Our budget began to get our attention again, especially if we wanted

to eat! Serious stuff, eating. While kidding around about eating, Sandia and I came up with the idea of opening a restaurant—one with a nice warm kitchen and "hot" Mexican food.

I talked our idea over with Ted and Dick and they said it was all right with them if I quit. They wanted to spread the work out a little bit anyway. They assured me they would eat at our restaurant, as they loved Mexican food. So we had our first two customers. All we needed was the restaurant. Small matter!

We did our restaurant homework, getting most excited over a small fast food hamburger place that was closed for the winter. It was attached to a mini-market store type of operation that remained open all year round. The restaurant was run by the mini-mart owner in the summer only, the peak season in Grand Lake. It appeared to be our best option, so we invited the owner and his wife over to our place for a homemade Mexican meal and a discussion of the restaurant business. Sandia and I cooked the entire meal from scratch on top of our woodstove and they loved it—fresh flour tortillas, refried beans, Spanish rice, and the killer, green chile made from Anaheim chiles and pork. All of this was garnished with a flavorful salsa, seasoned with fresh cilantro. This was the way to do business, on well-satisfied stomachs. They'd never leased out their summer restaurant before, but I guess our determination convinced them. Besides, they would be right next door and could keep an eye on us, eat our food, and if we did well, they would see the spin off business. We agreed with what seemed like a fair rent, shook hands on the deal and it was done.

That night after our new landlords left, we did a little dance around our place. We found ourselves suddenly in the restaurant business for the first time in either of our lives. Doesn't everyone, at one time or another want to own a restaurant? We would find that it is a lot easier from the outside looking in, than it is to actually run a good restaurant business! That night we talked into the wee hours and settled on a name—*La Cocina en las Montañas*, the kitchen in the mountains, to reflect our cuisine. I started designing the sign, while Sandia worked on the menu. We relied heavily on Sandia's heritage and family recipes for the majority of our menu offerings, with the standard burger, fries, hot dogs, etc. for those captivated only by that kind of food. It remained mostly Mexican. The next few days were busy ones, getting in supplies and inventory, checking out the equipment, and in general figuring out the operation. Then, with a new sign above the door, we opened for business.

Maybe it was the hot food in the cold winter that helped us, probably though more like the unbelievable flavors of the food, but at any rate, we soon worked hard to keep up with the business. On the only day we were closed, Mondays, we used to drive the blue van a hundred miles each way to Denver for supplies. We made everything from scratch; "nothing out of a can" became our motto. I soon found out that I could not keep up with the number of tortillas required, by hand, so we started buying handmade ones from a small factory in Denver each week on our supply run. Pinto beans cooked all night, every night, on our wonderful and versatile woodstove. Sandia's mom coached us on recipes, even gave us seeds to sprout our own secret special spices to season the salsa with. She helped us so much in putting out flavorful authentic Mexican food.

Both Sandia's mom and dad showed up on weekends that spring to help us. Mom would put on an apron and dig right into whatever she saw that needed doing—cleaning or cooking. Dad would sit for hours cleaning beans. With their help, we built the business to the point that we could again begin to buy building materials. And there is the truth of the story! We sold burritos to buy boards!

Sandia would hold down the "fort" at *La Cocina* in the afternoons while I went to work up at *La Casa*. The restaurant work proved tedious, and took most of our motivation, but we kept the house building going, which was our first priority at the time. It made for long hours, tired bodies, but good deep sleeps each night.

Late on one of those still winter, not quite spring, afternoons, when I returned from the house to pitch in with the supper hour at *La Cocina*, Sandia tried to get me to guess who she had met in my absence. After failing with answers like Clint Eastwood and Linda Ronstadt, I finally gave up. She jumped up and down when she told me that she met David Klein!

No bells rang in my head, so I said something really profound like, "Who the hell is David Klein?"

She was still jumping up and down when she told me, "He's a stained glass expert and he is going to help us!" Then I understood why she felt so excited. Sandia had accumulated all the tools, glass, and design for her first window to go in the front door, but lacked the confidence it took to go from there. "He's coming by tonight before we close and will come up to the house with us to teach the art of the stained glass window," she explained with obvious excitement.

Sure enough, as I mopped up, David came into *La Cocina* and Sandia introduced us. The long hair and short beard certainly gave him the look of an artist. David explained to me that he had given his brother a stained glass window in exchange for a round trip plane ticket from Berkeley, California, where he had a studio, to Colorado, for some cross-country skiing. His brother, Barry, a high school teacher, lived in the next closest town, about sixteen miles south of us. David had come to Grand Lake that morning to get in some back-country skiing near the national park and just happened to stop in for a burrito. To Sandia, it seemed some kind of fate or destiny; to me it just further demonstrated the power of the burrito!

I remember how reinforcing David's first impressions seemed when we got up to the house. To us, our progress on *La Casa* had really slowed, and here stood David looking around in amazement, saying he could not believe what we had accomplished in so short a time by ourselves. Even telling him that friends and family had pitched in also did not diminish his enthusiasm. It really made us feel good to see things from another fresh perspective, especially that of an artist.

Then David sat down and began to teach. He cut the first piece, then sat back to coach us after that. Ted's wife, Deborah, joined us to learn also. We started at about 9:00 p.m. and by 4:00 a.m., we had cut every piece for our window and the majority of that needed for a design that Deborah brought along for her first window. David taught us as much of his three years in the business that night as he could, and then he was gone—on his way back to California the very next day. He would stop back a year later to say hello and photograph all the windows Sandia had completed. *La Casa* would ultimately contain seven of Sandia's stained glass windows. They were masterpieces to me. And David proved to be another masterpiece, of the human vintage, an individual willing to share his knowledge and skills with other people. I've met so many from the other side of the coin, who hide their arts and skills in a very selfish way. David's name was added to our growing "friends list."

Sandia and I talked off and on about taking on some help in the restaurant, especially at night when we would fall exhausted into our

bed. I worked on the concrete block core of our rock mass at that time. If we had help at *La Cocina*, it would give me a little more time to concentrate on the work at *La Casa*. Just about that time, a very friendly and eager young lady walked into our restaurant looking for a job. Her husband worked on the new Grand Lake Elementary School construction project and Kim wanted to fill in her time and at the same time, help their budget. They had no children and Kim was available for work pretty much anytime.

We hired Kim, mostly due to her outgoing personality and energy, and she turned out to be an asset from the start. She worked beyond our expectations and really lifted some of the burden from our shoulders. Her husband Rick used to come and pick her up from work each night. That was how I found out that he worked as a brick mason. He used to give me clues on mortar mix and block sequences, while he waited for Kim to finish up. Learning from Rick and two do-it-yourself fireplace books, I soon had our large Rumsford fireplace mortared up. There were two flues in that eighteen-foot high concrete block core. The mass stood in the center of the house, just a few feet behind our glass solar south wall. It ended two feet below the ceiling and was carried out the roof using insulated pipe through a wooden chimney box. Never having mortared a fireplace firebox before, I followed the directions to the letter. It was a wide, tall, but shallow firebox like in the old New England houses. Its object was primarily to heat the house, not to incite romanticism. Modern fireplaces are very inefficient—for looks only. Our Rumsford design promised heat on a cold winter's night. I designed a way to bring in outside air and preheat it to use for firebox combustion, instead of the usual method of using heated room air. An additional core up through the mass was installed through which hot air from a later greenhouse could be ducted and the heat stored in the mass.

I had just started facing the entire four-sided concrete block mass with those rocks that Sandia and Pablo collected earlier on, when Kim told us she had to quit at the restaurant. It seemed that Rick got into a labor dispute with the Bricklayer's Union and walked off the job, along with another friend of his. They planned to head for another job, they knew was in progress, about 150 miles away. Sandia, in particular, said she was going to sorely miss Kim's energetic help at the restaurant, but they needed to do what was best for them.

Before they left, I asked Rick if he would give me one day as a paid moss rock consultant. He answered in the affirmative and came by the next morning to help. I figured one day of watching and taking notes would put me in good stead to finish the rock-facing task. Well, Rick got involved with our rock mass that day, and he did not leave for ten days. His buddy Ron, even pitched in and helped as a "hog carrier," as Rick called him. Ron kept us constantly supplied with fresh mortar of a consistent quality. We paid them what we could and fed them good Mexican food. The three of us worked about fourteen hours a day on the rock facing, while Sandia and Kim kept *La Cocina* going full tilt.

All of a sudden, we mortared the last few, small, moss rocks into place and removed the scaffolding. We were done and it was party time. Time to celebrate a picturesque pile of rocks! With the ladies help, we blitzed the mortar mess and then lit the first real fire in the new Rumsford fireplace. Rick and I sat there for no less than three hours, oblivious to the activities of the others, and watched those flames. The firebox vented perfectly and not a drop of smoke came into the house. We were covered with

mortar, but couldn't seem to move to clean up, despite everyone's repeated urgings. While draining several cold ones, and staring into the flames, Rick told me that, before he married Kim, on nights after work when he cleaned up before going to the bar, none of the ladies would pay him any attention. So one night he just went to

Rumsford firebox completed

That first fire

the bar straight from work covered with mortar, like we were. He insisted that night the women wouldn't leave him alone. Rick and I made a secret pact after his story, not to clean up that night, no matter how animated our wives pleas became! A tired beer pact, we called it. Sandia called Ted and Dick and their families and the celebration went on around us. Someone played the guitar, others sang, and Rick and I just stared exhaustedly, mesmerized by the flames. I never knew that a fire in a fireplace could be so fantastic!

As spring neared its end, it brought to us a noteworthy character. I was fencing in an adjacent outside eating area, El Patio, in anticipation of larger summer crowds at *La Cocina*, when one of our customers walked out of the restaurant and approached my effort. I don't recall his name, but let's call him Bob for the lack of identity now. Bob was in his early thirties and appeared physically fit. He had just lunched on our green chile burrito menu and appeared to be well satisfied with the food and the surroundings.

"Are you Bill?" he asked me.

"You bet", I responded. "What can I help you with?"

"My name is Bob and they told me inside that you had just picked up from the city and moved up here to the mountains to live! Is that true?"

"A little more complicated than that, but in a manner of speaking, it's pretty much the truth."

"Well, I'm a guy that's unhappy with my job and my life down in Denver and have been thinking of chucking it all and heading up here to live. I've thought about it for the last couple of years and really want to do it," Bob lamented.

Our conversation went on in that manner for the better part of an hour, with me trying to

give him all the positive aspects, as well as some of the negatives, of mountain life. Bob became so excited at one point, I thought he was ready to drive to Denver and pack up his belongings and head back up to begin a new life. I went on trying to answer his questions as honestly as I could, but probably a little biased on the mountain life because that's where my head was at. Bob seemed unable to make a final decision on his dilemma and I certainly wasn't going to make it for him.

Finally he commented, "But what if things don't work out up here and I'm unable to get my job back?"

"You get another job," I answered him matter-of-factly.

He thanked me rather half-heartedly and walked off shaking his head with indecision. I turned back to my fencing task. I never saw him again and believe to this day that he never moved to the mountains. There are no guarantees in life. The risks we take have to be our own doing and are the spices that add that unique and beautiful flavor to life! So what if it doesn't always turn out fantastic? They are our own lives to live. So we need to live them with a passion for the opportunity!

Summer came to Grand Lake, as only can occur at the elevations of the Colorado Mountains. It is best described as spring-like anywhere else, fresh, green, and just pleasurable to be immersed in. My son Gary came back to be with us. Kirsten went off to be with her dad in Europe again for the summer. We hired several more staff to help us take care of the *La Cocina*. Our business volume was really up as the plains east of us got hotter and hotter, driving people to the coolness of our mountains. Our rent was higher for the summer, so we needed those tourists. Most Grand Lake businesses had only one season–Memorial Day to Labor Day.

If you didn't make it then, it became a winter of starvation! Pablo, Carlos, and Tomas visited us again the first two weeks of June to help us celebrate our anniversary. Pablo spent most of his time in the kitchen of *La Cocina*, helping us keep up with the food orders. Pablo, what a friend!

My mom and younger sister Dottie visited us that summer. I was a little worried about my mom, who was in her late sixties, at our 8,800-foot elevation, but she was spry as a chicken. The elevation didn't phase her in the least. I took her to the Hot Sulphur mineral springs, a few towns away, and she loved the experience and the zest she felt after being in the baths. We didn't have as much time to spend with her and my sister as we would have liked, because the restaurant demanded so much of our time. Anyway, when two owner-builder lady friends of ours came and asked for our help with their wall raising, I took my mom and sis along. In the back of my mind, I thought perhaps they would be bored.

We had been helping and encouraging these two Shelter grads, Sandy and Beth, all along as they built their own house in a beautiful Aspen grove about fifteen miles from us. They used our pier foundation forms and were also building a solar shed design. So when they needed help raising a wall, off we went.

There were ten additional women at the site, ready to help, when we arrived. They were all Denver teachers, as were Sandy and Beth. They asked me how I thought everything looked. As I took in their preparations, I could see the pains they had taken to be ready. A block and tackle was rigged to a nearby tree, just in case it was needed. I couldn't see anything they'd overlooked, so we all got ready to lift. One volunteer stood by the block and tackle and I made sure my mom and sis were off to the side, out of harms way. "Let's go for it," we yelled and up it went. The second of two sections went up just as

easily. As we fastened the two sections together in the air and plumbed them up, I remember thinking that those ladies didn't even need me around. They could have done equally well by themselves, they were so eager! I guess I represented the confidence factor, with our wall raising experiences behind us.

The raising seemed to last only moments and there the wall stood, eighteen feet tall by twenty-four feet wide, with about eight solar window openings in it. In the wall's background was a whole grove of beautiful Aspen trees, and it seemed they were all fluttering in appreciation of their new neighbor, the post and beam wall. Then I looked around from the wall and the trees to see Sandy and Beth gazing up at their wall with tears streaming down their cheeks. I looked over at my sister and mom. It must have been contagious, because both of them were crying also. Then all the helpers started hugging, while Sandy and Beth broke out a bottle of champagne. They had iced it down to toast the wall in celebration. What a feeling!

All the way back to the restaurant my mom kept talking about the raising. She said, "Those girls are doing it all themselves. This is just like the old days, when people helped each other." I never realized she would be so deeply moved by it. But that is what a wall raising is all about, beyond the technical part—a deeply moving experience. My mom and sister left the next day to return to Massachusetts, and they were still talking about it at the Denver airport.

At the pace we were leading, it seemed no wonder that the summer passed like a bullet. Before we knew it, September fell upon us. Kirsten had returned, and this time my Deborah wanted to go back to Connecticut. Gary would stay with us and go to our mountain high school as a freshman.

At the end of the summer also, we decided

photos by Esther Harms

Sequence of the Sandy and Beth wall raising

our interests would be best served out of the restaurant business. We made a deal with the owner that he would take over the business and buy out our inventory. He had seen the business volume we did in the summer and appeared anxious to keep it going. To us, the prospect of long hours for the approaching winter, with a small hourly return, helped us make our decision to move on to other things.

I had some small remodel carpentry jobs lined up and also sold and installed woodstoves. So we had a decent basis to fall back on, especially with our low overheads. The additional time in the winter would allow us to work on things at *La Casa* such as cabinets, furniture, and the other unfinished items in the house. Also, in balance, we wanted to learn cross-country skiing. After working day and night since arriving in those mountains eighteen months earlier, it was time for a little mountain fun!

chapter eighteen

18

Toward Self Sufficiency—My First Hunt

Fall, in the mountains, has two main priorities. The first and foremost is preparation for winter. That means insulating your plumbing, checking your heating system, installing a woodstove, if you don't already have one, or upgrading to a more efficient model, and finally, getting in two or three, or more, cords of wood, depending on the square footage and insulated quality of your winter shelter. Fireplaces and the old Franklin stoves required, further, that the logs be split into smaller pieces. The coming of winter kept most of us mountain people pretty busy. The second priority, for most locals, was hunting season. The bagging of an elk or deer meant, that even when work became scarce, you would still have sustenance, a very important matter during a long cold winter.

Having met most everyone in our town through the restaurant, we found it really helped our woodstove business. People knew whom they were dealing with when we ran our stove ads in the local weekly paper. Most of what we did after that followed by "word of mouth." I studied hard and became familiar with all the aspects of a woodstove, in particular, the installation,

your breath all exhaled, cross hairs in place

squeeze off the shot; then winter, simpler to face

operation, and maintenance. Our little company, Rocky Mountain Homesteaders, handling the new and efficient airtight Earthstove, did enough stove business to keep us going that winter.

While I worked on stoves, Sandia always seemed to be involved with a new stained glass project. When she wasn't working on a window for La Casa, she was either helping someone else make a window, or else making a gift of stained glass for a friend's baby or maybe a wedding. I suggested she give classes to teach others on a regular basis, for a modest fee, and she took me up on it.

Our workshop became a classroom that winter, a prophecy of things to come. We built four lightboxes and set up stations so she could accommodate four students at a time. Most of those that came were females, but several males took her course also. Among those were a carpenter and the village blacksmith. Everyone had to make a small window to complete the course. The window the blacksmith made during the class hangs proudly in his shop—a huge muscular arm and hammer pounding hot steel on an anvil—very fitting. Sandia would ultimately teach a total of fifty-five students that winter.

As I installed woodstoves in the fall, most conversations finally got around to the approaching hunting season, deer and elk mostly. It seemed like some of the local guys lived all year for those few weeks of hunting. Most talk now turned to hunting stories of the past, the ones they had bagged and the big ones that had somehow escaped. Like fishermen, an element of the truth was always there, but amplified over the repeated storytelling with the passage of time.

I listened to the stories and slowly got intrigued. The previous year, I walked the forest with Ted during the elk hunting season, but had been too busy getting the house closed in to get serious about the hunt. This year, knowing we could really use the meat and its nourishment, I began to rationalize the quest of an animal. The locals were serious hunters, not just for trophies, but for the meat, hide, liver, heart, and anything else they could use. They did not like the city hunters, or the out-of-staters, a whole lot. Seems like those guys were just there for the sport of it. The locals told stories of the city guys just mounting the dead animal on the vehicle so the world could see what a great hunter they were. Sometimes, they didn't know enough to field dress the animal before slinging it up into view for that proud ride home. The meat wouldn't be worth a hoot after that kind of treatment. And after all, the locals sort of felt they had first rites to the hunting grounds as they lived there all year round and sort of earned that privilege.

As I became more and more convinced to hunt an elk, Dick took time to explain a lot to me about the animal, its habits, and how to dress it out if you got one. He showed me the knives and saws that a good hunter should carry. We talked about rifles and different calibers and the merits of each. I finally decided to hunt, although I didn't know if I could kill anything.

One of Sandia's creations

Colorado Mountain elk

Besides, I'd never laid eyes on an elk, cow or bull, at that point.

It happened about that time that I contracted to put a woodstove in the parsonage of our local church. During the installation, I got to talking to the minister, J. R., about hunting. Mostly he asked me how I felt about killing an animal.

"Could you pull the trigger?" he asked.

I expressed my strong feelings about the balance in nature as managed and sometimes harvested by man. Since we would use every bit of the animal, without waste, and not just hunt for the sport of it, I answered that I probably could pull the trigger, but would really just have to wait for the time to come. One of our forest ranger friends explained to me that the number of licenses issued was purposeful to harvest a certain number of the mountain elk herd, otherwise winter would take this same toll. The remaining mountain land, not covered by resorts, condominiums, and cabins, was only capable of supporting a diminishing number of these unique animals.

The end of October approached, and with it, elk season. Most of the locals would not commit to any work during the hunting season. The hunt took top priority. Dick would guide again at a hunting camp for out-of-staters, as he did each year. Ted and I made a pact to hunt together.

The night before "opening day" of elk season, we could hear the elk bugling in the nearby forest. They sounded close and mysterious to me. That bugle is melodious at first, but ends in a sort of grunting and snorting. I'm sure the cow elk thought it was beautiful and "macho." Only the strongest bull, with the greatest rack, or antlers, and the mightiest of bugles, became the herd bull. Only he could mate with the cows. In this way, nature built the instincts to propagate the fittest of the species. The stereotype of

two bull elk with their antlers locked together in mortal combat is untrue. It is actually more like arm wrestling, when one displays superior strength, the other backs down and heads for the fringe of the herd to wait for a better day. When all challenges have been repulsed, the herd bull is ready for mating with his "harem." When the day comes that a younger bull successfully dethrones the herd bull, that "old" bull is relegated to the outskirts of the herd to graze with the cows only out of mating season, and finally meets his end by predators or the severity of winter in the high mountains. I later witnessed elk with broken legs struggling for survival through deep snows, only to lose the battle and succumb to what we called, "winter kill." Such is the balance in nature.

I awoke to the alarm, while it still remained dark outside. I dressed quickly in the warm clothes Sandia laid out for me the night before. After eating a little bit and drinking two cups of wake up coffee, I double checked my gear—buck knife, bone saw, and skinning knife. I had two borrowed rifles, both small bore, a 300 Savage and a 308 Savage, both lever action, one with a scope (308), and one without (300). I had sighted them both in at a nearby target range. Without the scope, I could pop a soda can at one hundred yards. Which one should I take? I had not made up my mind yet, except I knew I did not want to carry them both.

Ted showed up as I still looked at the rifles. He had a friend, Mike, with him who worked with Ted at the time. It didn't matter how many of us there were, as we would all probably end up in different places anyway. Sandia was awake now, offering coffee, filling a thermos for me, putting sandwiches in my backpack and wishing us all good luck. I kissed her goodbye and picked up both rifles. I would decide in the truck which one to carry into the forest.

We drove only about a mile and a half and parked. The fun of being a local. The quiet dark forest lay all around us. I could hear the North Fork of the Colorado River flowing just off to our right. As we stood outside Ted's truck, no sounds could be heard above that of the steady flow of the river. My feet were barely visible.

I finally opted for the 308 Savage with the scope thinking of its light gathering capabilities in the early dawn and filled my ammo belt with a half dozen rounds of 308 shells. I shouldn't need anymore than that. Off we went, as quietly as possible, single file, slowly into the dark forest. We soon found an old logging road and walked carefully along it. Ted and Mike seemed to know where we were. I had no idea; it was all new and exciting to me, as I just followed along, peering into the darkness among the trees.

Soon, the sunrise began to light our way. An occasional elk would bugle in the distance to break the silence of the forest. It became lighter and I found myself crouching next to Ted in the brush, trying to detect any movement at all in our surroundings. All of a sudden, an elk bugle broke the silence not more than 150 yards in front of us. Immediately following the bugle, I thought the third world war had started, as several hunters, whose presence was unknown to us, started firing at an elk I couldn't even see. That many shots whizzing around made me nervous. Ted, picking himself off the ground, agreed. I told him I'd head back along the road we'd come in on and he said he would make a big circle and meet me later. Mike had gone off to sit somewhere and wait for an elk to run by. I have too much internal energy to approach it that way, so I headed off up the road trying to make like Daniel Boone.

At least it got quiet again. It seemed so peaceful out there by myself. After a while, I de-cided to get off the road and crept carefully into the adjacent forest. Moving quietly through the trees, I spied a ridge up in front of me so I slowly crawled up to a log near the top. It reminded me of marine boot camp a long time ago, except that I was alone in the quiet of the forest. My nostrils filled with the scents of pine needles and damp clumps of grass that grew intermittently. I stopped my crawl several times, lying there to listen to the absolute silence.

I reached the log and lifted my head just enough to peer over it, down into the draw in front of me. As my eyes moved up the far side of the draw, I was startled to see four or five cow elk, just "munching" on grass and gawk-ing around. There must be a herd bull around; this had to be his harem. I slowly raised my rifle and rested it on the log so I could study the scene through the telescopic sight. The cows were about 150 yards in front of me, at the same elevation as I was. I slowly scanned the forest around them. As I moved the scope above the cows, I saw first, a hoof, then a leg, and then a huge muscular body. A pine branch shielded his head, but I could see his tremendous rack above the branch. By then, my heart pounded so hard; I thought surely those elk could hear it. I wanted a head shot because I didn't want to take a chance and wound the animal. I put the cross hairs of the scope on his neck and waited. Maybe he would turn from the branches so I could get a clear shot at his head. I waited and watched with my heart still beating at an accelerated pace.

Off in the distance another hunter fired at something. Now I thought, what if he spooks because of some nearer shot. Without any fur-ther hesitation, I exhaled, held my breath, and squeezed off a shot at his vulnerable neck. The bull just dropped in my scope as the report echoed loudly through my head and the cow elk bolted into the cover of the deeper forest. I raised up from my log cover, put the rifle over my head and charged down the draw and up the other side. Suddenly I stood over him. He was bigger than I had even imagined. His rack had six beautifully polished symmetric "silver tips" on each side. As I gazed down at him, I realized how much my own body shook. I reflected then that the rifle with the scope had been a good choice. I also felt happy to have brought him down with a single shot.

Now the real work began and I was totally on my own. All the talks that Ted and Dick gave me were running through my head. They had told me, "Get his hind end up high so you can bleed him." I tried to move him, but I could hardly budge him. He must have weighed over nine hundred pounds. I then sat, trying to relax and think. This bull had to be dressed out and carefully done. I was on my own and that was all there was to it. I would have to think it out, one logical step at a time.

I had rope and belts and used their mechanical advantage around a tree to finally move his hind end up higher. After that the field dressing went well, a lot of it being common sense. You didn't have to be a skilled surgeon, just needed sharp knives. There was too much good meat to waste any of it. Before I knew it, I'd almost completed the task. I ran for the river to get water for the final rinsing out of the body cavity. Mike saw me from his sitting spot down river and waved. I signaled that I had an elk, bringing him on the run. Mike helped me with the last of the cleanup and the field dressing was done.

There was no way I could ever have his head mounted, but I did take that beautiful rack and the two ivory teeth he bugled with. The field dressing remains stayed in the forest to feed the scavengers. The area would be clean as a whistle in a few days. This is the way nature works.

Ted showed up then and between the three of us, we carried that elk, Elvis, as Mike named him, in sections to the pickup. We used freshly cut green lodge poles to tie the sections for easier carrying, taking turns on the pole ends.

Sandia could not believe it—enough meat to last us a year! She helped us take the sections to get them hung in the shed for a little aging. The neighbors kidded me saying how lucky I was. "A six point on opening morning and the first bull elk you ever saw." At the same time I felt pretty blessed for the whole opportunity. The balance of the day became a bit euphoric. Word travels quickly in a small town and I had to tell my first hunting story many times that day. In later years, I bagged an elk each hunting season, until I gave up the hunt in preference to a mainly vegetarian diet.

Dick, his wife Mary Pat, Ted and his wife Deborah, helped us butcher the meat into steaks, roasts, elkburger, and even the scraps for dog food. We shared the meat with everyone who helped us and put the rest away in the freezer. Sandia and I looked into that full freezer and had the security of knowing that we wouldn't be hungry that winter.

chapter nineteen

Our Second Winter in Mountain Paradise

Up until now, I hope I haven't been making you think that we were "goody two shoes," or anything like it, because we could party with the best of them. It's just that we didn't do it that much. We wouldn't have been able to get the priorities accomplished, partying all the time, but you have to do it on occasion, just to keep things in balance. Balance, that's my keyword in life. Hell, I remember Labor Day weekend, before we sold the *La Cocina*, I had a big party night. Pablo was there, helping us again, and he and I challenged Dick and Ted to a golfing match. Nine holes and the losers had to buy a case of beer. Well, they beat Pablo and me (They must have cheated on the score!), and we drove to town to pick up a case of Lowenbrau. Pablo and I brought the case back and met them on the deck of *La Casa* overlooking the eighth fairway. It was a nice sunny afternoon and the cold ones went down easily. We started yelling down to people on the golf course, being a bit obnoxious. Two young lady golfers, not only endured our whistling, but also obliged our loud requests for a show by lifting their T-shirts up for a quick flash. As they golfed on past, our cheers must have rung in their

*winter's grip is here
heavy coats and warm
gloves too
time to snuggle, true*

ears. Towards evening, we were out of beer and really hungry. Time to head to town for burritos at *La Cocina,* where Sandia held down the fort, and then to maybe the Stagecoach or Lariat Saloon for a few more beers. It had been a long hard summer on the work schedule and letting off a little steam wouldn't hurt any of us. The burritos went down quickly and pretty soon we got into arm wrestling.

Sandia muttered something like, "Boys will be boys!"

Dick and I got to wrestling which evolved into pushing and shoving. That soon got a bit out of hand. Meantime, Ted picked a fight with some old stable nemesis of his out on the main street and Dick and I ran out there to break that one up. Time to head for the nearest bar and a cold one. Pablo stuck to me like glue trying to watch out for my safety, I guess. Then across the street from the Stagecoach Saloon, Dick spotted a young blonde lady on the pay phone. He surprised us all by grabbing her up and throwing her over his shoulder, leaving her conversation dangling, and headed for the bar. When we all came through the door at once, with a kicking female on Dick's shoulder, no need to say the bar patrons shut up and turned to stare. Dick proceeded up to the bar, threw the young lady across it, face down, and bit her on the butt.

The big bartender, Fetch, raised his arms up and shouted, "I ain't serving you guys!"

So of course we had to climb up on the bar to challenge that ungracious welcome and at the same time so we could get above his head level. In the ensuing fracas, Pablo disappeared, probably giving up on me, and that young blonde lady also left, with a big smile on her face, maybe to go back and continue her telephone conversation. We never did get beers from Fetch, so we ambled down to the Lariat Saloon for a little more of what we really didn't need any more of. I'm pretty sure we quieted down after that and Sandia and Pablo found me after they closed the restaurant to make sure I got home to bed. You have to let loose sometime, otherwise things build up. Who the hell can be good all the time?

Hunting season ended and early winter moved in on us. Sunny crisp days and cold nights became the norm. Sandia and I used the pickup and our new chainsaw to get in about four chords of firewood from the surrounding forest. Exhausting work by the time it's done, but what a feeling seeing it all stacked there, neatly under the deck. With the woodstove our only backup to the sun, those rows of stacked firewood gave a warmth and confidence as winter approached. The previous winter, in February, the woodpile got down to fragments and bark. We had to borrow a chainsaw and snowshoes from friends and trudge to the nearest forest on top of four feet of snow. There we dropped standing dead pine trees, cut them into eight-foot lengths, and dragged them back to the house. When we dragged enough lengths back, we bucked them up with the chainsaw and stacked them under the deck. The lesson of that

long hard day, last winter, was to get in enough wood in the fall, while the pickup could still navigate those logging roads!

Thanksgiving was going to be special that year as Sandia's parents accepted our invitation to join us for a mountain celebration. Sandia went to work on some early pies and I, after consulting our growing do-it-yourself library, got down to basics on building a dining room table. After all, we'd used a large wooden electric cable spool, on its side, as a table ever since moving into *La Casa*. Company coming was good motivation to get a large table constructed. You know how you always run around fixing up the house when guests are coming. I had never built any furniture before, except an end table in high school shop, where they put me when I got kicked out of Spanish class. With the budding resolve and confidence of an owner-builder, I jumped right into the table building. There remained enough spare wood in the shop to complete it, while the local hardware store had all the fittings I would need, so I just had to engineer the table and input the labor.

That was an occasion when it was nice to have an attached but separate workshop. A guy could make a mess without getting sawdust into the living part of the house and the pumpkin pies. Sandia came in periodically from her tasks, giving me encouragement and an occasional cup of coffee. The construction went well and the next night, Thanksgiving eve, I stood proudly looking at the finished trestle table. All it lacked was a few coats of polyurethane for a protective coating and it would be ready to be eaten and spilt upon.

Sandia was always my cheerleader, so reinforcing when she viewed my work. She danced excitedly around the table describing its beauty. Well, I thought, it would be out of place in a modern furniture shop, but it was all ours and it really did have a bit of character. The top was built of sanded roughsawn boards, with blue and purple streaks of "beetle kill" stain visible. It fit the setting of our mountain home nicely. We both pitched in and gave it one good coat of urethane, which would dry by the next day's feast time. The other coats could be added after the holiday.

The next morning we arose to a forecast of snow, but we optimistically put the finishing touches on our Thanksgiving banquet. There were pies, turkey, a little elk, vegetables, heaps of mashed potatoes, my favorite, candied yams, and lots more in the works. As we worked in the kitchen, the snow began falling heavily and started piling up quickly. It just kept snowing and snowing. The telephone rang and it was Sandia's family apologizing for not wanting to attempt to drive over Berthoud Pass in the storm. We didn't blame them, but still felt the loss in our hearts. Better they stayed out of harm's way on that day. There would be other Thanksgivings; we knew that in our minds.

So Gary, Kirsten, Sandia and I sat down to our new table covered with abundance and celebrated, along with our ten-month old husky shepherd mix pup, Meshika. It continued to snow heavily. Soon friends joined us, at Sandia's invitation, as their families didn't make the drive either. We sat around the table, with well-satisfied stomachs, afterwards discussing the negatives and positives of mountain life, deciding that our lives definitely were inked in on the plus side of the accounting ledger.

One evening, several days after Thanksgiving, I worked on the one interior wall left unfinished—the center piece wall behind our thermal

The new table and abundance

rock mass and fireplace. It remained one of those projects that I left alone until we came up with a good creative idea for its completion. The wall sat right in the center of the house and was viewed from most of the downstairs areas. That afternoon, while working on a project in the shop, the design idea struck me clear as a bell. I planned it out, deciding to surprise Sandia with the finished product. I found the boards that I previously set aside for that special wall and measured them out, noting the great colors, blues and purples, they contained as a result of "beetle kill."

That night, as Sandia slept soundly, on my promise to be "right up in a few minutes," I worked on my idea for the wall—a log cabin pattern, done in honor of our special quilt! I worked as quietly as I could, making all my cuts in the workshop. Sandia is a deep sleeper and my finish nailing didn't wake her. It probably took me about six hours to complete and trim out the wall. Unable to contain my own excitement until morning, I woke Sandia up and guided her drowsy footsteps downstairs to look at the finished project.

Sandia stood sleepily in front of the wall (it was about 3:00 A.M.), and I watched her eyes light up as she recognized the pattern's design. Ever the cheerleader, she cried out, "Oh, Bill, it's just like our quilt! The wall is beautiful."

We cried together and hugged, both remembering those dreaming days of quilting and school in Maine. Now we stood at that wall, symbolic of those feelings, surrounded by *La Casa del Sol*—the true fruit of all those earlier dreams. We had done it—we had done it!! What great warmth flooded our minds and bodies at that moment. There was no holding back the tears of joy that poured down our smiling cheeks as we looked around and then into each other's eyes. I slept a tired, but exhilarated sleep that night!

Winter continued. The snow kept on falling. We did a lot of cross-country skiing and really strengthened our cardiovascular systems, as well as our leg and upper body muscles. I contracted sufficient work to keep our expenses paid. Most of the work consisted of woodstove installations and house designs. Several other builders approached me about drawing plans after I did my first "for hire" set for Ted and one of his house clients. I loved working on the drawing board. It was set up on my desk, which faced the fireplace, and also angled to look out our huge expanse of south facing windows. Elvis's (the elk) large rack hung high up on the fireplace mass, reminding me of our quest for reasonable self-reliance. The house was always warm and the view unbeatable. We didn't have any complaints about life!

I should remark here that the passive solar rock mass worked very well. Sometimes, the portion in the direct winter sunlight took my imbedded thermometer for a ride up to 106 degrees Fahrenheit. The rock mass stored that heat away only to give it back at night when we needed it.

Fifteen tons of mass, heated thirty plus degrees above room temperature, is a lot of BTUs of heat energy. Our inside air temperatures that winter never exceeded eighty degrees and were never lower than sixty degrees. The fifteen tons of rock acted like a giant thermal flywheel, keeping everything really constant. Without the mass the winter before, we experienced interior air temperatures as high as 110 degrees—not real comfortable! The mass just soaked up any excess heat and gave it back slowly when the house temperature fell below that of the rock.

Another later winter morning, Sandia and I figured that the time was right to replace the curtained doorway in our downstairs bathroom with a real door. I challenged her to a race. Could she finish a hexagonal stained glass window for the door, with a single red rose set in a field of opaque white, faster than I could build the heavy timber door? She took the challenge and off we ran to the workshop. We worked feverishly, but quietly, each at our own task. That afternoon turned into an energetic one. I tried persuading her to make us some lunch. Sandia said that that wouldn't be fair, so we did not eat. Six hours later, we finished. She officially beat me by ten minutes, as I still had a few bolts left to insert and tighten. We laughed together. It was fun, and we had our door.

While Sandia made food for our growling stomachs, I inset the stained glass window into the door and hung it on the hinges of the prepared door opening. Sandia then fashioned and engraved the wooden door handles and it was completely done in one very long day and evening burst of creative energy. A store bought door just wouldn't have been the same.

Spring approached and we experienced a lot of wet, heavy spring snowstorms. A friend from Albuquerque called and asked if we would check the roof of his nearby cabin for snow loading.

He offered to pay us. I told him not to worry. Gary and I would check the roof and if it needed shoveling, we would take care of it.

Gary and I left the next morning with shovels, just in case they would be needed, and headed for the cabin. We took Meshika along to let her run and play in the snow. She was a husky/shepherd mix and did she ever love the snow! She actually remained a pup at thirteen months, but pretty big in size. We finally made it to Randy's cabin through the very heavy and deep snow. The cabin appeared almost invisible under the blanket of snow. The total snowfall that winter, up to that point, had been just less than twenty feet.

We climbed up on the roof and started shoveling. Gary threw a few playful shovelfuls of snow at me, so I got him back good. It turned out to be fun as well as hard work. The bright Colorado Mountain sunshine shone down on us for several hours as we broke a sweat shoveling the snow off the roof structure.

Suddenly the acute silence was broken by a rifle report. A few seconds later, there was another shot, and then silence set in. I looked off in the direction that the shots seemed to have come from, but I could not see anything. An eerie feeling came over me and the hair went up on the back of my neck. I called down to Meshika. No response. Not wanting to alarm Gary, I slowly laid my shovel down and climbed off the roof. Gary asked, "Dad, where are you going?"

"I'm just going to go have a check on Meshika."

Meshika was nowhere to be found. Her tracks circled the house where she had been running around, but she didn't answer my calls. We had assumed that she was napping in the snow as she often did. Gary stood beside me now. He had heard the shots and had grown wary, also.

I chose the direction I thought the shots had

come from and headed off, my heart pounding. I sent Gary in the opposite direction. I ran through that deep snow as fast as I could go, calling out Meshika's name; hoping she would come bounding toward me, leaving some puppy adventure behind when she heard her name. The sounds of Gary calling her name got too far away to hear anymore.

A snowmobiler came along and I flagged him down. I described Meshika to him and asked if he had seen her. No, he had not, but offered to ride me around the area for a look. Accepting his offer, I climbed up behind on the passenger saddle and held on as he drove away. We found no sign of her, no fresh dog prints, nothing at all. I finally gave up and thanked him for his help.

I walked slowly back down the plowed portion of the road. Running in that deep snow had been tiring. Maybe she had dug a snow cave near Randy's cabin and just slept soundly all this time. I headed for the cabin.

Then I saw Gary walking toward me. He carried Meshika in his arms. Her head lay limply and hung to one side. Tears rolled down Gary's face. He was so choked up that he couldn't get any words to form on his lips. He finally took a deep breath and blurted out, "That rancher up there shot her, Dad!"

The anguish I felt at seeing Meshika, dead in Gary's arms, turned to pure fury.

"Who, Gary? Who did it?"

"That guy at the next ranch. He said she was chasing elk."

I ran all the way to that ranch house and stormed up to the door. I fought through tear filled eyes and a choking chest. I knew the man; he was a friend. He recoiled at my onslaught. "I'm sorry," he said over and over. "She was chasing the elk. I didn't know she was yours. I thought she was a stray," he offered.

I just raged and shouted, "But why did you

have to shoot her?"

He kept saying, "I'm sorry."

It finally crept into my numb brain that we couldn't bring Meshika back and couldn't do anything there but cause more grief. I turned to Gary, who did not understand, and we went to get our shovels and drove off.

Gary and I buried the pup that night under the deck of *La Casa* and covered her grave with big rocks and a handmade wooden cross. Meshika had been an enjoyable part of our lives up in those mountains. Gary and Deborah, before she left, had taught her lots of dog tricks. She'd been a really good-natured and spirited dog.

I called the Sheriff's office to report the shooting across a county road, which was not allowed. Later that night, a deputy and a forest service guy showed up to talk to us. They explained to us that there was nothing that could be done.

At least six or eight dogs were shot every winter chasing wild game or cattle. The game became so weak toward the end of winter, that a dog's chasing it could literally kill the animal from overexertion. That rancher had been feeding hay bales to about twenty elk, thus keeping them alive. Along came Meshika, saw her first elk, and followed her natural instincts to give chase. The rancher saw her and was within shooting range, so it was Meshika's end. No malice, just the way of the mountains. It had to be that way!

The knowledge helped to understand, but it didn't ease the hurting inside. The only good I could ever find in Meshika's death was the way we all came together that spring. Some of the strongest bonds of relationship are woven during the tough times. The good times are always easy to deal with; it's coping with the tough times that builds character in youngsters.

The Institute—Teaching and Sharing

The snow still remained on the ground when we started to build our greenhouse. This would be our last project before we could officially say, to those always asking when we'd be done, "The house is completed!" Working on the deck, on the south side of the house, where the greenhouse was located, on those sunny spring days, proved to be a pure joy. We had designed and drawn the greenhouse plans and received our building permit in late winter; stockpiled the roughsawn lumber we would need and ordered the glass. The windows, this time, were factory-made thermal pane, with tempered glass, replacement sliding glass door units. These units were available in a few sizes only, but were relatively inexpensive, so we designed around those sizes. I figured out that it would have cost us the same money to construct equivalent units from scratch, so why expend the labor?

The greenhouse was a necessity for growing food that high in the mountains, as Grand Lake only averaged about thirty frost-free days each year. In other words, 335 nights the temperatures could reach down to 32° F, or below. This is a really short growing season, to say the least. Our

come into the mountains, to learn and share

plan a house, with nature; show that you care

outside gardening efforts were only successful with greens like snow peas, spinach, nice crispy lettuce, radishes, and carrots, while attempts at fruity vegetables, like tomatoes, resulted in disaster. The working compost heap even froze solid at our low winter temperatures. We needed the greenhouse if we were going to have any semblance of a self-reliant lifestyle. With our material estimates figured at about $800.00, it seemed like a wise investment of labor. Also, when it was not growing, in the dead of winter, it would serve as a "walk-in solar collector." As we planned it, visions of winter morning coffee in a warm sunny greenhouse, surrounded by jungles of flowering plants, dreamily rushed through our heads.

So here we stood, raising another wall—our greenhouse wall. Terry, both an architectural draftsman and an ex-building inspector, and his wife, Janeen, were visiting from the next town and gave us a hand. We raised the wall, braced it temporarily, and cut a few roof rafters to hold it in place. As we worked together, I happened to discuss our school idea with Terry—an owner/builder school in the mountains of Colorado,

Sandia's final touch of glass for the greenhouse door-our mountain wildflowers

Greenhouse framing

specifically oriented to people wanting to build in the Rockies, or other outlying regions; kind of like homesteading, or modern pioneering. Sandia and I remained committed to the idea, always had been; it was only a matter of timing. Well, Terry got so fired up on the idea that we left the greenhouse framing and went inside the

house to talk some serious "school talk."

Up until that day, we had had only limited support for our school idea. A few people said that they would help, maybe! Quite a few locals had expressed an interest in attending. The vacant original Grand Lake log schoolhouse had been offered to us at a reasonable lease fee. I guess all we lacked at that point in time was bona fide support for the idea. And here was Terry, talking a mile a minute, offering to take time from his architectural duties to help me teach. He thought he could justify his absence from the office on the "if come" that one student might hire him to draw plans, which did happen in the first class! We literally caught on fire that night with the idea.

The following week, I arranged to lease the classroom, lavatory, office, and potential library and shop space in that old log schoolhouse. I opened book accounts and ordered a basic

 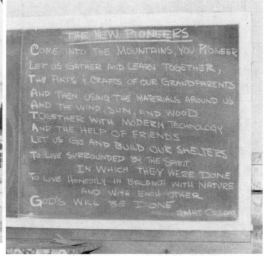

THE NEW PIONEERS
COME INTO THE MOUNTAINS, YOU PIONEER
LET US GATHER AND LEARN TOGETHER,
THE ARTS & CRAFTS OF OUR GRANDPARENTS
AND THEN USING THE MATERIALS AROUND US
AND THE WIND, SUN, AND WOOD
TOGETHER WITH MODERN TECHNOLOGY
AND THE HELP OF FRIENDS
LET US GO AND BUILD OUR SHELTERS
TO LIVE SURROUNDED BY THE SPIRIT
IN WHICH THEY WERE DONE
TO LIVE HONESTLY IN BALANCE WITH NATURE
AND WITH EACH OTHER
GOD'S WILL BE DONE
RMHI CREDO

The Institute and our credo

bookstore inventory. Terry and I built library and bookstore shelving the next weekend. The following week, I finished closing in the greenhouse, while Sandia started a stained glass mountain wildflower window for the east greenhouse door. In between greenhouse carpentry and stained glass, we wrote press releases and called potential students. Several students became really excited about the opportunity and committed to take classes, while others opted for later sessions. Several mountain papers and one large Midwestern newspaper promised to print special reports on the school's founding and it's scope, as well as that summer's class schedule. They seemed intrigued with the idea of a school devoted to those people who wanted to build their own homes—the owner/builder. Their published articles evolved into a great help by putting us on the map!

Rocky Mountain Homesteader's Institute was founded in those few weeks, after being in the embryonic stage for years. We had thought so much of it out, it just required putting the wheels in motion, and the small matter of getting *La Casa* close to finished! I had even spent time the previous winter working on course content and session outlines. Now, about twelve hours of inspired time yielded a huge, routed, chiseled and painted institute sign, complete with a blazing spirit sun at each side of the institute's name. In a short ceremony, the sign was raised and secured to the side of our log schoolhouse, right beside the main entry doors. Years of dreaming; now became reality. The sign hung in testimony of the fact. Rocky Mountain Homesteader's Institute was open for teaching and learning!

A friend at a nearby health and dude ranch offered her old mimeo machine at a good price. We took her up on the offer and started printing handouts and information sheets, complete with everything from Institute rules to scads of example house building problems. Every student would learn how to calculate joist and rafter sizes from the basic principles of wood physics, and not be dependent on other people's sizing tables. Even if they used the charts, the students would understand their basis.

At the time, I had quite a few local construction jobs lining up. After all the bid negotiations, I was under contract to complete a passive solar retrofit to a recreational building and to build from scratch, a large maintenance building. These jobs would help support the institute and at the same time, give the student a chance at some valuable "hands on" experience. It was pretty easy to put together a crew as a lot of people needed work, so I got a building permit and went to work on the solar retrofit.

Within the month, I stood in front of the students in Rocky Mountain Homesteader's Institute's first session. It was a small class of six—a rancher, a psychologist, a carpenter, a local apprentice, and a young couple. The butterflies left my stomach quickly after getting started. One can't be nervous while living a dream! Anyway, these people were serious, attentive, and appreciative. This was a step along the way to their dreams also! We kept the coffee and tea always on, and found insufficient time in each day for all we had planned. Questions were encouraged and those asked prompted some great discussions. For me, I felt so natural in the teaching, notwithstanding my five years of college teaching experience, but more so, because it was a subject I believed in and truly loved.

As the days moved on in our scheduled two-week session, the small class size allowed us to emphasize individual needs, without diminishing the general content of what we wanted each student to learn for their basic "toolbox." We toured some owner built houses and also framed several walls that session. People got a chance to cut and nail boards together. That is so much of it—just getting to feel comfortable with tools and knowing what they can

and cannot do. Seeing what other owner/builders have done helps bring the magnitude of the whole thought process into the realm of "I believe I can build my own home!" Seeing and doing is believing!

Then, almost as quickly as it began, it ended. We finished with a student barbecue, lots of final questions and the expression of several dreams. It turned out to be a sad time for us. The session had been intense in hours and content. A representative from our county building department, Sandia, and Terry had given me several breaks from the brunt of the teaching. All of us had learned too—those who teach learn the most! From that first class, two houses have been built. One was constructed locally, and we would visit it many times in future sessions and the other on Vancouver Island in British Columbia.

A quick student project

Students were already signing up and calling for information about our three remaining sessions for that first summer. A local bank president volunteered to come and lecture each session on home building finances and his bank's experiences with owner/builders. A magazine, Rodale's New Shelter, was coming to do photographs and a story, which I would end up writing. As we have so often said–we are so lucky in life!!

A few nights after that first Institute session ended, the telephone woke us after midnight. I groped for the receiver, finally getting it to my ear. Sometimes people called from other time zones, and a few times, from out of the country, so I wasn't really alarmed. My ex-wife's words on the other end, though, cut through my sleepiness very quickly. I found myself sitting bolt upright straining to hear that distant voice. There had been an automobile accident. My daughter Deborah had been in the passenger seat of a Volkswagen bug that had hit a tree at high speed. Deborah had been transferred only moments before from the local hospital near the accident to the neurological emergency unit at Hartford Hospital. She remained in critical condition and the prognosis was bad!

The race to Denver's Stapleton Airport became a blur of Deborah's laughing and spirited image mixed in with those of a Volkswagen wrapping itself around a large immovable tree. Sandia kept saying to me that it was going to be all right; all we could do was pray. Anxious time passed before I finally kissed Sandia goodbye and walked down the entry platform onto my flight. Then we were airborne and I headed toward Deborah, my baby girl.

So many things flashed through my mind on that flight. The image of Deborah's face came to me so clearly. I remembered how, as a toddler,

she used to rock back and forth so energetically on her little rocking horse, with such reckless glee sparkling in her eyes. In my mind, I could see her standing there, as a little girl, in one of those white lace smocks she wore for dress-up. "Please God, if you can hear me, please help her! She is so young. She is only seventeen now. She has so much in front of her–please?"

I prayed and prayed as hard as I knew how. It is so true, how we turn to the Creator when we're helpless in situations that are totally out of our hands. The waiting was so very difficult. Those words seemed like a neon sign in my mind, "There has been an automobile accident and Deborah was hurt badly!" I kept seeing those words and hearing them over and over. Still an hours time to go until I got to Hartford.

I took out a sheet of paper and started writing Deborah a poem. I often wrote her poems and she responded with verse of her own. It became a means of communication between the two of us. She was such a spirit, my baby girl. She used to like me to call her that, even as a teenager. My pen scribbled out words about the pain and the love in my heart. My cheeks wetted with tears that I could not hold back. "Please God, please!"

The airplane finally touched down near Hartford, after what seemed like a really long trip. My legs didn't stand for a slow pace as I left the aircraft. I literally bounded onto the concourse and there stood beautiful Pablo waiting for me. Sandia had called ahead and here was our anxious friend, waiting to drive me straight to the Hartford Hospital.

We didn't talk a lot as the highway flashed by. I told Pablo what I knew and we left it at that. It wasn't a time for catching up on life's little things, when a precious life hung in the balance. He told me not to worry; he would have me at the hospital as fast as his Bronco and the highway patrol would allow. What a friend! I promised to call him with news as soon as I found out anything. Then we arrived at the entrance to Hartford Hospital and I ran up the entry steps.

I found Deborah's mom in the Intensive Care Unit (ICU) waiting room, pacing around. She filled me in on the details, as she knew them. Seems like Deborah and her friends had gone to a party after school. The car belonged to the driver's dad. He was thrown clear, as was the girl in the back seat, but they found Deborah, lying like a lump under the dashboard. The police estimated their speed at the time of impact with the tree at about seventy miles per hour. Deborah sustained lots of cuts and bruises, an injured ankle, and a deep gash in one leg. These proved totally treatable in time and would heal. The big unknown lay in the extent of her head injuries. They had found at least two impact spots in her skull. We would just have to wait to see the extent of her brain injuries.

At the ICU desk, the nurse agreed to let me see my Deborah, after I put on a mask and gown. She then led me into the unit. Deborah lay there so still. The room was dimly lit, so I focused only on my Deborah lying there in front of me. Her breathing seemed so slow. I began to study the monitors set up behind her. Wires hooked up to electrodes attached to various spots on her body ran up to those instruments. Alarms were set up to measure her vital signs. If her heartbeat increased or decreased, red lights and alarm bells would go off.

After an hour of watching her slow labored breathing, I went back into the waiting room to talk with her mom. She seemed a little worried about her work schedule and replacements on this short notice. It occurred to me that I wasn't going anywhere, so I told her I would just stay right on through. I could call her if there ap-

peared any change in Deborah's condition. She did not want to go, but I convinced her that I could stay now and she could take over as soon as Deborah started recovering. It seemed certain that any recovery was not going to be an overnight thing and would probably be measured in months, but we only guessed as the nurses were baffled by her condition. We finally agreed to do it that way, at least until Deborah's condition changed. Then we could reevaluate the coverage. She left the hospital then, very tiredly, and I went back to sit by Deborah in the Intensive Care Unit.

I sat for days watching her. I read her my poems. I talked to her, but I'm sure she didn't hear me. In her unconsciousness, her breathing would move from very slow and deliberate, to very excited, periodically. The heartbeat monitor would go off on the low side and then, every once in a while, on the high side. The nurses on duty would run in each time, reset it, and check on her. I think maybe during those times the high side alarm went off and she thrashed about, with a grimace on her face, that her subconscious saw that big tree looming up into the windshield again.

The doctor on duty checked her periodically and told me it remained a "wait and see" proposition. I remember thinking it was only a matter of time. She would regain consciousness again. She had to. Deborah was so young. She had so much life to live. I kept reading her my poems and reciting others I could remember. I talked to her and told her stories. She gave no hint that she could hear me, but I kept on talking. "Please God, please. Let her be well again!"

I slept those nights on the uncomfortable waiting room couches and ate from those unnourishing vending machines. Deborah's exbeau, Lenny, came whenever he could. One morning, he woke me up with two peanut butter and jelly sandwiches. He obviously remembered what Deborah must have told him about one of my habits! Those sandwiches tasted a lot better than the stale peanut butter crackers I ate out of those handy machines. Lenny told me that their break-up was only a temporary thing; he cared so much about her. I could see that he cared. Even on his lunch hours, Lenny would come, even when he could stay only a few minutes. He was not even allowed to go into the Intensive Care Unit and would just ask me for news, or any changes in her condition. Never being one to try and judge my daughters' relationships, I, nevertheless, could see Lenny's interests stemmed genuinely from his heart.

I felt really tired. Those couches in the waiting room were meant for anything but deep restful sleeping. Early on the fourth night, a friend showed up, Marty, and offered me the extra bedroom at her place nearby. I was reluctant to leave, but the nurses promised to call me at Marty's if Deborah's condition changed even a little bit from it's constancy. So off we went to Marty's. Pablo was there. Along with a few cold beers, we all caught up on the latest developments in each of our worlds. They must have put me to bed because I don't even remember it. What a neat friend Marty is. Instead of waking me at 6:00 a.m., as promised, she let me sleep until 10:00 a.m. When I panicked upon seeing the time, she assured me that no one had called, so Deborah's condition must have been the same. I relaxed a little, but I still headed quickly for the hospital, thankful for Marty's friendship and the sleep she had coaxed me into. Marty was right; Deborah laid there the same as when I had left.

Although that waiting room was not meant to be a social club, we all felt an attachment for each other. I was a reformed smoker, but started going through them like candy during the ordeal of waiting. On my frequent returns from

Deborah, to set for awhile and have a smoke break, the other occupants of the room would always ask how she was doing. There formed such a bond between us. When good news or bad news came to one of us, it was felt by all. One woman lost her husband to a heart attack while I was there. The anguish she couldn't hold inside, when they came in to tell her, tore into all of our hearts. My heart and mind resolved that Deborah would make it. She had to!

It happened in that ICU waiting room, on about the sixth day, that the nurse came in to tell me that Deborah had, only a moment ago, said something and appeared to be regaining consciousness. With tears of joy running down my cheeks, I went to her side and talked to her once again, as she struggled, this time, against the restraining straps and tried to lift herself up. She expressed disconnected thoughts and did not even recognize that I stood there, but she was regaining consciousness. Thank you, God! I waited a few more minutes before running to the telephone to let her mother know the change.

Later in the day, Deborah was transferred from Intensive Care to the neurological ward on a different floor. She was out of the emergency unit. All those wires and monitoring instruments were disconnected. Her sentences came together better, but she sounded like a little girl learning to talk all over again. The doctors said that this was pretty standard behavior after a severe head injury. I remember when my daughter Andrea came to see her sister the next night. Deborah acted a little silly and was laughing. That behavior came in between frequent huge yawns, which the nurses explained was the brain trying to obtain extra oxygen.

Deborah was going to make it! There went up a collective sigh of relief from the entire extended family. I left to go back to Colorado on the ninth day. She would never remember my having been there, but I knew she would make it. Time would tell with regard to the extent of her recovery, but she made progress every day. Her mom and her sisters would take over periodic visitations as their schedules allowed. The important thing was she had pulled through and was on her way to recovery.

That third summer in the mountains went by too quickly. Gary and I had a really deep talk about his schooling. He didn't like the small high school in the mountains for a number of reasons. No baseball team, too few kids, not enough to do, etc., he had all the reasons. Figuring all of his reasoning, along with the fact that Deborah would be out of the hospital soon, and would need extra family help and tolerance, I agreed that he should return to Connecticut. I remember too well that empty feeling as I embraced my son goodbye in the driveway of *La Casa*. I was glad for once that I would be really busy. Gary's spirit and laughter had so much become a part of me.

Our remaining Institute sessions filled up and I began to teach a schedule of courses for Colorado Mountain College at night. C.M.C. was a community college concept, utilizing community facilities, so their administration allowed me to use our own building and classrooms to teach in, rather than the public school accommodations that were available. I'm probably the only adjunct faculty (part-timer) that came to teach, complete with his own schoolhouse. Sandia taught stained glass for them, while I taught several courses in greenhouse design and construction.

At the conclusion of our Institute's second session, several of the students asked if there was any way they could stay on in a work-for-hire capacity. I think they had fallen in love with our mountains and wanted to spend the rest of the summer there. At the time there was a retired mountain couple asking me to design and build

them a greenhouse. So why not put the two needs together? It seemed like a good chance to put some of the latest thinking regarding greenhouses to the practical test and at the same time create a win-win situation for the students and that retired couple. I told both sides, yes, let's get to work.

Now committed to both sides, students and clients, I designed a "pit" greenhouse to complement their house design. We broke ground and got started. So that no big machinery would tear up their landscaping and fences, we dug the pit greenhouse foundation by hand. I made my usual joke about how strong we'd be when we finished and someone threw a shovelful of dirt at me. It's good the digging came at the beginning of the project, when they were all full of that initial energy when you are starting out on a new project! It proved hard work, but we joked and planned the structure, along with reviews of their school lessons, as we dug and moved earth. Two days later, it was done. Even our one female student, who hailed from Cape Cod, said she felt stronger.

Those first two days turned into two months and at the end of that time, we stood proudly in front of the south facing glass of our pit greenhouse, a first for all of us. The fan and ductwork worked on a thermostat to automatically bring the excess ceiling hot air down to be stored in the six-ton rockbed under the concrete slab floor. The diagonally installed pine boards on the inside, above the stuccoed foundation hip wall gave the place an earthy appearance. The white reflective ceiling, in between the massive roof timbered rafters, would ensure that reflected sunlight would reach the backs of the plants as well as the fronts.

We felt proud and sad at the same time. It proved a bittersweet time. Our project was complete and waiting for the owner's green thumb to give it a colorful floral life. My total pay for the

Pit greenhouse framing

The completed pit greenhouse

project was the 308 caliber, lever action Savage rifle I had borrowed from the owner the year before to bring down my first elk. Trading reflected a mountain way of life. The students were all going off in different directions. We had related and shared in a very intense way. Sandia had become a part of that greenhouse as well. A hand-

made door, foam filled, with a beautiful flowered stained glass window insert, gave testimony to her part. We got together for a little farewell party that night at *La Casa*. We often received post cards from the group in the future. They wouldn't forget that special summer high up in the majestic Colorado Mountains.

As fast as the summer had arrived, it was all of a sudden coming to an end. Our last teaching session wound down. It felt uniquely different, as each session had been, because the students were all different in needs and dreams. That last session, we put heavy emphasis on log house building because it confirmed a common student interest. One local couple, Hal and Brenda, were determined to build a log house. To them, it seemed the only way to build and live in those mountains. So we covered the wood physics and structural calculations for round logs, or beams. We talked of the additional foundation requirements due to the uneven loading of the log corners during the first few years of settling. Our friend, Jimmy Reed, who made his living building fine original log homes, loaned us several carousels of his slides for classroom use. They showed several of his homes during the construction stages so students could study the progression of the log building sequence. Our house tour that session purposely included three of Jimmy's houses. He made himself available at the last house to answer student questions.

Hal and Brenda, the locals who so stubbornly wanted to build their own log house, sowed some very excited seeds in their meeting with Jimmy. He would ultimately agree to do the log work on their home. They did most of the rest, but their indomitable spirits infected Jimmy in such a way that he would later tell me that his work on their house ended up to be his finest effort. I drew the plans, Jimmy did the log work, and Hal and Brenda put together the rest, and all

of us became the deepest of friends in the process. It had been a deeply emotional and sharing
season, that Institute summer of 1980.

Hal and Brenda's passive solar log house

chapter twenty-one

When the Seed Dies, then It Blossoms

A beautiful fall season was upon us then. The aspen trees turned the mountains into patches of reddish gold spread between the stands of evergreen. Those golden leaves in late September and early October fluttered in the breezes like thousands of tiny pieces of golden glass moving in a gigantic wind chime. Elk bugling pierced the crisp, cold nights as nature followed its plan. Indian summer days became the rule, rather than the exception. Hunting season came again with all of the local excitement, and when it ended, we fortunately had a freezer replenished with hundreds of pounds of fresh elk meat. Four cords of wood were cut and stacked under the deck in preparation for the impending winter. Carpentry work remained plentiful. The Institute looked forward to building several houses under contract.

Sandia and I reflected on our lives one of

the message, red cloud fish, high in the sky

in life, there are times to laugh, times to cry

Rumsford fireplace and thermal rock mass

those crisp fall nights in front of the fireplace. We remembered the uncertainties back when we made the decision to come to those mountains. So many people continually asked, "But what will you do in the mountains?" The answer to that question became a short, standard reply—"Whatever it takes to stay there, for as long as it's good!" That answer said it all for us. Our commitment remained total. We learned to laugh about the hard times and cry together, with the emotional ones. One thing was so evident to us. Building that homestead, from scratch, had not just resulted in a house to shelter us; it had, in a much greater sense, brought us into a new way of life. We were born with abilities we had never even thought of using in our past lives. Even beyond abilities and talents, which all of us have in different degrees, the spirit to cope with whatever came along—a

102

certain self-reliance—filled us that night as we talked. We shared not conceited or arrogant feelings of self glory, but rather assuredness, that we could and would reason out each new path and take the sensible route, no matter how much it seemed contrary to accepted practice. The taste of it all truly became the sweetest drink of life that we had ever savored.

November approached with the feeling of winter imminent. Sandia drove to Denver often to spend time with her sick dad. Her visits got longer each time as she found it increasingly difficult to leave him. He moved in and out of hospitals, having had part of his stomach removed in an effort to stem the growth of cancer. At that time, chemotherapy treatments left him sick and nauseated. Dad was sixty-three and near retirement. He dreamed of fishing those idle days away. How he loved to fish; the casting, the waiting while talking, and then the excitement of the bite. In the past, it had been only a weekend pleasure, but upon retirement, the thoughts of endless days of fishing would become a reality. If anyone deserved his dreams, it was Sandia's dad.

La Casa del Sol

Photos in this chapter by Karl H. Riek, courtesy of Helma Riek

Some La Casa interior views

He spent eighteen years in the coal mines until every cough yielded black mucus from his lungs, then twenty-four years as a laborer for paving and concrete companies. Those jobs would have been enough for most, but Dad always took on extra work in the fields around Fort Lupton, mostly in the crouch position, or with his back bent, for additional long hours. He provided well, though, for his wife and five children. With Mom's additional income, they owned their home outright as well as a summer place in the mountains. Everything had been purchased only when the price had been earned—never a mortgage or a credit card! Now all the burdens of the past that he carried on those magnificent shoulders were consuming him. The cancer was spreading.

Frequent chemotherapy treatments took away weight from Dad, along with his hair, and a little of his dignity. As a family, we all shared Thanksgiving together at Sandia's sister's house in Denver. Dad was sick that day, but I am sure he hung in there in order not to spoil the holiday mood for anyone else. We all worried—not yet ready to accept the inevitable, somehow hoping for a miracle.

The day after Thanksgiving, Dad checked into the cancer ward at Mercy Hospital in Denver. The prognosis looked unforgiving—he had only a matter of time. The family took turns visiting Dad in the ensuing days. We stayed on in Denver to be close to the hospital. In less than two weeks, he lapsed into unconsciousness. We could no longer communicate with him.

I will never forget the last night Sandia and I visited the hospital. Dad fought to hold on so hard, even in his unconsciousness. We finally talked Mom into going home with Sandia's sister Irene to try to get some rest. We would stay and call her if there seemed any change at all. Mom's face and eyes showed the strain she was under. She needed rest in big way.

Sandia held on to her dad's hand most of

that night trying to soothe his troubled struggle to retain life. Then just as dawn broke and the sun began to rise; a peace came into Dad. His breathing quieted down, and he didn't strain and fight anymore. The change proved so startling that Sandia cried aloud for her mom. We both felt afraid to leave him, to let go of him. Kneeling by the bed, we prayed as hard as we knew how for her mom to know about Dad's peace. His entire body lay in a restful composure, with long, slow breathing. Sandia's mom, at that moment, rushed into the room. She knelt between us, at the bedside, as Dad's peaceful breathing came to an end. The Creator embraced him then.

The next hour became a blur. Other family members showed up. The grief clutched at those hearts. This man was so truly loved! No amount of thought can prepare a person for the finality of a precious life.

Later in the day, Sandia and I drove toward Fort Lupton and her parents' house. We drove numbly along, seeing the road and surroundings through tear-filled eyes, chests burning and choking. Then Sandia turned to me and said through all the grief she felt, "Do you think we could build Dad's coffin?"

I pondered her question for only an instant, understanding that this beautiful lady of mine, filled with love for her dad, my dad too, only wanted to create from that love, a personal thing, an expression of that love. "Of course we can," I told her. "But first we'd better check with your mom to see if it would be all right."

The responsibility of the funeral arrangements had fallen to Sandia's brother Bob, who had flown in from Las Cruces, New Mexico, only a few days before. He was a State Farm agent and, as such, was the family insurance man and advisor. When we got to the house in Fort Lupton, I tried our question on Bob first. In fact, I didn't really make it a question—Sandia and I wanted to build Dad's coffin—what did he think about it before we talked to Mom? Bob told us that there wouldn't be enough time, with the wake in two days, and besides, he didn't think we should burden ourselves with what he saw to be a huge project.

Beautiful Mom responded to us in such a positive way. She said, "Your dad would love it, but are you sure you want to attempt it?" Sandia was already creating as she described the stained glass that would become part of it.

"Dad would never be comfortable in one of those fancy metal boxes with padded velvet inside," she cried out to her mom. "He was a simple man and loved the beauty of simple things."

With our magnificent and responsive family's agreement in our minds and our little pickup loaded with special pieces of redwood, Sandia and I headed for the mountains toward our workshop for perhaps the biggest project of all. I looked skyward at strangely forming clouds as sunset approached, and we drove up the eastern slope of the Rockies. The sky seemed to boil with red brilliance as a parade of clouds moved by. Then with a defining splendor neither of us could miss, the most perfect cloud fish appeared in the sky. It filled the heavens with a bright red-orange color. It seemed to be the Creator telling us that our fisherman resided with Him now. We became so overcome by the spectacle that I had to pull off the road, where we sat and stared at that message in the sky. Peace replaced our grief. A peace that came from knowing it was all part of His plan. Now Dad could fish with the greatest fishermen of all time.

We reached home and unloaded the redwood. Sandia went right to work on the stained glass window design. It suddenly dawned on me the task I had before me. For planning, I had only a few measurements reluctantly given to me by the funeral director's wife. I got the distinct impression that the director did not want to talk to me when I made my request for simple dimensions of height, width, and depth.

I made a few sketches and started with only a vague idea of what I was doing. The sound of workshop tools echoed in my ears. My hands held the tools, but some other carpenter's spirit truly guided them. Pieces fit together like a glove. Throughout the night and on into the next day, those tools cut, routed, and sanded. Sandia's window was suddenly done and framed near the top of the coffin. It displayed a fish leaping up from a lake surrounded by snow capped peaks—Dad's favorite fishing environment.

Now we worked together on the finish, with me doweling the cover into place and Sandia with her engraving tools and tiny paint brushes. We used peeled aspen wood handrails for both sides as carrying bars. She engraved flowers, especially clusters of columbine, into the redwood and highlighted each engraving with paint. Her tool inscribed his name, Francisco Yañez Gomez, along with the Spanish words for "we love you"— "te amamos." Then a cross on the very top to signify Dad's spiritual commitment and it was finished. As I gazed down at that coffin, I truly could not remember building it.

Footsteps on our front porch, followed by a knock, interrupted our thoughts as we stood there in the workshop. I walked out and opened the door. Our local minister J.R. stepped in and began to explain how he had heard of Sandia's dad's sickness and made the trip to Denver to see him, only to arrive about three hours too late. J.R. felt badly and had waited until then to come over to offer his condolences. As he talked, he followed me back into the workshop, where he suddenly noticed the coffin and asked about it. He seemed astonished that such a thing could be done—building a coffin for a loved one. Sandia told him that we had just a moment before finished it. We told him we would be greatly honored if he would say a prayer over it, which he did with much exuberance. It seemed to lift him up considerably in contributing to the funerary process. J.R. is a true believer.

We slept soundly that night. We had only to get the coffin to the funeral parlor by the next afternoon. Up early, and with the help of two great friends, Ron and Georgie, we loaded the coffin into our little Toyota pickup and headed for Fort Lupton. Sandia had already called her mom that morning, and several members of the family waited at the house to help line and finish the inside of the coffin.

Once unloaded behind the house, so many hands reached in to put the finishing touches on the bare wooden insides. A Mexican blanket was inlaid over foam padding and fixed with upholstery pins. A Mexican flag, to depict Dad's roots, was sewn and stuffed to a finished pillow. Dad's fishing tackle box and gear was placed inside, along with the last dime "fishing pool" that had accumulated. "He would have won it anyway," Sandia's brother Fred commented. As I stood there, I realized that everyone was contributing, everyone felt a part of this expression. It was not the building of a coffin, which is just a box, it was loving the person and reaching out as Dad had always done. I saw little sparkles in eyes. Sure, there was profound grief, but I saw joy also. Joy that this great man had been a part of all of our lives and had left seeds amongst us that could only grow into brilliant flowering fruit.

When the coffin was ready, we loaded it up and headed the few blocks to the funeral parlor. The funeral director immediately came out to the truck and peered into the back. He walked away, rubbing his hands together in a nervous way. Pulling his garage door up, he pointed to the rear of his hearse and exclaimed, "That thing won't fit in here. We can't use it!"

I stood dumbfounded. I felt devastated. My tired mind raced. I had let the whole family down. They had depended on me. Then I heard Bob's poignant words, "If it won't fit, then we won't use the hearse. We'll use Dad's pickup truck!" Bob had a determined look on his face.

Now it was the director's turn to look dumbfounded at the turn of events. I found out later that our daughter Kirsten had asked earlier, from her youthful viewpoint, why we weren't using Dad's pickup, which seemed natural to her. Now her seed of thought blossomed in a strongly rooted family.

Returning to the house, the family swarmed over the old blue Ford pickup, washing and waxing until that dependable truck virtually glowed in a bright aura reflecting all the smiles and elation. Two priests arrived at the house to discuss the evening's rosary and how it would proceed. Sandia had another idea now, and she posed it to the priests. "Why couldn't there be a time when people stood and told things, personal things, they shared with my dad?" she asked. "Does it all have to be so solemn?"

They had never done anything like that before, but bowed to family wishes and agreed to announce such a time during the evening service.

I remember the church that night, jammed with family and friends, as they put Dad's coffin up in front. Beautiful flowers surrounded the closed redwood casket. He loved all things of nature—trees, flowers, and animals. On trips together, he would always spot animals first in the distance and point them out to us. He had nature's eye.

The service progressed and then the priest announced the family's wish that people could take a moment to stand and speak in a personal way about Dad. The priest appeared a little nervous in his announcement, as it was not a routine part of the process. It seemed like minutes went by, and no one stood in that crowded, yet very quiet sanctuary. They probably did not understand the nature of the request. Then Sandia nudged me with her elbow and whispered, "You've got to start it because they don't understand what it's about."

Not at my best in crowds, but filled with the love of this man, I slowly rose to my feet, turning to face the greatest portion of family and friends. I told about Dad's reaching out, how he waved to everyone, which I am sure they all knew. I told of a day, while riding as a passenger in his pickup, when we passed two male backpackers with long hair. Dad waved to them and they waved back, smiling.

He turned to me after passing them and said, "I sure don't understand those hippies."

Even though he didn't understand them, it never kept him from reaching out with a friendly greeting. Reaching out was all that mattered to him. It was that simple.

Now people had the idea, and one after another stood and told personal stories. We learned a lot of things we had never known before, all on the same theme—reaching out. Rudy, a good fishing buddy of Dad's, told of a cold stormy night at Red Feather Lakes when Dad peered out from their warm tent at a distant light.

"I think I know those people!"

"You're crazy. That light is half a mile away and it's raining!"

Dad went off into that stormy night anyway to reach the distant light. When he returned an hour or so later, he told Rudy he had known them and had had a good visit.

Finally, with hands still raised in the air, the priest brought us back to ritual; the personalizing

was over. I sat reflecting on those times friends and family had, only a moment ago, brought to life and shared with so many. Dad lived on in our memories. The shared stories provided such revealing and fitting moments to the service.

Dad was buried the next morning. The old steady blue Ford pickup led at least a mile of cars to the cemetery. People walking along town sidewalks, stopped, took off their hats and held them over their hearts as they recognized the blue pickup and the significance of its passing by. Baskets of flowers shared the back of the pickup bed with the redwood coffin. Even though that panicky funeral director tried to speed things up, the procession proceeded, as it should, at a slow pace. Irene's husband Dave was at the wheel of the pickup, and no one would rattle him out of the appropriate speed.

Then it was over. Dad was buried. We were all emotionally drained, but with a certain glow. Sandia's brother explained his feelings to me before flying back to Las Cruces, "When I flew up, I tried to prepare for a real wrenching time of grief. Now, though, I really can't tell you how good I feel about everything!"

I understood what he meant. I felt the same way. It is really hard to explain to people. For Sandia and me, however, it is a way of life.

22

Sometimes, It is the Right Time to Move On

The Spring of '82 arrived with all of its usual mountain splendor. Only those humans coming out of a high mountain winter could appreciate the vision of springtime that I still hold in awe with my myriad of memories. The snow melted quickly under the influence of the higher-in-the-sky, brilliant, clear sunshine and resulted in what the locals dubbed "mud season." For Sandia and I most of the mud lodged in our thinking. No question that we loved our handmade house, *La Casa*, but the mountain subdivision in which it was located, Columbine Lake, seemed to be closing in around us and choking our lifestyle ever tighter. More and more people built houses and the already small lots, all of a sudden, seemed even smaller. More people and their vacation homes coming in made the subdivision administration get "pickier" about the enforcement of covenants. For instance, we purchased an old, but still operable, International tractor out of the Illinois farm country and had it trucked out with the help of a couple of friends, only to be told that the covenants wouldn't allow us to park it at our home. These and a few other things, not the least of which grew from our desire to have a

mountain in front, bike underneath, bear down,

climb steady, keep those gears, turning around

lot more space around us to flex our newfound muscles of independence and self-reliance, made us seriously consider selling *La Casa* and looking for more land on which to build again.

For most people, building one house from scratch in a lifetime would be more than enough. Here we stood, only four years down the road from beginning *La Casa* and not even finished with it, thinking of starting another. I have to admit, honestly, it was a whole lot more me than Sandia this time. She loved *La Casa*. I slowly convinced her of the difficulty and the engineering required to move that beloved house; it made more sense to finish the odds and ends, sell it, using the financial gain to start another from scratch. She finally agreed, while making it clear to me that the next house would be mostly my responsibility. Sandia felt that she could best help our common goal by seeking outside employment to help with the building finances and living expenses. That plan would allow me to work full-time in the construction of our new home—an exciting prospect for my mind and energy.

I started looking for land, while at the same time putting out the word that *La Casa* was for sale. Mixed in with the land search and completing our own house, I contracted to finish off three log houses in our same subdivision. The original builder had gone "belly up" and the lending bank agreed to a time and materials contract with me to finish those houses, which were in pretty sad shape. The county building department had actually condemned one of them.

So that spring, between juggling engineers, subcontractors, materials, and the bank, I finished *La Casa*, with Ted's help and found an exciting location for a new home. Ted and Deborah and their two kids, Elijah and Rachel, had returned to the Colorado mountains after a short absence in which they spent time back in their home state of Illinois. Their return only proved an old adage that once you had those mountains in your "blood," so to speak, they were hard to stay away from. We shared *La Casa* with them and Ted became my "main man" on the log house effort. He and I made all the decisions daily on the best and most efficient way to remedy, remodel, and finish the log house interiors. We did not always agree. Several times it got downright ornery, but cool heads prevailed and we finished those houses by the end of summer, got them sold, and settled up with a very happy and relieved bank manager.

The new potential home site I focused on lay in a remote corner of a thousand plus acre ranch just outside of Grand Lake. I had come upon the location while hunting for elk and actually thought it belonged to the National Forest. A study of maps at the county seat, though, indicated that it belonged to the Winding River Ranch and made up its extreme southwestern corner, nestled up against 2.5 million acres of National Forest. The most exciting part of that remote ranch corner lay in the fact that it was cut off from the ranch by the flow of the Colorado River's North Fork as it flowed out of Rocky Mountain National Park. The water flowing by that land parcel ended up in Mexico/California and finally, the Pacific Ocean. About fifty feet above the river, with a view south downriver, was an almost ready cleared level spot ideal for a home. The trick would be to clear trees and build a switchback roadway to provide access to the building site!

I talked to the ranch owners and, after quite a few discussions, they agreed to sell it to us at what I felt was in the reasonable to high priced range. I would have to accomplish the legal subdivision with the county, in addition to building a fifty-foot bridge across the Colorado in order to have access. I would also be on my own to obtain a well permit for the land—an always uncertain project in a water conscious state. Colorado River land for purchase, then as now, is a difficult commodity to find.

Taking it all one step at a time, I began with the county commissioners in the quest for the subdivision exemption, as the parcel was less than 35 acres, and hence could not be subdivided from the ranch without an exemption from the existing state laws. Armed with newly drawn and surveyor certified maps, I stepped to the podium for presentations at two successive county commissioner meetings. At the second meeting, the gavel came down in our favor. The commissioners granted a subdivision exemption to build a home and a school-Rocky Mountain Homesteaders Institute-on that parcel. The excitement continued to build.

The next step consisted of a trip to the State Water Resources offices in Denver. The first day, a clerk told me that there was no way we'd ever get a well permit for a land parcel under 35 acres in our location. I stayed on in Denver, going to those offices everyday for three more days. Finally they let me see a higher up official. I'd like to think the meeting came about through perseverance, but maybe they just became tired of seeing me sitting around in their office reception areas. Anyway, that administrator told me to take out my calculator to figure out how much water we would be using under maximum conditions each year. He would return for my numbers in twenty minutes.

I started cranking, without panic, as numbers have always been my forte, figuring the maximum land occupancy; us, students, and visitors, number of daily toilet flushes, drinking, cooking, and gardening. I came out with a number: 0.31 acre-feet per year (the volume of water measuring 0.31 foot high covering an acre of land-about 100,000 gallons). The administrator returned, asked for my number, looked at it without comment, and said he would take it to his superior for discussion. I was to sit and wait.

The waiting seemed like forever, but in a little less than an hour he returned to ask me my well driller's name. We only had one well driller in town, but I hadn't even asked him about the job, let alone commissioned him to drill the well. I told the administrator the local well driller's name, Jack Dale, as he sat at his desk writing things down on some form. Then he pulled out an ink stamp, banged it down, and held out an 8 1/2 by 11-inch manila form to me saying, "Here is your well permit. We've put you in the Commercial Exempt category, since you are under one-third of an acre-foot per year. Any greater usage, we would not have been able to issue you a permit!"

I thanked him and walked calmly out of his office and the building. On the sidewalk outside, I let a shout of joy rip from deep down inside. Passerbys looked at me funny, but I didn't care. So many people, including one county commissioner, told me that a well permit for our subdivision exemption appeared next to impossible. There it was, permission to drill a well, still

clutched tightly in the fingers of my right hand! I tucked it away in my ever-carried backpack's file system, while heading for a telephone to share the great news with my lady. On the way to a payphone, I started thinking of the next project steps—the sale of *La Casa* and the new land parcel contract. There didn't seem to be any hassle in the land contract as I had a signed memo of understanding, which included the price and mortgage terms, and besides, we owned the subdivision exemption and the well permit rights, so no one else could buy the land. Not much could go wrong in that vein, so I decided to concentrate on the house sale.

La Casa had been listed with a real estate firm for a few months, but in that span of time they had only brought by one older couple, who were obviously not suited for life in that floor plan. When the exclusive listing came up for renewal, I told them we weren't signing on again for an exclusive, despite their eager and optimistic plans to get it sold. When they had the exclusive sale rights earlier, they always seemed busy with other things. I didn't want to be tied up for the approaching summer season, when most mountain properties sell.

The events of the following weekend, after the exclusive listing contract ended, had us wondering about words like "destiny" and "someone up there looking out for us." It all happened so quickly. J. R., our local minister, stopped in to use the telephone. I was off in another part of *La Casa*, while J. R. talked to Ted. J. R. had come into the subdivision to look at a house and property for sale. Seems like his church parsonage lease was up and he and his family wanted to buy their own home.

Next thing I knew, Ted and J. R. stood in front of me saying that J. R. had interest in buying *La Casa*. Ted had shown him around. He loved what he saw. I told him what Sandia and

I thought would be a fair price and he agreed to it. He just needed a few days to put together his financial package and walk his wife through the house. We shook hands and it appeared virtually a "done deal."

After J. R. left, Sandia and I stood there in kind of double shock—the swiftness of the sale after months of waiting for a real estate company's inactivity to pass and, more so, the reality of giving up *La Casa*, into which we had put so much of ourselves. We tried to rationalize the loss of *La Casa* by saying, and trying numbly to believe, that it only consisted of concrete, wood, and glass. We would still have each other, along with our shared dreams of the future. It still hurt deep inside. A few weeks later, at the closing of the sale of *La Casa* to J. R. and his family, we both felt very sad. Sandia, in fact, wept openly and sobbed as the papers passed back and forth across the table. Despite all my resolve, the tears ran down my cheeks also. When all the papers were signed, we left the room at Town Hall quickly, going out into the bright mountain sunshine, where we cried onto each other's shoulders while locked in a tight embrace. I remember saying out loud, "It was only concrete, wood, and glass. We have each other and the future together." The statement did not take away the pain. Only time would do that!

J. R. took over my V. A. Mortgage. We had the cash difference. The cash provided enough to pay off about one-third of the new land with enough left over to buy all the materials for the shell of the new house and the bridge. A civil engineering friend had already designed the log trussed bridge for me while another log supplier agreed to trade the long bridge logs we would need in exchange for my structural design and drawings of his new log house. We were on our way. The ranch owners agreed to the final land

mortgage terms, we had previously negotiated, for the rest of the land payment. They assured me they worked on the sale papers. I gave them a $20,000.00 check as a deposit, or "earnest money," for the land sale. Their son-in-law worked as a real estate broker and was drawing up the papers. They indicated that everything was being taken care of on their end. There was no way to anticipate what happened next.

Weeks went by. Weeks turned into months. I couldn't figure out what took so long on a straightforward land sale and mortgage papers. Each time I asked about a closing date, I was told, "We're working on it."

It took well into the summer building season before the ranch owners leveled with me that they had a problem, a "glitch" in the land sale. Seems like there was another minority owner, who refused to sign the papers—one of their sons! I knew him slightly, in a small town way, as he ran a sand, gravel, and ready-mix operation from a river location on the ranch. I had often purchased his services in my own construction efforts, but didn't know him well.

I went by his equipment repair shop on the ranch one evening soon after I became aware of the land sale glitch and found him working on one of his pieces of earth moving equipment. I took the direct approach and asked him straight out about his refusal to sign our land papers. His response to me that night can best be summarized, in my opinion, as, "I'm using you and your land sale papers as a catalyst to get my own share of the ranch that my parents have promised, but haven't followed through on!" His interest in the ranch consisted of eleven percent, which I believe made up an early inheritance or for services rendered, or maybe a bit of both, I don't really know. It stood as a family matter. He wanted his land, eleven percent of the ranch, to be deeded to him—then he would sign our papers. Simple as that!

I had no previous idea that this family conflict brewed, actually more like festered, and there appeared not a lot we could do about it. I went to talk to the ranch "father" and got the feeling that he seemed very reluctant to give up that much land to his son, just to sell us seven plus acres. Our dreams of building a home on that little land plateau above the river suddenly seemed to crash in flames to the earth. Remembering the determination in the son's face and seeing the reluctance in the father's eyes, I asked for my deposit check back. Maybe, having taken the $20,000.00 back out of the father's hands would spur on a family resolution. Sandia and I needed to step back and rethink our plans. After pushing everything so hard, for so many months, and having had such great success, suddenly we had come up against a brick wall—a family juggernaut!!

Summer neared conclusion and the crispness of fall definitely filled the air. We finished the last log house for the bank and a buyer negotiated its purchase. Sandia's parent's cabin became our temporary home again, with most of our possessions stored in a small rental garage. With our land purchase in limbo, it appeared the perfect time in life to do something different, just to take a break.

When I suggested to Sandia that we take our "found" time to ride our bicycles to California so as to take a swim in the Pacific Ocean, she looked at me like I was totally crazy. I had just bought her a new twelve speed Peugeot and I had my trusty twelve speed Kabuki from the Connecticut days. I proposed the ride at first purely out of jest, but then got a little serious about the potential trip as I thought more about it. My friends picked up on the idea with one friend in particular, Hal, kidding Sandia that he would drive us to the top of Rabbit Ears Pass,

above Steamboat Springs, where she could coast downhill all the way to California. I don't think she really believed Hal, but she began to weaken. Sandia even started to talk about the basic camping gear we would have to carry. Then, ever the seamstress, she ordered Frostline Kits and began sewing up two sets of bicycle carrier bags. I pitched into the sewing effort by putting together and sewing up her front handlebar bag. Our enthusiasm grew by the hour. Sandia's, however, always had a tint of reluctance mixed in with her eagerness. "Would I stop whenever she got too tired to peddle? Could we stop to eat when she became hungry? Could we stay in motels a few nights so as to take hot showers and sleep on real mattresses?"

"Of course," became my standard answer. I knew she asked because of my innate stubbornness and resolve when it came to doing things.

"Next time, I get to pick the holiday scenario," she told me. "Otherwise you'll have us trekking across Siberia!!"

It all came together and suddenly, we stood ready for the bicycle trip. It was the first week in October. Hal, true to his word, drove us to the top of Rabbit Ear's Pass, waving goodbye as we began our descent down that steep slope into Steamboat Springs. It probably consisted of a ten to fifteen mile downhill, followed by more or less the same distance on the "level" into town.

The first part of the descent from the summit would best be described by the word, "plummet." I didn't want to hold the brakes on during the steep stretches, as they would get hot, thus becoming ineffective. So I could only clamp firmly on the brake levers every minute or so while "flying" in between. Thankfully, there was not a lot of automobile traffic to contend with, so it became just us and the mountain. I couldn't even look behind me for Sandia at those speeds because turning in the saddle could have certainly upset my stability.

We made it down without any major mishaps and pulled off the road for a needed breather. It seemed a good time to let the heart slow down. Sandia's brakes were too hot to touch, as she had held them on most of the way down. My bike, loaded, weighed in at 100 pounds, while Sandia's tipped the scales at 40 pounds—that put me and my bike together at 250 pounds, and Sandia and her loaded two wheeler at 150 pounds. Gravity definitely placed a greater effect on my downhill speeds while in the retarding sense, uphill speeds, also. I felt unbelievably happy, though. We were on our way! The trip was my idea and I was a male, so my load necessarily had to be heavier in the balance of things. It appeared only fair! I had my best traveling buddy pedaling along with me. My spirits soared so high, I'm not sure my tires even touched the pavement.

That first night we stayed in Steamboat. Our odometers showed a first day mileage of thirty-five. Not that far, but we had to break in our butts slowly. We ate at a cozy café, letting their specialty stew fill the hungry voids in our stomachs. The waitress seemed amazed that we would even attempt to pedal the 1300 plus miles to the Pacific. Sandia kept pointing at me while saying, "His idea!"

I asked the waitress for directions to a good camping spot, anxious to get settled in before the impending nightfall. She responded with, "Use my yard out back of the cafe. It's getting too dark for you to go any further. This way, you can use my bathroom and kitchen in the morning." Then she had second thoughts on that offer, when another waitress mentioned that a storm was moving in. We ended up sleeping on a couch in her living room!

We awoke early, gathered up our gear, and quietly left her house, leaving a big thank you note on her kitchen counter. Our eyes blinked and opened wide as the sight of several inches of newly fallen snow gave our morning a cool reception. To make things a little worse, my rear tire was flat! What an ominous beginning!

Undaunted, we walked our bikes a few blocks to find a gas station with an air compressor. There was a small hand pump in our gear, but a compressor, when available, is so much easier. I fixed the flat under the shelter of their canopy, as it still lightly snowed on us. While I used the compressor to put the right amount of air back in the repaired tire, two of their mechanics joked with us as they drank their early morning coffee. "You guys should put your snow tires on," they quipped. Other comments like, "Don't you know it is easier to drive to California! Whose crazy idea was this anyway?" Again Sandia pointed at me. She looked pretty skeptical about the whole thing as we pushed off, westward, out of Steamboat. It proved pretty sloppy going for a while, to say the least!

On the western edge of town, the driver of a car slowed his vehicle, pulled over, and yelled to us, "Do you guys want hot coffee? I live just ahead and I'm a biker, so I know you must be a bit on the chilly side!"

I looked over at Sandia and she slowly shook her head negatively and said, "No thank you. I just want to keep going and get out of this stuff." I also gestured my thankful decline of his offer and we went steadily on, at least warmed slightly by the stranger's generosity. Sandia set as fast a pace as she could hold, while I followed.

A few miles up the road, I pulled up along side her and asked if she wanted to stop and change socks or anything. Her response was a classic. "The only thing I want to change now, is husbands!!!" Without a word, I fell in behind her, keeping at her steady pace. I knew it was a "fragile" time and figured quiet on my part would be the best of all worlds. In that silent, single file mode, we eventually got out of the snow and opted to stay the night in a warm, small town motel in the town of Maybell, Colorado. The hot showers felt like heaven to our somewhat murky, wet, and tired bodies. We decided to sneak our bikes into the tub to rinse the accumulated grime off of their frames. The next morning we arose, refreshed and respirited, to begin the leg that would take us to the Colorado/Utah border.

Things went pretty steadily for a few days as our body strengths grew and our backsides toughened to the bike saddles. The fact that we left the snow behind us, and the weather warmed a bit, also helped a whole bunch! We pedaled across the Utah border and on through the towns of Vernal, Roosevelt, Heber City, then south through Provo and Springville. Our travels took us down to old route 89, running between two mountain ranges. Using the old routes became necessary because the interstates would not allow bicycle traffic. The Utah State Police would have kicked us off the interstate highways. It felt better this way, because we didn't have to fight a lot of traffic. Also there were lots of small scenic towns to pedal through. The only drawback to the older roads is they tended to add miles to the trip, not being the most direct route between major points.

As we started south on route 89, it had become late in the day. Sandia felt tired. We were in a deep gorge when she told me she couldn't go another 100 yards. Looking around there appeared no place to set up camp, as the gorge bottom was filled with the highway, a river, and a set of railroad tracks. It was so narrow, there weren't even emergency lanes on the highway. The canyon sides went up steeply on both sides. Sandia assured me she could not go any further—this was it!

Bridal Veil Falls in Utah (crooked self-timer)

The railside bike camp

It was cold on the road in the early morning

Awesome scenery

She "wooden" talk to me!

I found a small bridge across the river to the railroad tracks. The tracks looked very rusty with apparent lack of use. Maybe they were abandoned, I reasoned. We found a small flat spot in the railbed between the tracks and the riverbank. We set up camp there, several feet away from the tracks, right on the edge of the riverbank. Inside the tent, sleep pretty much came easily, with our arms wrapped around each other for warmth. We had done quite a few uphills that day and our spot seemed so quiet and peaceful.

Sometime in the middle of that very cold night, we abruptly awakened to the shrill whistle of a train bearing down on us. It's headlight lit

up our tent like daylight and then it roared on past, shaking the ground like an earthquake. It felt like we might get sucked into the train's vortex. We held tightly onto each other as it passed on by, once more giving us a whistle blast in the distance. The only sound, after the whistled farewell, in our tent proved to be the mutual rapid beat of our hearts.

I crawled outside into the frigid cold, to confirm that there was no damage done to any of our gear. We'd located just far enough from the tracks, obviously, for clearance. We had a good laugh, tinged with relief, and snuggled back into each other's warmth. What a screamer that had been! The train engineer must have still been shaking his head at the unexpected daring of our camp's location.

Sandia got up first in the morning. I hadn't slept well as I kept thinking another train might

Approaching Zion National Park

come barreling through as soon as I dosed off. Sandia was going to surprise me with a cup of hot coffee, but when she came back in the tent all she carried was the news that the little stove wouldn't light and the water had frozen solid in the bottles. Time to head on down the road. The pedaling would warm us and wake us at the same time.

The sun came up, we got warmer from the exertion, and we finally stopped in a Mormon Church parking lot in a town called Birdseye. The town obviously got its name for the fantastic view the location gave of the surrounding mountains. On that warm black pavement, we made coffee and tasted its steaming hotness through grateful lips. We toasted the events of the previous night with laughter. That's easy when it is behind you! Pedaling due south now brought us ever warmer temperatures. It felt like an appropriate time to take off the jackets.

One day, in southern Utah, we pedaled the entire day uphill. It proved slow going, but we'd become strong enough to keep a steady pace. A good thing about uphills, which we tried to keep in mind, is that we knew they would be complemented with downhills. They definitely were, but none as steep as Rabbit Ear's Pass, our bike trip baptismal.

We passed through St. George, Utah and then the northwestern corner of Arizona, heading for Las Vegas. Here bicycles were allowed on the interstate as there were no other roads. Someone told me at a visitor's rest area that that short piece of highway, up in the corner of Arizona, had the most expensive per mile price tag of any highway in the country. It was so beautiful—the canyons, the river flowing into Lake Mead. Every bend in the road brought us a new and phenomenal vista.

Sandia and I had one of those nonsense fights at the Nevada border. I saw nothing but her back all the way into Las Vegas. Can't even remember what it was all about, but I do know one thing. She sure can pedal hard and strong, when she is angry! I knew we needed a break! So we got a motel in Vegas and walked around the whole next day watching the glitz and glitter, along with people gambling. Food proved cheap enough, so we splurged on prime rib and had a fantastic and much needed rest day.

The next day, we were up and strongly pedaling for the California border—the last state to get across, albeit, a wide one. Our plan now was to pedal Interstate 15 until they kicked us off. The alternate routes across the California desert were hundreds of miles out of the way and, besides, there wasn't much traffic out there on the interstate anyway. Interstate 15 looked the most direct route to our destination—Newport Beach and the Pacific Ocean. Hopefully our friend Linnea, who lived in Newport Beach, would be up for some surprise company and my sister, Helen, lived just up the coast in Rancho Palos Verdes. That would be the fun part, the visiting; now we just had to go that last distance. A friendly California based marine, who shared a love of bicycling, had flagged us down from his car back in Utah, near Zion National Park to ask about our trip. He and his girl friend had given us directions for a bike path through Los Angeles, so we wouldn't have to fight street traffic. The path followed the Santa Ana River west of the San Gabriel Mountains and the San Bernardino National Forest right to the Pacific Ocean! With that routing knowledge for peace of mind, we crossed into California knowing we had only about 200 plus miles in front of us, approximately two or three days of hard pedaling.

The desert made for a lonely trip with the infrequent car passing us by, usually with a friendly wave. We had come over a mountain pass towards the Utah/California border, just under 5000 feet at its summit, but pedaled now in the flats called "Devil's Playground." We were somewhere southwest of Baker and its nearby dry lakes. I saw a rest area ahead and signaled Sandia for a stop. She pulled up beside me to express a desire to keep going, as we had just recently made a "Snickers" stop. What a great nutritional diet we maintained! At that point, I think, she wanted to get the trip finished, but something in my mind really urged me to get off the highway there with Sandia reluctantly following me into that desert rest area.

As we pedaled into the remote rest spot, we saw a single vehicle sitting there, a white van with lots of gray primer covering obvious areas of rust. It was parked next to the bathrooms. As we approached closer around the front of the van, we saw a crudely lettered, hand printed cardboard sign in the front windshield, which read, 'Out of gas and money. Have not eaten in two days!' That's the first time we saw Lee as he stepped out of the van and looked at us. I remember Sandia speaking first with a light-hearted question, "What are you doing out here in the middle of the desert without any money?"

"What you be doing out here on them bicycles?" came Lee's response delivered with a huge white toothy smile, contrasted against his brown skin.

He was an African-American standing about six foot four, probably weighed in at 260

pounds, and maybe "fiftyish" in age. The passenger door to the van opened and out stepped his young wife Sarah, also with a big happy smile. I could see that her side of the van, including the dashboard, looked cluttered with a multitude of stuffed animals, in all shapes and sizes.

We listened to their hard luck story, incredulous to the fact that no passer through had helped them or even talked to them for over two days in that rest area, in spite of the fact that several cars had stopped in there. I told them we had a little trip money left and could certainly buy them a tank of gas and a meal. Lee said he knew of a gas station a few miles west of there and he had enough gas left to just make it there. I tried to hand him some money, but he wouldn't take it. Lee wanted to give us a ride west, amongst all of his rather tattered belongings, in that old Ford van, in payment for the gas money. I tried to explain our bike trip's purpose, but to him it seemed all nonsense. No one would ride bikes in the desert for the sport of it. Finally, we agreed to accept a ride to the gas station and turned to see Lee pick up both our bikes at the same time, gear and all, and walk over to put them inside his van. We found comfortable spots on cushions he placed on the van floor, leaning back on their old mattress, as he eased out onto the interstate heading west.

At the gas station, Lee explained to me that the gas tank leaked at approximately the three-quarter full level while asking if I could lay under the rear of the van to yell when it started to squirt out as he filled it from the gas pump. I chuckled to myself, lying under the van, when I saw it start to spray out of a rusted tank area. Upon my quick holler, I heard Lee stop the gas nozzle with a snap! Their old van, loaded with all the stuff, reminded me about the book, "Grapes of Wrath," except they came from Texas, not Oklahoma.

We went inside where I got in line to pay for the gas. Sandia picked up a half-dozen, ready-made sandwiches along with a couple of cold Cokes to add to the gas bill. Coming out of the air-conditioned store and cashier's booth made the desert outside seem even hotter. Sandia handed each of them two sandwiches and a Coke. We had our own drinking water to wash down the two remaining sandwiches after we unloaded our bikes from the van's interior.

Lee, by now, wouldn't hear of us pedaling when he could be driving us instead. I tried in vain to explain about the exercise, which he good heartedly laughed off again as a nonsensical effort. Then, after consulting my California map, I struck a deal with him. They traveled to Marysville in the northwest and we were headed southwest. Ahead about 50 miles lay the junction at Barstow. We would accept a ride to the road junction and then part company. Lee grinned as he accepted our terms.

"Just make yourselves comfortable back there and leave the driving to old Lee," he proclaimed as we pulled out onto the interstate. Lee had fixed us up with a bunch of couch cushions and as I looked over at Sandia lying into the softness of the pillows, I knew she, and her quadriceps, were enjoying a break from the bicycle saddle position.

Pretty soon, Sandia whispered over to me, "Did you see how quickly Sarah ate both those sandwiches?"

I replied, "I couldn't see from where I'm at, but she must've been really hungry." I remember reflecting on hunger, and the fact that I had had only one time in my life where I needed to go a few days without food. That time taught me that hunger is not a "fun" prospect. Lee and Sarah had just gone several days without food, but never complained to us of their hunger. Lee only talked about how good their lives were. He

was anxious to see his mom in Marysville and take care of her for a while. Lee had a passle of kids and grandkids and had been a widower before his kids fixed him up with young Sarah. She obviously enjoyed his company. Lee told us that he had previously been a gardener for a wealthy man in Texas, I think he said Lamar Hunt, for quite a few years. His employer had told Lee that he envied Lee's happy and spirited lifestyle. I found myself in awe of his charisma, listening with a smile to his stories as we drove towards Barstow.

The old white van rolled into Barstow in about an hour. It saved us between four and five hours of pedaling, the better part of a day. Lee reluctantly let us take our bikes out of the van, offering instead, to drive us to Los Angeles for safety reasons. From there he said they'd find some way to earn gas money to make it up north to Marysville. Sandia and I politely refused, but decided to split the money we had left with them. After final hugs and a farewell wave, we pedaled south for the San Gabriel Mountains. Lee and Sarah, for us, had been a fresh breeze blowing across the hot California desert lands!

The state police finally caught up to us on the downhill stretch of those mountains near San Bernardino, telling us we had to leave the interstate. It had begun to get a little too congested for us anyway, so leaving the interstate didn't seem that big a deal. I asked one of the policemen, "Has there been a forest fire around here lately?" as I could smell kind of a smoky pungent odor. The smell made my eyes water a little.

"No, that's just our everyday ordinary smog!" he answered to my query.

Wow, that smog smelled bad and you could swear there'd been a recent, and still smoldering, fire. Breathing that stuff wasn't pleasant. Years before, I had been in Southern California and remembered nothing that resembled the air we plowed through that day. Time to find a campground and build a smoky fire which no one would even take note of. Time for a night's rest in a snuggly tent anyway. Maybe a wind would blow the smog away while we slept—an optimistic thought!

We awoke to a little less smog; or else we were getting used to it already. Another freeze dried breakfast, washed down with awesome camp coffee—the kind you put the grounds in an old sock and hang it in the hot water—and we were on our way. Twenty or so miles later, on an alternate route to the interstate, we found a bike path which headed southwest toward Los Angeles. Later on, it connected to the Santa Ana River path that the marine and his girlfriend had told us about back in Utah. It felt great skirting through the fringes of L. A. without having to stop for a single traffic light or heavy street traffic. The bike path followed along the riverbank going under all the crossover streets. We cruised. Just about dusk, that same day, sixteen days after leaving our Colorado Mountains, we saw the "Newport Beach-City Limit" sign ahead.

Sandia had her first flat tire approaching the beach that evening, so I fixed it, thinking that one flat each for the whole trip wasn't all that bad. Mine had happened way back in Steamboat Springs at the beginning and hers was here, at the beach approach, at the end of the trip. Our bikes had logged a cumulative twenty six hundred miles, through some horrendous territory and hazards, with only two flat tires! Time to party hardy!

Our bikes managed to find their way, through the falling darkness, to a bar/lounge at the corner of Balboa and Pacific Coast Highway. After ordering and draining a couple of cold ones, we called Linnea. She answered the phone, but wouldn't believe we were so close and on our bicycles. When I described the intersection

outside in great detail, then she believed us and even knew which establishment we called from. "Hang on there my crazy friends. I'll borrow my dad's Volkswagen van and come and get you and your bicycles," she laughingly instructed. Sandia already had ordered two more frosty mugs. We tipped a few cold ones that night.

Visiting with our old and good friend Linnea proved fantastic. We stayed a couple of days, caught up on old and new times. Then Sandia and I pedaled up north to Redondo Beach and Rancho Palos Verdes to visit my sister Helen and family. After our visits, we packed up the bicycles in special airline boxes and flew back to Denver in a little under two hours! Sixteen days out versus two hours back. What a contrast! What strength also. Without panniers and gear, I had ridden my stripped down bike up the steep hills around Rancho Palos Verdes like they amounted to nothing! It felt so stimulating. Both

We made Newport Beach

of us felt so healthy and strong. Sandia told me she felt ready to run a marathon (26.2 miler) with me when she got back. I started kidding her by calling her, "Thunder Thighs!"

In reflection, during the plane ride back, we both commented on how the general public had been so supportive of our trip. The two questions, "Where are you coming from? Where are you headed?" were asked of us so many times. Restaurants always seemed to send bigger portions out to our table, once they were aware of our mode of travel. Sandia said she was amazed, that with all the exercise, to have gained five pounds on the trip. I think, in that, I felt a bit guilty for talking her into so many Snicker's breaks.

People used to slow down and pull along side us for a chat along the road, mostly in small towns. I remember one lady in Utah, in particular, telling us she had always wanted to do a bike trip and could she buy us a soda or cup of coffee. We politely refused, but I told her, "Just go out and do it. Life is short. You've got to do what you want to do!" She smiled knowingly, assuring us she would one day do it. I hope she did!

People had offered us their yards to camp in, refreshments, and always conversation and questions about our travels. Maybe our spirits just broke into their daily routines, giving them

Congratulations to each other

a little energy of thought and reflection, I don't know. One thing I did know for sure, however, was that we didn't want to live a life that would end with lots of regrets and apologies. The bicycle trip had been fun and invigorating for both of us. The hardest part lay in getting out on the road. After that, it came down to just a physical and common sense thing. Me for the physical leadership and Sandia for the common sense things!

chapter twenty-three

23

La Casita del Rio

When that incredible bike trip ended, the family disparity/land purchase situation hadn't changed one iota. It looked like our dreams of a mountain home and school next to the headwaters of the Colorado River near Grand Lake village were becoming just that—an unrealizable dream! Time to move on to Plan B. It didn't make sense to whine about the land effort that we'd expended. Some things are just not meant to be and you can't force them, or exert your will. Do what you can, make sure you didn't overlook anything, and then relax with the results!

With winter approaching, we decided to head up to northern Idaho to look at the land situation up there. The fuel for the Idaho trip was furnished by a very profound dream I had regarding that state. The dream probably stemmed in part from a short summer trip we'd recently taken to Coeur d'Alene with my son Gary and grandson Edward. We wanted to show them some of the northwestern country. At the time, Gary was sixteen and Edward, my oldest daughter Sherrie's firstborn, was seven. The boys both possessed an exploring mindset and with the exception of a bit of good natured fighting,

night stars, gazing down, through the teepee hole

river sounds, flowing by; peace for the soul

which one night actually caused their camping tent to cave in around them, they provided spirited company. The beauty of northern Idaho—the lush green forests, the huge, clear pristine lakes, and the various hot springs—obviously stuck in our minds. Sandia and I decided to go back for a second look to see how the winters felt. Maybe our dreams would become reality by following another dream?

The only way to experience a place is to live there on a day to day basis, so, upon arrival, Sandia, Kirsten, and I rented a small cottage on a 100-acre farm near Sandpoint and moved in. This location put us about forty miles south of British Columbia and the Canadian border. Kirsten attended the local school in Kootenai, while Sandia and I tried to fit into the community life as we began our search for land. Actually, there turned out to be a lot of acreage available, with rivers and creeks flowing through—a basic criterion for us, water flow. Something, however, seemed missing! I guess the best way to explain it is that once you've lived in the sunshine of those Colorado Rockies, it's a tough standard to compare other places to. It just felt too damp, too cold, too dark, and too icy for us. I often had illusions of one of those big logging trucks skidding on the narrow icy roads and taking out our van, head on! After three months, we mutually agreed that leaving northern Idaho would be in all our best interests of spirit.

I gave our notice to the landlord, and since we rented on a monthly schedule, he said we were free to go. The three of us pitched in on some rapid packing. Only three excited hours later, we headed the blue van south toward Colorado. I made one quick stop at a music store to surprise Sandia and Kirsten with a "Best of John Denver" cassette tape. Those beautiful ballads played over and over as we rolled south to the Colorado Mountains that January of 1983. Sometimes you need to go away for a while, to really know where you belong. It gives you a better perspective on things.

After a few short side trips in Denver, the three of us ended up as volunteer caretakers back up at the Winding River Ranch, while the owners Elaine and Bob Busse Sr. took a much needed Arizona vacation. They left in January and didn't return until the end of April. We home schooled Kirsten there, fed chickens, fought off the roosters, brought hay everyday to the barnyard corrals for the horses, kept all the ranch buildings with plumbing heated with woodstoves and solar collectors, and did the mailings for Elaine's mail order vitamin and mineral supplement business.

In our few telephone conversations with the ranch owners, we did not press, nor did we even mention, the land sale. We figured if it worked out, that would be exciting, and if it didn't, we'd move onto something else. Sandia always called me "flexi-Bill" to denote my willingness to roll with the punches. Anyway, with the land money safely in the bank and the subdivision exemption, as well as the well permit, approvals still valid and solely in our names, the dream yet retained a bit of life.

When Bob Sr. and Elaine returned in late April, they asked if we still had interest in the land back on the river. Answering in the affirmative, Elaine advised us that they probably had found a solution to the family standoff. As it turned out, by early summer, we moved back to the land and pitched tents up on that plateau above the river.

My first notion at a means to cross the river turned out to be a little harrowing and not real practical, but a lot of fun. With the help of a friend, Dave, we built a big log raft, figuring to set up kind of an old-west log-ferry operation. Dave and I pulled the completed raft to the riverbank and went off to cut some long stout poles to use as pushers off the river bottom. Well, when we pushed off on our maiden trip into the fast river current, without any previous poling experience, little did I know that those watching would end up bursting with laughter and glee. The river current grabbed us and started to spin us around. I guess we started to whip our long poles around, as the raft spun, and Dave's pole almost knocked me into the river. I, in turn, ended up whacking him in the back before we made the other shore, too far downstream! The curious onlookers rolled in mirth by the time we tied up the raft on the far side. Oh well, the raft logs did make good firewood the following winter. We definitely needed some kind of a bridge!

Ted and Deborah Burch and their two kids, Elijah and Rachel, moved back to the land with us. We established kind of a "hippie" tent community, complete with a newly dug outhouse and solar showers. The river seldom felt warm enough to bathe in and, besides, we didn't want the trout to get indigestion from the soap suds. Ted and I both had outside carpentry work, so we built a narrow foot-bridge on temporary river pilings and parked vehicles across the river. All supplies and visitors came by way of that three-foot wide swaying bridge. Fishing for German Brown, Rainbow, and the native Cutthroat Trout proved awesome. We often fried fresh fish on our campstove setup. Elijah and his young friend, Gabriel Cook, when barefoot and headed down to the river with their poles slung up on their shoulders, often reminded me of Tom Sawyer and Huckleberry Finn. Deborah got so handy with her hammer, she soon had installed food and storage "cabinets" outside their tents, off the ground, set up on old tree stumps. We referred to their area as "Camp Burch."

Despite the fact that we all kept ourselves pretty clean and tidy most of the time, a neighbor, downstream on the other side of the river, called the county building department to turn us in for living in "unclean" conditions. Out marched the chief building inspector to check us out. The inspector told us that he was only doing his duty when he red tagged our outhouse. He made me stand there holding the red tag in front of the outhouse, while he took a Polaroid picture for the record. He sort of insinuated that the weekenders didn't have much else to do but stir up trouble. The inspector told us to get and maintain a chemical toilet on site in case anyone else started complaining. We lived so remotely and had so much acreage around us, it all seemed kind of funny. That turned out to be the one and only visit from authorities telling us how we could live on our own land!

Sandia and I built a small storage shed, with lots of shelving, and brought most of our belongings out to the land. One box at a time, we carried across that less than stable foot bridge, until a lot of hours of carrying had all our "stuff" marked and packed neatly into our permanent new shed. Through our friend Hal, we bought a sixteen by seven foot used camper trailer and towed it across an upstream ranch bridge and

down to our land using our big FarmAll tractor. I hooked up a small hand pump and black poly piping from the river to the trailer and presto—we had sort of running water allowing us to take cold river water showers in the privacy of our little trailer home.

Our next priority fell to getting the local electric company to set five power poles to reach from the nearest available power junction, with the last pole on our side of the river. After they strung the electric cables along the tops of the newly installed poles, they gave us a temporary construction power drop and outlets at the bottom of the last pole. Our payment for the pole installations would be to guarantee the power company a thirty-dollar per month minimum usage fee for five years. If we used less, we would still have to pay the thirty bucks, but if we used more, it would be billed at the normal rate. Mission accomplished!! I promptly hooked up the construction power to the trailer circuitry and activated the hot water tank—what a trip—a hot filtered river water shower luxury!

A short time later, we went in together with the ranch, which also needed two wells drilled, to get a well driller and his heavy drilling rig out to our remote location. You would think, right beside the river, that we'd hit a shallow well. For days, those diamond bits augured their way through solid rock, until finally at about 120 feet below the river level, we hit some awesome crystal clear pure mountain water. Close to four thousand dollars poorer, we watched that 30 ton well drilling rig disappear upstream toward the far distant ranch access bridge. Our homestead, however, had potable water. Two days later, I had the submersible well pump and black poly pipe in place, along with a temporary faucet mounted on a post above the well. All you had to do was flip a tree mounted, outdoor electrical switch, turn on the faucet, and you had non-stop drinking water. It came from the tap so cold and pure, it hurt your teeth as you drank it. The big deal for us was how the well ended the era of filling water jugs at various faucets in town and carrying them back out to the land. Electric power and now, the water supply, became realities. Next on the priority list, we needed a bridge, a real bridge, to drive vehicles across!

A civil engineering friend, Rudi, who I worked with on various jobs which required a professional engineer's stamp, had drawn up a log-trussed bridge that would clearspan our river. I negotiated a trade for the required logs, figuring to come up with a way to handle those big fifty-foot logs in the meantime. Using a similar design to that of our local log house builders, I commissioned the town blacksmith and welder to build our log handling rig, dubbed a "log boom." The designed boom mounted on the front of the tractor, in place of the bucket, and would operate using the bucket hydraulics. As I lifted the first fifty-foot log with the newly fabricated log boom, the welder and I watched as the boom buckled under the huge cantilevered weight. "No problem. I can fix that," he told me as he jumped into his truck and headed to town to pick up some additional reinforcing angled steel. Hours later, with the new strengthening struts welded into place using his portable welding rig, our tractor deftly picked up a fifty foot by fourteen inch diameter log and held it aloft horizontally for ample test time.

The tractor and log boom apparatus were ready to begin the log superstructure work on the concrete bridge foundations we had poured either side of the river. The clearspan distance would be 45 feet. We didn't put anything to support the bridge center in the river, as that would have required a U. S. Army Corps of Engineers approval. I didn't even want to contemplate the paperwork that would have been required for

that approval—so clearspan it became—private land to private land. Rudi's bridge design had taken the clearspan into account. The far, west side concrete had been poured using a concrete pipe boom and a pumper truck. I used my trusty K&E Builder's Transit to shoot the top of concrete in at one foot above the one hundred-year flood level. Only two years later would the spring melt and mountain run-offs actually rise to the bridge floor level, but without any damage, as the bridge fasteners held adequately to the concrete foundations and footers.

The reinforced log boom on the front of the tractor worked like a charm allowing me to set the first of seven clearspan, twelve to sixteen inch diameter, logs in place. Once I anchored that first log into place, Sandia held me to my earlier boastful pledge to "walk" the first bridge log across the river. I ventured out onto that solitary log, stopped, looked at the long span, then down at the cold water moving rapidly below me, and returned to the riverbank—not as a quitter, but only to get a long "cheater" pole like the high wire stuntmen use. The physics of rotation and moments of inertia, surging up into my consciousness, told me balance would be easier done holding a long horizontal pole. Physics always works. I pretty much walked slowly, but steadily, right across that log, focusing ahead on the log, without looking down at the hypnotic flow of the Colorado River. I didn't get wet that day!

Working essentially by myself, as Ted, Deborah, and their kids had once more moved back to Illinois, with Sandia's occasional help when I needed two additional hands, it took over eight weeks to complete that majestic log-trussed bridge. Another three weeks went into the labor of the second smaller bridge, which spanned a twenty-foot beaver diversion off the river. The second bridge didn't need any trusses and proved easier to build. My nephew, Mark, peeled the

Even concrete needs a touch

Bridge log truss framing

bark from all the bridge logs. He came to the mountains from the shores of Massachusetts. What a contrast he found in our high peaks. Mark pitched his tent back on our land, near the forest, and went off each day to work with Jimmy Reed, the log house builder. Mark turned twenty in those mountains at the end of summer having grown stronger physically and mentally from the experience. He earned about ten cents a foot for peeling logs all day. Then he would come back in the evenings and peel the bridge logs, just to help contribute to our bridge project. Mark must have dreamed draw knives and bark those nights back in his tent. I remember he always wanted to arm wrestle me, but I managed to talk my way out of that macho confrontation, as it would have been a lose/lose situation for both of us. The final log bridge definitely stood more aesthetically pleasing because of Mark's effort.

My only setback on the big bridge came when I struggled a twelve-foot long log to the top of the upstream truss, about twelve feet above the bridge decking, only to lose my grip and plunge, log and all, into the cold river water. I held onto a post from the old temporary footbridge and managed to keep that truss log from floating away. Sandia responded to my calls for help on the run and between us, we managed to get the log out of the current, over to the riverbank.

As we sat there on the "saved" log, Sandia looked over at me and asked, "I know you're stubborn, but why didn't you just let the log float away. You could have made another one or maybe picked this one up someplace downstream and floated it back?"

I showed her the cut and scribed notches at both ends that had taken me hours to complete. It surely would have gotten banged up on some of the protruding rocks of the downstream rapids. I told her, "Too much work in this 250 pound log to let go of it!" Sandia shook her head sideways as she walked off back to the trailer to resume her own work. I turned to my pulleys and block and tackle rig to start hoisting that log successfully up into place the second time.

I don't know about most people, but for me, completing those bridges, virtually by hand, and then driving the old blue van across them to the west forest side of the river became a truly exhilarating experience. Some of us, I guess, never outgrow that need to build things with "Lincoln logs," or these days "Legos." The boy in me loved the old tractor and the whole process of building a fifteen-ton capacity log bridge across the Colorado River. An experience like that becomes indelibly woven into one's multi-colored tapestry of life.

After the celebration of spirit for being able to drive back and forth across the river and thus bring construction materials that much closer to our home site, the next task focused on building a road up to the actual plateau above the river. The only reasonable way to engineer it was to use a gradual slope upward downriver for a hundred, or so, yards, a switchback, then the same distance back, sloping up to our proposed house location. Any steeper roadway would have been undrivable after the mountain winter set in. The tractor could accomplish the grading and gravel work in a straightforward manner, but the trees would be the hard part. About thirty or forty large lodge pole pine trees grew in our proposed access road.

Only one way to attack it. One tree at a time, starting from the bottom, moving to the top Each tree that had to go, we flagged with bright orange surveyor ribbon. Sandia helped me on this project, saving me lots of time getting down and back up onto that big old tractor. We worked out a sequence on the first tree: using a chainsaw to drop the tree, leaving a high stump,

A rainbow on the log bridge

followed by trimming the branches, or "slash" as the loggers called it, then bucking up the trunk into eight foot lengths and stacking them in future firewood piles off the road. The last step used tractor bucket hydraulics, together with "choker" cables, to pull out the stumps. Most of the stumps, I hauled across the river to a wide graveled area and made an "ugly" pile for later burning. Some people just dig a deep hole and bury stumps, as they are hard things to get rid of.

I had to smile during the tree removal process, as I watched Sandia hook the chokers onto one of the stumps and turn to give me the thumbs up signal. She had leather gloves on and dirt smudges on her smiling, but serious, face. The words of advice that mountain man had given me years earlier came back to me. He had told me, "What you need to survive in these mountains is a good chainsaw, a decent pickup, and a warm woman—in that order!" Sandia probably wondered why I laughed as I pulled out

Our roadway cleared of trees and stumps

that particular stump with the tractor!

The better part of a week later, the roadway was done. The road surface proved a little rough in spots, and needed a bit more gravel, but that could come later. A truck could drive right up to the building site of "*La Casita del Rio*," the little house by the river, as we had dubbed it. At that point in time, however, the actual start of building *La Casita* would have to wait until spring as winter moved in on us so quickly. Our new access road soon lay under more than a foot of the white powdery stuff.

My nephew Mark decided to return home to Massachusetts that late fall. Maybe his tent became a tad cool at night, but it seemed in his mind a good time to go. We saw him off on his journey east. He had turned twenty there in our forest by the river, became a whole lot stronger physically, and seemed to have picked up a mountain sense of maturity. Mark's timing turned out to be very special as it gave him a few months of working with his dad back east, before his dad died suddenly of a heart attack. We need to listen to those inner voices that sometimes talk to us.

Having focused so totally on the bridges and

roadways, I didn't have any winter work lined up. Also, the trailer was getting mighty cold at night. Sandia and I decided to take her sister up on the offer of living in their partially finished basement down in Denver. We both could certainly find work in the city. Kirsten also seemed anxious to stop the home schooling program she worked on and socialize with kids her own age. So down the mountains we went in the old blue van, with a few clothes and belongings to see us through the rest of the winter.

Sandia found work as a dental assistant during the day and as a waitress in a newly opened Mexican food restaurant by night. I worked the early shift as a tuxedoed room service waiter at the downtown Marriott Hotel, taught mathematics at Metropolitan State College in the afternoons, and again taught night algebra classes at Red Rocks Community College. Seemed like we only saw each other every few days and the time passed too quickly. Suddenly, I turned in all my spring semester grades and the semester ended. I remember keeping a picture of our log trussed bridge always handy in my upper pocket, so that when some of the "mightier-than-thou" hotel guests would tell me things like, "Clean up my mess, boy, and get it out of here," I'd pat my pocket. Pulling out my picture later in the elevator always had an immediate calming effect on me. I knew in my heart that I had become a "mountain man" of sorts.

I headed back to those mountains a few weeks before Sandia, as she had to wait for Kirsten to finish up at Lake Junior High School. So, in the middle of May 1984, Sunshine, our wolf/shepherd mixed lady dog and I climbed into our blue van to head up to springtime in the Rockies. I hummed, sang, and breathed in the clean mountain air all the way over Berthoud Pass and down to the western slope. Sunshine sat up in the other captain's chair looking out the windshield as the scenery passed. Her wagging tail always answered me as I talked to her. I still swear she could smile when I told her things.

That summer we previously decided Kirsten would live in the trailer and have her own teen aged space. To that end, we bought a sixteen-foot diameter used teepee, which Sandia and I would call home—a teepee by the river. I cut and peeled a bunch of lodge poles, and with some engineering physics figured out how to get that huge teepee erected on my own. I built three levels of lofts inside using small downfall trees. Only a small portion of the floor was left dirt, to accommodate a small sheet metal stove for use on the cooler nights and when some cooking was required, like morning coffee. We would sleep on the upper loft level, highest from the ground, in case creeping and crawling critters explored our teepee at night. Sunshine loved the forest and the river. She chased chipmunks, field mice, and ground squirrels incessantly while I worked. Sometimes catching the mice, she would chew and gulp them down whole, following her wolf instincts. She never had to be tied up. If I told her to "stay," I could return two or three days later, and there she'd be, pretty much right where I left her, "staying."

Sandia and Kirsten soon joined me back on the land and Denver became a memory, quickly fading into the brilliant mountain sunshine. Sandia easily found waitressing work, as her friendliness and hard work ethic was well known in our small mountain community. She was there to help on the housebuilding when I needed more than my own two hands, from mixing concrete in that same putzy-putz, which now belonged to Dick, to sanding and oiling each of my hand chiseled timbers just before they would be lifted into place. I won't bore the reader with the construction details on *La Casita*, but will include a photograph of the completed

Our teepee and some timber framing joinery

The completed timber frame of La Casita del Rio

timber frame. The frame had two dormers, 523 wood joints, some mortise and tenon, some dovetails, some tongue and fork, and lots of oak dowels. It took seven weeks, working about fourteen to eighteen hours a day, with a little help from quite a few beautiful friends on raising days, to finish that artwork. The only thing not present in the final frame was the use of a single "modern" steel nail. The timber frame stood as a monument to timbersmiths and their historical artistry. In keeping with that ancient ritual, we even had a "pine bough" ceremony when the last piece of the frame was gently fitted into place using my "commander"—a big heavy wooden mallet. The ceremony consisted of nail-

ing a fresh pine branch to the top of the frame and then celebrating, with the occasional tankard of brew lifted toward that beautiful and mighty frame in a toast for its longevity. Sandia and I got a little tipsy with our friends that night, staring up at the complexity and enormity of the timber frame. To that point in my life, I thought the U.S. Patent I had once earned with two fellow workers for an invention in physics was my greatest accomplishment, but that timber frame, done with the hands, as well as the head, made the patent pale in comparison.

The morning after the celebration, I started putting the roof on, because in the mountains, old man winter is always lurking around the corner. *La Casita's* framing timbers had been delivered from the roughsawn mill in mid-August and it was already the first week in October. The roofing work needed the occasional sweeping off of snowstorms at times, but was soon enough finished and waterproofed, even with the additional work required to "flash" in the valleys created by the timber framed dormers.

The next closing in step was covering the walls and, here, I just nailed shiplapped knotty pine boards into place on the outside of the timber frame. I didn't even cut out the windows. They could be located, sized, framed, and cut out in the springtime. By late November, with the snowstorms rolling in all too frequently, I accepted a job to oversee the construction of a small office/retail center in Las Cruces, New Mexico, about forty miles west of El Paso, Texas

and Jaurez, Mexico. The center would be owned by Sandia's mom, her sister Irene and husband Dave, and her brother Bob, who lived in Las Cruces and would locate his insurance agency office in the complex.

So we would be busy that winter, but plenty warm down there near the border. For the family, to have us watching over the project and the subcontractors represented a great alternative. We brought the whole project in at a great bottom line price, with the owners' interests totally foremost. For us, the job became a super deal, as the income was good and the work warm. I guess when you keep your "windows of opportunity" open, things can "fly" in for your scrutiny. Not that one has to act on every chance that comes along, but it sure is nice to look at your options during the voyage of life.

chapter twenty-four

The Addiction to Running

My story, actually our story, wouldn't be complete without a chapter on our running craze.

Having been raised in an era when you weren't cool unless you had a Lucky Strike dangling from your lips, I always had an on-again, off-again relationship with cigarettes. As a tough teenager, they provided a necessary Jimmie Dean emulation. Then in the military they became a part of life, just like the coffee locker. At the university, I quit smoking because it proved easier to study without clouds of smoke swirling around outside my head and inside my lungs. Then, with the pressure of getting my thesis written to a deadline, I started puffing on butts again, only to quit again soon after upon acceptance of my position working with radioisotopes for five years. After that it evolved into smoking "borrowed or bummed" cigarettes at parties. They seemed to naturally go together with a couple of cold beers socially.

Anyway, there I sat one Sunday morning on the deck at *La Casa*, smoking a bummed cigarette from one of my visiting daughters, when I realized that it tasted horrible. I ground it out in a nearby ashtray. My niece Shellie and her hus-

to run the paths on which elk tread last night

gives spring to leg, to foot, and lifts heads high

band Roger sat nearby. Roger, at the time, quietly completed marathons (26.2-mile races) in times under two and one-half hours. Shellie told me he was thinking "Olympics '84." I remember asking him, after putting out that last cigarette, "Roger, can you teach a post-forty year old to run?"

"Sure," he said. "Why not start right now. We'll run to town."

I protested only slightly, as town stood at least two to three miles away. The road, however, sloped slightly downhill most of the way. I pulled on some old running shoes and a few minutes later we started on our way. I tried to talk as we ran, but had trouble breathing and talking at the same time. Roger clued me in that, if you can't talk easily, then you are running too fast! Something about "not building oxygen debt, because you can't make it up."

Roger and I made it slowly to town. I felt exhausted, but at the same time exhilarated for having done the distance. Sandia and the rest of the family came to pick us up and found Roger and I sharing a pitcher of cold beer in one of the local outdoor beer gardens. I toasted the unbelievable high my body experienced. Maybe the euphoria resulted just from the joy of having stopped running, I don't know. Later, I learned that the good feeling came about due to endorphins being released into the system during a hard cardiovascular workout, resulting in the so called "runner's high."

All our visitors soon went down the mountains from that running baptismal visit, but I found myself smitten by the running disease. I would never smoke another cigarette and began running just about every day, whenever I had a chance. At first, a few miles seemed so far. Running seemed akin to hitting your hand with a hammer—it felt so good when you stopped—but it started to grow on me. I looked forward to my time on the road or trails. After a month or so, it started to get easier, allowing me to run faster without gasping for breath at the end. My friend, Ron Cook, got caught up in running at about the same time. He had a friend, who had completed a marathon in Denver and described all the intriguing details to Ron.

The first day Ron and I did a five-miler up into Rocky Mountain National Park and back—five whole miles—we had a party afterwards. During the celebration, we even got in Ron's truck to use the odometer and remeasured the course we had run earlier, only to find it measured about one-tenth of a mile short of a true "fiver." We kidded about running it over again, on the spot, and adding the one-tenth, but cool heads prevailed, keeping us from running it with a couple of cold beers sloshing around in our stomachs.

In later days, we would run ten and fifteen milers. We started thinking we could maybe run a marathon. There was one scheduled two months hence down in Denver. The run was aptly called "The Mile High Marathon." Ron and I naively, and boldly, pledged to each other

to run it, even though our training program seemed amateurish and at best, grossly inadequate. I've always found, however, that a lot can be accomplished when it's fueled by pure enthusiasm!

On race day in Denver, there had to be, at least, two thousand runners lining up in the marathon starting area. It was early morning. The smell of Ben Gay and other remedy salves permeated the air. The excitement and energy levels amongst those runners seemed so high. Right there on top of those highs stood Ron and I, jumping up and down, stretching out our tightened muscles, and tasting a sweet mixture of fear and anticipation. We lined up for an optimistic four-hour finish, while they started playing the "William Tell Overture" on big booming outdoor loudspeakers. At the crescendo of the Overture, we heard the loud report of the starter's cannon up on the State House lawn. We took off running. Actually, our pace seemed more like a fast walk, as that whole sea of running humanity had to move cautiously at first, until each could find room for a full stride. The time for the first mile would be slow. We hadn't learned at that point that it was good to hold back a little. Ron and I wanted to go full-tilt-boogie all the way to the finish line. I clutched my little plastic baggies of vitamins that Elaine Busse had given me from her health ranch to swallow at intervals along the marathon route—big mistake!

Ron and I had worked out the sequence into highlighting the five, ten, thirteen point one (half-way), sixteen (only single digit miles to go), and twenty mile points as focus goals within the race. After the twenty-mile point, it would be only ten kilometers to the finish, and who couldn't run ten "K's?"

Just past the sixteen-mile marker, after the ingestion of a large baggie of vitamins, I began to lose it. We'd been running harder than we had ever trained up to that point in the race. We both slowed our pace. At twenty miles, Sandia and Ron's wife Georgi, met us in City Park to "run us in." I began to hallucinate, unable to communicate with Sandia. She told me to stay quiet and save my energy for moving one foot in front of the other. Ron fell behind us, doing little more than a fast walk. I didn't realize that my body suffered from dehydration in the heat of the day, brought on by swallowing so many vitamins and not enough water. Sandia told me later that soon after the twenty-three mile post in City Park I passed out, going down in a twitching, legs still moving, heap.

The Emergency Medical Technicians put me in an ambulance. I ended up at Porter Memorial Hospital, where the nurses pumped a gallon of sugar/water (dextrose) into me. Then I felt fine. I even asked the nurse if I could get a ride to City Park, so I could finish the race. She laughed and said, "No rides for any of you runners. It's too hot. There's too many of you ending up here today. You are all crazy!"

My buddy Ron showed up later. He limped in to a five plus hour finish and somehow managed to get us each a finisher's "T-shirt"—the ultimate prize. We hugged together, as only friends who had been through something like that, could appreciate. Ron had finished. I felt so proud for him. Sandia, at least, proved nice enough not to rub in the $200.00 hospital bill I ended up having to pay to get out of that episode. I promised her I would never be ill prepared for another marathon. I wouldn't go down again. She responded with something like, "Oh no—are you really thinking of running another one?"

"You bet I am!"

Ron and I vowed to run the Summit County Marathon, three and one-half months later, in

August, and began training the next day—albeit a slow day. During the week, Ron and I trained on our own, because of differing work schedules, but on the weekends, we usually managed to get in a long run together. I was soon referred to in our mountain community as "the guy who runs with the dog." Sunshine loved to run with me. She learned to heel quickly and mostly ran beside my right leg, at my pace. Sandia would later sew her up some doggie packs, which she would proudly bring to me in her mouth whenever she spied me lacing up my running shoes. Sunshine always looked anxious to get out on the road and didn't have a lot of patience with me dawdling around for one last swig of coffee.

I finished that Summit County race in a little over four hours; feeling strong despite the fact that much of the 26.2 mile distance was near the ten thousand foot elevation mark. My niece Shellie finished that race too, her first and last marathon, with her coach/husband Roger running at her side. She took, I believe, a third place female finishers medal. My friend Ron finished also, but walking in, having been really sick around the twenty-four mile marker.

I became a running fool after that, completing a total of eleven marathons through subsequent years, along with lots of half-marathons, 10 K, and 5 K races. I liked the long ones the best. I liked the endurance part of them, never running to win a race—just to challenge myself to a strong finish—for me, finishing became truly winning! The marathon itself, on race day, proved to be just a victory lap for a great training program. My best race happened under very cold, drizzling conditions when I finished 200th out of approximately 2300 runners in three hours, thirty minutes. That's about one hour, fifteen minutes behind world class finish times!

Sandia got caught up in the running with me, as she could sense the energy it gave me, especially after our bike trip to California. She sat there in Newport Beach, California drinking coffee and eating double chocolate donuts with me, when she suddenly looked at me to say, "I think I can run a marathon!!" She went on to run four marathons. Her best time clocked also at three hours, thirty minutes flat–actually twenty seconds better than my best. Sandia turned out to be such a natural runner, she never seemed to train as hard as I did, never got injured, and would run like a flowing deer on race day. She won many individual medals, while the only award I ever earned, was one-half of a husband/wife trophy for the best combined times in a New Mexico 10 K race. No worries though, as my main goal focused on running for spirit and well being, not glory.

One Denver Marathon, I was running by myself and hurting a bit as I approached the twenty-mile point at the entrance to City Park. My old running buddy, Ron, had moved away to Michigan a few years earlier. As I looked ahead at the park entrance, I saw a runner jogging in place that looked like my man, Ron Cook. At first I thought, "Oh no, I'm starting to hallucinate again!" but when I got to the entrance, it was Ron. He had flown in from Michigan as a surprise and ran with me that last 10 K. What a friend. What can I say? In that last 6.2 miles, he told me a story, I will never forget. It had to do with butterflies and emergence from their cocoons. Seems like some scientists did an experiment where they surgically removed the butterflies from their cocoons instead of allowing the natural struggle to open the fabric of their enclosure. Those butterflies that found the easy way out turned out weak, with their colors dull and faded. They died prematurely, without enough strength to cope with their surroundings. In contrast, the scientists observed that of the

butterflies left to their own struggle to break out of the cocoon, those that struggled the hardest and longest, turned out to be the most brilliantly colored, physically strongest, and longest lived of all. Ron and I applied the lesson of nature to our own lives, and the lives of others, from those that live on social welfare to those hard working immigrants that built this great nation of ours. Suddenly, the finish line appeared, ever beautiful, in front of us. I raised both arms, fists clenched, in my own tradition, and ran in the final 100 meters, feeling great about the struggles I'd been through in life, as well as the wealth and strength of friendships.

Again, race day provided fun, but the best part of running would always be the training. So many miles on mountain trails, feeling the softness of pine needles under foot. The quietness of the forests, the gentle sound of the wind through the trees, the occasional grazing wildlife looking up, undisturbed, at the peculiar human animal running by, all became a part of it. In order to be ready for a marathon race day, I had to put in running a total of about 650 miles in the three to four months prior to the race. I started out with about twenty miles a week, building to sixty plus at the end of the sixteen-week training program. A by-product of the program is that I felt well all the time—energized, healthy, vibrant, and alive. Sometimes I took my Walkman and listened to classical tapes or my favorite, in the forest, Navajo flute music. When I pushed real hard, like running up a mountain in the snow, I used to listen to all the theme music from the Rocky movies. That music has a great training rhythm.

One early winter morning, Sunshine and I began a training run in several inches of new powder snow. Only a dim gray light showed the way as we headed toward our front gate, about one-half mile from the *La Casita*, across the bridge and river. I mostly ran early mornings as it started my day off right. Sunshine, or "Burner" as she was nicknamed by Ted, ran near my right foot as we came through that open log gateway. I reflected that ours were the only footfalls marking that crispy cold new snowfall as I focused downward on the snow at that moment. Then I heard startled, snorting noises right in front of us and looked up to see that we had turned the gateway corner to run right into a herd of migrating cow elk, with a few young bulls. By chance, they started moving in the same direction we ran. I whispered "heel" down to Burner and kept my pace. She didn't need the command to stay with me as I think the hooves of twenty some odd big elk pounding around her seemed scary enough to keep her right beside me. We ran that way, surrounded by elk for at least one-quarter mile. Then they bounded, as a group, following a designated leader, off the gravel road and up an embankment, into the forest, leaving behind their strong damp scent in the air. For that brief few moments, Burner and I ran with a wild elk herd, immersed somewhere in its center, smelling its smells, feeling its energy and spirit, and moving forward with their dark heavy masses, as the sun had just begun to light our morning.

When they broke away from us, probably in fright, Burner and I stopped and watched their retreat up the hill. Burner came over to me, with tail and butt wagging in exaggerated relief. Sunshine certainly was no coward, as she often proved, but with that many large bodies around her, it must have made a profound impression on her instincts. We finished that morning's run with a very excited entry into my journals. Sandia said she could still smell the elk on us when we returned home.

Sometime after completion of my second marathon, I started showing blood in my urine. It usually only occurred after long runs, with dis-

tances in excess of twelve miles. I didn't say anything to Sandia at first, but later told her about it when I saw that it kept happening. I didn't want to quit running, but went to see a doctor at Sandia's prodding. She made an appointment and I drove forty miles to see a local doctor in Kremmling, Colorado.

Dr. Ceriani did tests, concluding that I might be beating up my kidneys by running long distances. He said with my six-foot tall and 146-pound frame, there wasn't much body to cushion the effect of the road jarring on my kidneys. The doc said I could keep running, just not to overdo it, whatever that meant. I felt so good in those days. There seemed no way I could quit running!

It happened the last hard day of the bicycle trip to California, when I really got concerned about the blood. While we waited at that bar for Linnea to pick us up in the van, I walked into the "used beer department" (the men's room), and lined up for a little relief into the urinal. As I looked straight ahead and up a little at the different writings and poems on the wall, as is customary at the urinal, I heard the guy at the urinal next to me audibly gasp. I glanced sideways to see him looking down into my urinal. I looked down to see my stream of almost pure red urine splashing against the contrasting white porcelain. I finished quickly, zipped up, and got out of there, admittedly, a little embarrassed. I told Sandia, again not feeling any internal pain, and vowed to have it thoroughly checked out when we got back to Denver. It only seemed to happen after really hard vigorous exercise.

I turned myself into the Lutheran Hospital near Denver upon returning to start a whole series of tests under the auspices of a urologist, Dr. Defalco. He was very acquainted with runners and their special maladies as he treated several world class runners out of Boulder, Colorado, among them Frank Shorter. The tests included

*Completing a marathon run
together in the Arizona desert*

Finish it in the sunshine

*Finish it in the cold drizzle,
but just finish that marathon!*

kidney x-rays and cystoscopy of the bladder—a
fancy word for sending a light pipe, or fiber
optics, into the bladder for a look around. It
turned out to be a small low-grade cancerous
tumor in my bladder, which I aggravated by running, thus causing it to bleed. After Dr. Defalco
described the situation to me, along with the
straightforward operation to remove it surgically,
sort of like using a "roto-rooter," I asked him
what causes bladder tumors. He quickly replied,
"Usually a pack of cigarettes a day for ten years!"
Oh, those Lucky Strike coffin nails had finally
caught up with me.

"Can I run again?"

"Give the operation a week's rest, then you
can start running again, slowly! We wouldn't
have been able to find it so early, except that
your running made it show up."

I ran again for sure, logging in almost 9,000
total miles for Burner and me in my running
journals. I would have several more operations
in the years to come, always indicated by blood
in my urine when a new tumor would grow and
I would aggravate it by running long distances.
I changed my eating habits to became mostly a
vegetarian. I tried to eliminate stress, which is
a self-perpetuating attitude, from my life. The

condition finally cleared up and no new tumors grew. Cystoscopic exams, periodically, showed no further tumor growths. I remember later on asking the doctor, "How does a non-runner know when he or she has bladder cancer?"

He turned to me and said, "They don't until later!"

When people still ask me, "Why do you run? Why do you play tennis so much? Why do you exercise so hard at your age?"

I always answer, without reservation, "For my health, both physical and spiritual, now more than ever!"

The Marathon

The race I've chosen to take part and run

The time is now; we're all lined up to start

This doubt of mine will go upon the gun

I'll bolt with all the speed my legs impart

I'm running now too fast; my face is red

It is hard to keep to a slower pace

To carry me the many miles ahead

Oh, why did I decide to run this race?

Stride constant now, my breath at steady rate

Those days of training made this body strong

One foot, then the other, just hold the gait

Hold true, the last few miles will be along

Now, finish line in sight; fist pump and shout

Belief in self, what this race is all about!

the second aside

Fine Wine and Miles to Drive Before We Stop

One early summer in the middle eighties, I found myself finishing details at *La Casita*, as an owner-builder is never finished with his house, and bidding the odd carpentry job that came up in our mountain area. Sandia had several waitressing opportunities lined up, but hadn't committed to any of them yet.

Friends from Connecticut, knowing our free type of lifestyle, called with an unusual offer of work. They had invested in a particular bottling run of a Reserve Chardonnay at a vineyard out in the wine country of the Sonoma and Napa Valleys. Notwithstanding the financial details, the bottom line turned out to be, would we be available to get one hundred fourteen cases (twelve bottles to the case) moved from the San Jose area to their home in Connecticut. There would also be bonus carpentry work at their home which involved removing all interior doors and replacing them with upgraded solid oak six-panel doors—about two dozen total. All travel expenses would be taken care of, plus a salary for driving and carpentry work. As I mulled the details on my end of the telephone conversation,

fine wine and miles to drive before we stop

from coast to coast, with vintage love on top

another comment came through the earpiece in a comical way, "And you can't drink more than one case on the way across the country!"

I answered the request in the affirmative, "We would be interested in the project. I'll check out the best way to accomplish the move, our timing, and get back to you."

It turned out that the highway proved the most economical transport mode, and after checking out weights and volumes with the vineyard, appropriate truck rental rates, and flight details to get to San Jose from Denver, we had an accurate estimate of the total financial costs involved. I also called the Wine Council of America, who assured me that the transportation of the wine for private consumption would be legitimate, as long as the wine was not meant for resale. After Sandia and I worked out our own timing, we called our friends with the details and received their go ahead; their wine cellar would await our arrival.

A few days later, in San Jose, we backed our newly rented, heavy duty, one ton, yellow van up to the loading dock of the vineyard warehouse

139

to begin loading the wine, one case at a time. We distributed most of the load between and over the two axles, with a smaller rear load. The last few cases had to go between the two front seats, sort of up to armrest height. As soon as the loading ended, overload springs checked okay for clearance, all consignment papers properly signed, Sandia and I looked at each other, gave a thumbs up, and rolled out onto the pavement of the California roadways. Sandia's expert map reading from our road atlas got us to the interstate, where we turned east toward Nevada.

After several hundred miles, with quite a few stops to check the cases in back, the overload springs, and the tires, I began to relax into the driving part, satisfied with the weights and balances. As we rolled past the first truck weigh station without stopping, I felt happy, as a novice freight man, with our choice of the van which wasn't required to stop for weighing. The rental company had offered us a bigger truck for the same price, but we insisted, waiting until they came up with our current heavy duty van, as reserved days earlier.

Rolling through Nevada that first evening, we did some multiplying. One of the warehouse administrators mentioned that the wine's value figured at more than one hundred dollars per bottle. When we multiplied it out, the number of zeros scared us. We should have rented an armored van!

Finally pulling into a generic Nevada motel, I backed the van almost up to our door. We used one of those thick quilted moving blankets that came with the van to cover up the rear door windows. The other quilted blanket, we threw over the cases of wine between our seats. You couldn't tell the nature of the cargo from the outside of the van. You'd have to break in. We felt the responsibility of the trust our friends had left with us.

Even though Sandia brought a bottle of that Reserve Chardonnay inside for a nightcap, neither of us slept very well that first night. Every time I awoke, I felt compelled to quietly walk to the motel door to assure myself that the van sat there unmolested.

On the road the next morning, Sandia and I remarked on what a fine tasting wine our nightcap had been. Next, we made a plan of night stops for the rest of the trip that would put us into friendly garages each night, leaving us to sleep a bit more soundly and restfully. We'd call ahead to several friends along our route and set it up. Can you imagine if a friend called you to ask about spending the night along with one thousand three hundred and sixty eight, oops, make that sixty seven, bottles of a fine Reserve Chardonnay? What would you say?

On we rolled toward our next stop—Mom's house near Denver. Sandia never drove much, spelling me an hour here or there, but she read to me constantly from newspapers, magazines, and a couple of novels we'd brought along. The scenery in the rest of Nevada, Utah, and on into Colorado became a wonderful focus.

We reached the Denver area that evening, stopping at Mom's for some well needed rest. We visited with mom and Kirsten, as she remained under mom's tutelage until we would get back. A fine wine nightcap and a soft pillow brought me quickly to the soft billowy clouds of slumber.

Sandia woke me up, as planned, while it remained dark outside. We faced a twenty plus hour stretch in order to make our friends', Ted and Deborah, place in southern Illinois. A big thermos of hot coffee and a load of mom's burritos, wrapped in aluminum foil, would sustain us for a good many miles, leaving us to stop only for gasoline and the toilet, which could easily be a combined stop.

The miles rolled by freely. By late afternoon,

Sandia had her legs stretched out to the dashboard, reading away, with a glass of wine balanced on our wine case console. I kept my vow to have no wine until the van moved into secure parking each night. Then a few glasses would be my reward. Actually, I preferred cold beer, but I had to admit the stuff we carried proved very easy on the palate.

Our wine laden van rolled into Ted and Deborah's little farm setup well past midnight. They'd finally gone to bed, leaving the door open for us. With the van safely put away in their barn, we found our way to the bedding they had laid out for us in a spare room. I think I continued driving in my sleep that night. It had been a long day behind the wheel!

After several hours of visiting over a not so early breakfast, we left our friends a bottle of wine, and hit the road again, this time aiming for friends, John and Linda, in Akron, Ohio. That provided a shorter day's trek for a change.

Sandia continued to read a novel aloud as we drank coffee and rolled on down the highway. Eastern Illinois showed us a beautiful sunny morning. The country driving passed leisurely. Then the novel moved into a pretty descriptive and torrid love scene. Our pulses quickened as Sandia invitingly read with emphasis. Then there appeared ahead an easy pull off spot. I guided the fine wine van to a stop in the shade of some big oak trees in the lush farm country.

We both ran around to the rear doors to climb in on top of the rear wine cases. Those big moving quilts softened the hard cases of cargo as we "christened" the wine, in a manner of speaking. Entwined in each other's arms, afterward, we spoke softly of our love for each other and the life we'd woven together. Never would we be rich in the monetary sense, but in spiritual zest for life, our "bank account" certainly runneth over with unending deposits of love.

Sandia didn't read for a while. The miles quietly passed under our rental wine van, while she slipped into a relaxed siesta and I into reflections on life. Indiana passed behind us, bringing the pavement of Ohio beneath our spinning wheels. A few hours later, toward early evening, road signs told us we'd reached Akron.

At John and Linda's house, in a gated community, we parked the fine wine van in their garage and began catching up on our lives, of course, over a bottle of wine. They laughed at our travel mission, remarking, "Only you two would find something like this to get involved in!"

We ate dinner, made brownies, a favorite of Linda's and mine, and talked into the wee hours about life and the choices we make. After two bottles of our wine, they uncorked one of theirs. We all remarked the difference, the fine bouquet of the Reserve Chardonnay. The talking blurred and sleep took over.

The following evening, I carried the cases of wine down into our friend's cellar in Connecticut. When the last case sat peacefully stacked into place, the count showed one hundred thirteen cases plus seven bottles. So we'd depleted only five bottles coming across the whole country, and that included the half-bottle we'd accidentally tipped over back in the Nevada motel! Our friends seemed very pleased with the results of our mission. After finishing all the interior door work, they slipped several bottles of the wine into our luggage and we flew back to Denver and our mountains. We heard years later, that the wine lasted them the better part of three years and their dinner guests always loved the wine, along with the stories that went with it.

the third aside

The Bare and the Bear

Living in the forest, beside the river, we had lots of encounters with the animal life of the mountains. There occurred the elk, deer, and moose on the shy side of things and then the predators and scavengers showed up also. The presence of our faithful wolf-shepherd Sunshine kept a lot of the easily spooked animal life at bay, but the odd predator sometimes would challenge her domain.

One morning, rising with the sun, I heard Sunshine's low growl of challenge from outside. I walked sleepily to our bedroom window and peered out into the dawning morning light. My eyes found Sunshine in a low crouch, with her back to La Casita, her teeth bared, growling a challenge at a nearby stand of lodgepole pines. My first thought was, "What are you growling at silly girl?" as I could not make out any movement amongst the timber. Maybe a porcupine waddled by some distance off. Ever since I pulled those quills from Sunshine's nose with pliers one morning, back when she still remained a pup, she steered clear of that animal species, but would growl her defiance when one got in the vicinity.

Then I saw movement, and then another,

sometime, when you live at one with nature

you might just meet, one of greater stature

amongst the trees. The animal coats looked yellowish and shaggy. The stealthy movement appeared definitely coming in Sunshine's direction. I saw more slow movement. More than one animal lurked in those trees. I squinted, trying to focus into the dim forest light, maybe sixty feet away.

Suddenly, I saw enough to know that several coyotes crept silently toward Sunshine and our house. What they wanted, I didn't know, but Sunshine clearly would be outnumbered. I bolted down the stairs, dressed only in shorts, and threw open the front door.

Sunshine stood her ground, never looking back toward me. Her low growl now sounded more like a snarl. My vision counted three mangy coyotes moving toward her, a leader in the middle, flanked by two others in the rear. Sunshine inched forward toward the leader. The coyotes stopped in their tracks, unsure now of the human interloper standing maybe thirty feet behind their adversary.

Almost as if my dog and I had mental telepathy, Sunshine lunged forward at the same instant I threw my arms in the air and shouted a guttural scream. The coyotes broke into a swift retreat

142

and in an instant their footfalls tearing through the forest came as the only sounds. Sunshine gave chase, but stopped and returned at my command. Her tail wagged and her eyes smiled as she wiggled up to me for stroking and acknowledgment that she had performed well. As I caressed her thick coat, I wondered how she would have fared if I had not been there. The coyotes bested her in individual size and in their number.

Sunshine, at peace with the nature of her domain

We'd never know, but her instincts to protect her domain proved unquestionable and I knew she would probably have died fighting those mangy scavengers. Who knows, maybe if she got the best of that leader, the others would have run off. At any rate, we knew she remained our faithful protector!

Years later, while Sunshine stayed at our friend's ranch, one fall evening, we had another predator encounter. The month was September and the nights felt cool for sleeping. Sandia and I hadn't been snuggled down under our comforter very long when we heard rummaging outside that sounded as if it came from the proximity of the humming bird feeder on the front deck. Even though mounted fairly high, over the deck rail, the red colored sugar water had probably attracted a skunk or maybe a raccoon. I flipped off the comforter from my uncluttered sleeping mode and headed down the stairs to shout away our intruder.

Opening our front door, I stepped naked out into the cool night air onto our front deck, squinting into the darkened area of the deck rail

where the humming bird feeder was located. All I saw was blackness, until a huge darkened form turned toward me with a low growl and yellow-white teeth, very evident in the star-lit darkness. My eyes were startled into instant awakened night vision. A black bear raised onto his hind paws right in front of me, maybe six feet away. He stood as tall as me and his growling made him seem even larger. My heart pounded as I realized I had him trapped in a corner by the deck rail. For an instant my bare feet seemed glued to the deck. What a rush!

Then he lunged toward me. My feet came unglued quickly and I beat feet back through the front door with a loud slam as I closed the door. Inside, knowing that the bear had an open escape, I thought I'd see the bear in retreat down the deck stairs and off toward the adjacent forest. Instead, as I stood at the window, staring out, he suddenly raised up in front of me, the claws of his front paws clicking against the glass of the window as he leaned against the double thermal pane. He growled again, moving his head from side to side, leaving vapor from his breath and saliva streaking the glass. I backed away slowly, not wanting to make any sudden movements to excite him further. Having made his show of male might, he dropped down again to all fours and ambled off the deck. As I stared out at his slowly retreating dark form, my hands started to shake. What ifs ran through my nervous brain, but that's all they were, "what ifs." I had cornered a black bear, in search of food to prepare for hibernation, and his instincts had been those of self-preservation. The stand at the window left his statement that he certainly stood mightier than any puny naked human, which he outweighed by a good hundred plus pounds. Go

with nature Mr. Black Bear. Have a good winter sleep. Good dreams. Tomorrow at dawn the humming bird feeder comes down!

As I started up the stairs to our bedroom, I heard Sandia's sleepy voice, "What was all that commotion down there? What was out there?"

Did I have a story to tell her! We would laugh later at the naked truth of it, as we snuggled into the safety of each other's arms, under the warmth of our down comforter. Visions of snarling teeth and clicking claws lasted far into the dark night until sleep finally came.

chapter twenty-five

The Road to New Guinea

Sandia, Kirsten, and I arrived in Las Cruces, New Mexico, early in December '84 and found a small furnished house to rent. Kirsten enrolled in the ninth grade at the nearest public school a few days later and almost immediately began days off for Christmas holidays. While Sandia set up housekeeping, I went right to work on designing the building that would house seven office/retail spaces of varying sizes. Several weeks of research in the library and city building department yielded enough data for me to draw up the construction plans. The building would be a standard forty-foot deep structure, with concrete block walls, topped with front-to-back clear-span steel-web trusses. Several similar buildings already existed around town. My drawings obtained building department approval after a local engineer certified their structural content with his special ink stamp. I also worked with a licensed General Contractor as a project consultant.

Again, I won't bore the reader with the gory construction details, but the project, for the most part, moved along smoothly. I set up a

leave the window of chance, slightly ajar

something could float through, a venture afar

spread sheet "tally" on all the costs—projected and the actual expenditures as we made them. In those days, an Apple IIe computer, along with the AppleWorks software did it all. We always knew exactly where our budget stood and could make quick decisions on alternatives, based on the tally sheet.

I hired a lot of Mexican laborers on the job and didn't always check their papers thoroughly. I really liked the way they worked and the fact that they never wanted to take coffee breaks. They also never complained about the hard or dirty jobs that I asked them do. Another benefit of the Mexican-American labor force turned out to be the improvement in my Spanish language capabilities. Workers like Angel, Baldo, Anacleto, and others taught me lots of vocabulary as we worked together every day. Lots of subcontractors that I hired also had Mexican-American crews. I never checked a "subbie's" worker's papers. That responsibility lay with the sub-contractor.

One day I worked in our little job office trailer when I heard a commotion outside. I

145

looked out the window to see several workers running in different directions with immigration people, "*migras,*" in hot pursuit. They rounded up five illegals that first raid on our job, four from the subcontractors and one of my guys. The immigration people made sure the five had received all pay due and owing them, after which they promptly put them in one of those light green vans for transport to the border, adjacent to Juarez. I noted the next morning at eight o'clock sharp, all four of the sub-contractor's il-legals showed up back on the job and even my guy, a real hard worker, showed up to work. It hurt me, but I had to send my guy away, while letting the subcontractors deal with their own workers.

The *migras* made their raids around town in a random fashion and one day timed a hit on a big bank construction job just as the ready mix trucks arrived with a huge number of cubic yards of wet concrete. Most of the laborers standing by to put the concrete into place were loaded into light green vans for transport to Juarez. The word coming out of the bank construction job a few days later told how much concrete had been wasted. I fully realized the immigration depart-ment had a legitimate job to accomplish, and for the most part, we co-operated. I did, however, on one of their raids of our job, have a run-in with an over zealous, and seemingly sadistic, agent, who appeared to love his work a little bit too much. His mightier-

than-thou attitude got to me. Statements of his like, "I ask them how many eggs are in a dozen! That always gets 'em!" The funniest part of his bragging conversation that day was while he focused on impressing me, I could see, behind him, an obvious illegal creep out of a hiding place in one of our job port-a-johns and run into the safety of the tall grass on the adjoining land. Almost laughing out loud, I cut off his superior type stories, asking if he was finished, did he mind if we got back to work.

We named the center, Mission Solano, a combination of its location on Solano Boulevard and the fact that the finished building looked like the replication of an old adobe mission. We installed phony protruding roof timbers to look like authentic rafters, or "*vigas,*" a bell tower, complete with iron bells from Mexico, hand carved wood entry doors with Sandia's stained glass installed in each, and a timber framed entry porch along two sides of the building. The porch was topped with authentic red clay roofing

The completed Mission Solano office center

tiles. When the light brown stucco-sided center neared completion, we used to walk across the boulevard to look at it. With your eyes squinted just right, the building looked like an old southwestern colonial mission.

Surrounding, and throughout, Las Cruces existed systems of irrigation ditches and dry riverbeds which are maintained for run-off purposes during flash flooding times. These made great running trails for those of us addicted to that pursuit. Sandia and I would awaken very early morning—the time depended on the number of miles we would run on that particular day—have a cup of coffee and head out the door to run those graveled ditches and riverbanks. It always amazed me after getting into running, well after getting past those starting agonies, how energized I felt the rest of the day. The sluggish days turned out to be the ones when I skipped a morning run for whatever reason.

Sandia and I, over a period of four months, each logged in about six hundred plus miles on those gravel pathways, building up for another Mile High Marathon. They actually changed the name of the race to the Mayor's Cup Marathon when Denver's mayor Frederico Peña got into running and organizing things. He ran at least three of the marathons himself; usually completing them in a very respectable three-hour fifteen-minute time frame. Anyway, we took a few days off from Mission Solano duties the first week in May and drove to Denver, ran the twenty-six mile race, and then drove the six or seven hundred miles back down to Las Cruces. Sandia's brother Bob couldn't understand why we didn't let him mark out a 26.2-mile course in the desert and just run it, without all the travel back and forth to Denver. Only another runner would understand all the driving to run an organized race with all the hoopla emanating from the crowds of spectators, urging you on to a better finish,

versus the solitude of the lonely desert.

After the marathon, while Sandia and I finished up the last details of Mission Solano, I had the strongest urge or "calling" to go see my mom in Massachusetts. I knew we needed to get on up to the Colorado Mountains to work on *La Casita*, but it could certainly wait a few weeks longer. I hadn't seen my mom in a while and really felt strongly that this needed to be the time. We have to set our own priorities in life; there will consistently be the day to day stuff to keep our tails wagging.

With our old blue Dodge van on its last legs, we decided to use the "drive-away" method to get to Massachusetts. Drive away services are located around the country and deal in moving cars and trucks from city to city. They frequently need drivers. The vehicles involved are usually new cars, belonging to people wealthy enough to pay a service to move them. The service checked all of our references, etc., to make sure we demonstrated responsibility. Then the process became a matter of which cars they needed driven from El Paso to New York City or Boston. The cars and destinations change daily at the drive-away companies, but we found one to the Connecticut Shore from El Paso and posted the necessary bond.

We happen to enjoy driving cross-country. You can take roads other than the interstates, see lots of sights, talk, listen to music, read newspapers, and not have anyone calling you (unless you happen to carry a cell phone). To us, it seemed literally, a time to get away from the routines of life.

The car needed to be turned in at a Connecticut Shore town. From there, we caught a bus to the nearby town of Essex to see our friends, Marti and Jack, and play some tennis on their private court before heading north to Massachusetts. Sandia and I figured on using the bus lines to get to my mom's place, a little south of Boston, but Jack and Marti wouldn't hear of it. Jack told me, "We have an extra Mercedes in the garage. Take it and use it!" He wasn't kidding. They had a small 450SL convertible, a medium sized, and a full sized Mercedes with cushy leather seats, in their big garage.

I ended up reluctantly agreeing; a little scared to get any scratches on the car, and Jack insisted we take the big car as it was the most comfortable on a long drive. Promising to bring back fresh lobsters from the South Shore of Massachusetts, where my mom lived, for a big dinner party, we rolled out of Jack and Marti's driveway in that big Mercedes Benz.

Always a poor boy at heart, it took a while to not feel conspicuous in that luxury car. Jack proved correct about the comfort. It was awesome. That car traveled so smoothly, even on a bumpy road. The Benz did just about everything for you, except drive on autopilot. It did have cruise control, which felt nice on the highway.

When my Mom came to the door of her house on Wollaston Beach (twenty miles south of Boston), I had to first explain to her that the car wasn't ours, but belonged to some very sharing friends of ours. She didn't care. She was happy to see us. It had been a while.

For the next three or four days, I played chauffeur, taking my mom, along with Sandia in the co-pilot's seat, to each and every place Mom wanted to visit. Mom sat in the big comfortable leather back seat and I would ask her, "Where to next, Mom?"

We ordered fried clams at the old Clambox restaurant, right on the beach, then sat on the seawall eating them, while the tide came in. After that we drove south along the shore to visit my younger sister in Hull (Nantasket Beach) for an afternoon. We even visited the bar where my dad used to have a "snort" with friends on his way

home from work some nights. My older brother Roy met us for breakfast one of those mornings right across from our old high school—North Quincy High School. Sandia couldn't miss the photo opportunity and snapped a picture of Roy, Mom, and I with the high school in the background.

All in all, we put together a super visit with Mom. My nephew Mark fixed us up with a full crate of fresh lobsters from his contacts down Hull way. I remember feeling so good about it as we headed south to Connecticut, remarking to Sandia that I wished we lived closer so we could see my mom more often, but not wanting to give up our mountains at the same time.

After the big lobster dinner party in Essex, we found another drive-away car that needed to be delivered to Dallas, Texas. In Dallas, we subsequently found another car that needed to get to El Paso. From there, we hitchhiked to Las Cruces.

The old blue van was almost loaded with our stuff for the trip north to the mountains, when the telephone call came from my daughter, Lynne. My mom had died only a few days after we left her to head back. Something about her blood pressure medicine's dosage and a stroke. I was struck numb. I was in shock. I could still see her smiling and hear her laughter from only a few days before.

Sandia made flight arrangements for me and within hours, I headed back to my mom's again—this time to help my sisters and brother bury her. On the flight, I tried to pull together the pieces of my heart. Mom stood as my symbol of the centerpiece of our family. Her spirit, her humanness, her oil painting expressions, but mostly the love and pride she had for her children, grandchildren and great grandchildren, showed in her day to day life. My suddenly orphaned state-of-mind tried to dwell on the fact that we'd been lucky to have such a devoted mom for as long as we did, and not on the fact that we just lost her. That single thought became my mainstay. I would try and share that blessing with my sisters and brother.

We buried Mom next to my dad and after hugs and farewells, while still filled with disbelief, I headed back to Las Cruces to gather up Sandia and Kirsten. I longed for the solitude and sanctuary of the mountains—the quiet forest and the sound of the Colorado River flowing past. I felt grateful and gifted to have had those last five days with Mom before she died. I could see her face so clearly from that last visit. The vision went with me up into our mountain retreat. One has to go with the leadings of the heart. If we don't chart our own course in life, we're just blowing along through the different storms that always occur. Keep your hand on the rudder and your eyes on the map. Break the routines. Discover a new port. Feel the wind on your face! Go with your leanings.

Sandia and I struggled that summer as the mountain economy reflected the general downturn in the Colorado business outlook. The old "overbuilding" phenomenon hit the mountain resort areas. The word around the village spread that builders couldn't give away condos they started earlier in the better times. Unsold units glutted the mountain market. Lending institutions wouldn't finance any more Colorado Mountain development. Sandia waited tables for dwindling tips while I worked

La Casita looking from the east

A completed La Casita facing solar south

on *La Casita* along with odd jobs. We perpetually had food, however, fresh trout from the river and elk meat from the freezer. By keeping our overheads low, we never panicked. Lots of people headed out of the mountains late summer of '85 in search of work. I got in several cords of wood and we battened down for the winter. Cross-country skiing would soon enough be the exercise of choice.

That winter ('85 - '86) our well silted up and our water stopped. Our local well driller said it would be no big deal to fix, but he couldn't get into it until late spring. If you've ever lived without water, you know what a drag it is. We didn't quit the homestead though. We carried in drinking water and drew river water for non-drinking chores. My early morning routine, after stoking up the woodstove, turned into trudging through the snow down to the river, which became thick with ice and topped with several feet of snow. At one spot over the river, we cut a circular staircase into the snow and ice leading down to a black hole at the bottom about two feet in diameter. I would then grab a heavy wood splitting mallet, that we left down there, to break through the new ice that had formed since the last water quest. Then I would fill two five- gallon pails about two thirds full and start up the ice stairs, then the hill up to *La Casita*. Kirsten would heat up her bathing water on the wood stove and just let it go down the bathtub drain as the septic and leach field worked fine. A flush bucket of river water sat next to the toilet. In spite of adverse conditions, Kirsten consistently headed off to school looking clean and tidy.

A revealing thing happened in late spring. We had one of those heavy wet snowstorms that toppled trees which took out power lines, leav-

An interior view of La Casita

ing our community without power for about five days. Most kids that showed up at school appeared totally out of sorts, looking really disheveled, unable to handle life without our modern conveniences. They started asking Kirsten how she continued to look so clean and tidy throughout that stretch of time. When she told them we'd been living without running water for most of the winter, she said

Sandia's stained glass

they seemed kind of "freaked out!" We do take so many things for granted in this magnificent country of ours!

While I'm on the subject, my son Gary would later relate another story to me. Seems he went on a two-week, military survival-training mission, with a dozen others, in the Florida Everglades. None of them had eaten anything substantial for days, living on tree bark and grasses. Gary trapped and caught a sizable ant-eater with his hands and his wit. He proceeded to field dress it, section it up, and cook it over an open campfire. As the other enlisted guys gobbled up their shared good fortune, the officer in charge asked him where he learned his survival skills. Gary told him about his life in the mountains with us, which included elk hunting, field dressing, and cooking. Gary had also learned how to survive in the winter by building snow caves. He spent the night in one as part of the regular mountain high school program. I think that turned out to be the time he and his buddy got caught tunneling into the high school girl's snow cave! Ah, the lessons of life.

Sandia and I ran another Mayor's Cup Marathon in the spring of '86 and went on to enjoy another summer, fall, and winter despite a continuing bleak local economy.

La Casa had changed hands back while we worked in Las Cruces and the new owners, an Australian man with an American lady friend, had asked me to build them an addition, carrying out the timber framed theme of the original house. When Jim Wright first told me he wanted an addition to *La Casa* so he could build an airplane, I thought he meant a model airplane, figuring it to be a hobby of his. Turned out though, he intended to build a real airplane—one he could fly eastward, to end up in the South Pacific islands, where he owned and operated businesses.

I think I may have rolled my eyes skyward as he briefly described his flying plan. This Australian looked like my kind of person, certainly not cut and sewed up from any ordinary kind of cloth!

I jotted down the working dimensions Jim would need and headed for my drawing board. After a few days of intense planning, drawing, and compilations of material estimates, I returned to *La Casa* to give him the sketches, along with a firm price bid to do the work. After some consideration with a few additions to the design, Jim accepted my bid and asked me how soon I could start the work.

I didn't have any problem putting together a small hard working crew as most guys in the mountains needed work in 1986. I hired my good friend Hal Simmons as my number one hand, along with a couple more laborers. Dick subcontracted the concrete foundation work and Bobbie Busse, from the ranch, did the excavation. I put in a timber order to the roughsawn mill in nearby Granby and, not being busy, they started right away on the required timbers.

It provided good steady work, while we had fun at that job. Jim proved a great owner and didn't try and push us to an unrealistic completion date. In fact, he took off for the South Pacific to oversee his business interests. He didn't come back for about three months. Jim mailed us regular progress payments in his absence. When he returned, we just about had the job wrapped up. There ended up about nine hundred plus square feet of useful shop space including a storage loft above, and a three-zone heated concrete slab floor. Nothing better than warm feet when you work on a concrete floor in the wintertime! The structure included two automatic garage doors—one oversized—so the space could also serve to park cars when airplane building was not in progress.

Jim and Mary Ann, his American lady friend,

liked the workmanship on the addition and gave me more work during the following winter ('86 - '87) to go along with the other work we had contracted. Life held a spirited quality, even in the lean times, if you worked hard at it.

We got a kick out of Mary Ann's story of how she met Jim on the South Pacific Island of Papua New Guinea. She had worked for Sears Roebuck in some capacity with fabrics and domestics on a high numbered floor of the Sear's Tower in downtown Chicago. One work day, totally fed up with the mediocrity of her life, she gathered up all the papers on her desk, throwing them into the air as she uttered, "I quit!"

Her friend, Connie, at the next desk, looked over in amazement saying something like, "But what will you do?"

Mary Ann looked at the ceiling, while answering her friend, "I'm going to take a trip around the world!"

Connie reflected only a moment, gathered up all the papers on her own desk and stood to heave them upward as she exclaimed, "And I'm going with you!"

They walked out of that office, and immediately thereafter, made plans for their trip. They left some startled, bewildered, and, perhaps, envious office staff behind them. Mary Ann, or M. A., as we came to call her, obviously had some "moxie" to break away from the routine in that fashion.

Starting their trip westward, New Guinea made only about their third stop after California and Hawaii. In the small mountain town of Mt. Hagen, located in the Western Highlands Province of Papua New Guinea, M. A. met Jim Wright, an Australian businessman. She didn't continue her trip any further. Connie, I believe, went on without her after a few months.

Jim came to New Guinea in the Australian colonial days as an army civil engineer, a gradu-

ate of Australia's Duntroon, similar to our West Point. He headed up an army contingent that built the bridges of the Highlands Highway, the one road into the rugged New Guinea Mountains from the coastal port city of Lae, on the Huon Gulf. Later on, after fourteen years in the military, Jim decided to give up his army career, along with his pension benefits to "go it on his own" in New Guinea. He had established a thriving saw mill, lumber, and hardware business in Mt. Hagen by the time tourist M. A. rolled into town. Jim, previously divorced, had two grown sons, Garth and Rohan, in those New Guinea Mountains with him. Both sons worked in their dad's business in varying capacities. Jim's daughter, Anneleis, had gone south to Australia, with her "mum." Another daughter, Karen, had died in those mountains at the young age of seven years after being run over by some sort of construction vehicle. Mary Ann, also divorced, found a kindred spirit in those mountains of New Guinea, before her trip around the world hardly even started. I guess it became a match put together in the heavens of the South Pacific Island Gods. Beautiful blonde American lady tourist meets handsome Australian pilot/businessman in the remote mountains of New Guinea—what an out of the ordinary story about two non-conforming people—our kind of people!

Of course, we didn't know all of Jim and M.A.'s circumstances and history back in '86 and '87, only a few shared stories then. I ran the Mayor's Cup Marathon the first weekend of May '87, with Sandia opting for the half-marathon alternative, doing my personal best under miserable, cold, wet, weather conditions. The week following, I had finished up a chimney repair job at *La Casa*, suggesting to M. A. that they use their homeowner's insurance to cover the cost of the repair work. I remember Jim was getting ready to once again head for Papua New Guinea the following week. Right in the middle of our "wrap up" job conversation, Mary Ann looked at me and said, "You wouldn't consider going to New Guinea to run our construction business there, would you?"

I think I just grunted or gasped, sort of, in response, as it seemed a startling question, catching me unexpectedly.

"No, I didn't think so," she said in response to my uttered gasp.

"No, no," I quickly answered. "I just want to talk it over with my lady. I'll be back in the morning to give you a firm answer. Thanks for asking me!"

I left *La Casa* excitedly driving immediately to the restaurant at Soda Springs Ranch, a condominium development on the shores of Lake Granby, where Sandia worked. She brought me a cup of coffee as I tried to be nonchalant asking her, "How do you feel about going to the mountains of New Guinea to work for a few years?"

Sandia looked me right in the eye, reflected only an instant, and answered, "It sounds great to me. Is it really true?"

I told her what facts I knew, which were few, and headed off to do another job I had promised. Sandia and I talked late that night about the excitement of the opportunity. We looked up New Guinea in our rather sparse library, but found a few additional facts, like it is the second biggest island in the world, after Greenland, and had mountains that rose more than fourteen thousand feet above sea level. Sandia finally fell asleep while I laid awake the rest of the night with blurred visions of tropical mountain rainforests and native villages going round and round in my head. I never slept a wink the rest of the night and when I finally couldn't stand the excitement of it alone anymore, I woke Sandia with a cup of hot coffee asking her, "How do you

feel about New Guinea after a night's sleep?"

She sipped her coffee sleepily and answered me, "Now I'm afraid we won't be able to go!" Mirroring my own feelings, the opportunity seemed too exciting to let pass by, but, at the same time, what if it turned out to be a false hope? I wolfed down my breakfast and headed over to tell Jim and M. A. that we would definitely go to Papua New Guinea, if the job remained open. I told him the truth that I had not slept at all, thinking about the offer.

Jim related to me that his General Manager, Lindsay, had called during the night and amongst other business details they had discussed, Lindsay thought he already had someone to replace their "sacked" building manager. Jim headed to New Guinea, or P.N.G. as it was referred to, a few days hence to check things out himself, while promising to get back to me as soon as he assessed the situation. So Sandia and I began to walk around with our fingers crossed, so to speak, for quite a few weeks. I kept busy with big timber framed signs I contracted to build for the town of Grand Lake. My hammer beam truss design, taken on a smaller scale from London's Parliament House, won a defacto design contest to do the signs. The work kept me busy, chiseling the wooden joints to fit together. The sign/marquees would stand twenty-eight feet tall and about eighteen feet wide with only oak dowels and wood joints to hold all the timbers together.

I worked, totally engrossed in chiseling a wood sign joint to fit, one night in the middle of June, when Sandia called to me that the phone was ringing and could I get to it. I picked it up, a little out of breath from my run into the house, to hear Jim's distant voice say, "G'day Bill. How are you doing?" He then asked right away if I still had an interest in the job, and if so, how soon could I be ready to come over?

153

"Yes to the interest part and for the other question, it will take me about eight weeks to finish my last contracted sign!"

"Good on you," he remarked. "It'll take close to eight weeks to get you cleared for a work permit through the New Guinea Embassy in Washington, D.C., anyway. I'll mail you an information packet with visa application forms right away. Get your passport started. Keep a record of any expenses. I need you as soon as possible!"

When I hung the phone back in its cradle, Sandia stood there, staring at me, waiting for details. I jumped high with excitement.

"We're going to the mountains of New Guinea! It's a go for eight weeks!"

Sandia wouldn't be able to go with me right away as Kirsten had one last semester to complete in order to receive her high school diploma by January '88. Then Sandia would fly to join me in those so far away mountains, just south of the equator, half way around the world. Some of our friends thought we'd always been a bit loony and this decision just served to demonstrate the fact even further. Others seemed indifferent, with a very few, envious. Sandia and I knew it would prove right for us. Life is to live, touch, learn, explore, and discover, even if it's a little scary when you first step out into a new and unknown place.

All my life, to that point, had been an "apprenticeship" for this new encounter. Life goes by so fast! You have to decide what's important, what you want to do, and be about doing it!

Timber framed entry sign

154

PART II
Papua New Guinea

Papua New Guinea

Islands, where mountains rise out of the sea
Where birds of brilliant hues, fly tree to tree
In lush green jungles that run down to the beach
Where sounds rise from villages, with childlike glee,
Laughter as light as white clouds, to the heavens reach.

Centers of life, in the village are found
Women, children, and pigs moving around
Men always planning, while women toil
In gardens, where fruit and sweet yams abound
No hunger occurs, in this land of prolific soil.

Islands, where pigs are not, just a source of meat
Taste of its flesh, only the final treat
Ritual first, then the feast, on this animal species
Which yields the aboriginal life complete
These converters of waste and human feces.

The young swine are stroked and petted from birth
The more value it has, the greater its girth
Bride price is even paid in pigs, for taking a wife
Payment in pigs can change dispute to mirth
The swine, in short, can buy anything in life.

Islands, where volcanoes belch to the skies
Towns buried in dust, before they realize.
Expatriates work beside the turquoise sea
Missionaries, who toil to proselytize,
And mercenaries, and misfits like me.

Islands, where numbers seem ever to expand
Three plus years, I worked there; it was never bland
Copper and gold mining, now oil drilling rigs
Suck up the riches, from this primitive land,
While a "big" man's wealth is still measured in pigs!

photos by Laurel (Appleton) Luebkeman

chapter twenty-six

The Journey

From my window seat, I gazed down at those rugged peaks of our Colorado Rocky Mountains. Even in the middle of August, the "perma-snow" on the high peaks seemed to reflect the bright Colorado sunshine right up to my aircraft. My mind buzzed with a myriad of thoughts. I shuddered as yet another vibration of my parting embrace with Sandia coursed through my body. The flight attendant's voice still sounded in my head— telling me that I had to get on board—they needed to shut the jetway door! One last squeeze and I headed onto the waiting aircraft, pausing at the plane's hatchway for one last urgent look back at my lady. She stood there, trying to smile, still waving, with the moisture of tears so evident on her cheeks. Throwing her one last kiss, I turned to step aboard. Now, I sat looking down at those magnificent mountains, amongst which we had shared the pursuit of so many dreams together. I knew in my mind, the heartsick loss of my lovely lady would only be balanced by the ecstatic gain of her when she, in six months time, would walk off an aircraft in Papua New Guinea into my waiting and aching arms.

on wings of steel, clouds below, long hours flown,

screech of wheels, touching down in land unknown

Often, while at work down there, amongst the distinctly scented pine, aspen, and spruce trees, with the sound of our peaceful flowing river in my ears, I would gaze skyward at a distant vapor trail to wonder about the travelers, their lives, and where they might be going. What dreams did they have or were they just in lockstep, existing in a manner so accepted by today's society—going through it in a way their parents or others said was the best way? Then it occurred to me that I'd now become a vapor trail, heading west to the South Pacific, with a mind and spirit filled with anticipation and excitement. I was lead scout! Sandia would join me in approximately six months. The separation would pay the price we had to pledge for the opportunity. I wondered if anyone gazed up at my vapor trail with a longing for adventure. At that, I started to scribble dreamily in my journal as those mountains fell behind.

My son Gary, on military leave, had come to the airport in Denver to see me off, as had Kirsten, and my grandson Edward, who spent his third summer vacation with us. All of their faces were in my mind. Gary had assured me that

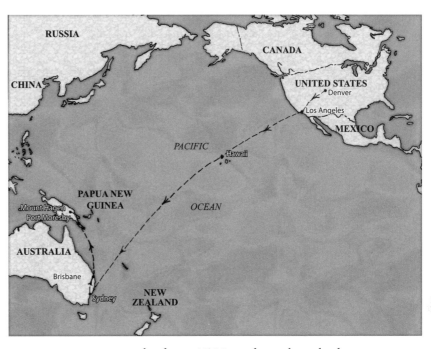

he had enough "leave" time left to help Sandia close up *La Casita* for a several year hiatus, or hibernation, while we would be gone. Then Sandia and Kirsten would head down the mountains to stay at her mom's house in Denver while Kirsten finished her last semester of high school. Gary, in turn, would take Edward back to his home in Connecticut before reporting to his next duty station. He had just finished several years stationed out of Guam with a Naval Patrol Squadron. Gary seemed anxious for some stateside duty along with some of the creature comforts it would bring him, not the least of which included dating U.S.A. women, for a change. There had been so many details to finish before leaving; I didn't get to all of them. I knew Gary and Sandia would handle them fine!

Beside all the requirements for passports, medical examinations, and work permit bureaucracy, I managed to fit in some time before leaving to complete a short language course in the neo-melanasian, or New Guinea pidgin, tongue. It is a remarkable language, born out of the necessity of native islanders to communicate when they were thrown together in plantation environments, each bringing a different native tongue. History refers to that colonial period as the time of "blackbirding"—when different islands were sourced for native labor forces needed to work the big sugar plantations of the region. This common South Pacific pidgin has a bit of German, Dutch, and a lot of English mixed into it. It basically reflects the language and dialects of the plantation bosses, or "masters." There are only about 1500 total words and takes a person maybe three or four months to become proficient in its use—if you work at it. I listened to the tapes Jim sent me for a few weeks and could only get along at a very basic level. I could say simple sentences such as, *"Mi gat wonpela pikinini man na fivpela pikinini meri"*— I have one son and five daughters. Later, I would learn to put a whole bunch of words together to say, for example "piano"—*"emi bikpela bokis, emi gat teet, yu paitim, na emi kri!"* This literally means it is a big box, with teeth, and when you pound on them, it makes sounds. I never would learn the words for violin, but I understand it takes the better part of a full page to write it down. What a fun language!

My limited encyclopedic research had told me that half the languages of the world were spoken in Papua New Guinea, with over 700 separate and distinct languages being spoken there. Each remote village and its surrounding people had through the centuries developed their own spoken, but non-written, language. Now as a result of the colonial period, the Territory of New Guinea, the northeastern one-quarter of the country had adopted pidgin as a common language. The southeastern quarter of the island, formerly the Australian colony of Papua spoke a police "motu" as a common language. Upon independence, mandated by the United Nations, in 1975, the two colonial territories became the independent commonwealth nation of Papua New Guinea. The only accepted languages in parliament were motu, pidgin, or English. To be a politician, you had to be fluent in one of these three tongues. Me, I just wanted to find a good history book on P.N.G. to learn what I could of its maybe 40,000 years of habitation.

Our friend Linnea met me at the Los Angeles International Airport. We had time for only one cold Michelob before the departure of my Qantas flight for Sydney, Australia, by way of Hawaii. I passed through the airport in Honolulu with impressions of solicitors wooing vacationers and flower necklaces being hung around arriving passengers' necks. The smell of flowers filled the warm, moisture-laden air. Hoping that my duffel bags followed me, I boarded my flight for Sydney. Then someplace over the South Pacific, when my body itched for a long exercise run, a magical thing happened. At the end of an Australian news segment on the in-flight movie screen, they showed a clip from Elton John's recently concluded Australian tour. He sang one song in the clip, "Your Song"—our song, Sandia's and mine! It was the first song to which we danced together and it became our song. What a message! As the piano notes played the melody and his voice crooned out our love song, the tears cascaded down my cheeks. I didn't give a hoot what my fellow travelers thought, I just let the tears and deep breaths come, as the joy and happiness of our relationship welled up into my chest to overflow through my tear ducts. Thank you Elton for our song. Thank you,

Maker of the Universe for letting me know the profound and true love of my soulmate!

Sydney consisted of a blur as I headed north again for a plane change in Brisbane, in the State of Queensland, Australia. The long hours of travel and catnaps caught up to me. I had entered the world of the comatose "jetlag." Brisbane came and went with nothing more than a late departure. My planned two-hour customs clearance time in the coastal capital city of Port Moresby, P.N.G. would be down to less than one hour in order to make my Air Niugini flight up into the mountains. Not to worry! Nothing I could do. No sense in getting stressed out over it. Something would work out.

As we flew toward the Coral Sea, the ocean appeared such a rich blue-green, in stark contrast to the white of so many coral reefs I saw east and north of Queensland. The ocean seemed so tranquil from the plane's high elevation. A few other passengers were also heading for P.N.G and Mt. Hagen to witness a huge annual festival, or *"sing-sing,"* of the mountain tribal people. Jim had told me the *sing-sing* would be my baptism, but I didn't know what he meant by it.

The descent into Port Moresby, Papua New Guinea started. Flight attendants began spraying the cabin with a sweet smelling non-toxic chemical. I guess it was intended to kill our foreign, or expatriate, germs before we could enter the country.

After landing, I found my two big duffel bags, cleared customs/immigration, and made my Air Niugini flight with an extra payment of $52 U.S. for overweight luggage, all in the 55 minutes that remained between flights. I settled back into my seat trying to accurately tally the thirty plus hours and one international date change of my trip to that point. As I looked around the cabin, I realized, with the exception

of the one expatriate couple heading for the Hagen Show, my "white" skin appeared in a definite minority to the dark skin around me. Then my native, or as they prefer to be called, national seatmate struck up a conversation with me in English.

His name was Paul Morris. He worked for the Department of Forestry in Mount Hagen. Paul looked young, but full bearded—a mark of the highlanders' manliness, or maybe machismo, as we call it. Paul's conversation and questions indicated to me that he was a very educated person. I couldn't resist laying a little bit of my newly acquired pidgin on him after which he seemed genuinely happy that I tried to learn the language. He said most expats preferred to speak English, expecting the nationals they worked with to learn it also. Paul corrected some of my pronunciations and added a few words to my vo-

cabulary. When I mentioned tennis, he responded that he played also as a member of the Hagen Tennis Club and that we should play sometime in the future. Paul then pointed out the window to tell me Hagen lay just ahead.

I focused on the terrain outside my window as we began to descend from a climb over a pretty high mountain range. My reading told me those mountains in Papua New Guinea reached heights in excess of fourteen thousand feet. The mountains I looked down upon seemed rugged, but unlike my Rockies. They looked steep with deep canyons and ravines, but covered with lush green trees and other growth. Many of the ravines had a river or creek flowing in their bottoms and I saw several spectacular waterfalls cascading down the mountainsides. Absent were the huge outcroppings of rocks, which so distinguished my home mountains. I did see some formations that appeared to be limestone as they reflected a chalky white color, so outstanding against the rich green tropical background. A quick glance at the P.N.G. map in the seat pocket booklet showed me that we were six degrees below the equator, in the Southern Hemisphere. We then dropped into an expansive green fertile valley, which stood in marked contrast to the hot, brown, and dry area we left behind in the Port Moresby countryside. Paul leaned over to explain this was the Wahgi Valley with the Wahgi River the main water flow that fed and nourished the vast agricultural effort so visible below. About two-thirds of the valley was filled with cleared rectangular farming plots. The rest looked to be a mix of forest and a few industrial metal buildings, with occasional clusters of grass roofed houses marking the different village locations. Many large tea and coffee plantations were visible from our low flying aircraft. Paul explained to me that most people used to live in the hills and slopes above a swampy valley floor. In more recent times they had drained the swamps to recover a very fertile agricultural area. Expatriate engineers furnished a lot of the expertise that went into the swamp drainage.

I noted at least a dozen, isolated fires that belched smoke into the valley sky. Paul answered my query saying the smoke probably originated from villagers burning the debris and residue from the clearing of land. Later I would learn that the nationals just like to light fires, sometimes for heat; for even in the tropical highlands, they felt cold.

As we circled Kagamuga Airport in Mt. Hagen for a landing, Paul Morris said a curious thing to me. It was roughly, "You probably won't remember me!" At first I thought it seemed odd, or maybe some other expatriate had forgotten his acquaintance in the past. Or maybe he was telling me a tale of "we will all look alike to you."

I reflected on it for a moment and then left it alone, too tired and excited at the same time, to ponder it another day. The funny thing is, Paul turned out to be prophetic in that two months after I arrived, at the Hagen Tennis Club, he walked up to remind me we'd met, much to my embarrassment, as I clearly remembered his statement, even noting it in my journal entries. Later on, I would learn to tell what part of the country a person originated from just by seeing distinctive facial and body features, and I always remembered my friend Paul after our second meeting!

It was late afternoon. Our plane made the last flight into Kagamuga for the day. I easily recognized Jim standing in the small crowded reception area of the airport. There were mobs of nationals, making the few light-skinned expats easy to distinguish. My very tired brain did notice the sights, sounds, and smells around me. The peoples clothing was so filled with bright colors, predominantly reds, and the different languages blended into a rapid-fire machine gun like speaking level. The air carried a distinctive people smell—not overly offensive, but strong, pungent, and different from any previous experience. My eyes worked like a photographer's rapid triggering of a shutter to take in all the unique happenings around me. I saw lots of smiles and heard plenty of laughter. A reoccurring "*ayiii*" also rang in my ears.

Jim came through the crowd to meet me, with another expat tagging along. "Welcome to New Guinea," Jim greeted me as he grasped my hand. He introduced me to Craig Dobkin, a United Nations Volunteer from the U.S.A. Craig was a "*wontok*" of mine in their language, or a countryman in ours. We spoke the same language (one talk). A village language was called *plestok*, and if two nationals shared the same *plestok*, they were *wontoks*.

Anyway, Jim had told Craig I was a runner, and Craig came to ask if I might help organize some Hagen foot races in the future. He worked as the national sports organizer in the Mt. Hagen area. I told him I would certainly enjoy helping with the races and we said our goodbye while Jim instructed a couple of his national workers to carry my luggage to his waiting truck.

In the forced guise of a jet lagged zombie, I put my stuff away in a temporary bedroom at Jim's flat smack in the middle of his construction, lumber, and hardware business. I felt sleepy, but I wasn't at the same time. Everything was so new and came at me in such a rush, shaking hands with workers and trying to remember their names. Jim toured me through the domain that he had built up over the past twenty years. He showed me what would be my office at the construction yard. He said I would see the house, in which I'd live, by the native outdoor market, in a few days. First we had to get ready for the Hagen Show, or the so-called, Hagen *sing-sing*. It started in about 36 hours! My baptism would start the morning after—what an excited mental overload consumed my tired brain!

chapter twenty-seven

The Hagen Sing-Sing

My eyes drank in the scene in front of me. I stood on the small verandah of a pre-fabricated model display house my company had spent the better part of a month erecting. Early morning brightened the mobs of people that moved about the showgrounds around me. Most of the crowd consisted of nationals dressed in the western style of trousers and T-shirts. Footwear varied from nothing at all to cheap foam soled sandals with a single toe thong. The sandals made a distinctive "flip - flop" sound from which they derived their name. Mixed in with the men's western style dress was the traditional native wear consisting of a wide bark waist belt from which hung "*arse*" grass in the back and a short *lap-lap* (cloth) cover in the front. This skirt-like arrangement usually was worn without footwear or shirt. The men in traditional tribal costume wore varying types of headgear, usually consisting of large colorful bird feathers and sometimes only a large bright flower behind the ear. The women in traditional wear mostly wore a brightly colored wrap around *lap-lap* skirt, kind of like a sarong. Nothing was worn above the waist except various types of what ap-

body paint, colors bold, on skin of brown

beat of drums, dancing feet, shouts all around

peared to be seashell neck-laces. Down most of their backs hung very colorfully designed *bilums*, or hand woven string bags, filled with different items, which even included babies. These bags were supported using a wide top band around the head, mainly the forehead. The erect posture the national women exhibited struck me immediately. Maybe carrying loads in those head-supported *bilums* since childhood did the trick. There didn't appear to be a slouchy female posture in view, except the odd expat, or female tourist.

A few hundred meters in front of the model house stood an arena and staging area where it seemed many groups of nationals, in unique traditional dress, gathered. Some groups danced in a jumping up and down sort of way keeping time to drumbeats and a rhythmic chanting that almost sounded like birds squawking.

All the sights, sounds, and smells permeated my tired, but alert and excited morning senses. I took another swig from my cup of instant coffee and thought about the rush since arriving. The entire day and night before had been spent putting together brochures explaining the virtues of

164

Hailans Homes Kit House at the Hagen Sing Sing

the pre-fabricated house I manned for this weekend *sing-sing*. The idea was to get some interest and house orders, if possible. The pre-fabricated, or kit house, idea originated in Australia. The concept consisted of bolting together pre-built wall panels in a specific sequence, nailing pre-cut roof rafters into place over the wall panels, fastening on corrugated iron roofing sheets, and finally fixing pre-constructed window and door units into their respective locations. These houses were small by our western standards. The average two-bedroom kit house in P.N.G. measured a bit less than 350 square feet. A nominal two-bedroom in the U.S.A. is about 1500 square feet. The entire kit house package, including the treated wood foundation posts, could be delivered on the flatbed of one large four-ton truck. Smaller houses fill the requirements in the tropics where most living takes place outdoors.

As I wrote up the house sales information the day before, I needed to do a rapid review of my metric system. Everything in Papua New Guinea was measured and built using meters, millimeters, and kilograms. Gasoline, or petrol as it was

called, sold by the liter. All my science background made it easier to make the mental transition. The hardest units for me to master would be in figuring timber beam loadings. Pounds per square inch (psi) had to be converted to megapascals, or millions of newtons per square meter. I'd deal with that later, when I found myself absolutely forced into it!

The metric system consisted of only numbers and conversion factors. I could learn that a sheet of plywood measured 1220 by 2440 millimeters without causing myself any bodily harm. The more difficult lesson I needed to learn proved to be driving on the "wrong" side of the road. My first full day in the country I made a driving run to the airport to drop Jim at his Cessna aircraft. He drove on the way out, and when he boarded his airplane, I was left on my own to get back to town. *Ayiii*, the baptism of new culture! Driving on the left side of the road and floor shifting with the left hand seemed so backwards. I told myself, *"The steering wheel is on the right side of the truck (looking forward), so just keep it next to the center line of the road at all times, never driving with it next to the ditch!"* I did great on the straight stretch back to Mt. Hagen, but while turning through the first intersection in town, my impulses led me astray. Luckily for me, there wasn't very much traffic and I pulled back to the "right" side-the left side! It would definitely take some getting used to. Jim laughingly had told me to put the truck in the ditch if an emergency bailout became necessary! Of course when I approached the truck to drive the second time I started to get in on the wrong side-the passenger side. Oh well, it would come to me; then I'd go back to the U.S. and have to do it the other way around. Why were the Brits so contrary—or could it be us?

After two exhausted nights of sleep, my "jet lag" didn't seem as bad. Maybe it lay in the anticipation, followed by the excitement of this new and so different country that kept me from feeling fatigued. Later trips would teach me that traveling with the sun (westward) seemed a whole lot easier than traveling against the sun (eastward)!

I was suddenly snapped out of my reflective trance by an Australian voice asking, "Do you have any information and prices on these kit houses that I can carry away with me?"

It turned out to be an Australian medical doctor who did volunteer work at one of the fledgling Highlands hospitals up the Baiyer River Valley. "You bet," came my reply as I jumped inside to my neatly stacked pile of handouts and turned to hand him one. He flipped through the few pages quickly and asked the price of the two-bedroom model we stood in. I told him the price in *kina*, the P.N.G. currency, and then followed him as he looked throughout the house. The doctor told me they were thinking of housing some of their senior national staff. This type of house might work out very well. They needed to submit a budget request for Australian funding and that could take a few months. For my part, I found myself happy to have a first inquiry. You can't sell something without first having someone express an interest.

I went on to ask about his impressions of the country and his work, but he seemed in a bit of a hurry saying he had to return to the hospital for duty. Seems they had a problem keeping the volunteer Australian contingent happy with the conditions and were currently short handed. Then as he left the verandah, the doctor turned and asked, "What brings an American to these New Guinea Mountains selling kit houses?"

I briefly told him about the mechanics of it, but the spirit part lay in the adventure, exploration, and discovery that really brought me there. The same question would be asked of me many times in the future.

The good doctor left me with one last thought as he ambled off. "You know there's a saying in New Guinea that all expats here fit into one of the three "m" categories—missionaries, mercenaries, and misfits. Which one are you?"

"That's easy. A misfit! I've never been accused of fitting into the normal scheme of things!"

He laughed and waved as he walked off towards the arena leaving me thinking about those three categories and my own motivations.

It turned out I didn't have a whole lot of time to think about it as many people started walking up the verandah steps and looking through our display house. I began handing out those information sheets very rapidly. Most inquiries that weekend came from nationals who viewed our little kit house as a "proper" house, when compared to their traditional *kunai* grass houses. Western influence had certainly taken a foothold in P.N.G.

As happy as I'd been to field that first expat doctor's inquiry on Saturday morning, by late the next day, I didn't want to answer another question. On Saturday night, I had to make up several hundred more copies of our handout back on the lumber office copy machine. I kept notes, however, and did have several good leads to sell some houses. I made a mental note to follow up the legitimate inquiries with phone calls or letters in the weeks to follow. I felt excited that the small construction arm of the lumber and hardware business, that was mine to manage, had some real potential. I felt sure I could get some kit house orders.

Jim and M.A. spelled me from the model

house on Sunday afternoon for a while, so I could walk around gawking and acting like a tourist with an itchy trigger finger on my camera shutter button. Sandia was not going to believe some of the tribal scenes I witnessed. The face and body painting must have taken many hours to apply. The headgear looked as if many days, or weeks, went into its assemblage. Long beautiful feathers taken from New Guinea's birds of paradise were the centerpieces of most of the headgear. During their dances, which again were mostly up and down jumping, the long feathers billowed in a rhythmic fashion. When many dancers' head feathers moved in unison, the sight proved awesome and, for me, totally unique.

A contest was staged, complete with national judges, for the most traditional tribal presentation. I didn't understand then what most of it was about, only that the different villages and regions sent groups to compete in hopes of returning with some sort of prestigious award or monetary prize. One expat told me that the *sing-sing* was originally conceived to bring tribal groups together in sort of a rendezvous to promote national harmony. Many times in the past it manifested just the opposite effect as fighting between long-established enemies broke out to end the *sing-sing*. The original concept, however, had prevailed, and every few years the tribes still came together in the in-

A couple of Hagen meris at the Sing Sing

terests of maintaining cultural ties to the past.

The make-up of the Hagen *sing-sing* crowd consisted of several thousand nationals and maybe a few dozen expatriates. Several of the tourists were couples and seeing them holding hands had an incredible effect on my heart. I stood there, halfway around the world from my lady! I forced myself to look away and tried hard to change my focus from the long, lonely distance of separation to the work at hand. Another national approached shyly to ask about our model house and helped break me away from my nostalgic thoughts.

The housing inquiries fell into two groups. The first constituted the serious group and consisted of mostly expats. They came from mission groups, hospital administrators, plantation owners and managers, and U.S. Peace Corps workers. Most of their development funding came from overseas. The second group consisted of nationals and included policemen, army personnel, mineworkers, and schoolteachers. Their funding was based in their salaries, which turned out to be rather meager. One primary school teacher told me that after five years of teaching, his salary brought him a whopping K100 each fortnight. Since one *kina* equaled about $1.15 U.S. at the time, he made approximately fifty-eight dollars U.S. per week. Even our cheaper priced kit house options at maybe five or six thousand *kina* reached well beyond the means of most nationals. There also did not exist any big home mortgage business available from the mostly overseas-owned banks. The few carpenters that Jim handed over to me with the building business were supposedly well paid at about K1.25 per hour. To me, and my maybe-naive quick assessment, there existed a huge gulf between earnings and the cost of goods. Maybe it remained that way because so many of the goods had to be imported and were not manufactured in the country. It seemed that even though P.N.G. had recently become an independent nation, Australia had a "captive" market for Australian manufactured items here in her old colony.

I found most of the nationals to be a bit on the shy side as they approached me to ask about the display house. My thoughts reflected that even though the price of the kit house was

Some Wahgi Valley men in their traditional dress for the Sing Sing

Hagen Sing Sing warriors

168

Huli men (Southern Highlands) preparing to dance

Coastal meris at the Hagen Sing Sing

A splendid feathered headdress on a Hagen meri with Kundu drum

well beyond their means, they wanted to walk through it and dream a little—the Papua New Guinea dream, scaled down from, but much like our American dream. I broke the ice with a few by showing them pictures of our *La Casita* on the Colorado River and the log trussed bridge. A few of my photos included our deep snowy winter scenes and one close-up of a big bull elk. They seemed in awe of the snow and the tall pine and spruce trees. They acted out shivering from the cold. Too cold for them, they told me. Several told me of high mountains in P.N.G. where snow was seen to fall on rare occasions. My time to show dismay as they assured me it was true. Maybe even here, just below the equator, if you climbed up to 4500+ meters (15,000 feet); it was possible to see a snowflake. The national men I showed the Colorado Mountain photos to seemed keenly interested in the bull elk and asked, "How big?"

I replied, "Maybe 450 kilos." Ooohs and *ayiiis* followed my response.

Once I broke through the average national's timidity and shyness, I found a very eager, laughing, and an almost child-like joy of life. As I watched from the vantagepoint of the model house's verandah, I noted the spontaneous laughter coming from various small groups of nationals. The shyness, I guess, seemed only to be reserved for their approach to us "*whiteskins*," as they called us. I also felt puzzled when I kept noticing, in contrast to the few tourist couples holding hands, that national couples didn't hold hands, but many pairs of men did. Those few days of the Hagen *sing-sing* threw me right into the middle of an entirely different culture. I made another mental note to ask later about the male handholding. Maybe it constituted a sensitive issue. I didn't know.

The Hagen Show ended and I found my bed in the flat above the lumber yard a very comfortable place to settle into and let the images go round and round in my head—the dancing, the body painting, the shell decorations, the bird of paradise feathers in rhythmic motion above a sea of dancing and chanting heads, the infectious smiles, the masses of dark-skinned people, my voice selling the virtues of a kit house I had only laid eyes on two days before, and so many more visions—Elton John at the piano, singing "Your Song"—our song—then welcome sleep finally came.

chapter twenty-eight

Settling in and Sizing Up

With the panic of the Hagen *Sing-Sing* behind me, I turned my focus to the day to day routines, with an eye toward future work. My predecessor left me a gigantic mess of unfinished business. He had been "sacked" for incompetence and left the country in rapid fashion. Seems like he bid a catholic girls' school library construction job in the Baiyer River Valley for K30,000, and brought it in at K81,000, still unfinished. Guess he tried to hide the cost overruns in with the lumber/hardware side of things, but the accountant figured it out. It would not be a hard act to follow!

Jim drove me from one end of the Wahgi Valley to the other, showing me the unfinished jobs my predecessor left me. I scribbled notes on each job, hoping I'd be able to find my way back to each location via my crude map sketches. Then Jim headed down to the coast to work on another business he was getting started—office and home furnishings. He left me with one old blue Toyota pickup, seven carpenters of questionable skill levels, and with the charge, "Do the best you can with what I showed you. Treat it like it is your own business. Call me if you need

with space to write, space to sleep, built of wood

with glass to view, the house on hilltop stood

to!" With those words uttered over a warm handshake, Jim hopped into the Aero Club Cessna 172, strapped himself in, started the engine, and taxied out for a take-off from Mt. Hagen's Kagamuga Airport. He headed east for the Huon Gulf and the coastal city of Lae. I stood and watched his lift-off against the backdrop of the lush green forest and mountains. Jim loved his flying!

I headed back to my office and factory/shop. My excitement for this new country and the work challenge felt only tempered by the deep homesickness in my heart. I could feel it in my stomach. Just to hold Sandia in my arms for a brief moment would be breathtaking. I concentrated on the fact that she would join me after the first of the year. My focus snapped back to the road into Hagen. I had inadvertently drifted to the wrong side of the road, while immersed in my thoughts. The sudden sight of an oncoming truck reminded me to get back to the left side. I'd get it soon—this driving on the "wrong" side!

The next day I took a ride with Lindsay Mackney up into the Enga Province. Our destination, the town of Wabag, lay high in the

Myself and Lindsay seeing Jim (l to r) off on one of his flying trips. This one was over water.

his Queenslander accent, but believe me it proved really difficult at first. We truly were separated by a common language. His accent sounded kind of like a cross between a Maine and Alabama dialect, but still totally unique. Mine, of course, consisted of certified perfect American English!

"So you're a bloody Yank", was about the first thing that came out of Lindsay's mouth as he catapulted us out of town in his twincab yellow Toyota pickup, leaving a cloud of dust behind us hanging over the gravel road. I answered in the affirmative to his query and soon learned there were also Kiwis (New Zealanders), bleeding, whinging Poms (Great Britain), Frogs (French), Euros (Europeans, in general), and, like himself, Aussies. Guess the labels all came about from the Allies' slang during the two world wars.

This Yank sat back, listened mostly, asked a few questions, and watched the road ahead as each new twist and turn brought a new spectacular vista into view. Most of the ground looked to be a mix of red clay and sand, without many stones. They didn't use the word "rocks" much at all over there, just stones. The vegetation appeared lush green and the trees, mostly gum and casuarina species, grew to great heights. Most houses, or shelters, which showed up infrequently along the road, were constructed of bamboo framework, with covering walls of woven young bamboo or sugar cane fiber called "*pit-pit.*" The roofs were thatched in layers of long *kunai* grass, without a vent hole at the top, similar, for instance, to the American Indian Teepee smokehole. The New Guinea Highlanders didn't want to lose any heat from their smoky "green" wood

mountains at the western extreme of the Hailans Highway, which originated in the port city of Lae. Lindsay was General Manager of Jim's lumber/hardware operation and previously had run the Tomba Sawmill, which started the lumber business. Lindsay worked that sawmill for six years. During that stint, he did most of the work of bargaining for trees in the adjacent hardwood forests, dropping them with a chain saw, hauling them to the sawmill, and, finally, rough sawing the green logs into useful timber sizes to sell. That length of time had been a bit too long for Lindsay's wife to handle the rugged, sparse, third world mountain life, so she opted to go back to their home in Queensland, Australia. Lindsay stayed on in P.N.G., periodically taking a trip down to Tin Can Bay in Queensland to see his wife. He obviously enjoyed the rough and tumble life in the New Guinea mountains. He told me that he once ran a sawmill in Fiji for twelve years. Lindsay, in his late fifties, was a big rugged physical man with a seemingly gentle heart.

I pieced together his history by deciphering

fires, and used the ceiling soot buildup to seal out the raindrops. They said their eyes got used to the smoky, acrid, *kunai* hut interiors! Euro eye doctors found many eye problems in older Highlanders, which they attributed to the smoke filled interiors. For the most part, however, the highlanders spent most of their days outside in the clean fresh air, only seeking out their smoke polluted shacks in heavy downpours and at night for supper and sleeping.

Even though we'd drop into quite a few small valleys, we seemed to be constantly gaining elevation as we rolled on toward Enga Province. Lindsay filled me in on the history of the company, starting with Jim's original purchase from a few missionaries. Then, Glen Eildon Timbers, as it was named, consisted of the Tomba Sawmill, about twenty miles west of Hagen at about the 8,000-foot (2,400-meter) elevation, and a small timber retailing property in the town itself. They ran the lumber operation efficiently and profitably, enabling purchase of other properties adjacent to the timber sales lot. Now Jim and Lindsay had closed the sawmill in the Tomba village, buying timber wholesale from larger sawmill operations, mostly down on the coast. Jim later added imported hardware, plumbing, and electrical supplies to his now complete building supply business and renamed it, Total Hardware, Ltd. My construction yard overlaid the original timber sales yard that the missionaries built.

We reached the town of Wabag and Lindsay did some wheeling and dealing at the Public Works Office. He emerged from the administration office with a big check for previously delivered items and K30,000 in new orders. I left some of the kit house show flyers with the administrators to whom Lindsay introduced me. I then talked him into going by the two banks in town and I went inside each to introduce myself as the new manager of Hailans Homes and

handed out some more kit house flyers to the bank managers. Then we were finished!

I offered to drive on the way back to Hagen and Lindsay, looking a bit weary, took me up on it. Rounding those narrow road curves, along with climbing into and dropping out of those steep mountains required focus and stamina. By the time we reached Mt. Hagen, I felt physically and mentally drained.

Back at the lumberyard Lindsay showed me a stash of South Pacific Lager, about a dozen cases. He told me to help myself to one, but I'd have to buy my own after that. Free beer didn't come with the job description. I would soon find out that most other things did however, like living quarters, truck, petrol (gasoline), tools, and just about all work related items, as well as one membership in the private club of your choice. I basically had to pay for food and entertainment, both of which were fairly expensive by U.S. standards. Private clubs came about as a place to buy "grog." Most members were expatriates, with a few wealthy nationals mixed in for flavor. Membership fees were set high and certainly not affordable for the average national. There was the lawn bowling club, the golf club, the pioneer club, and the tennis club. The tennis club turned out to be the only club without a pub. It had six clay (New Guinea dirt!) courts. I chose the tennis club and would go into the others as a guest when I felt the need, or thirst!

My first established priority lay in getting set up in my own flat. The flat stood in a section dubbed "Siberia" by the other expatriates because of its location far from the center of town. I loved the location. The tennis club was a half-mile away (about 0.8 km) and there existed an outdoor market with fresh produce and handmade local handicrafts only a short distance beyond the tennis courts.

The flat consisted of one-half a duplex owned

by the local commuter airlines, Talair. No one lived in the other half and hadn't for quite a while. It was located on top of a small hill. From the flat you could look down the long driveway to the entry gate, across the access road into a squatters' village built around a small muddy creek, which served as the village water supply, and then, lifting your eyes, to gaze upon a splendid mountain range beyond, called Kuta Ridge, on the far side of Mt. Hagen. Situated in the center of the squatters' village, a small tradestore did a business, which produced a scene of constant activity. I had Australian/Scottish neighbors on one side of me, New Zealanders behind me, and open space on the other side. A small decaying deck, which overlooked the described view, was accessed from the living room. I later rebuilt the deck a bit bigger. In my new yard, I had a gum tree, a pine tree, a stand of bamboo, and a big poinsettia bush that flowered all the time, not just around Christmas time. The large galvanized water tanks that caught water from the metal roof (cistern system) still sat there for emergency, but a town water system had finally reached Siberia, which made the tanks obsolete.

The flat consisted of two bedrooms, a bathroom—complete with a clothes washer, a living room/dining room combination, a little kitchen, and, outside, a rotary clothesline for hanging out the wet laundry. Huge satellite dishes were evident in the neighbors' yards, but I'd get along with my newly purchased short-wave radio for a while.

I found a few pieces of furniture around the lumberyard and my carpentry shop to basically outfit the flat. I borrowed an extra single bed from Jim's flat

above the lumber yard, while telling my men that they could build me a double bed when my lady came. Empty, cold space in a big bed would only serve to make my longing to hold Sandia in my arms at night and in the early mornings that much worse. Yaupas, the deaf mute who worked in my shop, helped me move my "new" furniture to the flat. I took notice of what an excellent worker he was that night as we communicated

The duplex on the hill. Our flat is the half on the right side

The view from our flat's little deck looking toward Kuta Ridge

with our eyes and hands.

Into my sparsely furnished quarters, I moved with commitment, determined to make a "go" of this whole opportunity. I brought from work, the scattered, and no longer used, pieces of an old Apple computer and printer, along with a step-down transformer, from P.N.G.'s 220V system to the U.S. equipment required 110V. Several late nights later, I had it working; the data base and word processor parts anyway, thanks to finding some Appleworks software in a file at the accountant's office.

My days and nights soon fell into a routine. I awoke at 5:30 A.M., stumbled out the door for a three to five kilometer run, showered, dressed in shorts, short sleeved sport shirt, hiking boots, ate some fresh fruit, and headed for my office about 7 A.M. Those first weeks, I concentrated on cleaning up my predecessors unfinished jobs, while I made my own plans for the future of Hailans Homes. When I returned to the flat at night, usually around 5:30 or 6 P.M., I would write in my journal first, regarding the days activities and acquired lessons of the P.N.G. culture, then I'd fix something to eat. My evening meals always consisted of vegetables in some form, usually stir fried in a big Chinese wok, followed by the cracking of a cold South Pacific brownie (a lager beer so called because of its stubby brown bottle—the tall green ones were for export and cost more, notwithstanding the taste of the preservative!). The late hours found me finishing up letters to family and friends, or reading a big fat book until I couldn't keep my eyes open any longer. Then sleep would come to help hide the voids within my spirit.

My letters to Sandia consisted pretty much of daily photocopies of my journal pages, which became a long series of descriptive letters filling several fat spiral bound notebooks. It made me feel as if I talked to her when I'd come back to

the flat at night and sit down in my desk chair to write. Several framed photos of her, and us together, were spread across the desktop. There was a photo of us crossing the finish line, holding hands, at a marathon we'd run a few years earlier in the desert outside Scottsdale, Arizona. The photo reminded me that we were a tough pair of Colorado Mountain people, able to handle most anything, including this period of separation. Then I'd scribble out words to create a written image of my day in the mountains of New Guinea. Each day following, before going to get my men started, I'd photocopy my writings, double-sided for mailing economy, then post them to Sandia about every third day, or so. I longed for her replies, the sight of her handwritten words on stationary, but in the beginning they were delayed by an inefficient P.N.G. postal system trying to figure out who I was. Our address, thanks to those missionary founders, was P. O. Box 1, Mt. Hagen, Western Highlands Province (W.H.P. usually got it done!), Papua New Guinea. I haunted our accountant, an Aussie named Jock, who served as the company mailman and the only one with a key to that first mailbox, every afternoon when he returned from the Hagen Post Office, but for several weeks it remained all for naught. The huge void in my heart and stomach grew bigger. Burrowing deeply into my work kept me going.

Three plus weeks in New Guinea, without mail from home, I decided to try out my newly installed phone at the flat and dial up those beautiful Colorado Mountains. Taking into account the time difference, P.N.G. was a day ahead, but eight hours behind, or a net of sixteen hours difference, I picked up the phone to place a long distance, person-to-person call to Sandia. Suddenly I heard her voice on the other end of the line, identifying herself to the New Guinean operator, and then we actually talked. Her voice was absolutely the sweetest sound I've ever heard. Just to hear her say, "I love you, sweetheart," lifted me ten feet off the ground! We talked a few minutes and Sandia brought me up to date on how she was managing the closing up of *La Casita del Rio*. My friend, Ron, finished the log slab siding on a small rear room addition that I'd almost completed before heading overseas. Sandia coped nicely with lots of unfinished details in the mountains and enrolled Kirsten in Jefferson High School, down near her mom, so she could finish her last semester, in order to graduate at the end of the year. We ended the call, noting that we could talk maybe once a month for about twenty minutes. The charges cost approximately K5 (~$5) per minute and the company would pay the first K100 of my phone bill. The rest of the bill fell to my responsibility. I would run it over many times in the future!

That "phone calling" morning, I felt so buoyed up in spirit, I ran four miles (about 6.4 km) up a nearby mountain and back. My feet flew easily over the red clay path, while my heart pulled me up the inclines. Sandia's sweet voice stayed in my mind, echoing through the voids, the rest of the day as I worked. Then, almost the same as winning double jeopardy, Jock, our accountant, came running into my office that afternoon with Sandia's first letter—complete with some photos of our mountains. She had written and mailed it the day I boarded the flight west for the South Pacific.

Days later, buried in my work, focusing on finishing up my predecessor's residuals, I tried to do some long-term thinking. Jim's words, "Run it like your own business," stayed posted on my mental bulletin board. What direction should I try to aim "my" Hailans Homes toward? Other expats called New Guinea, "Murphy's Law Country—if something could be constructed or installed wrong, it would be! Nothing was going

to be easy to accomplish. I ran into evidence of this law, my first week in the country. Checking on materials over at the Total Hardware lumber yard, I was amazed at the actions of two of their in-house carpenters, who had just hung an exterior door, out of plumb, or askew. The door hit the concrete slab threshold as they tried to open it. So here they kneeled, as I came upon them, with cold chisels and hammers, starting to chip away the concrete! I motioned for them to stop what they attempted to do and spent the next hour working with them. We shimmed the door opening until it measured square and then re-installed the door. This time the door opened easily above the concrete with plenty of clearance. Both carpenters grabbed my hand, pumping it up and down as they saw the door swinging easy and level. I laughed together with them and their expressed joy at seeing how to do it correctly. As I walked away, I wondered how much and what kind of teaching they'd had. They sure seemed eager enough to learn.

Only a few days later, the hardware sales manager asked me to build them some shelving for plumbing supplies. I told them it would be my pleasure and headed back to my shop to put Buka and Lavalle on the task. I wrote down the dimensions on a shelving sketch I'd drawn, and showed them how to install the shelf cleats on the side boards—a simple bookcase idea, only bigger. I carefully explained everything in half *pisin*/half English, as the two nodded with apparent understanding. Then I headed back to my office to work on another job estimate.

An hour later, I walked out to the shop to check on the progress of the shelving. To my chagrin, I saw they had it all "buggered up" (an Aussie expression similar to our fouled up). This time I went to great lengths to calmly explain and show them how I wanted the shelving done. I even used model pieces of wood scraps to illustrate my sketches. Buka and Lavalle again nodded understanding and began taking apart their first attempts at the shelving.

Forty-five minutes later, I strolled out to the shop to find them again building the shelving wrong. I explained again slowly, using those model wood pieces again to show how things should fit together. I walked slowly back to my office, feeling more than a little frustrated with my inability to communicate. I sat down at my desk and waited another forty-five minutes, not really concentrating on the estimate in front of me. Would it always be this hard to get a simple custom job completed correctly? I wondered about the future.

With my hands plunged deeply into the pockets of my cargo shorts, and an optimistic smile on my face, I ambled back to the shop area. My face truly lit up when I saw the almost completed shelving. It stood there, so simply splendid, framed correctly, using P.N.G. beech hardwood.

I quickly asked Buka and Lavalle, "What did I say that made you understand how to build them like this?"

They both looked at each other then turned to point at Yaupas standing nearby. "He told us," they replied in unison. My deaf mute's eyes twinkled as his mouth formed a grin. He rushed over to the model scraps of wood I used earlier for demonstrating to Lavalle and Buka, placing them like I'd previously done. Yaupas grunted and laughed as he pointed to the shelving, nodding his approval.

I stood there, smiling in utter amazement. Yaupas, or Terape, as we later came to call him, hadn't heard a word as I instructed my "carpenters" earlier. He only watched my hands, along with the movement of the scrap lumber to understand how the shelving needed to be built. Terape would become one of my most valuable

and trusted men. He taught me so much about New Guineans and the culture. Between all of us, we developed a sign language of our own so we could communicate with our "disadvantaged," but intelligent, co-worker. Terape became my eyes and ears around Hailans Homes. He taught me "body" language. If I ever showed up for work in a depressed mood, Terape would knock on my office door, enter grunting and laughing, and then proceed to do a dance until I finally laughed out loud. Only then would he give me the "thumbs up" sign and return to his job of making pallets. He made between thirty and fifty of them each day and we sold every one of them. From his corner of the yard, Terape saw all that went on at Hailans Homes, and he kept me posted on the security of the tools, machines, and supplies.

There existed another worker, Koki, who turned out coffins all day long, every day. We used plywood as the main coffin material, fastened over a framework of two by twos. The coffins sold for between K35 and K65, depending on size and embellishments, like fancy plastic handles. I added a more expensive line that came with all the fancy stuff and a window at the head position. The coffins sold fast enough to keep Koki busy all the time. Sometimes when we'd start to run low on the coffin inventory, I'd have to assign a helper to Koki. I wondered how they buried their dead before the arrival of the coffin concept from the missionaries. Some of my men told me they used to lower the dead into a prepared burial hole on a palm thatched stretcher type of carrier. If the person had been an important villager, the stretcher would be supported in the air by poles during the mourning and wailing period, before the burial, so that all people could observe the deceased. The sound of the wailing sometimes went on for days. The louder one wailed during mourning signified how important the deceased had been to the wailer. I heard wailing often enough from my flat, sometimes lasting the entire night. I think the people believed that the dead spirit observed the funeral ritual. Lots of shamanism preceded the arrival of the first Christian missionaries.

My administrative man, Bobby, handled the money and the invoices on the pallets and coffins. One day I noticed him pound a red ink stamp on a receipt he handed the leader of a group that just purchased one of our adult sized plywood coffins. I intercepted the receipt and saw that the red inked letters stated, "No Returns on Coffins." Puzzled, I handed the receipt back to the group's headman and waited for them to file out of the front office in their *arse* grass and traditional wear.

"Do we really need that red ink stamp?" I asked Bobby.

"Yes, we do."

Then Bobby went on to tell me, very descriptively, how before the stamp, a few groups would buy the most expensive coffin to impress the villagers at the funeral ceremony, then when everyone would leave after the speeches, and mourning, they would roll the deceased out into the naked burial hole, shovel in the dirt, then bring the coffin back for a refund!

I burst out laughing and told Bobby to keep on using the stamp. I told him, "Maybe we should keep one of the best coffins for rental use only!" When he finally caught on to my humor, he let out a good laugh. For me, I learned something new every hour in those early days.

The pallet, coffin, and a basic line of wood furniture business at Hailans Homes brought in a steady base income, but I had no idea how we did financially, as the way things were set up, the accounting lumped us in with lumber and hardware sales. My own figuring found that Hailans Homes definitely required entry on the nega-tive side of the ledger. I added up the materials, maintenance, and labor payroll we averaged. The sum certainly came out higher than our income- and we didn't even pay rent on our space, or taxes!

It seemed clear to me, as I finished my first month in P.N.G., that Hailans Homes needed to do repetitive work, not custom work, where every day I'd have to be on every job site explaining, teaching, and hoping my guys understood my ever improving, but still imperfect, *pisin*. We were happily close to finishing the obligations the former manager left me. Like the pallets, coffins, and our basic furniture line, I resolved to make the kit house concept into a business reality.

I spent a week drawing up kit house plans for three basic designs, ranging from about 30 square meters (320 square feet) to 42 square meters (450 square feet). Exterior wall panels were interchangeable and consisted of only three types, window, door, and solid filler panels. I scrounged around my office files for old drawings of the maybe a dozen kit houses Hailans Homes had built in the previous seven or eight years. What I found gave me ideas and places to start. Building repetitive panels in the shop under scrutiny, in an assembly line type of process, seemed to me the way to go. One man could build the same panel frame over and over. Another man could then fasten on the treated wood siding to the squared up frame. Other men could be building the window and door units that would fit into the appropriate panel openings. The panels could then be stood upright on the prepared plywood subfloor and bolted together in a planned sequence. Then a simple beamed roofing system could span the top of the secured wall panels, and finally the corrugated iron roofing panels would be fastened to the roof beams. The roof did not have to hold up heavy snow loads here in the quiet tropics near the tranquil equator.

My task, as manager, lay in the marketing of the kit houses. I knew we could get them built. All I needed to get started was a few orders. That's when Terry Smith, an expat village school principal showed up in my office. Terry was referred to me by the two Peace Corps *wontoks* I met at the Hagen *Sing Sing*. He needed a teacher's house out at his school in Gumine, in the Chimbu Mountains, just east of the Wahgi Valley—about a four-hour drive. Terry had a provincial school budget to work with. We made a deal on a two bedroom, 30 square meter kit house, complete with a solar hot water system on the roof to heat a portion of the collected rain water. We shook hands as Terry handed me a check for half the job, K5,000. I felt so excited when he left the office after giving me our first kit house order. It was all going to work. I could feel it in my heart.

I ran out to the shop to tell my men. They too became excited. Work for them meant they kept their jobs and could feed their families. That meant a lot in the teeth of high unemployment in the towns. Back in the villages, life proved fairly self-sufficient and money was not a high priority. Plentiful gardens supplied the basic needs of each village. All you had to do was pitch in and help the community labor requirements. When a teenager acquired a little schooling, however, it seemed they all wanted to go to the towns, earn big bucks, and reap all the benefits that money could buy in this emerging nation. They showed up every day, lining up outside my gate looking for work. Many carried faded and dirty letters of recommendations that some previous employer had written them. You couldn't be sure the bearer of the letter was even the person mentioned in the text. I think they traded the letters around always in the hope that one

of their *wontoks* would be successful in landing a job. Then he had to share his paychecks with his village group. Half the time they didn't even know what had been written in the letter. One time I received a letter by a smiling job seeker and it read, "if you hire this guy you should have your bloody brain examined. _____ is lazy and really a lousy worker…" I smiled politely, telling him, "*No gat wok. Tank yu plenti.*" Off he trudged, unaware of what his previous employer had written, ready to stand in another job seeking line, and then proudly hand the "treasured" recommendation letter to another potential employer. Some expats were cruel! I seldom hired from the daily job seeking line, depending rather on recommendations of my more trusted workers, but early one morning; an eager guy in the line just took my fancy. His eyes sparkled, his spirit showed, his letter was a good one, and on an impulse, I hired him. He was a Southern Highlander named Gibson Mondul Mondhaim. He became one of my better workers, always smilingly calling me "*wonwok*", meaning that we started work at the company at about the same time.

Getting back to the first kit house order—we actually used most of the panels from the *singsing* show house, after careful dismantling, and had Terry's house completely finished three weeks later. My guys loved getting out of the shop for a while and I ferried materials to them in Gumine using the lumberyard's six-ton truck. The building site had a million-dollar view of surrounding mountains in the very peaceful area near Gumine village. The Chimbu River (*Wara Chimbu*) flowed near the building site, but several hundred feet below us in a deep ravine. It provided a magnificent sight looking down into that mighty river. Those mountains were steep and rugged, obviously thrown up by huge volcanic uplifting of the ocean floor many, many thousands of years earlier.

We ended up depleting Terry's entire budget surplus for that year by adding another small kit classroom to his school. Hailans Homes prefabricated buildings were going to find many uses in the future. They would include police outposts, health aid stations, mission stations, offices, trading stores, but mostly houses for nationals to live and raise their families in and around.

Always armed with my trusty 35 mm Canon camera, I photographed our new buildings in Gumine along with a few plantation houses in the Wahgi Valley that Jim had built a few years earlier. The photos, along with a few simple language sales paragraphs, became Hailans Homes first color brochure. I had to send the printing order down to Australia to get it done, but when it came back two weeks later, and we opened the package, my men started hooping and laughing with great glee. There was their recent teacher's house construction effort on the cover of the foldout brochure. They all wanted one to take

home and show their families and *wontoks*. Two of them appeared in one of the construction photos I had included. No worries, I gave them each a couple as I had ordered five thousand. They treated the brochures like they were made of gold, cradling them with great care as they excitedly walked out of my office.

In the quiet of the men's aftermath, I gazed at the big package of brochures and smiled, feeling sure that we stood on the threshold of something great. I had a small crew of eager workers, located in the mountains of an emerging nation, rich in mineral resources, and greatly in need of housing. It had to work. Tomorrow I would start spreading the brochures throughout the highlands, to all the banks, schools, plantations, mining operations, and government offices. Hailans Homes was on the map! I felt so optimistic that we would get kit house orders and could reasonably control the repetitive prefabrication process right there in our little shop/factory space. The work potential made for an exciting time.

chapter twenty-nine

My Workforce and the First Contract Bid

The expansive Highlands region, with its interwoven valleys, actually makes up the most densely populated area in the entire country. The fertile Highlands valleys also constitute the most agriculturally productive areas of P.N.G., a fact manifested in numerous bountiful coffee and tea plantations. The former proves the better, more recent, cash crop, but the latter, introduced into the Highlands as one of the earliest European crops, still yields some great tasting teas. The staple crop of the Highlands villages is the sweet potato, or yam (*kau kau*), which came when the Spaniards, in the 16th century, introduced it into the Spice Islands, where it subsequently was traded through Irian Jaya, on up to the Highlands of Papua New Guinea. The introduction of the sweet potato must have had a major impact on the life of the Highlanders. Its tolerance of differing soil conditions and colder climates, while still producing abundant yields, allowed habitation at even higher elevations. The sweet potato crop surplus allowed the villagers to raise more pigs, which are extremely important in the Highlands culture, both for ritual and economic purposes.

round that curve of mountain road, there awaits

warriors bold, spears held high for fear creates

Pigs signified wealth, and still do, today. A village "big" man usually owned many pigs and they served as the symbol of his wealth and stature among his people. With pigs, he could buy more wives, who in turn could tend more garden area, raise, and feed more pigs. Throughout the protein deficient Highlands, when a pig was ritualistically slaughtered and fed to other villagers as part of, for example, a wedding feast, the people would literally gorge themselves on the meat. There existed no refrigeration, so all the pig meat had to be eaten before it spoiled. The groom, who paid for his bride with pigs, and in turn, the bride's family who shared the pig's protein, enjoyed the accolades extended by all the villagers taking part in the ceremony.

In between pig feasts, the Highlander's diet consisted mainly of the starchy carbohydrate of the sweet potato, mixed with some edible and tasty greens (*kumus*). The *kau kau* of the Highlands also is not the rich orange color of the sweet potato, as we know it in the States, but a creamy, off-white color. Historians place the arrival of the pig from Asia between 5,000 and

10,000 years ago. Excavations in the Highlands show farming began about 9,000 years ago, making the Highlanders of New Guinea some of the earliest farmers of the world. Their skills at farming, clever trading, and dealing with land ownership made them capitalistic long before western culture showed its pale face in the Highlands. Someone owns every tree and stone in P.N.G. Someone, or some village, owns even the coral reefs off the beautiful coastal beaches. Whenever we needed to cut down a Casuarina (named for its twigs resemblance to cassowary feathers) tree, or find stones for a soakage pit (similar to a leach field), we had to find the owner to commence bargaining to reach a reasonable price. You couldn't just take stuff without asking. Sometimes, after the negotiations, I had the distinct, but humorous, feeling that we didn't even pay the "right" landowner!

The Highlands is divided into five provinces, Eastern Highlands, Chimbu, Western Highlands, Southern Highlands, and Enga. As my workforce grew, I had men from all the Highlands Provinces, as well as, many of the Coastal Provinces. I wanted a diverse group so they would compete a bit, rather than hiring all *wontoks* from one province. Remember that *wontoks* remained culturally obligated to stick together and help each other. If my night security watch originated from Enga, for example, and an Engan burglar (*raskol*) showed up at night to rob the Hailans Homes yard, the security man could end up helping the *raskol* to our stuff. Believe me, it happened. It seemed much better to have a diverse group. The Coastal people thought the Highlanders exhibited aggressive and troublesome traits, while the Highlanders described the Coastals as lazy and unmotivated. I attribute the differing characteristics to the hot, humid Coastal climate as contrasted to the cooler Highlands environment. Besides the climate, the Coastals and Highlanders had totally different origins.

A majority of my foremen would end up being Coastals, but my fewer Highlander foremen also did great work. I only ever hired one female to my crew, my "pseudo" secretary, who I later found out worked as a prostitute at an expat club at night, and as my dependable girl "Friday" during the daytime. She finally got beat up badly one night; that's when word of her nighttime activities "leaked" back to me. After several weeks of healing, Kathy came back and quietly asked if she still had a job. I told her to sit down and get to work. She always proved a skilled worker, never giving me any problems. About two months later, she got beat up again, this time worse than before. I never saw her again.

We began landing kit house contracts here and there, usually one or sometimes two at a building site. The shop payroll, I could keep an eye on because it lay right under my, and Terape's, nose. The field construction payroll gave me fits, however. They camped at the remote construction sites, telling me they worked at night a lot. It became apparent that the foremen "padded" the field labor hours, especially in favor of their *wontok* laborers. Visiting every building site, all the time, would prove impossible for me. The field cost of erecting the same little house varied greatly from crew to crew. The "padding" wasn't a malicious, or a deeply criminal, thing, just an opportunity. That's why they are called *raskols* in the South Pacific, rather than criminals! Nonetheless, I had to figure some way to control our costs.

One night, sitting out on my little deck at the flat, with a cold S.P. brownie in my hand, watching the comings and goings of the squatter village below me, the solution on the field payroll came to me out of the cloudy New Guinea sky. I ran inside, turned on the computer, and pulled up my database on labor costs. I figured out the average cost to erect each of our three kit house models. I would add a small incentive bonus to the average cost and offer a subcontract to my foremen. For example, Hailans Homes would pay Mondul K650 to completely erect a thirty square meter kit house. He could hire whomever he wanted, paying them out of his sub-contract amount. If something had to be fixed, or reinstalled, Mondul had the responsibility without an increase in the sub-contract agreement amount. Hailans Homes would throw in one 25 kg. sack of rice and two cartons of tinned fish on each sub-contract, as well as getting the prefabricated house components delivered to the building site. If the foreman proved smart and efficient, he could make some *kina*. This method would create "big" men in the Hailans Homes' culture. No longer would I have to worry about legitimate field payrolls—I knew the final field costs of a house even before the erection, factoring those costs into my overall kit house contract price. Oh, it would work! I toasted the cool New Guinea night that evening with a big smiling sigh of relief. I wanted to dial up Sandia to explain it all to her, but the time difference would have had her asleep, the morning before!

The next kit house I contracted, my foreman appeared eager to become his own boss and hire his own workers. I only needed to deal with him and he, in turn, would control five or six others. Just once did a crew come to me after that, complaining that the foreman cheated his workers. I worked it out with the foreman, making

sure his workers got paid reasonably. The other foremen took note of that incident and didn't play any more hanky panky!

Lindsay clued me in one day that a contract (tender) bid for ten houses back in the Chimbu Mountains around Gumine was to be released forthwith. I drove over to the Chimbu Provincial Public Works in the town of Kundiawa to pick up a set of contract specifications from the expat manager, a cheery Pom by the name of Bob Eyles. He pointed out to me the construction sites on a big Chimbu Provincial map that hung on his drafting room wall. I eyeballed the spread out locations, with village names like Omkalai, Dirima, Gomgale, Yani, Dege, and Nomani. The geography looked a little scary, but the size of the contract would make it worthwhile—ten houses in one contract order! It would be a major feather in Hailans Home's little cap! If only I could put it together. . .

One of the stipulations of the Chimbu Tender was that the bidding company had to

Chimbu mountain country with early morning mist

visit each building site specified in the documents. To me, it sounded like a reasonable requirement. I surely couldn't work out the final costs without seeing if any site anomalies or delivery difficulties existed. I scheduled myself out of the office for a day, driving eastward for the Chimbu Mountains. I took a passenger named Robert, a Hagen teacher, who was returning to his village near Gumine to visit family.

Robert and I drove through the early morning mists, which were probably morning clouds settled in on our mountains. Robert shared his culture with me as we drove along by telling me about his own life. Raised in a remote Chimbu mountain village, he did well at primary school and was passed onto secondary school. Only those with the best grades went on. Distances from home to the village school were often long and difficult treks, so many pupils, including Robert, boarded at the schools. Robert said he loved school and, early on, decided he wanted to become a teacher. In secondary school, he studied hard and showed enough promise to be offered a coveted spot at the University of P.N.G. After graduation, Robert became a primary teacher in a village school near Mt. Hagen. His pay, after several years of teaching, added up to K150 each month. Whoa, and I thought our teachers in the U.S. were underpaid. Try teaching in the third world conditions of the New Guinea Highlands for less than forty bucks a week! To be fair though, Robert said they provided him with basic living quarters at the village school and the villagers did help him out with fresh produce from their gardens—all

the *kau kau* he could eat. Robert seemed happy enough, but told me he usually remained short of money. I guess that's why one of my men arranged for him to ride with me. He couldn't afford the P.M.V. (private inter-village mini-vans/buses) fare, which was only about K1.50 per hour, depending on distance. It got cheaper with distance.

Coming around the first mountain south of the town of Kundiawa, we saw a commotion ahead of us on the clay/gravel road. Several nationals signaled us to pull over and stop. Only moments before, a huge landslide took out a hundred meters of the road ahead. Robert and I leaned out to look down at the rubble and dust still settling about two or three hundred feet below us, on the edge of the *Wara Chimbu* (Chimbu River). My heart pounded, but I felt a sense of relief that it had given way before we got there! I'd heard plenty of expat horror stories of cars and trucks going down these steep gorges. One crazy expat in Hagen actually made his living with winches and cables, recovering vehicles

Wara Chimbu snaking through the mountains

which, too often, slid down mountainsides. New Guinea clay is treacherous during, and after, long periods of rain (*taim bilong ren*).

I turned back to Robert and laughingly said, "Guess we didn't want to go to Gumine today anyway?"

He looked a little puzzled at my American use of the negative to make humor, but smiled and said, "There is another older, winding road around the backside of this mountain, not as good as this one, but only a few miles out of the way."

Without hesitation, I replied, "Let's take it then. You show me the way. We'll get you home and I'll get to visit my construction sites."

Robert's description proved correct about the secondary road being inferior to the landslidden one. It exhibited deep ruts, many twists and turns, with frequent projecting stones, but the 4WD Toyota Hilux navigated it just fine, albeit slower. We passed through several remote villages on the backside of the mountain. Robert told me in approximately 15 kilometers (~10 miles) we would join back up with the better road, well south of the landslide.

Rounding the next curve, I had to slam on the brakes or run straight into a mass of several hundred warriors in full war regalia, glistening bodies, and brandishing bush knives (machetes), bows and arrows, and spears. My mind filled with shock and surprise as they quickly surrounded our truck and several young, very muscular warriors came up on the front bumper, thrusting their spears with great force back and forth at the windshield. I impulsively thought about gunning the engine and running the truck through them, but quickly abandoned the idea. There were just too many of them. Robert cowered down in the passenger seat with fear in his eyes. They could be enemies of his village, in which case, he'd be taken. My right hand slipped

down to clutch the hardwood axe handle, I kept under the truck seat for emergencies. With second thoughts, my nervous fingers released their grip on the axe handle. I reached instead for the door handle. *They must know I'm not their enemy*, I told myself as I felt the door opening.

Stepping out from the truck, the closest warriors backed away from me with fierce expressions on their faces. I raised both hands, hopefully, in a gesture of peace. I smiled as big as I could, while fear drained all sign of moisture from my mouth.

"*Mi lukim long bikpela man bilong yu,*" I blurted out trying to find their leader, not even knowing if they understood pidgin, especially mine! They continued to grunt and lunge at me with sharpened spear points, while continuing to display a very menacing body language. *What if one of them slips with those spears?* My mind raced.

Then I saw a warrior with several bird of paradise feathers held in place at the back of his head by means of a bright red head wrap, moving easily through the group in front of me. He was evidently the headman. As he came to a stop directly in front of me, I could see that he was greatly muscled, but a good head shorter than me. His facial expression was unsmiling, but questioning. Dabs of colored face paint made him look all the more ferocious.

Instinctively, I reached out and took his right hand in my own and told him, "*Mi pren* (friend) *bilong ol Chimbu manmeri* (people). *Yu mi sekan* (shake hands)!" I pumped his hand firmly in a friendly handshake, while holding my pasted smile.

Startled, he reached out his free left hand and pulled up my right short sleeve even higher to expose the tattoo of a bird and a heart on my right biceps. He broke out in a huge grin and said, "*Yu mi wontoks!*" With that declaration, he turned to point out my old Navy tattoo to those closest to him. They also began to laugh. I focused in on the facial tattoos that many of them exhibited. In New Guinea, tattooing serves as adornment, much as jewelry does in other parts of the world. Many men and, perhaps more so, women tattoo their faces and bodies.

By now, I had become aware that Robert had stepped from the truck and, understanding the warriors' *tokples* (village language), explained to them the main road landslide and our destination for the Gumine village area. Robert then turned to ask me if two of these fighters could ride in the back of the truck as far as the next village to search out signs of their enemies' whereabouts.

"Tell them to hop aboard. I'd just as soon get out of here as fast as we can!"

Robert turned and motioned two warriors standing there with homemade rifles to get up in the back. I grabbed the big man's hand, gave it a last shake, saying, "*Lukim yu behin* (sort of similar to 'see you later')," and turned for the sanctuary of the Toyota. Once inside, I fired up that engine, and we eased out of there with a last wave back to our recent tormentors.

As we drove toward the next village, leaving that armed mob behind us, I finally began to relax. My armpits were soaked with sweat. Even my forehead perspired, but the intense experience seemed over for the moment. The two warriors jumped out soon enough when I slowed for a sharp mountain turn. With their exit, I blurted out, "Ah, Papua New Guinea, what lies around the next curve in the road?" My travel mate smiled.

Robert told me what he learned talking to some of the fighters. They were returning to their home villages, not having encountered the enemy, at that moment when we came upon them. The whole dispute started, evidently, six

months earlier as an offshoot to a drunken conversation between two men from different villages. During the conversation, one man made disparaging remarks about one of the other man's wives. Thus it began from drunken remarks and had carried on for about six months, with no relief in sight. I later came to believe that tribal warfare was nothing but a macho thing, a male testosterone driven activity. Occasionally, someone got wounded, or even killed; then, the fighting would stop and negotiations would begin. A settlement of pigs would then go to the "wronged" party, the wounded man, or the family of any warrior who had died in the tribal fighting. Pigs would also have to be paid in compensation to allied villages that supported the main village war effort. It never appeared the tribes would negotiate until a reasonable show of macho warfare had been completed. Sort of reminded me of the Rocky Mountain bull elk locking horns to demonstrate prowess, but then the elk never negotiated afterwards—he, the weaker male elk, just went away vowing to return stronger another day.

Robert also answered my query about the glistening bodies by telling me they rubbed themselves down with pig grease, or fat. Some even used motor oil in more recent times. Similarly, the traditional face and body paints used to be extracted from all natural local sources, such as clay, berries, and ochre. Now it could be purchased in many trade stores, imported from factories outside New Guinea.

I dropped Robert in his village, but before we said our goodbyes, he drew me a rough map of the route to my *wontoks'* (U.S. Peace Corps) house in the bush near Gumine. After thanking each other, me for his teachings, and him, for the ride, I drove off to find David, and his wife Melynda, the Peace Corps volunteers from Iowa. I first met them at the Hagen *Sing-Sing*, a few months earlier.

Melynda displayed surprise, and delight, to see me knocking at the door of their little one bedroom house. I'm sure they didn't get much expat company, especially from the States. I smelled something good, and familiar, baking in the oven. Melynda asked, "I've got some brownies coming out of the oven in a minute. Would you like some with a cup of tea?"

Wow, good old American brownies, warm out of the oven, in the New Guinea bush, right on the heels of an intense tribal war encounter. What a treat!

"You bet I would!"

David returned to the house shortly thereafter, having heard village talk about a "*whiteskin*" in the area, and guessing it was someone looking for him. We all had a laugh regarding my first tribal war encounter, while agreeing it was best to keep our distance from such occurrences! Then David agreed to hop in my truck and navigate me to each of the proposed contract building sites. What an aid his help would be, as he knew the most efficient route to take to all the proposed locations. Off we went into those Chimbu peaks.

Toward evening, I was ready to retrace my morning drive and get back to Hagen. David and Melynda offered their little *kunai* shack, dubbed "The Gumine Guest Haus," but I politely refused. I explained that I had lots of work to do at my desk in Hagen, if I intended to get the contract bid finished, and submitted on time.

So I waved so long to my *wontoks* and headed back to Hagen the way I'd come only that morning. David arranged for four Gumine young men to ride as far as Kundiawa with

Wara Chimbu **below a pig fenced garden near Gumine**

me. One of them was in training to make the P.N.G. boxing squad for the upcoming South Pacific Games and looked quite formidable. All four seemed friendly enough, telling me that if Hailans Homes won the contract, they'd make sure my men got fresh garden food. We drove through more heavy rain and slid a bit on the wet clay roads coming back around the mountain. In the dark and the driving rain, it felt good to have company. I never saw a trace of a warrior on the return trip.

I dropped the four of them at the Kundiawa disco, a hall with music, soda pop, and other young people. It sounded noisy and spirited at the disco, although dark and sparse by Western standards. The rest of the way, from Kundiawa to Hagen, the road was paved and I put the "pedal to the metal." The Toyota speedometer hung on 120 kmph as I stared into the dark ahead of my headlights. Didn't need to hit some national on a *wokabaut* along the road. My day already runneth over. The events whirled in my head. I felt tired. Warriors' faces, glistening bodies, threatening spears, the headman smiling at my tattoos, Melynda's brownies—so American, the building sites, and finally the four spirited young men, who escorted me out of the South Chimbu Mountains. Then my driveway appeared, my single bed, and blessed sleep. . .

The next two weeks, I worked almost non-stop on the figures for the South Chimbu Rural Development Project contract bid. I figured the materials and then re-figured them again. The pre-fabrication costs, I had a descent handle on. To the material and factory labor costs, I added my estimated foreman sub-contract erection prices, leaving a little extra room in case we got into a re-negotiation debate. To these numbers, I added a fair profit, overheads, and then another fifteen percent for contingencies—after all, it remained a long way into those Chimbu Mountains. Expect the unexpected in Papua New Guinea. The final total was right at, but just below K120,000.00. I had one night left to sleep on it, as the bid deadline loomed the very next day, Friday, by 2 P.M. in Kundiawa at the Provincial Secretary's Office.

The next morning, after getting my men lined out on the day's work, I sat down at my desk to double-check all my numbers again. I came up with the same total again, just below the K120,000.00 figure, and decided to leave it without rounding it up to the even thousand. I sat looking at the figure, reflecting on the whole bid. Hailans Homes could sure use the work. I felt responsible for my men. Word had gotten back to me from David, in Gumine, that no other contractors visited the construction sites. Could I be alone in this bid submittal? I heard from Lindsay at least two other companies, one based near Kundiawa, and the other from Goroka, wanted the job. It was obviously a sizable contract. Maybe, for some reason, they didn't need to visit the sites. Maybe they knew something I didn't know? No more time for wondering, however; the clock was ticking.

I'd go with my numbers. I began to fill in my legitimate final figures to the bid form blanks. Finishing that, I headed up to get our new accountant, Ray West (Jock had been recently sacked by Jim!), to sign as company secretary, sealed it in the submittal envelope, and jumped into my trusty blue Hilux for the one and a half hour drive to Kundiawa in order to deliver the bid.

After arrival at the Provincial Headquarters Building, an aide ushered me into the Secretary's Office. The Secretary rose from his chair and came out from behind his desk to greet me. We exchanged pleasantries and I assured him that I had adhered to the "letter" of the bid instructions throughout, including visitation of each and every construction site. He smiled politely and reached for my envelope. Thanking me, he headed for his desk, while telling me that I would be informed of the contract outcome. As I left his office, I glanced back through the door and could swear the Secretary and his aide were opening my bid. I walked back to my truck puzzled, as all bids were to be opened simultaneously, the next day at high noon. Maybe I was mistaken? Maybe there was another similar envelope on his desk?

The following Wednesday rolled around before I found out what had transpired regarding the bid opening. One company threw in a really high bid without even working it out, in the event there were no other bidders—they'd have a nice "fat" contract. The only other bidders were Hailans Homes and the Kundiawa based construction firm, also managed by an expat. Well, the Kundiawa outfit, by some happenstance, was precisely and exactly K500, to the *toea* (penny), below my odd *kina* number. Bob Eyles, the pom Public Works Manager, suspecting a little payola, but unable to speak out against the elected, and nationally connected, Provincial Secretary, threw out the Kundiawa company's bid saying they already had too much work going and wouldn't be able to bring this new contract in on time. Hailans Homes became the official recipient of the contract after a "closed door" session of the Chimbu Provincial Government.

We won the contract! Hailans Homes had ten houses to build on one governmental order. I knew the money could be collected. In the process, I had found a straight shooting Public Works Manager to work with. I walked out to the shop and called all my men together, carpenters, security men, Bobby, and, of course, Terape. When I told them we had won the contract, pure joy lit up their faces. Several of them let tears run down their cheeks. Terape, sizing up the situation by reading the faces, ran over to me, grabbed my hand, and kissed it. Embarrassed at his display, I pulled my hand away, but gave him a hug and tousled his head. The men all laughed. They were patting each other on the shoulders and shaking hands. It meant several months of work in front of them. I gave them a little pep talk and told them to sharpen their saws and chisels, clean up the shop area, as tomorrow we would begin.

I walked over to the lumberyard and on up to the offices to tell Ray and Lindsay the good news. Lindsay picked up the phone and called Jim in Lae. He handed the phone to me right after telling Jim the news. "Good on you, mate," Jim told me. I went on to tell him about the Chimbu "hanky-panky" that had transpired. He laughed knowingly. "Serves them right."

"No wonder they never visited the building sites, they had me to do it for 'em."

That night, on my little deck overlooking the squatter's village, with a cold S.P. brownie to toast the night sky, I celebrated by myself, our first contract won. My excitement became a little tempered by knowing that the responsibility fell on my shoulders to get it all done—the planning, the materials, the pre-fabrication, the deliveries, and the erection—all on schedule.

I grinned to myself, cracked another brownie and vowed out loud to the few stars that showed themselves through the clouds, "We'll get it done—me and my men. South Chimbu will be happy that Hailans Homes will engineer and construct their new rural development project!" I lifted my bottle skyward, with a little pride, but at the same time, in awe of the circumstances and toasted the feeling that could bring a tear and a grin, simultaneously. Papua New Guinea certainly posed a tremendous challenge. I could only wonder that night, what lay ahead!

chapter thirty

Airfreight, Malaria, and Holidays

Hailans Homes remained hard at work on supplying and erecting the South Chimbu Rural Development Project houses, when another challenge walked into my office. It showed up in the person of a Baptist minister who needed a house built in the village of Laplama, located in the mountains of the Enga Province. The problem to be figured out lay in getting the building materials into the village, since there was no road. In the past, they'd always carried materials in on foot, or used airfreight into their little grass airstrip. It had been an expensive chore to construct the few buildings that comprised the minister's present mission complex. Several of the existing buildings had been built from bush materials. The minister had an assistant pastor arriving to help with the mission effort and wanted to house him in a substantial house—at least one without constant roof leaks. He heard about our kit houses and liked the concept, as well as the prices. The minister told me the kit house cost would fit his mission budget, but the problem consisted of figuring a way to get the house panels into his village, and erected.

through the evening dusk there flies, tiny wings

with feverish dose, and bite that barely stings

A small river ran near Laplama, but the steep climb up to the village from the river would have been prohibitive. The trek in from the nearest clay road downriver, carrying building materials through dense bush, would also prove prohibitive. The pastor held out slim chance for getting the kit house components into Laplama via a water route.

Then the pastor puzzled out loud, "Too bad the components I saw in your shop wouldn't fit into a twin otter, as MAF (Mission Aviation Fellowship) would fly them into my village at no cost!"

"How big is the twin otter's freight door?"

"I don't remember the exact dimensions, but your panels would never fit in!"

I picked up the telephone on my desk and dialed the MAF Office at Hagen's Kagamuga Airport. After a few telephone referrals, I reached their freight office and one of their administrators. He told me the biggest width the freight door could handle was 1200 mm (4 ft.), but material lengths on up to 3000 mm (10 ft.) would fit inside the fuselage of the rugged STOL (short takeoff and landing) aircraft. The freight man

190

also gave me the maximum weight in kilograms that the plane could carry on any one load. I thanked him and hung up the phone.

After a few size calculations, and knowing the approximate weights of the kit house components, I looked up from my scratch pad at the pastor sitting anxiously beside my desk. I asked him if delivery and commencement of erection in three weeks would work for him. A big smile lit up his face as he glanced skyward. I went on to explain that we would have to cut the panels sizes in half vertically, creating twice as many panels. The panel joints would be covered every 1200 mm around the house with vertical cover strips. The pastor kept smiling as he asked me if he could sign anything, like a contract. I told him he could sign a check for half the price and the balance would be due upon our successful completion of his new assistant's house. We shook hands on the deal and after he left, still smiling, I went out to tell my men we needed to fit another house into our prefabrication schedule. I would give the shop foreman the sizing details the next day. They made their happy sounds – "*ayiii*" – fill the shop as they looked around at each other grinning. They felt busy, but obviously pleased by the security more work brought to their jobs.

From the shop, I sprinted over and up to Ray West's office to give him the Baptist pastor's check for deposit. Ray joked with me that the way Hailans Homes was bringing in housing orders, we soon would be the lumberyard's biggest customer. We had a little laugh as I showed him my crossed fingers and said, "I hope so!"

Ray and I had worked out an accounting system that separated Hailans Homes from the lumber and hardware business. I wanted to know how we did on our own. From housing profits, I now paid rent on my factory/shop space, an administrative fee for his monthly accounting

services, and a reasonable contribution into the company overhead costs for telephone, office supplies, postage, and other items. In return, the lumber/hardware sales office gave me a good contractor's discount on my purchased materials. Each house we now finished, I could check my costs and overheads, then adjust my future estimates accordingly. Jim had tried to give me a raise when I landed the Chimbu contract, but I told him I'd rather have a small percentage of the profits to add to my basic salary. I felt it would be an incentive for me and would be a "win – win" situation for him. We agreed on ten percent and both were happy. If I made him a hundred grand in net profits, he'd give me ten grand and keep ninety for the company. If I didn't do well, he'd only have to pay me a base salary. To me, the challenge of the New Guinea mountains represented the best part, with whatever followed in remuneration, a definite plus.

Ray West had hired on from the Gold Coast of Australia, south of Brisbane, in Queensland. He and his wife Meg decided the adventure would be a worthwhile experience for both them, and their three kids – Tracey (10 yrs.), Joanne (8 yrs.), and Glenn (5 yrs.). He took a two-year contract and came on board to replace Jock at putting the company's financial affairs in order.

I saw in Ray's paperwork that he played tennis and swam for recreation. I invited him to the Hagen Tennis Club to hit some balls, soon after he arrived. Ray turned out to be a "Clark Kent" on the tennis court. The first set we played, I was lucky to win two games, and my game is actually pretty good at the club level. Ray wears glasses and looks the part of the quiet accountant. Later, I found out from his wife Meg, that he played doubles one year in the French Open and he, with an American partner, knocked out the top tournament seeds, Ian Tiriac and Ile Nastase! Ray was also a gold medal swimmer from his Gold Coast competitive days in Australia. The two of us went on to play a lot of fun tennis on weekends. He tried to teach me to relax on the court and become more fluid in my motions. He proved semi-successful with his effort, but it was like trying to teach a deer not to tense up with a mountain lion on the prowl nearby. My energy levels were high, and still are! When I got good and tired, then I became a bit more fluid. Maybe it was the great tasting New Guinea coffee and tea that kept my engine running at a high idle! Who knows?

The West family—Ray, Meg, and Tracey in back, shy Glenn and Joanne in front

Each night after scribbling in my journal, I would cross another day off the calendar that hung on the wall beside my living room desk. Some nights seemed so long and the void caused by the distance between myself and my family and friends made the void pulse an aching beat. I talked with Sandia, and some of my kids, by telephone periodically, but usually got withdrawal pangs after hanging up. I wrote my daughters and my son as often as I could. How I wished they would listen to the lessons that life had taught me. I could tell, however, from their lack of genuine interest, that my children would have to experience life themselves. My stories, and philosophies, just didn't appear as profound as what life brought to each of their doorsteps. I guess all of us parents want to save the heartaches and explain the joys in this life, but words are just that, words. I guess we need to live what we tell them is important, let them witness our commitment to our stated values, without double standards, and just hope they see the truth of it!

Sandia's arrival date, at that point, was only a little more than a month away. I found myself increasingly nervous and tense at times, needing so badly to hold my lady in my arms. Four and one-half months had passed without seeing her, holding her, with the beautiful exception of looking at her photographs on my desks at the office and at home. Try going months without a hug!

My men must have sensed my irritability, and discussed a solution, because one evening one of the lumberyard truck drivers, Tommie, showed up at my gate with two young New Guinea ladies. He thought he was doing me a favor and told me they came from his village and would spend the night with me. I didn't want to hurt his feelings and tried to explain that I wanted to wait for my own lady to arrive. Tommie couldn't understand, or believe me, and pointed to their naked breasts to show me they didn't sag, and were full and uplifted. "*Yonpela susu, emi gutpela*," he said (Young breasts are good!) The two young ladies smiled and poked their chests

192

out even further.

"Tommie, thank you and please tell them thank you for the offer, but I want to wait for my own *meri*. It is very important to me!"

I turned and walked up toward my flat, waving back at their questioning faces on the other side of the chainlink gate. They still stood there, by the padlocked entry gate, when I got up to the flat and looked out the window. Finally, they got into Tommie's lumberyard truck and drove away. My heart was still beating from the unexpected pleasure offering of these New Guinea Mountains. My men probably had a hand in this, but none the less, I felt good. The stubbornness and resolve in my heart, to me, represented a measure of my deep love for Sandia. I didn't want to cheapen that love with a one-nighter. Maybe she'd never know, but I would. I walked over to my calendar and again counted the days remaining.

One morning, about a month before Thanksgiving, I stood in the shop lining out the men on the day's workload, when I noticed tears rolling down the cheeks of one of my new hires, Steven. I asked Mondul, my "*wonwok*" foreman to find out what had happened to the man and let me know.

Mondul caught up with me a few minutes later and explained, "*Nupela pikinini meri bilong Steven, emi dai pinis!* (Steven's baby girl had died.)

I asked Mondul, "*Bebi bilong em gat hamas mun?*" (How many months old was his baby?)

"*Emi gat tripela mun, tasol,*" he responded telling me the baby was just three months old.

"Mondul," I instructed, "*Tokim long mi, sori tumas long bebi bilong em! Yu kisim bokis bilong putim skin bilong bebi e dai pinis na givim long* Hailans Homes. *Tokim Steven, emi no wok dispela de na tumaro. Emi go long ples bilong em nau.*" (Tell him, I mourn for his baby girl. You get a

baby coffin and present it to him from Hailans Homes. Tell him not to work today or tomorrow. He should go to his village now.)

Mondul turned and trotted back to the shop to carry out my wishes. A few minutes later, Steven walked out the security gate, carrying one of our Hailans Homes plywood child's coffins on his shoulder. He waved to me, trying to smile a thank you through his tears. My heart did a tumble. It is no small thing to lose such a young life, even in a country where many infants die. I heard stories that when the white man came to Papua New Guinea, six out of every ten babies died. Western teaching of hygiene and medicines had cut the number of infant deaths in half, but still, too many died. I reflected on some of the squatter's villages that I ran through on my early morning runs. Usually they were built around a water source, in a ravine, for instance, or beside a small creek. The creeks always looked muddy and dirty to me. No telling what was dumped into them upstream of each village. They used the water for drinking, cooking, washing, and everything else. Hygiene was definitely lacking in those crowded conditions.

That same afternoon, I got word Lindsay had been stricken with malaria. The office girls cooked up chicken soup for him and I volunteered to drive them over to Lindsay's house with their "Samaritan" soup. Poor Lindsay was scheduled to go home to Australia in only six more weeks when his present contract finished. He had explained to me one day that this time he intended to really go finish. He had two grandsons that were already teenagers. Lindsay had been gone so much, he hardly knew them.

At Lindsay's bedside, I grabbed his big hand in both of mine and told him, "Lindsay, you've got to get better so you can go home and see those grandkids you told me about. No lousy mosquito can keep you down!"

He looked up at me through half-opened, very bloodshot, and swollen eyes, with a hint of a smile from his mouth. His strained voice sounded barely audible as he told me, "Bill, you have to take cloroquin. I've never been so sick in my life. It is bloody hell, this malaria stuff. My body, mind, everything is all buggered up!"

We didn't talk too much more because one of the office girls, Maggie, told Lindsay to, "Hush up now, you can talk to Bill later" and started spooning in their chicken soup, bite by bite, to his parched lips.

A few minutes after getting a small portion of the soup down his throat, Lindsay drifted off into a feverish sleep. The two office girls, along with his *haus meri* (maid), told me to go ahead and leave. They would stay and watch him until he woke again, or until the night watch came on.

I drove away, hearing Lindsay's words about the cloroquin and decided I'd better get on a schedule with the malaria medicine. Lindsay's sickbed advice had a certain persuasive power about it. I aimed my truck down the road toward the Government Pharmaceutical Building, where my *wontok*, Charles Fishman, held the position of head pharmacist. After parking and finding Charles, he gladly counted me out a year's supply of the cloroquin pills. Two per week was the dosage he explained as he typed out a label and affixed it to the pill jar. "There's a water fountain over there. Take your first two right now, then once a week, every Thursday, from now on!"

As I swallowed the first two pills, I asked him, "I've heard some people can't handle the cloroquin. They have adverse reactions. How true is that?"

"Very few people have bad reactions. When they do, it usually affects their sight and hearing. You'll know if it affects you."

"I heard a story of a big strapping athlete from Australia that died from the side effects of cloroquin!"

"Very rare. Would you rather get malaria?"

"Nope. I just saw an Aussie friend of mine sick as a dog with it. Doesn't look like fun at all. How much do I owe you for the pills?"

"On the house, *wontok*."

"*Tank yu, maracin man bilong mi*!" (Thanks, my medicine man!)

I headed back to work with a head full of thoughts spinning around—malaria, Lindsay, cloroquin drugs, and the fact that I'd just as soon not get sick like Lindsay, and then have to deal with the ongoing relapses that malaria brought on. I knew Jim's philosophy with regard to the disease was that "healthy people didn't get sick!" Mosquitoes didn't check your health chart, however, before they sunk their trusty sticker into you; and if the female anopheles mosquito bit a person carrying the malaria parasite and then came along, in short order, and stuck their little sharp sucker thing into your body— welcome to the nasty world of malaria. That's how an insect carrier transmits it, from one human to the next. The mosquito never even gets sick. Even though the disease proved more prevalent in the coastal regions, than in the highlands, Lindsay was sick with it, as were other highlanders. I finally decided not to worry about it anymore. Take the two pills every Thursday evening and forget about all the controversy.

That weekend I felt like I caught a mild cold, with sniffles and watery eyes, but it disappeared by Monday. I never gave the cloroquin a thought. The next weekend, though, I got a bit sicker and did begin to wonder if the cloroquin had anything to do with it. By Monday it passed again. The third weekend after starting the cloroquin regime, by Friday afternoon, I left work and went to the flat to crawl into my little single bed. I'd become a very sick "puppy" and hardly remember that weekend at all. I went through

My faithful man Terape

cycles of pounding headaches, fever, chills, and debilitating thirst. Getting to a sink for water proved a monster chore. A couple of bananas made up the only solid food that passed my parched lips. I slept for long periods of tossing and turning restless sleep. My body became so weak; I couldn't even sit up without tremendous effort. My ears rang a steady, high-pitched hum. Mid-morning on Monday, I came out of it a bit and stumbled my way into the shower. I stood with my mouth upturned to the shower rose drinking in the cool water. The shower felt so refreshing, as the fever had broken and my skin now felt cool to the touch.

I pulled on some clothes and drove my pick-up the short distance to the office. I sat weakly in my chair and looked around my domain. Looking at the stack of estimates waiting to be done on my desk seemed to take an effort, just in their contemplation. I stood from my desk chair and pulled the curtains almost shut. The decreased brightness made my eyes feel a little better. My ears still filled with a distant, steady ringing.

Terape came slowly through the office door, studying my face as he moved to the front of my desk. He frowned and signed me that he was worried about me in his heart. I signed back that I would be okay. None the less, Terape showed up about every half-hour and signed me to go home and sleep. I felt better there in the office with my men walking around outside than I would have back in the flat, alone.

A little later, I walked over to the bakery next door to buy a couple of scones and returned to my desk to eat them. The walk and the food nourishment felt good. I tackled a small job and actually got it done, although it took most of the afternoon. Finally Terape came in and told me it was quitting time. His signing consisted of pointing at his old beat up watch followed by an index finger slice across his throat. All the men were going home. They had worked well on their own. Some of them waved at my partially drawn curtains as they passed my office on their way out our security gate. I knew their looks of concerns were genuine. They thought I had come down with malaria—a disease of their country.

I did very little work that Monday, but the fact that I did anything at all seemed an accomplishment. My post-fevered mind worked out slowly that the cloroquin had to be the culpirt. Looking intently at the pile of work on the desk in front of me, I made a quiet, but firm, resolution that Monday afternoon—*muski maracin bilong malaria* (forget about the malaria medicine)!

I would take my chances with the female anopheles mosquito in those highlands. I had tough skin anyway. Cloroquin and my body didn't make good roommates, period.

My recovery proved slow, but steady. By the following Thursday, I neared ninety percent comeback. A pair of shorts arrived in a package from Sandia. I felt a little sad that there wasn't a letter in the box also, but I was super happy with the shorts. At my flat that evening, I tried them on to find a perfect fit. When I let my right hand slide into the cargo pocket of the shorts, I felt paper and pulled it out. It turned out to be a beautiful love note from my Sandia, hidden away in the pocket, for me to find upon wearing the shorts. My spirits lifted skyward. The note brought me past one hundred percent. No more cloroquin and away I'd go. Sandia always surprised me with subtle love messages like that. Weeks after entering New Guinea, I flipped my day timer open to the new date page to note down something and found a "post-it" message of love from my lady. What a sweet thoughtful person to share life with. How could I have been so lucky!

The following week was Thanksgiving, which is not even a holiday in Papua New Guinea, but a big deal in my lonely heart. I passed through Kagamuga Airport to pick up some airfreighted materials on Tuesday, when a missionary woman, a *wontok*, walked up and invited me for Thanksgiving dinner. She knew who I was, where I worked, and the fact that I lived in the country alone. After recovering from my initial surprise, I thanked her for the invitation. She went on to describe her house location to me. It was also in the "Siberia" area and only a few minutes from my own flat. I should note that missionary women and their dress—long skirts, long sleeve blouses, and no cosmetics—appeared very identifiable. They chose to act and dress in a

manner so as not to draw any attention to themselves.

I awoke the next morning very early with many reflections in my mind. I grabbed my journal and a cup of coffee and started to write:

25th of November 1987

When I awoke this morning,
My very first thought that struggled through was
"This is my 100th day in Papua New Guinea,"
And then slowly a second thought
Found its way into my waking mind,
"Tomorrow is Thanksgiving and I'm here alone
in a very strange land."
I laid there in sadness,
As I thought of all the families
That would gather together tomorrow
In the good old U. S. of A.
I could almost smell the aromas
Of turkey and that tasty seasoned dressing,
And mashed potatoes, all covered with gravy,
And my favorite yams, smothered in a candied
sauce,
And oh those beautifully delicious pumpkin pies.
Wow, how the depression set in!
How alone I felt,
How far away from it all I was!
Then I started to think-
As the first rays of sunshine,
Began to fill my little bedroom with light.
I am so very lucky
And I have so much to be thankful for,
And lest I forget,
I must put these thoughts to paper.
Thanks for whatever Divine Purpose
That gave me life.
I give thanks for the love of my wife,
Whose vibrations of caring reach me so strongly,
Across all the mountains and oceans between.
I give thanks for all my children

And their children,
For in giving them life,
My own life takes purpose.
And through their seeds,
My life is without end.
I am so thankful to be
Husband, Father, Grandfather, Brother, and Friend
To my so very special few,
Whose love I never doubt,
Regardless of the distance that separates us,
Or the lack of communication between us.
I give thanks for the health and the strength,
That has allowed me to run
To the top of the mountain
That fills my window view.
I feel thanks for the spirit of youth,
That keeps my body young
And my mind, still full of dreams.
I feel a special thanks for all the little things:
Like a pair of shoes,
When most around me, walk in bare feet.
Like a hot shower each morning,
While I see most around me
Only able to quench their thirst
From little muddy creeks.
Like fresh fruit and vegetables
When I see so many hungry every day,
Like my body's health that keeps me well,
While so many others are sick and die here every day.
Like having a good job,
While thousands in this land, seek work of any kind.
Like my invitation from an American missionary family,
To share their Thanksgiving meal.
Like just plain being free
To decide where I want to be,
To follow dreams and explore the world
For whatever seems
To be worth learning or teaching about,
To share with whom I please,
All my discoveries,

To try and live an example life
For others to see
To break out of their ritual shells
And smell the fragrance of the flowers,
And hear the crickets and the songs of the birds,
And just be free to choose!
Oh my Creator, I have so very much
Take from me this sadness,
And let me only smile!
Mipela no ken lusim ting ting! (We cannot forget!)

The next day, sitting at the missionaries' "table of plenty," during the blessing, I could not hold the tears back. Joining hands and giving Thanks, in the mountains of New Guinea, surrounded by countrymen, became so overwhelming. The table was set with turkey, dressing, mashed potatoes, yams, and gravy. There was even cranberry sauce and pumpkin pie. It is so difficult to find words to express my feelings on that afternoon. We talked of the hardships and the challenges of P.N.G.—theirs to save souls and mine, definitely more capitalistic, to get housing constructed. The rest of the group, maybe ten people, were all missionaries, but did seem interested in my P.N.G. experiences, albeit short in duration.

I met Rachel that week also. She was an Engan *meri* and the mother of two small children. Rachel approached me outside the office, on the street, asking if I needed a "*haus meri.*" Her easy smile showed brilliant white teeth. She obviously didn't chew betelnut, or *buai*, which stained so many of the New Guinean's teeth a nasty red color. Rachel had a twinkle in her eye and showed a lot of animation and spirit. She seemed well mannered and obviously unafraid to speak to me quietly, yet boldly, on the street. Not many native women would approach an expatriate and speak out to him on the public street. Anyway, she caught me a little unaware, so I didn't give her a definite answer—

197

something like, "I don't think so, but I'll think about it later." My response ended her solicitation at that point and I walked on toward the lumberyard. I had indeed been thinking about hiring a *haus meri* as I didn't want to spend what little time I had for leisure scrubbing floors, but that's as far as I got in my thinking.

Early Sunday morning, after Thanksgiving, I felt strong enough to try my old constitutional run up Kuta Ridge Mountain near the edge of town. I headed out my door, thinking to hold it down to an easy run. I knew, once I began running, it would be easy to get carried away. "*Hold it down, hold it down, this is only a recovery run,*" I told myself silently.

There squatted Rachel, outside my security gate, smiling, and ready to make her case that she was the *haus meri*, I didn't know I needed, but really did. I told her I'd think about it as I ran—for her to come back in two hours, or so.

An hour and a half later, I trotted back to my flat to find Rachel still squatting in the same position as I had left her earlier. "Okay, today you can clean my place and I'll see what you can do!" I told her. Rachel's round face broke out in a radiant smile as she deciphered my meaning. I motioned for her to follow me through the chain link security gate.

As we walked up the drive to my little flat on the hill, my expatriate neighbor, Mary, stuck her head out her window and offered me the part-time services of her *haus meri*. Mary said to me, "You can't hire a girl off the street. She'll steal from you every time. An honest *haus meri* is very difficult to find!"

"Thank you, Mary, for the advice, but I'm going to give Rachel here a try. She'll only clean when I'm around on weekends anyway," I shouted up to her, fully realizing that Rachel understood enough English to get the gist of Mary's implication. I saw Mary shaking her head from

side to side as she retreated into her big house.

I showed Rachel where my cleaning stuff was located and coached her in its use, as she tried desperately to explain to me that she was an S.D.A.(Seventh Day Adventist) and didn't steal. I responded to her plea by telling her, "Don't worry about what Mary said. Just give my place a good cleanup and I'll be happy."

I left her alone, after a little bit, to go up to the tennis club for my Sunday game with Ray and Meg and whoever else happened to show up. We always played round robin tennis, switching partners, to keep it fun. I loved the running, the sweating, and the excellent competition. The dirt courts proved easy underfoot and one could play several hours without leg muscle fatigue. We usually followed the tennis with a cold beer from an ever present "eski" (cooler—Australian slang for Eskimo) and small talk after the tennis—mostly regarding the difficulties in getting work accomplished in P.N.G. and sometimes, the humor of it all! You had to learn to laugh at some of the situations that arose, rather than letting the circumstances stress you out!

I returned to my flat, unlocked the padlocked security gate, which I locked to keep others out, rather than Rachel in, and entered the house to find all five foot of Rachel down on her knees, just finishing polishing the hardwood floors by hand. I hoped leaving her alone in the flat made a statement of my trust. The place sparkled with cleanness. She had retrieved one of my empty, imported, ice cream containers from the trash, washed it, lined it with aluminum foil, and filled it with bright, fresh cut flowers. The place glowed with a woman's touch. Oh, how my heart wished it had been Sandia's touch, but that would have to wait a while longer.

I gave her a big smile and told her, "*Emi plenti gutpela wok!*" (You've done very good work!) From my pocket, I drew out some *kina*

Rachel showing her first pay

Rachel with baby (Note facial tattoos)

and paid her a *kina* fifty per hour. It became Rachel's turn to smile, as that was a good rate of pay—six *kina* for four hours work.

"Rachel, you come next Sunday at the same time and you can clean again. Do you understand?"

"Yes, I will come next Sunday to clean."

As I let her out the security gate at the bottom of the hill, she turned and said to me, "*Plenti white man no ken laugh.* You like to laugh. I am happy to work for you. *Lukim yu behin* (see you later)."

I watched her walk away, noting her upright, head held high, proud posture. Many New Guinea women had that posture, perhaps because of the heavy loads they often carried on their backs in *bilums* (string bags) supported from their foreheads. Rachel's walk was, however, just a bit more upright and spirited than most. I thought to myself as Rachel's form grew smaller in the distance, *The women here, as in many emerging societies, are the strength and backbone of this culture! They bear the brunt of the hard labor in New Guinea. They are the glue that holds this place together!*

Lindsay continued to recover from his bout with malaria and weakly went about cleaning up his affairs, in preparation for "going finish"—Aussie terminology signifying the expatriate contract had terminated and it was time to leave the country, usually for home, although sometimes for another expatriate contract somewhere else. Lindsay had been in P.N.G. for about seven years and had done it all. He'd managed the sawmill in Tomba from the start and helped Jim get the lumber business going, and then the hardware side of things. He'd done the fun things like deep-sea fishing and bush walking. He'd suffered the difficult times when beaten and robbed with axes, when his wife didn't want to stay in P.N.G. any longer and went home, and finally, the latest, contracting malaria. Lindsay proved a tough man and an honest man at the same time. I think that's why the nationals liked him so much. He was a fair man when it came to being "boss" man. Many of the national workers seemed saddened at the prospect of his leaving. Maggie, Roselynn, and the rest of the lumberyard office girls organized a "going finish" *mumu* for Lindsay. I told them I would help out in any way they needed. "Grunt labor" is what I ended up providing—carrying and digging. They were well versed in the *mumu* process and I became the student.

At a one of their clan sites, in the hills overlooking Hagen, a large deep hole was dug in the predominately clayish ground to start things out. When it measured maybe a meter (a little more than three feet) in depth, the office girls lined the bottom with two or three layers of banana palm leaves, then dropped in lots of hot stones they had heated on a nearby bonfire. They put another couple of layers of banana palm leaves, followed by the uncooked food—peeled *strongpela* cooking bananas, *kau kau* (sweet potatoes), carrots, *kumus* (tasty greens), and a bunch of plucked and prepared *kakaruks* (chickens). Coconut milk was then poured over the lot. More palm leaves, followed by more hot stones, another last layer of banana palms, and the process terminated by shoveling back the earth to fill the original hole to the top. Four hours, more or less, later, the girls would reverse the process and retrieve the cooked food for serving.

The taste and the tenderness of the food astounded me. It was moist and flavored by the coconut milk. Also astounding to me, was the amount of food the nationals piled, or mounded, on their plates. Surely they wouldn't be able to eat it all, but they did for the most part. I did see one man's *meri* putting some food into her ever-present *bilum*. The "feast or famine" mentality prevailed, ingrained in their society—especially when it came to meat, or protein. There was no nice little "three meals a day" thinking in Papua New Guinea. Just eat a lot when it's available. Stomachs must be able to expand at will, like those *bilums*. The more the women loaded into them, the bigger they became.

Lindsay appeared to be sad and happy with excitement at the same time. His going finish party found him very reflective on his challenging time in New Guinea, but anxious at the same time, to go home to Tin Can Bay in Queensland. The office girls and the lumberyard guys dressed Lindsay in the traditional dress of a Wahgi man, complete with *arse* grass and face paint, and made him one of their own. He did keep his skivie shorts on and they showed where the *arse* grass wasn't. He seemed a little sheepish posing for our cameras, but after downing a couple of S.P. brownies, Lindsay began to relax a little and get used to his native dress. Later he

Lindsay (center) in traditional dress

200

even tried to imitate some of the native dances. His dancing attempts brought hoots of laughter from his national hosts.

Some of the spokesmen for the different clans took turns making speeches about Lindsay, mostly in glowing terms and tinted with genuine sadness at his leaving. When the accolades were finished, we broke up into small groups, with S.P. *bia* as the catalyst and shared ideas and thoughts. I found myself wondering what these same people would think of me when it came my turn to "go *pinis*?"

I cornered one of the office girls, Annette, and asked her, "Was it a good thing that the white man came to New Guinea?"

"Oh yes," she answered in her best English. "We have so much more in our lives now. The big companies give us jobs and we earn money to buy things with. Even women can get jobs and help our families!"

Other nationals, men and women, began to gather around us to listen to the conversation and join the dialogue. The men probably didn't appreciate me asking opinions of a *meri*, but I went on, focusing on Annette.

"What man is considered successful in Papua New Guinea?"

"One who has many wives, much land, many pigs, and many children, especially girl children, who bring big bride price," Annette answered. The others around us nodded in agreement. "How does a man in your country become a big-man?" she asked me in return.

"Except for the many wives, as we are allowed only one, it's pretty much the same, except we use money instead of pigs."

I squatted down on the grass, holding my S.P. *bia* and talked with this national group how pretty much the world over, a man is judged by what he has, not what he does. I used Lindsay as an example to contradict what they were telling

me. They honored him for what he did in their country, not what he possessed. They puzzled over that for a little while and then one man said Lindsay had land and houses in Australia.

"Look," I offered, "at the missionaries. They don't get paid and live with only basic needs. Many are from my country and are here for an idea—just to help your *wontoks* to know the God they believe in and devote their lives to."

"But your churches collect money and send it to them," one man commented.

"Yes, you are right, but they don't keep the money for themselves. The missionaries use it to build churches here to teach about God."

"Why are you here, Bill?" one of the office girls asked.

"Do you know the word, adventure?" I asked looking at the faces around me. "I guess I came for the adventure and the challenge of it and to learn from your New Guinea culture about my own life and values. Maybe I can also teach something that will help you after I leave—like the building of a kit house!" They all laughed with me. The nationals liked to laugh, almost like children do.

Just then, the scene struck me. I stood surrounded by all nationals, while across the clearing a group of '*white skins*' gathered, partying together. Lindsay, in the middle of the white group, was the only contrast to the western clothes, still dressed in his native get-up. How we all gravitate to the security of our own kind. I guess it's a human thing! I silently vowed to not shut myself off from what the nationals of Papua New Guinea could teach me. We are all conceived and born in the same way, and we all die one day; there are no better or lesser people. We are just socialized a bit differently in between the first gasping inhale of breath upon entry into life and the last slow exhaling breath upon exit from it.

"Come on," I said to those around me, "let's go over and drink some of Lindsay's *bia* and wish him well!"

Lindsay went home as Christmas approached. Many other Australian expats took holidays (vacations) as the year neared its end. Most businesses put things into slow gear and let the festivities happen. I gave my men a Christmas party and put Rachel in charge of the *mumu*. She seemed happy to get the extra work and took responsibility for the food. I told one of my drivers to take her to the market in my truck and gave her some money from my "petty cash." Her instructions were to get enough food for all my men and their wives. Rachel walked proudly back to the shop to start counting the workers and ask about their marital status. She was a capable, no-nonsense, Engan *meri*. I, in turn, raided the company beer stash to come up with three *bias* per man. That would be a fair ration, otherwise, they'd drink too much and I'd end up with trouble in the ranks!

The Hailans Homes party in the shop area a few days before Christmas turned out great. Rachel portioned the food out in large piles on each plate. There turned out to be plenty to go around. I took the opportunity to go around and shake each of the wives hands, although I didn't do too well at remembering all their names. After eating most of the food and drinking a couple of beers, my normally quiet crew called for me to make a speech. When I stood up, obviously a little nervous, they started banging on the workbenches and yelling the familiar, "*ayiii!*"

Holding my hands up, palms forward, for quiet, I bowed my head and gave the Creator thanks for the chance to work together with them at Hailans Homes and to be in Papua New Guinea. I gave thanks for the work that had come to us and said "Amen." Looking out at their eager faces, I told them that I felt happy that we had plenty of houses to build. They would have work for many moons to come as long as we each did our part and paid attention to doing good work. Then more house orders would come to us. Now was the time to enjoy their families, as we would have to work hard, come the New Year. I turned to sit down and Mondul, my *wonwok* foreman, jumped up on the workbench. In New Guinea, men love to make speeches!

Mondul started by telling the men to rest up during the Christmas holidays, so they could work hard when they returned. He told them that many of the workers at the lumberyard wanted to now come to work at Hailans Homes because we had much work and good conditions. They'd better not be lazy, as other men wanted to take their jobs. Then Mondul turned toward me and said to the group in pisin, "*Taim nuigini man igat fivpela ten krismas, emi stap long tri. Olgeta man na meri, istap hia, gat hamamas yu no stap long tri. Tank yu plenti long wok bilong mipela olgeta.*" (When a New Guinea man reaches fifty years of age, he lies down under a tree. All the men and women, here, are happy that you don't lie under a tree. Thank you much for the work that you brought to all of us!)

I held up a beer to toast them all and told them to pick up their paychecks, with holiday bonus, and go home with their families. "Merry Christmas and I'll see you all the Monday after the New Year!"

Later that night, I bailed one of my men, Graham, out of the calaboose, where they held him for beating up his wife. He had evidently gone off with friends after our party and found a lot more to drink. Wife beating and drinking proved inherent problems in the New Guinea society. Wife beating had gone on long before alcohol came to the country, but drunkenness certainly exacerbated the fighting between marital partners. The New Guinean couldn't hold his liquor and didn't know when to stop drinking, kind of like our own native Americans, who were without any previous alcoholic experience. A New Guinean could, and would, sit down and drink a carton (case) of *bia*, and more, at one sitting. If some felt good, then more would be better. Feast or famine. Drink to oblivion. In fact, back in '75, when Papua New Guinea moved quickly toward independence, the expatriate population, of 50,000 plus, was very fearful of the chaos that would result when the nationals voted out the prohibition previously enforced by the Australian administration. The expatriates left in droves just prior to full independence in September of '75. Some reports show the expatriate numbers dropped below 10,000 shortly after independence. Many, in the exodus, expressed fear of what would happen under self-rule, which allowed wholesale liquor distribution throughout the country. Drunken debauchery turned out to be more of a paranoia than a reality, except in isolated cases, in a country where wife beating had always been a problem. Papua New Guinea demonstrated they could deal with the problems of self-rule in a reasonably responsible manner. Slowly, the expatriate population began to return, with much encouragement from the newly formed government. Administrators appealed for the expertise to return for the transitional phase of the new nation. Water supply plants, power plants, sewage disposal facilities, technical industries, —the infrastructure of the country, needed the expatriates to teach the technical end of things, along with a little westernization. The socialization, in a large way, was left to the missionaries and the new government. For example, a decree that all babies must be fed from the mother's breast; no artificial formulas allowed, except with medical certification.

The next day was Christmas Eve and I went into Hailans Homes to button things up and check on security guys. Sometimes they were apt to fall asleep! Satisfied to their alertness, I went to my desk and started to clean and organize the many piles on the top surface. There came a knock and I looked up to see the smiling face of my man, Mondul. He carried a neatly wrapped Christmas present, which he proudly held out to me. The homemade package label was done in Mondul's best printing and read, "Mary Christmas – this is a memorial present of Mary Christmas to you Mr. & Mrs. Bill Bruton from Mr. & Mrs. Mondul Mondhaim. May the Lord be with you and me through our Christmas Holiday. See you New Year – 1988." His English was great! I laughed with him, gave him a big hug, and told him I'd put it under my little Christmas tree (more like a branch off a pine tree) to open on the morrow. Mondul looked proud as he left my office.

Ray called me later in the morning to tell me two parcels had arrived in the mail for me. I ran all the way over and up to his office, with excited anticipation, to find a package from my Sandia and the other from Mary Pat, Dick's wife. My men had presented me with a joint little present also, so that "pine branch" tree would have a couple of things under it after all. I could wake the next morning, on Christmas, and sit down by the tree. You are never alone, if you love and are loved, no matter the distances that separate the physical bodies.

Later, as I locked up my office, my painter, Thomas, came to find me. He told me, "I have a Christmas present for you, but it's too heavy to carry. Can we use your truck?"

"Sure thing. Hop in and show me the way."

Thomas directed me to his nearby squatters' village and we pulled up near his little cardboard and grass shack. His smiling wife and several of his shy children appeared from behind their house, carrying a stalk of green bananas for me. Thomas helped them put it up into the truck bed. "They'll be ripe when your wife comes," he commented. I turned my attention to Thomas's family and took each of their hands, in turn, to ask their names and thank them for the Christmas present. Thomas once told me that seven of his twelve children had died very young.

Driving back to my flat, I thought about the difference between being alone and lonely. I was alone, as in being at a great distance from family and friends, but how could I really feel lonely when people in these remote mountains reached out to me. Old people often reached out to touch my arm with a smile as I passed them on my runs, or, sometimes, when I just walked by myself in town. Sure, I was alone, but I could focus on not being lonely. I could certainly focus on how fortunate I felt to be where I was, with the opportunity I had, to have my loved ones, however distant, and to have my health and energy.

While I stood engrossed in hanging the stalk of green bananas from the roof beam by my back door, the New Zealand neighbor behind me called over the fence to tell me she was hosting a Christmas Eve party that night. Would I please jump the fence to join the festivities? She said there was no need to bring anything except myself. I thanked her and told her, "Maybe I will," although the prospect of being with a bunch of married couples seemed less than intriguing at the time.

At dusk that night, I heard my gate shaking and rattling. Someone was down there and appeared to be a national in traditional attire – *arse* grass, no shirt, pig's tooth necklace, and bare feet. I headed down toward the gate. I recognized the security guard from next door, Amo. He spoke no English, but held out what appeared to

be an arrow in one hand and something white in the other.

"*Emi Krismas presen long yu,*" he told me with a huge smile, which seemed bright in the dim light of approaching darkness. The arrow was an intricately carved, ceremonial shaft and the white "something" turned out to be hand carved boar's tusks. Immediately struck with the compulsion to reciprocate, I dug down into the pockets of my shorts. After all, Amo didn't work for me and hadn't received a Christmas bonus in his paycheck – his gifts came from the heart. My left hand grasped some bills and I pulled them out, about five *kina*.

"*Emi moni tasol. Mi no gat sampela samting long yu,*" I said as I offered the *kina* bills through the chain link mesh of the security gate.

"*Tank yu, Masta Bill. Hamamas Krismas long yu,*" I heard Amo say as he waved and faded into the darkness, heading back to his duty post next door.

"*Hamamas Krismas,*" I shouted at his departing figure as I turned to walk up my long driveway, thinking of the cultural differences between Amo and me. He lived in a tiny grass sentry shack and worked for a few *kina* a week, while I lived in a "taj mahal" in comparison and earned hundreds of times his weekly income. Twenty or thirty New Guinea families and their houses could fit into my front yard alone. Most of the national families near me, lived along the creek banks in squatters' villages, while I lived on top of a hill. Yes, the companies gave the expats a lavish life style. It came with the job. Otherwise, the expats probably wouldn't stay on in P.N.G. On balance, I rationalized, the work proved tough and demanding. Many expats threw up their hands in utter despair, resigned, and left the country. Many others, however, adapted and toughed it out. Some of these expats would find it difficult in future years to return to the lifestyle of their homeland. Not the least of the difficulties were caused by getting used to the colonial lifestyle – never involving manual labor, house servants, and, mostly, living an elitist type of existence. Some expats I talked to refused to learn the relatively easy "*pisin*" language and would only deal with English speaking nationals, and then, only when they had to. This perspective formed the "we do it the right way, the only way, and these bloody nationals will do it my way, or not at all" attitude. The use of *bois* (boys) and *kanakas* (savages) were well salted into some of the expatriate vocabulary patterns. The nationals, on the other hand, felt total confusion by the whole westernization process. Take the missionaries, for example, in their zeal to save souls, very often left the nationals perplexed. My men, on more than one occasion, asked me, "Which church is telling the truth?" One church, in the Chimbu Mountains, paid ten *kina* to each national to leave the longer established church and come to their new one. Some missionaries required women in remote villages to start wearing brasseries! What a trip! Talk about confusion!

I decided to skip the expat Christmas Eve party over the fence behind me and went to bed early. It proved a homesick night. Sleep did not come easily. In between the party sounds of laughter and music, I still thought of Amo and my men, their gifts, and how far from home I was. The distance from family and friends seemed infinite. Ever the positive thinker, I concentrated on Sandia's arrival, now only a little more than three weeks away. Sleep came through the blurred images of my lady's smiling face and arms reaching out to encircle me. For all of you, whose relationships have become routine and mundane, try and visualize a long, distant separation and then watch the trivial "crud," or small stuff, fall away. Sandia's and my relationship had, and has even moreso now, value to both of us.

She is extraordinary to me and lets me know I am very important to her. Sleep came, as I centered all my smiling thoughts on my treasures in life.

Christmas morning, I awoke and stumbled my way to the electric water kettle. Soon I wrapped my hands around a mug of hot black New Guinea tea and walked out onto the small verandah to watch the squatters' village below me come to life. Smoke from some early morning fires hung above the grass rooftops. Kuta Ridge Mountain looked so beautiful with the early morning sun highlighting its shroud of misty fog. Soon the sun's rays would heat it enough to lift the veil of moisture skyward, revealing the lush green textures of the tree-laden mountain.

The phone rang inside, breaking into my quiet thoughts. I sat my tea on the rail and darted inside to my desk to answer it. Two lady friends from Grand Lake, Vivian and Wanda, sang "Merry Christmas to you" on the other end. They had worked out the time zone difference and figured they'd wake me up on Christmas morning with a harmonious serenade. The sunshine in their voices was truly a gift I will never forget. They took me from laughter to tears, and back again, describing winter in our Colorado Mountains, along with all the local gossip. Those moments are so special. Only a few years later, we lost Wanda, and her magic spirit, to breast cancer. She was only in her early forties! Live every second in time!

That Christmas day was bookended with another telephone conversation. Sandia called in the evening. We had an exciting conversation about the details of her journey to Papua New Guinea. I decided not to wait her arrival in the mountains, but to fly to the capital city of Port Moresby to meet her flight from Guam.

I told her I would have a hotel lined up where we could "crash" for the night and head up to the mountains the following day. She would be exhausted after traveling from Denver to New Guinea, via California, Hawaii, and Guam. Just make the Guam to Moresby flight. I'd take her from there!

After setting the telephone receiver back in its cradle, sleep proved impossible. My mind was in a rush. Sandia was really coming soon! I wanted to shout. Earlier attempts at persuading her to come at Christmas had proved futile. She had to get Kirsten lined out, after her high school completion, for her intended resettlement back east at her Connecticut grandma's house. Relationships sometimes have to take a back seat to the children's needs. Such is the way of us humans. To me, I had a date circled in red on my "X" hatched calendar – five months gone, three weeks to go. I could deal. I had to deal. My body finally stopped vibrating in the wee hours and a blissful sleep came.

New Years Eve found me at the Apple computer, I had pieced together, trying to express feelings in a form letter to friends and family:

Niuyia's Eve Ting-ting (THOUGHTS) 31 December '87

As I sit here on Niuyia's Eve, about to enter my sixth month in Papua New Guinea, it is certainly a time for reflection.

Sandia will join me in only 17 more days and I'm sure that will ease the feelings of isolation that I've experienced on many occasions. It is hard to explain the emotions of being alone in a native culture so radically different from anything I've ever known. You reach such exciting heights of exploration and discovery, only to find other times of extreme separation and loneliness. Oh, the balance of it all.

My first Krismas in P.N.G. was a whirlwind of

impressions. My men (29 of them), a few of their meris (women), some of their pikininies (children), and my haus meri, Rachel, prepared and shared an afternoon pre-Krismas mumu feast. Into a hole in the ground, lined with banana palm leaves, went strongpela bananas, kaukau (sweet potatoes), regular potatoes, squash, corn, cabbage, various greens, carrots, 14 freshly butchered chickens, and about 25 really hot stones. It was covered over with more banana palms and earth, then left to slowly cook for about three hours.

The smells and tastes of the kaikai (food) were so delicious. All the flavors permeated each other while cooking in the pit. I was the only one, by the way, who was honored with a fork to eat my share with. They wouldn't let me use my fingers to eat.

My last mail call before Krismas yielded two so appreciated packages – homemade Krismas cookies as only my friend Mary Pat could make them, and think to send them, and Bronco video tapes from my buddies, Vivian and Sandia. I went directly to my little flat on the hill, overlooking town, to put those gifts under my tropical Krismas tree.

In the dark of Krismas Eve, other presents were brought to my gate – a pair of pig's tusks and an intricately carved arrow. These gestures, along with a stalk of green bananas, I'd received a little earlier in the day, and the previous hand grasps of my men, with their expressions of Hamamas (Happy) Krismas, filled me with special warmth.

Then when Vivian and Wanda figured out the time difference to call me early Krismas morning, I was beside myself with joy. After hanging up the telephone and looking around at the many cards I'd also received, there was just one thought prevalent in my mind – no matter where you are, you are never alone, if you live in the thoughts of your so special friends!

Nothing is easy here in raw and rugged Papua New Guinea, but these people, for the most part, are a friendly, caring, and trying people. Only thir-

ty or forty years ago, here in these mountains, they were still in the virtual Stone Age. Now they are trying to speak English and rush headlong into the modern world. Sometimes I wonder if they would have been better off left alone, but of course the world won't allow it. The nationals (natives) have seen the "things" of civilization and want them. The appetite of our modern world also craves the rich store of minerals upon which these islanders sit – so there is no turning back now! Move past "GO" and don't even stop for the $200!

Perhaps there are things the Niuginians can teach us in our great rush to civilize them. For example, the nationals have pointed out to me, on more than one occasion, that most white people never laugh and smile – you think of the implication and what it means. Maybe we should learn to smile and laugh a little like these people so often do.

Most of the whites, or expatriates as they are called, arrived here first as missionaries and mercenaries, the profit seekers, and the occasional misfit, or non-conformist, like me,—here they call it the phenomenon of the three M's. Most I've met, do fit into one of these M's.

Sandia and I will be managing side by side businesses, furnishings and construction, respectively – in the purest capitalistic sense. I only hope, though, in addition to making the companies profitable, that we can teach our people well. I count on lots of patience, as the workings of a good company are completely foreign to the national here, as well it should be.

Before the white man showed up, the Niuginian lived, and still lives, a subsistent village life, where food is grown and shared by everyone. The young always eat first and the old eat last, whatever is left. A man's wealth is measured in the number of wives, pigs, and here in the mountains, seashells that he possesses. Bride prices can range up to thirty pigs, or the equivalent. A man with many daughters will become wealthy. An interesting aside on paying for your wife (bride price) is that if the parentally arranged bride doesn't work out and is sent home to her village (divorced), the village court works out a proportionate refund to the husband!

I'm getting off the track, but I hope Sandia and I can be meaningful in Papua New Guinea while we are here. I have spent much time contemplating why we decided to leave our beloved Rocky Mountains behind and come here. The long and the short of it is, while we'll probably end up buried in them thar hills, there is too much world out here to learn from, to look at, touch and share. Maybe, after all is said and thought about, it was just too exciting an offer to refuse!

Back to the present, as midnight approaches, the sound of drums has steadily increased in volume for the last hour or so, while I've been thinking and typing. All over town, people are beating drums, sing-sing drums, kundu drums, and empty oil barrel drums, to welcome in the Niuyia. It sounds like thousands of them in a steady beat, echoing off the mountainsides, filling this fertile mountain valley with an incredibly pulsating sound. My desktop is vibrating. A little different from the lighted ball dropping in Time's Square!

Hamamas Niuyia my friends – may you resolve to touch and share the Creation this year in a way you've never done before. Challenges and rainbows are what it's all about. All my best hopes for your 1988!

Niugini Bill

chapter thirty-one

The Touch of Sandia

A date for Sandia's arrival was marked and circled in red on my calendar. It approached quickly as the Christmas/New Year holidays fell behind me. The date was January 17, 1988.

the wait seemed long, ocean's span undefined

but time flowed past, then hearts once more entwined

Jim and Mary Ann started a new home and office furnishings business, Total Concept, in the coastal city of Lae. They planned a branch store of Total Concept in Mt. Hagen. Hailans Homes created, remodeled, and painted the new branch space from an old storage area adjacent to Hailans Homes shop space. The plan in place called for Sandia to apply for a work permit upon arrival and then manage the Hagen store for Total Concept. Her duties would include sales, delivery, installation, and teaching/managing a sewing room. The main ordering of inventory, as well as payroll and accounting, would be the responsibility of the main store in Lae. We all figured, with Sandia's enthusiastic approval, that she'd rather work than sit around our chainlink and barbed wire encircled flat each day while I worked. Sandia had always been a worker "beaver," starting when she was six years old helping the family with harvesting in the agricultural fields in Colorado.

Over the slow holiday season, Jim and Mary Ann really would have preferred to have Sandia around the new branch store, getting familiar with her responsibilities. In an effort to entice her to New Guinea earlier than planned, they offered, and booked us, accommodations at a tourist resort hotel on the northern coastal beaches at Madang, over Christmas week. I wanted it to happen, obviously, but it was Sandia's call. She reluctantly passed on it, trying to get our Kirsten set up for her move from Colorado to Connecticut. Kirsten would start out her life as a brand new high school graduate under the wing of her Connecticut grandmother and branch out from there. Her longer-term goal lay in New York City to work around music in some fashion. What a contrast, from the rugged and remote Rocky Mountains to New York City! Later, she would get a job in N.Y.C., bookkeeping for M.T.V., and meet a few famous people, only to discover they were just as human as the rest of us.

The long and short of Sandia's decision came down to the fact that she couldn't head for P.N.G. until the 10th of January. Jim and M.A.

208

figured a way to cover for her at the Hagen store and, as for myself, I took a really deep breath, circled the 10th on my calendar, and hunkered a little deeper into my work. Then a few days later the call came from Sandia saying she found it impossible to get all things done on time. She had to back up her travel another week, to arrive on the 17th. Poor Sandia must have been feeling the pressure. A week isn't a long stretch of time to most people, but to me, it honestly hit me right in the pit of my stomach. I went through the whole gamut from anger to frustration, then sucked it all in, focused on the love in my heart, crossed out the 10th, and circled the 17th on my trusty calendar. The 17th it was – no more wavering allowed!

Time is such a very different concept to people. Moments can be forever, when you are alone. Moments fly by for those wrapped up in their many pursuits. To them, there is never enough time. Later in my life, when I would find myself teaching physics to college students, I would often ask, on the first day of class, for my freshmen and sophomores to give me a quick paragraph defining the concept, "time." When they finished groaning at the assignment, the resulting writings always demonstrated the elusiveness of the human's concept of time. At the beginning of January 1988, however, the extra week until the 17th seemed a very long time indeed.

With no lack of work to focus on, I dug in. I kept the fabrication of the Chimbu contract houses rolling on schedule, loaded and delivered the assistant pastor's house, via twin otter, to Laplama, along with a foreman and crew to get it put together, and plowed into the many requested building estimates that littered the top of my desk. Using feedback from the accounting system, Ray and I set up, I developed an analog formula for housing bid estimates. I needed to

do a careful material takeoff that would translate into an accurate job material costing. Then my labor, overheads, and profit became a constant multiple factor of the material cost. The truth of it lay in the fact that a large portion of the housing estimates would never bear fruit, but you had to do them, as a smaller percentage of the estimates would turn into work and they had to be figured correctly. Nothing worse than finishing a difficult job and finding out that you lost money. When a client wanted to go ahead based on my numbers, I stuck, rather successfully, to the half-down and the other half of the bid cost, upon completion of a building project. I figured if we got the house fabricated and problems arose with the client, the half-down covered the initial fabrication work and then some. We could always sell the house down the line to someone else, and I did design interchangeable panels between the two, three, and four bedroom models. In the beginning of negotiations, if a customer seemed shaky at all, I would ask for all of the costs up front. We only got burnt on the second half of a payment once.

While I cranked out the estimates, Jim called from Lae and prevailed upon me to go out to a tea plantation near Hagen, owned by a "mate" of his, to look at moving a building. He presumed we'd have to dismantle, move the materials, and then, reassemble the building at the new location. I told him I'd take a look at the requirements of the job, as soon as possible, and not to worry, we'd get it done, if it could be done.

The next day, happy for a break from the paperwork, I grabbed one of my foremen, Paul, and we drove out to the plantation, about fifteen miles northeast of Hagen. The building, about four meters wide by eleven meters long (about 500 square feet) proved a fairly complicated construction, and I frowned at the thought of dismantling it without destroying much of the material. Thinking out loud, I said something like, "If only we could lift it in one piece and put it on a truck."

Paul, standing beside me, responded quietly, "Papua New Guinea men are very strong."

I looked at him, then back at the building. It sat on a treated post foundation, with the bottom carrying timbers strapped to the top of each post. We could easily unfasten the strapping and, then indeed, the house could be lifted free, and placed on a large flatbed truck. The wheels of my mind turned, driven by the desire not to dismantle the whole bloody building. If we could lift it straight up, with lots of men and get one end onto an adjacent flatbed truck, using lengths of pipe for rollers on the flatbed, it could work. As soon as we got one end onto the flatbed pipe rollers, the truck would take half the weight of the building. The initial lift would be the hardest part.

I grabbed Paul and headed back to Hailans Homes to start figuring the weight of the building. Using the measurements we took of the building, together with the published density of hardwoods from the P.N.G. Forestry Department, to calculate the volume of the buildings timbers, I came up with a weight a little under four tons. If each man could squat lift about 200 pounds (a bit under 100 kilograms), we'd need at least forty men. Hailans Homes could supply twenty men and upon telephoning the plantation manager, I was told, "No worries, mate. You can have all the "*bois*" you want from here."

Three afternoons later, we piled twenty Hailans Homes workers on the back of a borrowed six ton flatbed truck, belonging to the lumber yard, along with a half dozen pipe rollers we made up, and headed for the tea plantation. Paul and I, with a few laborers, already had set up the post foundation at the new location and

unfastened the carrying beams from the old foundation. Our chore, now, was to move the four-ton building from one spot to another, without "buggering" it up in the process.

We stopped at the plantation office to ask them to send twenty-five strong men to the existing building location as soon as they could. That would give me time to go over to the building and set up the truck, rollers, and double check underneath to make sure all fastenings were loose and only "gravity" was left to overcome.

An hour later, we were ready to go. We went over the plan once more. After the initial lift, we would only have to move the building forward about one foot (one-third meter) to catch the rear end of the flatbed and the first roller. The men at the back end, away from the truck, would then walk it forward as the front men peeled off and ran to the back end to help, if needed. It should just roll onto the back of the truck. The three-foot (one meter) lift would be the hard part.

I put Paul in charge of the pipe rollers and I took a position along one house side to help with the lifting. The men on either side of me smiled as I grabbed a hand hold while shouting, "*Olgeta man yu holim nau strongpela!*" (Everybody get a strong grip now!)

I tightened my grip on the building perimeter and again shouted, "*Wan, tu, tri, upim!*"

A bit to my amazement, the building lifted. The bulging muscles strained around me.

"*Nau, antap trak,*" I yelled with my own arms trembling from the exertion.

The building moved slowly forward and we caught the truck bed and the first roller. The building seemed to get a little lighter and it started to roll a bit faster onto the back of the truck. Men ran from the front sides to the building's rear as they lost their positions to the truck bed.

I was at a middle position on the building's

side and when I got to the truck bed, I let loose and ran to the back yelling, "*Isi, isi.*" We didn't want to bash the truck cab!

Then it was done. The building sat on the pipe rollers, snugged up against the front rails of the truck bed. Lots of "*ayiiis*" filled the air. As we secured the building for driving, with chains and "boomers" (snap levers), Paul came up to me with a big smile on his face. Unable to stop laughing, he finally blurted out that there was no word "*upim*" in the pisin language! The word for lift was "*haisapim.*" It was my turn to laugh as I told him, "There is now. Everybody lifted when I yelled '*upim*'!"

Paul kept smiling when he told me the plantation workers remained startled by the fact that I took a spot and lifted the building along with them. He said expats usually just shout and watch. I took it as a compliment.

We drove slowly on the gravel roads about two miles to the other side of the plantation and reversed the procedure. This time it took a little fine-tuning after we sat the building on the posts. Pulling the flatbed out of the way, we had muscle on all four sides. Two small moves, in the inch category, and the building sat positioned in its final resting place, at least as far as I was concerned. My men crawled underneath and began fastening the metal strapping from the top of each post to the carrying beams. The job was finished, done the New Guinea way – brute force. Paul was right. New Guinea men are very strong. Even *lapun* (old) men exhibited muscular bodies.

My eyes witnessed lots of hand shaking and excitement when the job was completed. I tried to say "*Tank yu*" to all the plantation workers and give them a slap on the arm. We loaded up our gear and men onto the flatbed and headed back to the lumberyard. I called Jim from my office after telling all the men to go home an hour early as a reward for their effort. Jim seemed

elated when I called to tell him his mate's building had been moved successfully.

"How did you get it done so quickly?"

"We did it the New Guinea way. Physically lifted it onto a flatbed and then reversed the process at the new site!"

"Bill, you're turning into a New Guinean!"

That night on my little verandah, the first S.P. brownie tasted wonderful. It hardly touched the sides of my throat going down. It would have taken us several weeks to disassemble and reassemble that building. Mission accomplished in a few hours with the muscle of New Guinea Highlanders and one lean expat shouting a reinvented *pisin* language. The adventures in meeting the challenges of New Guinea truly thrilled the heart and mind.

A few days later, I caught a flight to Moresby to attend a construction trade show. While at the Moresby Airport, I walked to the International terminal to reacquaint myself with the route Sandia would take through immigration and customs. I stood by the door she would come through with her luggage and into my welcoming arms. On my flight back to the mountains and Mt. Hagen, I felt like bursting. Only a few more days to wait. I couldn't even mail her copies of my journal pages anymore. She would be on her way before they could be "posted" to her.

The following Saturday morning one of my drivers took me to Kagamuga Airport so I could catch an Air Niugini flight to Moresby. There I lined up a hotel room at the Airporter Hotel, near where Sandia's Continental flight from Guam would land the next morning at 10 o'clock. The Airporter received Armed Forces Television, although only in black and white, so I busied myself through the evening gawking at some programming and news from the States.

The next morning, Sunday, at least an hour before Sandia's flight was due to arrive, I found a spot on a hill overlooking the airport terminal, under a palm tree. As I lay there waiting and watching, Mondul's words came into my mind – *"Taim niugini man igat fivpela ten Krismas's, emi stap long tri*!" (When a New Guinea man reaches 50 years of age, he lays down under a tree.) There I laid under a tree in my fiftieth year, finally. A laugh worked its way up from my stomach and I let it out. Life seemed awesome and soon would get even better. I felt a profound joy welling up inside me. Sandia was coming. She was really coming! In less than an hour, her feet would touch the ground of Papua New Guinea.

My eyes followed a few domestic flights landing and taking off. Then at about five minutes before ten, my eyes picked up a large aircraft overhead, approaching from the northeast, the direction of Guam. At first, I thought it would fly right over, but then it banked into a turn and began an approach to the Moresby Airport for a landing. As it came closer in, I could clearly see the Continental logo on the tail rudder section. My heartbeat picked up a notch. My mind uttered, *It must be her!*

My eyes fixed on the aircraft as it glided to the runway, landed smoothly, and taxied to its parking spot, next to an Air Nuigini flight that was pulling back for a departure to Brisbane, Australia. The ground crew chocked the wheels of the arriving Continental flight and ran around the plane pulling levers in preparation for passenger deplaning. By now, I had left the palm tree to do a "face plant" on the chainlink perimeter security fence that served to keep people away from arriving and departing aircraft. The fence was lined on my side with curious nationals. The rear stairway, under the tail, came down slowly and a moment later, the first passenger appeared and descended to the ground. A few people

later, I saw her stepping her way to the ground. Sandia was here. She was really here in Papua New Guinea. She turned toward the terminal entry canopy and the immigration aisles. Sandia looked so beautiful in the light early morning drizzle. She was dressed in a long blue denim skirt, black walking boots, and wore a three-quarter sleeved, high waisted jacket to match. I don't believe I've ever seen a more fantastic or beautiful sight in my entire life.

Our eyes found each other. She waved. I let go with my right hand from clutching the chain-link mesh and waved back. The tears flowed. They spilled down my cheeks. Many nationals turned to look at me, while I drank in thirstily the sight of her through the blur of tears, so joyfully flowing. The wait was over. The months of waiting and being alone were over. She was here. Sandia was here in this strange and beautifully mysterious land.

We walked toward the terminal together, but on opposite sides of the chainlink fence – 100 feet apart, but so close. We waved, slowly walked, and just looked at each other. Sandia's carry-on bag appeared heavy as she kept switching it back and forth between hands as she walked. Finally the brick wall of the immigration/customs building stopped my progress and I watched as Sandia continued inside to begin the International Arrivals process. I walked over to take up a vigil at the exit door, or as my mind called it, "the emergence door!"

I paced and peeked through the door whenever the security guard opened it to let someone out. Sandia got her entry permit stamped, found a cart for her luggage, and got in one of the customs lines.

Then the doors opened. Sandia came through them, pushing her luggage cart, and flew into my arms. The feeling was beyond description, even beyond all my anticipation.

People in the crowd stared at us and smiled. Our lips pressed together, arms tightly embraced, bodies vibrated in longing recognition of deep feelings for each other. I stepped back without letting go and looked into Sandia's eyes. My lady was in my aching arms at last. Whatever lay in store for us would be okay, as we would tackle it together.

The following days blended into a beautiful whirlwind of reunion, love, touching, and just looking at each other. Sandia told me at one point, "I feel like I've been here. Your journal pages were so colorful and descriptive." Even the Denver Broncos won the A.F.C. Championship on Armed Forces Television as we embraced in love. (Sorry, Cleveland!) Sandia lugged an American V.C.R. player and Bronco playoff tapes in that carry-on bag of hers as a gift for this die hard football fan.

We flew to Mt. Hagen later on Monday and I showed her the flat. Sandia fixed us a meal and as she hummed about the kitchen, I watched in total amazement that she moved about here in my (our) little flat on the hill. I pointed out all the sights and told her the neighbors' names. We unpacked her duffel bags, drove to the outdoor market for a few essentials, then back to the flat and into each other's arms again. Sleeping together the first night, in our new double bed, found my hand constantly reaching out to touch her to make sure she was really there.

The company booked us accommodations at Ambua Lodge in the rainforest on the Southern Highlands for four days. Those few days proved a short, but wonderful, honeymoon against the stunning backdrop of rainforest greenery that was so lush and beautifully humid. We took bushwalks, ate, when the urge told us to, at the lodge, held each other, and slept whenever we felt like it. Sandia did experience a bit of jetlag and needed some serious sleep. At times, I just

A hideaway in the rainforest

Beauty of a rainforest waterfall

213

Rainforest scenes with Sandia in front of our lodgings amongst the flowers

laid there beside her, watching her sleep and listening to her breathing. The beauty of my lady lay there for me to gaze upon, right next to me!

We discovered, on one bushwalk, the most breathtaking waterfall, cascading down 1000 feet into a clear pool. The impact of the water was so great, the air filled with water vapor and the rays of sun, streaming through the lush green canopy, created rainbows. What an incredible setting surrounded us, there in the high mountains of Papua New Guinea. Sandia and I, wet with the fine, clear droplets, held each other and let the sound, the tree filtered sunlight, and the vapor created by the waterfall permeate our beings. We were together again. My soul mate stood beside me.

chapter *thirty-two*

The Dark Side

I'd like to tell you that once Sandia arrived, everything turned to "peaches and cream," but about the time you thought things seemed under control, the culture had a way of rising up and slapping you hard in the face. Our slap, or sort of a baptism for Sandia, came in a way to demonstrate the subtle violence submerged within the culture of New Guinea.

A few days before Sandia's arrival, a fight happened in the park in front of Hailans Homes. By the time I got out of my office and across the street to the park, it had ended. One meri was left bloody and battered by another. My men told me, one wife, jealous of another wife, clobbered the latter upside the head with a 100 x 50 (a 2 by 4 in U.S.A lingo). During the fight between the wives, the husband, an employee of Total Hardware, looked on with indifference from the lumberyard across the street. Fighting between wives was not an uncommon occurrence in P.N.G. My man, Bobby, told me that you must treat all your wives the same; for example, if you gave one of them K5, then you must give each of the others K5, and so on; otherwise jealousy would surely result from the inequity.

marriage and a family, that's what is planned

the fighting part, is hard to understand

On the day I brought Sandia to Mt. Hagen from Port Morseby, we were touring the company buildings, when we ran into Jim at Total Hardware. He was excited to see Sandia and invited us to lunch. Eager to talk, we piled into a Total Hardware vehicle, proceeded out of the lumberyard, and headed for town. Jim drove and had to come to a stop right outside of Hailans Homes as several other cars stopped to watch some kind of a commotion on the edge of the park. In the blink of an eye, a woman, bleeding profusely from a head wound, ran and stumbled from the gathering mob, right onto the fender and hood of our little pickup truck. I jumped from the passenger door, the side the wounded meri was on, and grabbed her to keep her from collapsing to the road. Sandia's hands covered her face, in total disbelief that this whole scene was going down. I suddenly recognized the wounded meri as the wife who had wielded the 100 x 50 wooden club the week before. The wife she had clobbered earlier just retaliated with an axe! The bashing resulted in a huge open wound in the right side of her head.

Jim signaled for help and several of the yardmen brought a truck, lifted the wounded meri onto it, and sped off to the Hagen Hospital to get emergency treatment. We went on our way to lunch in varying degrees of shock. Jim, an old hand at the ways of New Guinea, acted as if nothing out of the ordinary had happened. Sandia's eyes reflected the "baptism of fire" she'd, only moments before, undergone.

Not more than two weeks later, marital violence would reach up and slap us again. This time it happened between a man and his wife. We slowed down to turn a corner one evening heading home to our flat only to come upon a national man punching and beating his wife with a piece of wood, like a club. I pulled on the emergency brake, reaching for my door handle. Sandia, seeing my intent, shouted to me, "Don't go near them. Let's go home!"

The man hit her again with the wooden club, hard, right on the top of the head. She went down in a heap at the side of the road, just ahead of my truck. I couldn't hold back. With trembling hands, I wrenched open my door, breaking away from Sandia's grip on the back of my shirt. I started toward the man and the woman on the ground before him, not even knowing what I intended to do. Sandia's shout of "Bill don't!" rang out from behind me. The man stood staring at my approach.

I was still six meters from the scene, when up popped the woman from the ground, with a big stone in her hand, and slammed it down with great force on her husband's head. I stopped my approach in amazement. Now he staggered away in obvious bloody pain. I turned, let out a big sigh of relief, and headed back to the truck.

"Sandia, did you see that? She hammered that big stone right down on his head and he didn't even lose consciousness. Just staggered away. Amazing!"

We would never get used to it, but it hap-

pened often enough – jealous wife beating another wife, husband beating wife, gang rape of village girls and women, never singular rape, always the men in numbers of four or five. Before we would leave New Guinea, the gang rape would begin to involve expatriate women – a retail shop manager we knew and, also, the wife of an Australian missionary friend, in front of her four children, after five national men knocked her husband senseless.

In the latter instance, the missionary family drove toward their home one night and came upon logs piled across an uninhabited section of the road. Sensing danger, the husband, Greg, tried to back up and quickly turn the car around. Before he could complete his escape maneuver, the five men fell upon them, knocking Greg unconscious. They then took turns at his wife, while the children screamed helplessly from the back seat. Needless to say, the family left the country a few days later, thankful that they were all alive.

Sandia and I agreed from that first "baptism" to try always to stay alert, not being naïve about situations that might occur. The retail shop manager, a Greek woman named Helen, was set up by some of her own male workers. Because so many of the nationals we knew, and came to know, proved pure, honest, hard working people, it was easy to forget about the infrequent violence that could, and did, occur.

The late Friday afternoon beer sessions with Ray and other expats usually evolved into storytelling affairs. Most expat conversations were spiced with "horror" stories. At times, it seemed to me, there appeared too much preoccupation with the dark side. I reminded myself that it couldn't be any worse than back home in our own cities.

We finally hired 24-hour security at our flat, as we came home one day for lunch and surprised some robber *raskols* in the process of cleaning out our stuff. They got away with a couple of big sheath knives I kept for whatever, and a brand new VCR we'd only recently purchased out of Singapore to watch the odd "pirated" rental movie some nights. Most of the other stuff they'd intended to steal remained in a stack inside the bathroom window they'd used to gain entrance. The robbers ran when we came through our entry gate, leaving lots of good stuff behind. After that Sandia and I decided to get security, as most other expatriates already had. Companies footed the tab, but the recipient had to manage the shifts of security men. My guys lined us out on plenty of good security men, who came with their own bows and arrows, spears, and tomahawks.

We never experienced another robbery again, but one night there sounded a loud thunk under our house, which turned out to be the security man hitting his head as he was awakened from a deep snooze by would-be robbers cutting their way through our chainlink fence! We repaired the fence the next day, but the security guy had a pretty ugly bump on the top of his head. Actually, the bump added a little humor to it all.

Pretty soon we got used to having a security guy marching around our yard with his bow and arrows on display. Our twelve-hour shift daytime guy, Kiagi, turned out to be a super help. He turned an old water tank into a sentry house by our gate. When it rained, or they got cold, they'd go into that galvanized hut and get a warm fire going. Smoke would billow out the small door opening, as I couldn't convince them to put a vent in the roof of that old metal tank. I would have choked to death in there, but they said it was fine.

Kiagi became adept at hanging out our laundry. He even invented a new way to use the waist tied clothespin bag. Sandia called me to the window one weekend day, to point out at Kiagi merrily hanging our wet laundry, with the clothespin bag tied around his neck! We decided— if it worked for him – no worries for us. He always tried to help with the gardening and whatever else had to be done. It got to be fun, and actually comforting, to have the different security guys around, especially the nights I had to spend away. I knew they would faithfully guard my *missus*, as they called her. They became the bright side of the dark side!

chapter thirty-three

Porgera – the Beginning

The first time I saw Francis Kaupa, he strode into my office after a quick knock on the always-open door. He was a national with a very focused expression on his face. Francis stopped in front of my desk and stated, "I'd like your company to bid a few dongas (Aussie slang for bunkhouses) up at the Porgera Gold Mine. I need two twelve man buildings and one ten man building. If you'll schedule a flight, I'll meet you at the Porgera airstrip and show you the building site. Here's my card. Call me when you line up a flight. I'm on my way back up to the mine right now."

I stood up from my desk and reached out to shake his hand. "Thanks for the opportunity. What kind of a time schedule do you have in mind for the project?"

"No drama. As soon as we can get it rolling."

"I'll check the flights for tomorrow and call you when I'm booked."

"Good on you. I'll leave it with you," Francis uttered as he turned to exit my door in an obvious hurry to get to the airport.

After Francis left, I looked down to study his business card. He was a civil engineer, work-

mountain bold, spots of white, so brown, so high

her peak, through the clouds, touching bright blue sky

ing for Placer Dome Mining Corporation up at the Porgera mine site, well west into the Engan Mountains. Gold mining – what an opportunity! I picked up the phone and dialed Talair, our local commuter airline, to get a seat on the next morning's flight up to Porgera. My omnipresent bid estimating paper work could wait.

The next day in Porgera, Francis showed me Top Camp, above the proposed deep shaft mining location. Top Camp, at the time, consisted of an appendage of crudely built temporary housing and mess quarters for a dozen or so start up workers, mostly nationals, with the occasional transient expat. Those existing buildings perched on the mountainside, maybe 50 meters (150 feet) above a small, but reasonably flat, area where Francis wanted the dongas built. There were steep mountains on three sides, with the east side open to the access road and the valley below. The major problem with the building area turned out to be the soil. It was mud! Francis had no clue how far under the mud to solid ground. He left it to me to figure out something as we headed down to the Engineering Area to look at a model bunkhouse built years earlier for a skeleton exploration staff. Francis explained to me that the Special Mining Lease would soon be approved and issued by the P.N.G. Government. After that, initial mining operations would begin. He needed the living quarters for those impending crews. He would, at a later date, let another contract to build the mess facilities and a few more dongas at Top Camp. My job was to figure a way to house 34 workers above the mud. The buildings needed to have a useful life of twenty-four months before

Mount Kajindi as seen from Porgera

they'd be phased out. Francis dropped me back at the gravel airstrip with instructions to call him as soon as I worked it all out.

As I waited for my Talair return flight to Hagen, my head whirled with the challenge of the project. Francis would be a straight forward, no nonsense, person to work with. That part was great. The location in the mountains was exciting. The main mining elevation stood at the 8,000 foot level, with Top Camp, a thousand feet above it. The mountains looked spectacular. I stared up at one dominant peak, in particular. We flew in right beside it on the morning flight. From the far side, the eastern side, it was another densely treed mountain, like so many in the highlands, but from this side, the western side, steep cliffs of exposed limestone gave it a majestic and towering appearance. The cliffs almost glowed as the afternoon sun highlighted the chalky limestone formations.

On the flight back to Hagen, on Talair's Bandeirante aircraft (built in San Paulo, Brazil), the pilot told me the mountain that so struck me

was named Mount Kajindi and its summit measured about 11,000 feet above sea level. What a great name for a splendid mountain—Kajindi.

The next few days, I did little else but work on the bid for the three Top Camp dongas. The buildings themselves seemed fairly simple, small cubicled rooms, with two power points (electrical receptacles) and one ceiling light in each, a corridor, dividing two rows of rooms, and leading to "ganged" bathroom/shower facilities and a common lounging room at the far end. Hailans Homes could do it using our prefabricated wall panel system with roof trusses to span the width between exterior sidewalls. My dilemma lay in the foundation. What to set the buildings on in all that mud? A regular concrete foundation wall would sink unevenly, and crack, depending on the varying consistency of the mud. Besides, there were no ready mix plants or concrete delivery trucks operating in the area. A post foundation would also sink unevenly, leaving the building's flooring heaving up in some areas and down in others. It wouldn't work. There appeared no argument for non-uniform mud!

The second night of what I began to call "donga madness," on my little verandah with Sandia, sharing cold S.P. brownies, I described the muddy building site to her and by chance remarked, "Too bad I can't float the buildings in the mud!" That's when the idea hit me. I could float them on a log raft, or sort of a "catamaran." The buildings would be narrow and long (20 feet wide by sixty-six feet long, approximately). We could get some large diameter, long, straight gum or casuarina trees, then build the first three tiers of a log cabin, notching the logs together at the corners, with some intermediate cross links. Next, we could span the top, the long way, with three continuous, steel "I" beams and build the buildings on top. Even if one corner sunk a little more than another did, it would all stay in one plane – a flat floor.

I became so excited, and probably animated, trying to explain it to Sandia. I drew her sketches and then she saw it. "Do you think they'll go for it?" she asked. "I've never seen anything like that before. A building sitting on top of logs!"

"Me neither, but Francis is an engineer. He'll see the merit of it, or he'll shoot the whole idea down in flames!"

The next morning, I explained my log crib foundation idea to Francis on the telephone. After a few questions, he admitted it seemed an interesting solution and could I get him preliminary plans and prices as soon as possible.

We won the donga contract. Francis didn't even cross bid me. He knew the numbers and the ideas would work. He faxed me a confirming order for the job. The project was bigger than the Chimbu contract and there'd be no worries regarding the payments, as Placer Dome was a huge Canadian based mining outfit. Jim's excited comment, when I called him with the news, was "We'd better get you a few big trucks of your own."

I always enjoyed telling my men about new contracts. They became so genuinely delighted and animated about the work guarantees each new job brought them. I guess most of them had bounced around previously on different jobs. I told them it was their good quality work that made Hailans Homes known in the Highlands. They patted each other on the back, shook hands, and sang out those happy "*ayiiis.*" I also mentioned to Mondul to keep his eyes and ears open for another good foreman. We were certainly going to need more good help.

Later, I sat at my desk, looking up at a huge status board that my guys built and hung for me. It took up most of the wall to the right of my desk and consisted of a green chalkboard, so I could write, erase, and fuss around with it. I had, only a moment before, finished drawing in a flow diagram for the Porgera Donga Project. The status board showed we then worked in seven different locations throughout the Highlands, from Chimbu locations in the East to the Porgera Gold Mine in the West. We were spread out. The facts seemed obvious; we needed more help and vehicles. I presently kept three dozen men busy. My old blue Toyota Hilux spent most of the time in the Chimbu Mountains, with a driver instructed to ferry supplies between the remote building sites. He came in for fuel, money, and supplies every few days. It seemed clear we needed a few more trucks to supply the Porgera effort. I always either walked or borrowed trucks from Total Hardware and Sandia to get around myself. We would be done with the Chimbu project in another four to six weeks, but the "bush grapevine," on good authority, had us getting another dozen houses and open garden produce market stalls, funded by Rural Development moneys from Australia. The status board showed us then working bigger on Eastern and Western fronts, with only several smaller local jobs in between.

Looking up at that status board, I heard Jim's words in my mind, 'Run it like it was your own business.' So it was my call. The wise move would be to bid the next Chimbu contract phase and see what developed in Porgera. If the Special Mining Lease came through, there would be plenty of work in Porgera. We could finish Phase II in Chimbu and pull out, concentrating all efforts at the mining site. If the government dragged its feet in Porgera, as often happened, we could hum and buzz along in Chimbu. That seemed to be the move; I would bid Chimbu Phase II as soon as the specifications became available.

In the meantime, the fun part of Porgera lay in the fact that Francis wasn't holding a sledge-hammer over my head to get the project done "post haste." Porgera felt raw and exciting. There existed only a few small villages, which happened to be located near a mountain of gold. With the preliminary assays predicting six billion dollars in gold reserves, the lives of those villagers would be greatly impacted and changed forever. There came a certain sadness with that thought, but there could be no turning back. The presence of gold was known. Trade stores were already springing up around the short tilted airstrip which dead ended into a mountain. One Talair pilot told me, "You can't do a 'go-around' on this strip. Once you are in the approach pattern, you have to put it on the ground, good or bad!"

The one-way airstrip measured about 600 meters long with a ten percent "up" grade for landing. When you took off, going downhill, the opposite way, the bottom of the runway dropped off rapidly into a deep valley. Take-offs from the Porgera airstrip always proved a bit startling as the stomach rushed upwards when the aircraft plunged downwards into that deep wide valley

which suddenly appeared before you.

The only full time expat at the mine site was a well-seasoned, tough Slovenian and ex-resistance fighter by the name of Rudi. He'd been there several years and liked doing the start up and exploration work in mining. Rudi said once all the smart young mining engineers came in; he would head off to another quiet exploration location. Rudi lived in a small house, next to a mining tunnel he'd helped dig. He christened his abode "Rudi's Bar and Grill." One morning, later on, he would offer me a shot of whiskey at only eight o'clock in the morning, which I politely refused, but saw that the name was apt for the supplies he kept in the pantry. Like Rudi, I felt intrigued with the start up, as opposed to the routine operations of the mining camp. It possessed an adventuresome challenge.

It took four days at Top Camp to get the first log foundation ready for building. I, with my foreman, Kivon, and six of his men, bargained for tall straight trees down in the villages, along the valley road. We bought and dropped trees along the road so we could winch and chain them up to the truck. I dropped them with Lindsay's old chainsaw and all my months of experience from logging in the Colorado Mountains. I knew if we missed on a tree drop, crushing a *kunai* shack or somebody's garden, we'd have to pay compensation to the owner, and possibly end up in village court. With probably more luck than skill, all dropped trees fell on, or near enough, to their marks.

Once we got all the logs hauled up to Top Camp, I gave Kivon a lesson in log notching. Most of my men did not like power tools, instead preferring handsaws and chisels for wood removal efforts. I roughed the notches quickly with the big chain saw and their sharp chisels did the rest. A builder's transit showed the finished log crib to be within millimeters of level.

We shimmed the three "I" beams to dead level and fastened them to the tops of the logs. Total Hardware trucks were already arriving with the flooring materials, when I caught a flight back to Mt. Hagen. Kivon could work on his own with the flooring and I would bring a set of final plans back to him in a few days. The shop guys were already pounding out the prefabricated wall panels.

The log crib foundation and steel "I" beams would hold the building floor above the mud by a good meter (three plus feet). The mud seemed to be drying a bit as the days went on. When we started, it would suck the yellow gumboots right off your feet. Since my guys wore those waterproof boots every day, all day, without socks, your nose would tell you when a man stepped out of his boots! It became a nose-pinching shocker, to say the least. I'd yell, "Get your boots back on, quiktime!" Maybe it stemmed from my tender expat nostrils, but the odor would snap your head back. You'd never let a man take his gumboots off in the truck cab, or any other closed area!

Right in the middle of my desk, upon returning to Hagen, sat the contract specifications for Chimbu, Phase II. Attached to it was a post-it note from George Hook, Total Hardware General Manager, who'd replaced Lindsay, to come up to the lumber yard. He'd parked a brand new Toyota Hilux next to his office. It turned out to be my new truck. Wow, I could look at the contract specs later. I trotted for the lumberyard and there it stood. A bright yellow cab with a wooden coffee body (flatbed) and gray metal pipe rails in back. It smelled so new. George saw me from his second floor office and brought down the keys. "It's even got a radio and tape deck, with stereo speakers," he told me.

"Wow, I like the color. They'll see me coming out in the bush."

Top Camp donga construction on log crib foundations

George joked with me, "If anyone spits *buai* (betel nut) on it, you'll know." *Buai* chewers frequently spit a bright red oily splatter. If you pulled up beside a P.M.V. bus, your car could get hit with the red spittle from the open bus windows.

"Jim told me to get you a new truck and it's done. We'll keep spare keys up on our keyboard in case you lose this set. Your overheads will more than cover this truck."

"Thanks George. I'm out of here. Gonna see if Sandia will take a break and go for a ride with me."

I'd only been gone four days, but it felt great to park my new truck by her store and walk inside to see her in the process of explaining a sewing machine procedure to a new girl she'd hired. Her staff always displayed joy and wonders when they saw us hugging and holding each other's hands. It wasn't in their culture. You might say it seemed "foreign" to them.

We took a short afternoon ride up to Maggie Leahy's Coffee Shop, where I filled Sandia in on the project at Top Camp. She brought me up to date on her own business. She definitely loved her job—what fun, the two of us, being able to work close by each other. We could, and did, take lunch together some of the time and an occasional break. Sandia and I did plenty of extra work to make up for it!

With the Porgera project under control, I headed my new yellow Hilux east for the Chimbu Mountains to look at the new Phase II building sites. I had called the South Chimbu Rural Development Project office in Kundiawa and they relayed a radio message to David, my Peace Corps *wontok*, that I was coming into his village of Gumine. The "bush drums" could get the message through from there.

David guided me to each of the different remote village building sites. We chatted about stateside news and he filled me in on the New Guinea Peace Corps effort. He only had six months remaining on his two-year assignment and appeared unsure of his next move. David's wife, Melynda, wanted to get out of the bush. The village, or bush, culture was very macho in nature and Melynda possessed more than a little independent streak. Her ideas, however intelligent, were not listened to the same way David's were in village meetings. It probably also made a difference that David stood six-foot three and two hundred plus pounds, while Melinda stood about five-foot three and petite.

I followed David's directions to the next village, but was startled as we came over a hill and

dropped down to a narrow log bridge crossing a deep ravine. The bridge looked barely wider than the Hilux. It looked strong enough, with two large main cross logs, topped with a smaller cross log decking and two smaller logs nailed to the top outside edges as sort of tire rails. The narrowness is what freaked me out, as well as both approaches being downhill onto the bridge. We navigated it okay and ascended from the far side to rise up over a hill and down toward the village we were searching for.

The rain started shortly after we talked to the village chief and he showed us a fairly flat spot where the contract specs called for a two-bedroom agricultural foreman's house. We thanked the "big man" and ran for the truck to escape the increasing downpour. This was our last building site, so we could head back to the shelter of David's house in Gumine.

I remarked to David, as we drove through the rain, "When I bid this thing, I'm going to make a condition that they rebuild the bridge up ahead to at least double the present width. I don't want to lose my men and trucks on that narrow span!"

In the next instant, we crested the hilltop approaching the bridge. I tapped the brakes on the downhill approach to slow the truck, but with the downpour, the approach had become a mass of glistening red clay. We slid toward the bridge and started into a skid. I steered into the skid, with windshield wipers whirring, but had to pull it back so we could hit the bridge. Otherwise, we would have slid right over the edge of the ravine. As soon as we hit the first log of the bridge decking, I pulled the steering wheel to bring the wheels straight onto the bridge. David went rigid in the passenger seat to my left. We came to a stop in the middle of the bridge, with David's side cocked out over the edge. Neither one of us moved. I couldn't tell if the front left wheel had gone over, or around, the guide rail log along the edge of the bridge. I shut off the engine and told David, "You sit still. I'm going out my window and over the hood to get a look at the situation on your wheel over there!" The bridge wasn't wide enough to get out my door.

I crawled out the driver's side window, onto the bright yellow hood, and over the grill to get my feet planted on the bridge. The bridge swayed a little with the weight of the truck sitting right in the middle of it. The heavy rain seemed to be letting up as I slid under the truck for a "look see." Sure enough, the guide rail log, which was pieced together, had come partially unfastened, with our tire somehow on the outside. If the remainder of the guide log could be pulled loose, there would be room ahead to get the front wheel turned back onto the bridge surface.

I yelled up to David, "I'm gonna shake the bridge. Don't worry!"

Grabbing onto the loose portion of the guide log and bracing my feet against the undercarriage of the truck, I gave a slow, strong pull on the loosened guide log segment. The log came free in my hands with a loud snap. David's voice could be heard, "What the hell are you doing under there?" as I carefully placed the log segment in the middle of the bridge, under the truck, out of our wheels' way. I crawled and reached around to each front wheel to snap in the locking hubs.

My feet stepped up onto the front bumper, as I tried to smile, and I slid over the wet yellow hood, grabbing onto the big rear view mirror bracket for support. As I slid around and into my window, my eyes glanced downward for the first time. My breath made a whistle as I sucked it in. The surface of the glowing, churning water glistened about fifty feet below us.

The rain had completely stopped as I started the engine, put it into four-wheel and eased for-

ward, turning the wheels inward as we started to move. The truck straightened onto the centerline of the bridge and we pulled forward, easing up the incline on the other side. At the top of the hill, I stopped and turned to look wide eyed at my *wontok*.

"You're a crazy man," David quietly uttered.

"This is my brand new truck. I don't want to lose it down some Chimbu gorge!"

We both agreed the bridge had to be replaced, otherwise Hailans Homes wouldn't do the job.

As we drove on toward Gumine, I finally got nervous. My hands started to shake and I began to perspire. The quick vision down that ravine played over and over in my mind. That would have been a mighty long plunge. David noticed my demeanor and commented, "So, he is human after all!"

A week later, I had the whole job figured and

Norbert with our trusty blue Hilux

submitted our bid for the Chimbu contract. This time, at the bid opening, no "payola" occurred and we won the work straight up. Jim's response to the new contract news was, "I've got you two 4 ½ ton, four wheel drive, Mitsubishi trucks all lined up. You'll need your own trucks and drivers for the amount of work you're bringing in. Congratulations!"

More work meant a fuller status board. I needed some more foremen, big time. Mondul came to my rescue. He walked into my office with a worker, who'd been laid off at Hagen Public Works because of a Government money shortage. That seemed a common happenstance in P.N.G. It didn't mean the laid off worker was a poor worker, just bad management of funding by the local administrators. Mondul introduced me to Norbert Huangile and I told him to sit down. I thanked Mondul, telling him I wanted to talk with Norbert for a while, alone. Norbert was a Sepik man from the northern coast, married, with two small children. As he described his work experience, I liked his attitude, bearing, and especially, his laugh. I read through several glowing reference letters, he lay in front of me. Norbert definitely had supervisory experience. I wrote an hourly wage figure on a notepad and slid it over to him.

Finished Top Camp dongas next to the "gold mountains." Note the activities of the locals chipping away for gold behind dongas

"Norbert, I'll start you at that figure and if things work out, I'll take care of you. Can you bring your toolbox and start tomorrow?"

"Yes, I can start tomorrow. Mondul told me you got plenty work here and you are good bossman. I will go back and meet the other workers and look at the shop tools for the rest of the afternoon. What time should I come tomorrow?"

"We start at 7:30 in the morning. Come

a little earlier if you want a cup of hot tea. We keep a pot brewing most of the time right outside my office, next to Bobby's desk. Happy to have you with us at Hailans Homes!"

I shook his hand firmly and Norbert headed out my door for the shop area.

I didn't know it then, but I'd just hired a lieutenant. Norbert would prove out to be one of my most valued men.

Jim felt so excited about the way his businesses were going. Every cent of profit that Hailans Homes made meant that his lumber hardware business prospered also, because they were our sole supplier of building materials. Jim saw the merit in purchasing an aircraft for the company and bought a used Cessna 182 from a Hagen mate of his. The plane, Romeo Papa Tango (call letters R.P.T.), was a single engine, four-seater.

Soon Jim began flying from Lae to Porgera, with a stop in Hagen to pick me up, to market office supplies at the burgeoning mine complex. I could check on my men's progress at the Top Camp dongas, while he did his sales presentations for Total Concept down at the engineering building. We could fly in by late morning and be out by early afternoon, before the clouds really socked in.

Jim loved to fly and learned the art years earlier, in those New Guinea Mountains. He told me, in the past, he'd make every excuse to get flight time. It didn't matter whose plane, just so long as the hours at the controls could be inked into his flight logbook. When you love something that much, you want others to love it too. I figure that's why he started telling me to take the controls of R.P.T. for periods of time during our Porgera trips, and elsewhere.

At first, I considered keeping us in straight and level flight to be an accomplishment. For a rookie, the controls seemed very touchy. Jim never panicked and calmly explained the basics of flight mechanics to me as we flew along, with an occasional demonstration sprinkled in. After several hours at the controls of R.P.T., I started to relax and feel comfortable.

Frequently, George Hook, and his sales manager, would fly up to Porgera with us to market lumber and hardware supplies at the mine. Jim didn't care about having passengers. He'd give me the controls and have me practice climbs, dives,

Morning above the mountains near Porgera

Saddle point approach into Porgera. Mount Kajindi is on the right. Porgera village and landing strip is just left of center, partially obscured by the foreground mountain.

and banking turns around mountains, while we flew in route. He even let me practice take-offs.

At one company luncheon, the sales manager jokingly told me how afraid of flying George felt and how he had commented, "Why does Jim have to teach Bill how to fly while I'm in the back seat of the plane?" Concerned about George's fear of flying, I talked with him and reminded him that Jim could always grab the controls quickly, if I buggered anything up. George laughed nervously and said he just plain didn't like to fly. It didn't matter who was flying, but he knew he had to and would suffer through it. On later flights, I noticed he would grab the seat back in front of him, during any turbulence, or maneuvers, and hang on for dear life. We kiddingly started calling him "White Knuckles."

For my own part, I took to flying like an eagle to the air. Maybe I'd never have the grace of an eagle, but the thrill and the spirit of flying belonged to me. I knew there'd be lots of flights in my future and maybe, just maybe, if a pilot ever got sick, or something, it would be great to be able to put the "bird" on the ground, safely. In another practical sense, my work was so spread out, flying between jobs would be much more efficient than hours in 4WD commuting twisting mountain roads between job sites. There existed lots of small grass and gravel airstrips throughout the highlands of New Guinea.

In that regard, and with Jim's blessings and sponsorship, I started taking flying lessons at Hagen's Kagamuga Airport from Mission Aviation Fellowship (M.A.F.) instructors. A Cessna 172, Hotel Foxtrot Golf (call letters H.F.G.) became my in-the-air classroom. I studied the flight manuals and took tests whenever I could fit them into my schedule. Flying, at that point in my life, became a welcome diversion from the hassles of getting buildings built, working with my labor force, and dealing with job administrators. And besides, I'd wanted to fly ever since I was a kid. You know, "Off we go into the wide blue yonder!" What a feeling to experience, to work toward, alone in the sky with your own wings, looking down at the beautiful earth, soaring above the mountaintops, reaching for the face of the sun! I made a solemn pact with myself to accomplish it.

chapter thirty-four

The Kare Gold Fields

The helicopter control stick vibrated in my right hand. My eyes stayed mostly fixed on the horizon beyond. I quickly glanced down at the altimeter and compass to get my bearings for maintaining straight and level flight. The mountains lay about five hundred feet below us. My body had slowly begun to relax after Phil, the chopper pilot, gave me the controls. When he found out I held a student pilot license, Phil decided to give me a lesson. So here I sat, my first time ever in a helicopter, at the controls.

The chopper "caper" had all started the previous day with a phone call from the manager of Rotorworks at Kagamuga Airport. "Could you build us a small bunkhouse to sleep four chopper pilots up at the new Mt. Kare gold strike? It's bloody soft soil up there in a high valley. We heard you blokes did a ripper job in the mud for that mob up in Porgera. One of our pilots stayed at Top Camp and saw your buildings. Be here at seven, tomorrow morning, mate, and one of my pilots will fly you up to Kare for a lookabout. Give us a reasonable plan. I'll leave it with you for now, mate," made up the gist of the conversation from the Rotorworks end.

a metal pan, with mud and water shakes

keen eyes, the contents search, for yellow flakes

Now we headed almost due west for Mt. Kare-Puge on the border between the Southern Highlands and Engan Provinces. As the crow flies, or maybe more fitting, as the chopper flies, Mt. Kare was located only about 25 to 30 miles southwest of the Porgera gold mine. Phil told me no roads existed into our destination. You went in by chopper, or on foot. Seems as if gold had been discovered recently in the small valley adjacent to Mt. Kare. Soon after, lots of national prospectors had walked into the area, lured by the "gold fever."

After holding the Bell helicopter fairly straight and level for the better part of an hour while Phil relaxed, drank coffee, and kept an eye on me, he took over the controls and pointed straight ahead through the clear bubble canopy. "That's where we're headed. Up the little valley over there on the right. Hang on! I'm gonna take us in closer to the ground," he warned me. Next thing I knew, we skimmed above the valley floor at maybe a hundred-foot above the ground.

The scene that came into view can best be described as a war zone. A small creek ran from a mountain base. On both sides of it lay random

The chopper pad with Mount Kare-Puge in the background.
This is a two photo overlay showing the effects of tropical humidity

holes, maybe fifty of them, that looked like mortar rounds had exploded, leaving craters with soil piled high all around each hole. The pattern of hole digging looked random, close together, but chaotic in appearance. In most of the holes, mud-covered people worked with shovels and other digging tools. On a ridge, overlooking the melee down by the streambed, stood a row of neat yellow plastic tents. Next to the tents, a large roped off area came into view, in the middle of which sat a huge raft of logs, to which Phil pointed and said, "There's our chopper pad!"

Phil set our small Bell helicopter smoothly down on those logs and cut her down to a slow idle. He motioned for me to get out and yelled that he would meet me later over by the yellow tents.

As I walked off the chopper pad, involuntarily ducking my head even though the rotor blades whirled well above me, I saw kind of a log walkway heading towards the tent area. Stepping to one side, off the logs, I discovered their purpose. The surrounding ground proved soft and muddy. Lots of foot traffic probably would have churned it into a quagmire. A network of the log walkways extended throughout the entire tented area. Phil revved up the chopper behind me and

lifted off for some mission.

I found a grassy area, a little firmer than where the soil was exposed, knelt down to get my bearings, and made a rough sketch of the area. My trusty compass showed north to be approximately down the valley in front of me. Mt. Kare lay to my right, or east, and another small mountain stood left of me, or west. The two gullies formed between the ridge on which I stood and the mountains to my left and right, fed water into one creek that flowed downstream, north, through the small valley. All the digging took place around that small, innocent looking creek.

My eyes began to take in the busy scene in the valley below when a voice behind me broke into my fixation. "Hey, Yank, Phil just radioed in to ask me to show you the spot for their bunkhouse. He's gonna be busy for a while flying sorties. Said to meet Grant Ward, another Kiwi chopper ace, here at 4:30 this afternoon. Grant will get you back to Hagen."

Paul was a young, lean, tall geologist for C.R.A. (Consolidated Riotintozinc Australia) mining. He showed me where to grab a cup of coffee in the yellow plastic mess tent. Then we walked over to the site for the chopper pilots' bunkhouse. Paul told me the story of how he and his boss, Colin, moved through the territory specified on their government exploration license, sampling soils and studying topographical formations. He said he'd yet to venture down to the creek.

"You've never been down there. Who discovered the gold then?"

Paul answered my query by pointing down into the creek area below. "They did. Everywhere we've set up camp for the last two months on this exploration license, some of those 'kanakas' (uncivilized natives) always followed and watched what we did. Kind of creepy, but they looked in every stream and river we've camped near, thinking we knew some kind of secrets. We were still setting up a new camp here on the ridge, when we heard all the commotion and fighting down below. They know what a gold nugget looks like! That was three bloody weeks ago. More 'kanakas' have been pouring in ever since. There are no roads. They've been walking in over the mountains. Two day's walk that way to the nearest village close to Porgera. Nobody ever wanted this high, cold valley. Now everybody wants the bloody place!"

Curiosity prompted me to ask him, "Hey Paul, is it also true what I've heard that they can only use alluvial techniques to get the gold?"

"You're right on, mate. They're entitled to all the gold in the first two meters of surface, but only using pans and shovels. No mechanized equipment allowed. We've got the exploration rights to all the rest. There was some *whiteskin* down there a week ago trying to tell them how to set up high-pressure hoses. Thought he'd be a hero and make himself rich at the same time. We got wind of it and radioed in. The government blokes got him out of here in a hurry on a chopper. They've probably thrown him out of the country by now. None of the chopper pilots brought him in. Must have had a bad case of the fever to walk all the way through the moun-

tains."

"Where do you think the nugget source is? Doesn't it usually move out from a single source, or maybe a few sources?"

"It often comes from one nugget source and moves out slowly through the soil. I'm sure it's on top of Kare over there, judging from the topography of this valley. Probably an ancient fissure spit up a whole lot of liquid stuff that congealed into the nuggets they're finding. I've heard one *kanaka* found one as big as your fist. The purity is high, too, maybe ninety- four percent. Most of the remaining is silver."

"Is it true an expat can get killed for touching the stuff?"

"You can buy it from them. You can't pan for it, though. Everything in that first two meters is theirs. And anyway, if you had some, it's bloody hell to get out of the country."

Paul showed me the area for the bunkhouse, which was a bit firmer than back at the ridge camp, but still near enough to the chopper pad for easy portage of building materials. A log crib foundation would work well in the silted soil we stood on.

I explained the log setup to Paul as he looked on. "The chopper guys can bring me in about six 20-meter casuarina trees and drop them right here. We'll take it from there, assembling the bunkhouse right on top of the log tiers. Even if they sink a little, or tilt in an earthquake, the floor will stay in one flat plane. They don't care if the house is exactly level, as long as they can take a hot shower and sleep in a real bed."

"Those bloody Kiwis (most chopper pilots in P.N.G. originated from New Zealand) are so spoiled. We gave them one of our best plastic tents and they said they couldn't get enough sleep – too damp and cold. They wouldn't be fit for flying. Then I heard they were bringing you in to build them a real bunkhouse. They must figure to be operating out of here for quite a while."

"When I get back to Hagen tonight, I'll draw it up and we can begin to prefab the building tomorrow. The pilots said they'd carry the prefabbed sections in cargo nets slung under the choppers."

"Well, they're paying for it. They can have bloody flush toilets as far as I'm concerned. My boss gave permission to put it here, so they're right on that."

"Don't mention flush toilets to them. A pit latrine is all they're getting for a 'dunny,' as you Aussies call it."

I went on to ask his approval to head down to the diggings for a closer look at the action. He asked if I spoke the language, which I confirmed. "I can't stop you, Yank, but watch your backside and let me know when you come back up. Also, a mixed race bloke George Leahy came in here by chopper a few days ago and will be asking you to build him a house across the valley there. If you hear from him, tell him we haven't got permission for his place yet from the big guys."

Paul turned and headed back to camp while I glanced down at my watch. A good six hours remained until my chopper ride back to Hagen. I took off for the other side of the valley, staying above the diggings, figuring to drop down from the Mt. Kare side, off to my right. Jumping from grass clump to grass clump kept my feet out of the soft soil for a little while, but I soon missed a clump and went in over my hiking boot tops. Oh well, it would wash off later. It actually proved easier to plod straight through the mud anyway.

As I headed for Mt. Kare, I reflected on the stories that I'd heard about the Leahy (pronounced "lay" in flat Australian) brothers regarding how they'd opened the Highlands of New Guinea to explorations in the 1930's. Times got bad in Australia after the big war (World War I) with the depression setting in. Mick Leahy, next to the oldest of the five Leahy brothers, headed north for Australia's colony of New Guinea to try his hand at prospecting for gold in the coastal areas of Bulolo and Lae. Those early prospectors had a saying, "There's a lot of gold in New Guinea, but there's a lot of New Guinea mixed in with it!" They referred, in part, to the fearsome Kukukuku tribe that would appear out of the foggy bush without warning to fill the air with arrows and club prospectors' heads with lethal stone axes. Most Australian prospectors never ventured far inland from the coast and when the "yellow" colors faded in 1929, the majority headed south to Australia and home. Mick Leahy and his brother Paddy, however, along with a few others, thought there must be more gold inland, up in the unexplored and uncon-

The Kare gold fields exhibiting the "gold fever"

trolled territory. Mick obtained financial backing and an Uncontrolled Areas' Permit, which allowed his party to head inland for the purpose of prospecting for gold.

Mick's initial foray up into the unexplored regions of Lamari and Purari River areas almost ended in disaster as they lost their way and were attacked by the Kukukuku. During the fighting, a stone club found its mark, knocking Mick senseless. His brother Paddy and the gun "*bois*" repulsed the attack as Mick lay writhing on the ground in pain. Other than recurring headaches in the future, the blow to the head did not diminish Mick's appetite for exploration and gold. Upon arrival back to coastal Lae, Mick sent word down to Queensland for his brother Danny to join him and brothers, Paddy and James, in New Guinea. He came by the next available ship. Thereafter, Danny, at nineteen years of age, excitedly joined his older brother Mick on later expeditions, further and further into the Highlands. James stayed mostly in Lae to arrange permits and to supply the exploration efforts by airdrops and an occasional landing, when possible. Mick carried a 16mm movie camera, as well as a still photo camera, to record their exploration adventures over the next three or four years. On several of the early expeditions, an Australian Patrol Officer (*kiap*) James Taylor accompanied them.

The *kiap* monitored the expedition's impact during encounters with tribal groups, trying to minimize any conflicts that occurred. Needless to say, the three *whiteskins* armed themselves with rifles, pistols, and employed several trusted Waria gun "*bois*" to back them up. The balance of the exploration party consisted of coastal native carriers. These coastals carried trade goods, camp supplies, and sometimes even carried the *whiteskins* across rivers to keep their boots dry.

Mick and Danny received credit for opening the Highlands of Papua New Guinea in that period of the 1930's. They found a vast number of inhabitants (500,000 plus) living there, unknown to the outside world. Quite a few of those Highlanders died in gunfire when they attacked Mick's exploration group in an effort to steal trade goods, such as steel axes, necklaces, and seashells. Most tribes they encountered, however, preferred peace, gladly offering pigs and other food for those wonderful trade goods. Many natives happily traded their wives and daughters for a few steel axes.

Two major things happened as a result of the Highlands explorations. First, the Stone Age tribal groups found out that an outside world existed far advanced to their own civilization, with lots of goodies. Second, the outside world found out there was "gold in them thar hills." The inevitable clash of cultures began. There was no turning back.

Mick later married an Australian lady and ended up raising chickens on his Zenag plantation in the hills near coastal Lae. Danny, on the other hand, worked a family gold claim until it ran out years later at Kuta Ridge, near Hagen, which was the richest ore they came upon. He married three native wives, reared ten mixed race children, and enjoyed a plentiful life on his plantation Korgua, outside Mt. Hagen, for the rest of his life. Danny would later tell Sandia and I that he had traveled the world over, including a visit to the 1938 Munich Olympics, and knew well that he lived in "paradise." Danny died only a few years ago, in his late seventies, and is buried on that plantation he loved so much. An honest and a fair man by reputation, Danny even raised and schooled his brother's mixed race children, in addition to his own brood. George Leahy, one of Danny's own children, was the man Paul referred to as wanting the small house up here in Mt. Kare for the purpose of buying gold. George would eventually get his permission to build and become a good friend of Sandia's and mine in the process.

I continued my trek over toward Mt. Kare, took some tree samples for later identification at the Forestry Department, and began to plod my muddy feet down toward the diggings. I greeted each national I came upon in *Tok Pisin* and found myself a bit astonished when one prospector, in a deep conversation with another, turned to answer me back in perfect English. His name turned out to be the same as mine, Bill. He asked if he could show me around. I gladly accepted his offer and asked him about his language skill. Bill was educated at Sydney University and had been assistant camp manager at the Porgera Mine for three years in the early eighties.

Anyway, Bill adopted me and showed me around the alluvial gold area. Everyone knew him and seemed to respect him, so they consequently accepted my being there. They showed me their panning techniques – sorting the mud out into its yield of gold, using the seepage water in the bottoms of their holes. Every pan of mud yielded gold in some quantity – not only flakes, but granules of gold about the size of half a pea. Prospectors produced nuggets from special plastic wrappings and bags in their pockets to proudly display their prizes for my perusal.

One particular prospector, Andana (meaning "big" in his Porgeran *ples tok*), specially posed for my camera and wanted to share his claim spot with me. Andana started his day by digging out the mud he covered his spot over with the night

before in fear someone would come there to dig during the night. Even his fill-in mud was laced with gold. After Andana offered me the use of an extra pan, I jumped down into his hole to try a technique I once practiced on the North Fork of the Colorado River back in my own mountains. Several minutes later, the last of the mud and gravel sloshed over the pan edge to reveal three good-sized granules of gold. All my hours in the Colorado River gravel had yielded only a few small flakes of gold, but here, in maybe three or four minutes, I stared down at about five grams (0.16 troy ounce) in my first pan.

Andana saw my smile and motioned for me to put the gold in my pocket. I looked into the

Andana digging mud out of his "claim" hole to get started panning

sincerity of his eyes, picked up the three pieces from my pan, reached over and dropped them into his pan, telling him the gold must go toward the school fees of his two sons which he had described to me earlier. His sharing gesture really touched me. I wasn't sure how my refusal would affect him. In life, a delicate sensitivity balances giving and being able to receive. In any regard, I thanked Andana for the experience he gave me and promised to bring him a copy of his photograph upon my return. He looked into my eyes and said he thought I wouldn't remember him. I grabbed his muddy hand and said, "Yes,

I will!" As I climbed up out of his hole, Andana offered an undug area near his for me to use and stay in the valley to pan for gold. He said his village people wouldn't mind. I felt sorry that I didn't have the language skills to explain the philosophies of expatriate rules of conduct while in his country on a work permit. I only told him thanks for the offer, but I couldn't accept and waved farewell. Oh the giving and sharing heart of a New Guinea national!

Bill and I walked on down toward the central creek, about two feet wide by maybe a foot deep. Bill shouted to the nearby prospectors in some *ples tok* and turned to me, "They said it's okay for you to walk in the middle of the creek. It's easier than the muddy edges!"

As I followed Bill downstream, the water felt refreshing on my feet as it washed away some of the mud caked on my boots, socks, and calves. I noticed various dams and diversions built into the creek and its banks to expedite the alluvial gold process in many of the adjacent small claim areas.

Bill brought me to his family's claim area – one section of the creek itself. He introduced me to his father, who claimed to have ten wives, was 68 years old, and the obvious respected patriarch of his family. His sons talked to me, but he went on working, stooped over with a shovel. The sons proudly showed me jars of gold from their work and explained that they had rights in this valley, as demonstrated by the location of their claim area in the main creek itself. Lesser claimants worked farther away from the creek. Engans and Southern Highlanders both now laid claim to this previously unwanted valley. Prospectors from outside those two provinces could dig only far above the creek in areas not yet desired by Engans or Southern Highlanders. There prevailed a definite digging order, regulated and maintained by ancient tribal laws but inseminated with the seeds of human greed.

I found myself wishing I had something to share with the brothers in return for letting me visit and photograph their claim area and part of their gold stash. Then I thought of a small photo album, always in my rucksack – pictures of *La Casita* on the Colorado River. Nationals love photographs. I dug into my rucksack and came out with the pictures. The brothers excitedly gathered around me to see the photographs. I explained in my best *Tok Pisin* about my home in the Colorado Rockies. They delighted over the photos and asked permission to take them over to show their father, who had by then stopped working. He studied each photo as one son flipped through them explaining in ples tok the

Bill (left), father, and brothers working their creek section

details as he knew them.

Then Bill became the interpreter and asked, "My father wants to know what kind of trees these are?"

"Tell him they are pine and spruce trees. We call them evergreens."

There proceeded more huddled discussion over the photographs. Next Bill emerged to ask, "They want to know if there is any gold in your river?"

"Tell them yes, I've taken out a little."

Then there occurred more animated and huddled discussion from which Bill turned to ask, "Now they want to know how much it costs to fly to your mountains in America?"

"About 1,800 dollars U.S. for one round trip," I answered with the hint of a grin as I began to see where their thought processes headed.

Bill turned back into his family group and reported the price. More discussions ensued. Finally he turned to me and said, "Now you've done it. They want to go there and look for gold where it is not muddy and crowded with many other gold seekers!"

With a smile, I told Bill, "Tell them that other gold seekers have already taken most of the big gold from my river. There is very little in contrast to what they have here. I panned my river for three weeks and only found about 15 grams. And besides, tell them it gets very cold in my mountains. Sometimes there is ice on my river!"

A few more minutes passed as their discussions ensued. Then they broke up and the father and brothers went back to their work. Bill approached me and said, "My father says to thank you. He said you are a good man, but he decided that we must stay here to work in this gold field. He also said you and I can talk longer if you have any other questions."

"Well only one and then I'd better head back up to the ridge camp. For my own journals and writing, I'm just curious what you think will happen to this little valley in the future?"

Bill answered me, with obvious bitterness creeping into his voice, "That's not hard to answer, mate. I've seen it happen before. The mining company has already paid off our politicians and they will be given a Special Mining Lease to begin mining the gold once their exploration license runs out. Our government will take a small five to ten percent of the total profit, which will go into too many willing pockets. My people, who own this land, will not see the benefit of the gold by way of schools and better housing. We're supposed to be happy and placated with these nuggets near the surface, while the mining com-

pany takes all the rest!"

"Not a lot you can do, Bill. Your government holds the mineral rights, just as in my country."

"But in your country, no one puts it all in their pockets. Here our politicians buy up some of the best beachfront property in Australia and end up living down there later with our money. There is no way to stop it. What belongs to all my people ends up in the pockets of a few. Most of the gold will go out of the country. In twenty or thirty years, there will be no more for our children, and their children!"

I tried to calm him a little with the realities of life, "Bill, many governments are like that, especially in developing countries. Even in my country, the U.S.A., there are some wide-open pockets. It's the nature of man, but most of my country's politicians are interested in the people, or maybe just the power of it all. I don't know all the answers. I wish for your people's sake, things worked better here."

"Look around you. See the gold fever. It's in my people's eyes. More gold seekers walk in every day. They've been paying those chopper pilots two or three nuggets for the thrill of a ten-minute ride in the sky. It costs seven dollars U.S. for a pack of cigarettes up here. A bloody scrawny chicken costs ten dollars. These diggers think they're rich and pay it. Scared to leave their holes for fear someone else will move in and

A jar of Kare gold nuggets. Sorry about the focus!

take it. You saw. Some fill their holes in at night, thinking no one will know where they're digging – then they have to dig it all out the next morning, just to get started. In a few months, all the nuggets will be gone and then what'll happen around here? When the mine opens, they think we should be happy for the lousy jobs as laborers, mining our own gold! At the other mines, there aren't that many jobs. They bring in outsiders for the real work. I'm telling my people we should shut down this area and learn how to mine the gold ourselves by working over at the Pogera Mine for a few years; then we can come back here and mine all this gold for Papua New Guineans! What do you think of my plan?"

I answered him, a bit taken aback by his passionate tirade, "I think it is noble and has some merit, but I don't know the politics of it all. The reality is your Engans and Southern Highlanders now fight over ownership for the surface nuggets while the rich lode probably lies beneath it all. If your own people can't come together, your plan will never work! Also, Bill, I think your father is motioning for you. And I'd better get up the hill."

As we shook hands in parting and I thanked him for his time and thoughts, Bill left me with his father's thinking, "My father wants me to get back to work. He doesn't like my ideas. Says we should work hard now, as a family, to get as much gold as we can. He says the government is too big to fight!"

I smiled and nodded in acknowledgement of his father's wisdom, waving to them all as I started up the hill toward the yellow plastic tent camp on the ridge above.

After checking in with Paul, I found a cup of coffee and an empty table in the mess tent. I scribbled pages of descriptions and reflections of the day in my journal. The words flowed easily onto the lined notebook pages. A hand on my shoulder startled me and brought me out of my writing trance.

The type of gold scales used by Kare gold buyers

It was Paul with another expat in tow, saying, "Bill, this is Richard Leahy. He wants to get a closer look at the diggings. I told him you'd already been down there today and might show him the way. Would you mind? You've still got an hour until your chopper gets here."

I turned to shake the extended hand of Richard Leahy. He was maybe five foot ten, with a strong, stout build. He was dressed in the standard hiking boots, shorts, and short sleeved shirt. On his head, though, he wore a different sort of short-billed Irish cap. Paul explained that Richard owned an air freighting business, Kiunga Airfreight, and might be doing some later business with C.R.A.

I gladly agreed and Richard followed me out of the tent. We went past the chopper pad down toward the diggings. I shared with Richard some of the things I'd seen on my earlier foray that day. He seemed keenly interested in the richness of the strike. I described my first pan of mud and the resulting five grams of gold. I told him the high purity figures I'd heard. Richard's eyes sparkled. I noticed he involuntarily rubbed his hands together as he digested my descriptions and took in the scene below us.

Several hundred meters from the mud of the creek, Richard was happy to stop, while he still had grass to walk on. His "*boi*" stood beside him.

As he gazed down at the alluvial activity, I heard him say, as he shook his head side to side, "Who would have thought – this high up!"

Knowing the irony of the situation with Richard being the son of Mick Leahy and his Australian wife, Jeanette, I asked Richard if I might take his photograph with the national gold seekers in the background. As soon as my shutter clicked, Richard turned to point up the valley and commented, "My father and uncle stopped their explorations of this land just over that mountain and went back to Kuta Ridge in Hagen. Imagine if they'd come over one more mountain!"

There was definitely some gold fever in Richard's eyes and understandably so. His father Mick and uncle Danny had first prospecting rights in the Highlands and missed this Mother Lode of nuggets by "one more mountain." Millions of dollars in gold nuggets lay undiscovered for another fifty plus years in this high, cold, unwanted little valley, until a couple of national camp followers poked up their yellow glint.

Waiting at the chopper pad later, I saw all the C.R.A. "v.i.p.s" flown off to warm and comfortable accommodations at the Ambua Lodge, near Tari, in the Southern Highlands, where Sandia and I had honeymooned a few months earlier. What blissful memories that brought back!

My designated Bell helicopter and pilot Grant Ward showed up pretty much on time. On the way to Hagen, though, we made one stop to drop off a national camp worker at the Tari Hospital with blankets and *kai* (food) for a *wontok* laborer, who'd mangled two fingers in a core drilling accident that same morning.

Grant decided to drop me at the seldom-used Hagen town chopper pad as I didn't have a car at Kagamuga Airport. As he circled and then hovered for his landing, hundreds of nationals rushed to circle the chopper pad with their unending curiosity. I hopped out, shouting thanks

Richard Leahy at the Kare gold fields

to Grant, and walked through the crowd staring at me, right into the nearby Highlander Hotel Bar and ordered a cold "*bia.*"

What a day it had been. Sandia joined me for dinner. I tried to describe to her my incredible day with all its historical meanings and significance.

Hailans Homes with Norbert as my main foreman got the chopper pilots' bunkhouse built. We also got George Leahy's place built for him in that valley at the base of Mt. Kare-Puge. The word up there told of 100 million dollars in gold nuggets coming out of the ground in the first six months after the initial strike. I'm not sure who kept track of value, or the ounces. I flew in and out of the valley quite a few times, keeping a check on progress. Yes, I did get Andana back his photo. Lots of horror stories and some humorous ones came out of that gold strike. A small earthquake caused a section of Mt. Kare to slide one day, exposing a new field of nuggets. Before the "mud" cleared, seven nationals died in an axe-fighting, greedy rush for the pieces of precious yellow metal. There occurred the usual cheating with dishonest scales by some of the gold buyers. Prospectors had to hire choppers to get them to the bank; otherwise, they stood a good chance of being ambushed if they tried to lug out their gold, or money, on foot. I heard of one expat bank manager who greedily bought some large nuggets for himself at what he thought seemed a moneymaking price, only to find out later, the "nuggets" were actually brass. Once, C.R.A. officials, in an attempt to "seduce" the local Kare landowners, went to the elaborate lengths of flying a representative group by chopper and then airplane all the way to Port Moresby for a lot of "wining and dining." While the "seduction" progressed, they discovered the national group they had brought turned out to be the wrong people, having absolutely nothing to do with the Mt. Kare valley ownership! It truly made for a "wild

Pilot Grant Ward landing at the muddy Mount Kare chopper pad

west" boomtown type happening, with the flavor of Papua New Guinea mixed in, to yield a distinctive sweet and sour taste.

chapter thirty-five

A New Direction in Porgera

I followed the slash-
ing sounds of the bush
knife wielded by one of
our guides up ahead as
we moved slowly through
the rainforest above
Tomba. Two hours ear-
lier, the four of us, Ray West, George Hook, the
new sales manager from Tasmania, Steve, and
myself, set out from the old sawmill outside of
Tomba village determined to reach the summit
of Mount Hagen at 12,450 feet. Tomba was at
about the 8,000-foot elevation, so we were at-
tempting an ascent of approximately 4,450 feet
and return on the same day, a Sunday.

The bush proved amazingly damp and dense.
Early on, I had tried my hand at bush slashing
with the machete and found it to be an artful
and demanding task. Our guide in the lead,
hired from Tomba village, however, made chop-
ping through the dense growth seem easy. In
everyday life that big bush knife likely never lay
far from his hand, as seemed the case for most
Highlands village men. Another Tomba man
followed in the rear, watching for what, I don't
know. Maybe he just wanted to keep his *wontok*,
or cousin-brother, company.

The guide told us we would soon come out

*eyes trained on the peak,
keep going, don't stop*

*muscles strain in one resolve,
"reach the top"*

of the bush to start climbing on open ground (*graun
no gat diwai*). That sounded
like good news to me, as
the humidity really seemed
to dampen my movements.
Perspiration wet my entire
body. I wondered about the light nylon jacket
in my rucksack-a recommended item for the
trip. Certainly I didn't need it there in the dark,
damp, tropical rain forest.

Then suddenly the forest ahead began to
brighten. All of us increased the uphill pace. The
bush began to thin noticeably. You could make
out the trunks of trees, no longer hidden by the
dense undergrowth. The sounds of birds began
to fill my ears. The movement of a jet-black bird
of paradise in a tree ahead of us caught my attention. Long black tail feathers, probably 18
inches in length, hung below the branch on
which he perched. His song sounded hauntingly
melodious. I had never heard a bird sing like that
before. Then our movements startled his melody.
He left quickly, to seek a more distant, peaceful
perch to continue his musical quest for a mate.
I'm sure he'd rarely been interrupted by *whiteskins* trekking through his domain.

Our hiking party broke out at tree line to

stand gawking at the view beyond. It truly made me suck in my breath. The guide pointed to a distant peak and said, "*Emi* Hagen!" We still had a ways to go yet, but it became a whole lot more fun when you could see the surrounding mountains and focus on the destination summit ahead.

As I continued walking, I thought of my lady and wondered how she was doing down in coastal Lae. Sandia had been sent on a three-day training session down to the main Total Concept store and warehouse. I'd have to describe our climb to her later. A separation of only a few days seemed so small, and so much easier to handle, after waiting nearly six months for her arrival in Papua New Guinea. And besides, it was fun to be with the guys on a macho type mission. Ray and I kidded seriously about how good an ice cold brownie would taste at the end of the day.

The time approached noon as we crested a summit to look ahead at the higher Mount Hagen peak. I felt dismayed to find we had to give up maybe 1,500 to 2,000 feet and then climb again to the Hagen summit. The peak looked so close, yet still so far. We stared at each other, gritted our teeth, and plunged downward, following the barefooted guide, so we could reach the point for the final ascent to Mount Hagen's summit. I guess, in life, there are times, when you have to give up some personal gains in sacrifice for a greater prize. On this principle, great relationships between humans can be built. Down we went, on our way to the higher prize of Hagen's peak.

When we climbed back up to within two hundred meters of our goal, Steve and I, almost simultaneously, driven by the exuberance of the finish so close above, ran together the final distance of the ascent and fell to the ground at the top, rolling in laughter and exhaustion at the same time. We got to our feet as the more

conservative Ray and George crested the summit with our two Tomba men.

After wolfing down the lunches we'd carried, Ray and I started looking off into the distance to see if we could identify any landmarks. As we turned to the north and focused our eyes, we could see the blue waters of the South Pacific, or actually the Bismark Sea. The Germans had named quite a few things, including the summit on which we stood. They sighted it from the sea and named it after a famous countryman named von Hagen. We yelled out to Steve and George to look as we pointed toward the ocean to the north. One of the Tomba men walked up, looked, and said, "*Emi blubush!*"

It took me a couple moments of reflection to comprehend what he had said. Since obviously he'd never been to the ocean to see it, he, and probably many other Highlanders, from that vantage point, thought the green bush of the jungle merely turned into blue bush as it became the horizon. The texture of the ocean, in fact, didn't appear much different from the far distant jungle textures. Most Highlanders had never touched the sea.

I shivered as a sudden cold wind blew across my moist body and clothing. Storm clouds engulfed our summit. None of us had a thermometer attached to our packs, but we knew it was cold. Time to break out the nylon windbreaker I'd carried up in my rucksack. We posed for a quick photograph at the Mt. Hagen summit signpost, as the storm began to lace us with little pellets of white ice. Here we stood only six degrees latitude below the equator, in the equatorial trough, shivering. George, who'd neglected to bring the recommended jacket, shivered as he said, "I'm ready to head down."

Our Tomba guide at that moment pointed skyward remarking, "*Emi sol.*" He thought the little ice balls were "salt!" We didn't try to explain, just headed down, and up, and down again. When we reached the earlier, lower summit, we looked back to see Mt. Hagen obliterated by the storm. *Ayiii*, great timing!

Going downhill quickly made all of us feel leg muscles that we hadn't been aware of before. By the time we reached our truck at the old sawmill, my leg muscles screamed obscenities at me. I volunteered to drive back to Hagen and, during the trip, moving my feet on the foot pedals became literally a "pain." Approaching Hagen, we decided each of us had just enough strength left in our arms to hoist a couple of cold brownies at the Highlander Hotel Bar in celebration of our mutual "macho" tour de force. How great they tasted, sharing those "earned" beers with your mates.

Sandia's trip to the Lae workshop ended up with a humorous aspect to it. Seems on the last day, Sunday, while we toughed it out on Mt. Hagen, the Total Concept expats took a break for a sail on a friend's boat out of the Lae Yacht Club. They returned for dinner at a private club and socialized, kind of a celebration of the work they'd accomplished. Well, the national newspaper photographer appeared at the club that night, probably at the instigation of Yvonne Leahy, one of Sandia's coworkers. Then, sure enough, in the next week's newspaper, in the "Who's Who in P.N.G. Society" section, there was my beautiful lady smiling up at me from the Society page. Did I ever rib her, only four months in the country, and already a P.N.G. socialite! The society thing made for a laugh in a developing country like Papua New Guinea, but some expats imported their own culture, holding onto it as if it was sacred. Sandia said she turned her head from the dinner table to look right into the camera lens. The occurrence became part of our education in human values, observing the contrasting realities and extremes of P.N.G. After

Ray, George, Steve, and myself (l to r) at the summit of Mount Hagen

all, isn't that what life is all about, searching for and defining what is important to each of us?

The beginning of summer '88, actually winter, found Sandia coming near her first half-year mark in Papua New Guinea. She worked hard to put her Total Concept branch store in the "black." Most of her customers consisted of expats shopping for home or office furnishings. Several other competing Hagen stores carried inexpensive furnishings designed to attract the national buyer, but Total Concept's inventory, by design, demonstrated a bit better quality and, hence, a little more expensive. Sandia's three sewing girls, who now included the opportunistic Rachel, turned out nice custom drapes, window coverings, and dunas (bed coverings). Sandia seemed always on the run, measuring peoples' windows for curtains and their floors for wall-to-wall carpeting. She did, however, find the time to teach her one male employee, Goi, how to drive the company pickup truck. The pride and happiness of accomplishment was etched in Goi's face when he returned from his driving test to proudly hold up his brand new driver's license. Goi's driving ability freed up Sandia from running all the Total Concept errands around Hagen. She fondly referred to Goi as, "my *boi* Goi."

In the meantime, Hailans Homes worked toward the completion of the Top Camp bunk-houses at Porgera. At the same time, my man Norbert supervised the chopper pilots' bunk-house in Mt. Kare, while I had three more crews in the Chimbu Mountains working on the Phase II contract houses and market stalls. It was about that time, while inundated with work and spread several hours flight time from west to east, that I decided to start charging a small, but reasonable, fee for building estimates and material take-offs (lists). We stood deep in work and the fee told me if the inquiry constituted a legitimate project or just "pie in the sky." There just wasn't time for extraneous work, and, besides, Hailans Homes then had solid work under contract for three months ahead.

A Sunday bush walk above the fertile Wahgi Valley

The time seemed right for a mini-break. Our eleventh wedding anniversary furnished the momentum. Queen's Birthday three-day weekend became the vehicle. The Windjammer Lodge on the beach on the north coast in a town named Wewak served as the place. (This location stood only about sixty miles east of where the "killer" tsunami would hit those defense-less nationals ten years later in '98.) Our little separate *kunai* lodge opened onto the white sand beach and the magical sound and rhythm of the waves became our back-ground music for a long weekend of love in the sun and surf. It was time to recharge our human batter-ies, renew our "vows," and remem-ber our friends and family who shared our wedding day. Sitting on a palm log, with my feet in the sand and the surf breaking in front of me, as Sandia napped an

Sandia and me on the beach in Wewak with some of the local youngsters

242

afternoon siesta in the shade of our *kunai* shelter, I scribbled down my reflections and mailed the following:

11 June 1988, Saturday

To Those Special Few:

Who shared this wedding day with us eleven years ago, we write to share this anniversary day and remembrance of you.

Some of you know the mountain journey, on which we embarked and even came to join us for a small part of what we undertook. Well, we left those mountains and our sanctuary above the Colorado River that we built and carved out of that peaceful forest land. The snows of last winter came and went, without any smoke from our chimney vent. Doors and windows boarded up, an empty house, save an occasional, hibernating, little furry mouse. We will go back one day, I guess, but for now, the world's too big a space, for us to stay in just one small place.

This special anniversary day finds us in a tiny town called Wewak, on the northern coast of Papua New Guinea. It's Queen's Birthday weekend and in a Commonwealth Country, we get an extra day off. Our jobs are high up in the mountains of New Guinea, but for the holiday, it's only a thirty- minute flight down here to paradise. Sun and surf, just below the equator, is not real hard to take. We took an early morning run along the beach with the palm trees swaying in the soft coastal breeze. Then a walk to town, along the beach, for supplies to stock our weekend retreat; followed by a nice long swim in the warm turquoise surf. The sound of waves pounding on the beach. I'm sure it won't be our last weekend here.

Yesterday, we spent most of the day with an American teacher, named Byron, who's traveling around the world. This morning we bade him farewell as he headed up the Sepik River in a dugout canoe into the jungles of New Guinea. A local guide supplied the canoe, a doctor supplied his malaria pills, bush villages will supply his sleeping needs, and for seven days he'll have to supply the nerve to see it through. What an opportunity, and to think he almost packed it in, but then said, with our cheering support, "What the hell, I'll probably never get the chance again!"

It kind of reminded us of the route we followed to get here. An opportunity, a quick bold decision, and now we live in the mountains of Papua New Guinea—about a mile above sea level, with some peaks around us towering up to 14,500 feet. Sometimes it's very difficult and the strong urge to leave sets in, but then some special excitement reminds us that, "What the hell, we may never get the chance again!"

I'm learning to become a pilot in these rugged mountains and, three weeks ago, I even got the chance to fly a chopper into a gold strike area at 9,100 feet up in a little valley at the base of Mt. Kare-Puge. Hundreds of natives, huddled over a little creek from which they've pulled out several million dollars in nuggets in seven short weeks. I bought some nuggets for souvenirs. The biggest gold nugget found so far weighed in at 3.6 kilograms (about eight pounds!). School kids had coffee jars full of gold.

Last week, we chopper-lifted our first kit house into the gold strike area. We'll probably build several more in the boomtown up there. My company has been given the contract to build bunkhouses at another gold mine, 25 miles away from the new gold strike. There, they'll remove a whole mountain over twenty years, again in the quest of gold—hundreds of tons of it.

In the other direction, I'm building kit houses/office stores in the bush of the Chimbu Mountains to support new vegetable growing efforts and a village market economy, funded by the World Bank. I'm meeting U.S. Peace Corps workers who astound me with their dedication. All in all, I guess you could say, for Sandia and I, there is hardly a dull moment here in "the land of the unexpected."

Sandia manages a business close to mine—carpets, furniture, and curtains. We both have totally indigenous staff. The language isn't difficult—neo-Melanesian, or pidgin, and many can speak decent English. We usually have lunch together a few times a week. She works Hagen town, while I spend most of my time in the bush. Ten months of my two-year contract have already gone by like a rocket, and with ten weeks of holiday someplace in front of us, it's really more like a year to go.

When we "go finish" our plan now is to travel around the world and take six to eight months to get home. We're thinking Australia, Hong Kong, Singapore, India, Turkey, Europe, followed by the good ole U.S. of A., but that's the future and it's fun to dream. Who knows where we'll all be a year from now?

Right now, we're here in Wewak, a beautiful, coastal, South Pacific town. The years have brought us much and our love has steadily grown. We remember often all our family and friends on that magical day we shared beside a lake in Marlborough and then the reception at the "Big Oak." Thanks then and thanks now for being special for us and to us. Know that although the years have passed, and miles have come between, and maybe correspondence has grown thin—you are

often thought of and often missed—as our very special few.

We love you.

B & S

PS, Please write sometime, when the moment and the thoughts are there—let us know how it is with your lives and what it's all about!

On our flight back to Hagen, Sandia and I reflected on the contrasting attitudes and personalities of the coastal people we had spent the long weekend amongst and the highlanders who we spent the majority of our time with. The coastal people seemed so "laid back" and peaceful in their demeanor. Our recent walks along the beach allowed us to observe the lifestyle of the nationals living around Wewak. Kids took us willingly into their beach games of kick ball and

Sunset on the Wewak beach

laughed so easily with us. We watched the fisher-men and women cast their small nets from waist deep water to catch the odd fish, crab, or cray-fish, for, I guess, their dinner. Women tended small garden plots, shaded by coconut palms. The coastal people seemed much in rhythm with the slow, steady wash of waves upon the clean, bright, beach sand. In contrast, the Highlanders appeared much more aggressive in their behav-ior. Maybe it all comes down to the weather, the cool highlands vs. the hotter, more humid coast, but apart from the physical differences in body types, the taller, thinner Coastals, vs. the shorter, stockier Highlanders, the national attitude to-ward life varied greatly with altitude, as well as, genetic heritage.

The next week in Porgera, while check-ing on the finishing touches on the Top Camp "dongas," I was approached with a new request. Fritz Robinson, an ex-agricultural of-ficer, now working as a consulting liaison be-tween the Placer Dome Mining Company and the Porgeran villagers, asked my help in coming up with a house design into which the mining company would relocate villagers presently liv-ing within the future mine boundaries. It seemed that back in the early days of the initial explora-tion of the area, only three or four families lived on or near the two gold laden mountains. Now, a few years later, in hopes of "cashing in," several hundred "relatives" of the initial families had moved onto the mountains. The mining com-pany now contemplated building each of those mountain dwelling families a new house, off site, and giving them each a generous garden allow-ance to replant a new garden away from the gold mountains. There existed no land ownership documents to be checked, only nebulous squat-ter family networking rights, again established by the cultural "pecking" order of ancestry.

I smiled, happy it wasn't me trying to do the liaison work, as Fritz described what they attempted to accomplish. What a task in front of him to get these hundreds of Porgerans to agree on one house design, because all had to receive an equal house, otherwise there would be charges of favoritism stemming from human jealousy followed by possible tribal fighting. All the years Fritz had spent as an agricultural officer (*didiman*) among the Highlanders was going to be put to the test in the pending negotiations to relocate nationals from the future mine site. The Special Mining Lease was rumored to be close to issuance, but the mining work couldn't begin until the people moved off the gold mountains.

Over the next two months, I drew no less than five sets of house plans for Fritz to use in his negotiations with the Porgeran villagers and their "big men." The final design, accepted by the people, proved cheaper to build than previ-ous designs as it called for imported metal siding ("V" crimp) vs. treated P.N.G. wooden tongue and groove exterior walls. One villager later told me he voted for the "V" crimp, as did many others, because of the common belief that dur-ing tribal wars, their houses couldn't be burned down! They neglected to notice that their foun-dation posts and all structural framing, as well as interior plywood walls, were combustible. They also thought the metal would protect them from axes and spears, even though it was only about one millimeter thick. I think, though, an over-riding reason for their choice lay in the belief that they thought it was modern, and the proper thing to do.

So there it was, the negotiations ended. Each designated family would receive a brand new four bedroom house, measuring approximately 500 square feet (about one-third the average American house), built at a new location in clus-ters of family groupings. Each would receive an

A Porgeran mother. Note the load on her back.

Two young Porgeran girls on a misty morning

additional garden allowance of K1500 (~$1,650 U.S.) to start a new garden in the vicinity of their relocation house. This settlement easily amounted to a seven or eight million-dollar undertaking by the mining company to "clear" the mine site. All I could surmise was they must have shown great core samples in the exploratory drilling. Figures of six billion dollars in reserves were being bandied about.

Can you imagine the impact on the lives in this remote mountain village, not removed from "Stone Age" culture by much more than fifty years since the Leahy brothers showed their pale faces in the Highlands of Papua New Guinea? Mick and Danny Leahys' impact, or baptism, seemed so minuscule in comparison to today's mining giants. Modern humans must have their precious metal chains and adornments, so Porgeran villagers hold on tight, your ride into the modern world is only beginning, and there will be no going back!

A village youngster and pig

chapter thirty-six

Picking up Steam in Porgera

There could be no denying the traces of blood in the toilet in front of me. I stood there staring down at the red color as it diluted into the toilet volume. How long had it been since I'd last seen the red urine. I watched the fading red color with anguish, as I mentally counted the three plus years that had passed without a sign of the bladder tumors. I finished three hard hours on the tennis court a little earlier, but I'd certainly done that kind of a workout, and then some, before. That Saturday night, the 2nd of July, 1988, I spent in reflection on what to do. A later trip to the bathroom to void my bladder showed the same red. Why had it come back on me? Why had it started again?

Two days later, I laid in a hospital bed in Brisbane, Australia. Mary Ann's brother, a U.S. urologist, recommended an Australian counterpart, experienced in the cystoscopy procedures, and the next day he would have a look into my bladder. So there I lay, on Independence Day, the 4th of July, hunkered down in my hospital bed, scribbling thoughts and reflections into my journal. Ever the optimist, I knew I'd be fine, but still your mind plays little "what if" games. These

beneath the waves, into the turquoise sea,

one slips, to touch the ocean's mystery

games can insert tiny seeds of doubt. *"No way, they're not going to find anything major. Must be one lousy little tumor that decided to grow in there just to bug me! What if there turns out to be more than one? A whole bunch of malignancy? No way, I've been eating tons of vegetables and exercising almost every day! I've been doing all the good stuff, except maybe keeping the stress to a minimum. I wonder?"*

I put it out of my mind. I gritted my teeth and told myself it would be routine and fine. No negative thoughts allowed in this head. I wrote a few passages to Sandia, who remained back in the mountains of Papua New Guinea, looking after her business and keeping an eye on mine. The company didn't provide health insurance, and State Farm had canceled mine, maybe thinking I'd get malaria, or some other tropical disease. So I was on my own with the hospital and doctor bills, but the company did book my round trip airfare to Brisbane from P.N.G. No worries, health is the highest of priorities, and besides, Australian medical costs are only a fraction of stateside billings.

I turned my analytical focus to the cause

of this reoccurrence with bladder tumor/s. My lifestyle seemed sound in the diet and exercise realm. I'd completed the 26 mile marathon distance in ten different races over eight years, with all the rigorous training that it required. Running logbooks, at that point, showed my total mileage in excess of 8,500 miles. My eating habits had changed drastically in response to the running, consisting of mostly fruit and vegetables, with occasional fish and white meat. The cause had to lie in the stress of it all—the deadlines, the job complexities, the flat out difficulties of getting work completed in a developing country. I promised myself that night, before falling asleep, to try to relax in my approach to Hailans Homes tasks. Just do the best, without the worries. A new theme to go along with deep breathing – "no worries!" It seemed a perfect saying for the Australian territory.

Two days later, I sat in a Brisbane shopping mall watching the civilization around me. The smile in my heart showed on my face. The doctor had removed one small tumor from the bladder wall itself, making me promise to get another examination when I got back to the States. He thought there might be a growth up the connecting tube to the right kidney and I should get another opinion, at least an exam. I felt great. Hearing my lady's voice on the telephone served as therapeutic recovery medicine. I would be holding her in my arms by the next night.

In the meantime, Jim's brother Bob, and his wife, who lived in Brisbane, graciously looked after me. They had reluctantly left me on my own in the shopping mall, with detailed instructions on which bus to catch to their house, a short distance away. I shopped for a few clothing items, and a gift for Sandia. After the hospital stay, I found it exhilarating to sit and watch people going about their routine shopping business. That trip constituted my first venture out of New Guinea in eleven months. The occurrence had a

*Sandia bargaining for a mud man statue
with an Assaro tribe craftsman*

memorable effect on my mind. *"Enjoy the moment,"* I told myself. *"Relax in the satisfaction that they didn't find any major health problems. Take deep breaths. Relax."*

Then I focused in on a sign advertising ear piercing at the chemist (pharmacist) nearby. In one crazy moment of rationale, I made up my mind, walked into the chemist shop, sat in the piercing chair, and then walked out sporting a gold earring in my left lob. That earring, I reasoned, would be my symbol to not take myself too seriously. I would wear it as my own badge of reminder to relax; eventually replacing the store bought stud with a gold nugget from Mt. Kare-Puge. Now my friends and family would confirm what they already knew, that I'm a crazy man! I headed back to P.N.G. the next day feeling good about life, happy with the challenge of my work, determined to keep stress out of my life, but mostly so anxious to hold my lady Sandia in my arms once again.

I jumped right back into work and soon stood up to my eyeballs in the South Chimbu Rural Development Project, the Mount Kare gold strike buildings, and the iterative design work for the Porgera Relocation Project. We also had several local houses going – at the Hagen Bakery next door, for our friend and bakery manager, Robert Jacobsen, and another house at the St. Anslem's School. An additional house was in the final bid stages with nearby Angco Coffee. Hailans Homes now employed about fifty people, counting drivers and security personnel. I took lots of deep breaths as I tried to keep all the projects busy and efficient. About that time, the company informed Sandia and I that we had accrued a mid-year week's holiday for the sole purpose of recuperation. It was understood we'd stay in the country, or at least nearby, like the Solomon Islands, for instance. We could stay at home if we wanted to. With a few weeks to think

about exciting options, Sandia and I had some fun brainstorming locations. We finally decided on a scuba diving school on the north coast of the island of New Britain, east of New Guinea's main island. The beach resort, Walindi, where the school was located, lay a little northeast of the main town of Kimbe. An interesting character named Max Benjamin owned and managed Walindi. His staff included head dive master, Frank Butler, a Pom, who would be our instructor. Sandia called to get us school reservations and lodgings for the five-day course. We had both dreamed and talked of diving in the waters of the South Pacific. Now it suddenly became a reality.

Jim offered to fly us in Romeo Papa Tango, from Lae out to the little Kimbe airport about 400 kilometers (250 miles) away. We crossed from mainland P.N.G., across the Vitiaz and Dampier Straits, then along the north coast of New Britain until we saw the Kimbe Airport. Jim was running late, and subsequently, dropped us off at the side of the runway and immediately took off for Lae, so he'd have time to get back before dusk.

Sandia and I carried our frame-packs from the runway over to the little terminal building, only to find it locked up for the night. The main gate was also locked. So over the chain-link and barbed wire we climbed, following our tossed over backpacks. It seemed desolate at first, then up pulled a "hire" car (taxi) offering to help. He got us to a telephone, where we called the Walindi Resort. They immediately sent their airport shuttle van to pick us up. The scuba school had expected us on an earlier scheduled flight, unaware we would arrive on a "private charter."

We fell asleep that night in our grass roofed and bamboo walled beach house after reading dive manuals and reflecting on our four classmates. Two originated from France, one from

England, and the other, from Australia. A small class of six would be just right for learning. On the morrow would be first day lessons with the scuba gear in the swimming pool, followed by the next few days exploring the wonders of the Bismark Sea. I was already learning to fly high above the earth, why not learn to submerge below the surface of the earth's oceans? To say we felt excited on scuba school eve would be a colossal understatement.

Sandia and I arose early the next morning, took a run and swim, showered, and headed for a breakfast served near the pool. Soon after, Frank Butler showed up, pushing a cart loaded with diving gear. It looks so easy when you see film of divers cruising beneath the sea, so effortlessly swimming with tanks on their backs, flippers on their feet, and the sound of a long streams of bubbles as they breathe through their mouthpieces. To the novice, that first day in the pool is a must. Sandia and I listened carefully and hung on every word Frank uttered, especially his expression of the dangers involved in diving when a person doesn't really understand his equipment or the dramatic pressures that the human body, in particular, the lungs, is subjected to in scuba diving. Every thirty-three feet of diving depth adds another atmosphere of pressure to the lungs, in addition to the atmospheric pressure above the water's surface.

We spent the first day learning the function and use of our B.C.D.s (buoyancy control devices), the air tanks and associated valving, masks, snorkels, and flippers. Frank told us about using gloves when touching coral, wearing lycra suits to ward off stinging undersea creatures, like jelly fish, and donning wet suits for extremely cold waters. During lunch and breaks from the pool, the six of us studied and talked together for a written test at the end of the first day, which we all passed with varying grades. Passing the test

served as a prerequisite for the next lessons, to be conducted in the adjacent ocean.

The next morning found us sitting on the sandy bottom of the Bismark Sea, on the edge of a coral reef about 30 feet below the surface. The water proved a bright turquoise color, so warm and clear. Occasionally we stirred up a bit of sand with our antics and maneuvers. The morning lessons included purposely losing our equipment, retrieving it, then recovering our buoyancy and breathing. In the unlikely, but possible, event of using up all the air in our tanks, while deeply submerged, we learned and practiced "buddy breathing," or taking turns calmly breathing from your diving partner's air supply. Loss of air added another reason why it's always safer to dive with at least one other person, and never alone. Too many things can happen when you're out there alone, no matter how experienced you are.

Well, we all passed our practical tests with the equipment and safety procedures at thirty feet that morning, so after lunch we were rewarded with a dive on an awesome coral reef. No tests or anything, just looked at the incredible undersea life that centers itself on the coral reefs of the South Pacific. As we swam away from our dive boat, toward the coral reef, the sky darkened and the wind blew in blustery gusts, but as you slipped below the gusty, choppy surface, it became an entrance to a different, more peaceful world. Time immediately seemed to slow down. All the visible sea life seemed to move calmly and slowly. Deep breaths were taken in and released slowly and deliberately. The only sound heard was one's own breathing. We were truly being spoiled, learning to become Open Water Divers in, perhaps, the finest diving area of the world. The undersea life proved abundant, the colors magnificent. Clown fish with their sea anemone, parrot fish, reef sharks, star fish, eels, sea cucumbers, and the colorful coral all existed there on the submerged reef for the novice diver to behold. Everyone seemed to excitedly signal at the same time regarding something new for each of us to come and have a look at. There seemed so much to focus on. It was truly a different world.

A glance down at my air gauge reading told me it was time to slowly head to the surface to return to the atmosphere of my human, non-fish existence. Others had already headed up. Our newly discovered undersea world seemed a difficult place to leave behind, but we headed up. Sandia and I swam side by side until we finally broke the ocean's surface to begin the short easy swim towards the dive boat ladder.

Once all were on board and accounted for, with our gear stowed away properly, Frank headed the boat for the shore and the Walindi Resort. Almost as a perfect culmination to our first unbelievable day in the sea, a school of dolphins appeared to lead our boat back to shore. They dipped and bobbed in apparent play all the way along our return route out in front of our prow and as we neared our pier, slipped below the surface and disappeared. We saw only a glint of their shimmering, sleek bodies as they headed back out to sea. The word "paradise" was used several times amongst our dive mates as we reflected on where we were lucky enough to be.

We dove multiple times in the next few days, each time on a different reef location. The sea, north of Walindi, certainly constituted a diving "mecca." Usually the most colorful and abundant observations of undersea life appeared in the ten to twenty meter (30 to 60 feet) depths. My few forays below that demonstrated how "gray" and less colorful the undersea life became, notwithstanding the fact that a diver used up his air supply much quicker at greater depths. Sandia and I decided, in all our "buddy" dives, that we liked the ten-meter depth above all others.

Our last night at Walindi, Frank Butler made a big ceremony out of presenting the class with our Open Water Diver Certificates and Logbooks. We hoisted a few cold beers to the tropical stars, while telling each other what exotic places we'd later dive. It's always fun to dream, as we did that night with our new dive cards clutched in our hands. Sandia and I would go on to dive several other locations in New Guinea, including Rabaul Harbor, and Madang, where we found a WWII B-25 Yank bomber in

Dolphins leading the way back to the Walindi Resort

Submerged dolphins heading back out to the Bismarck Sea

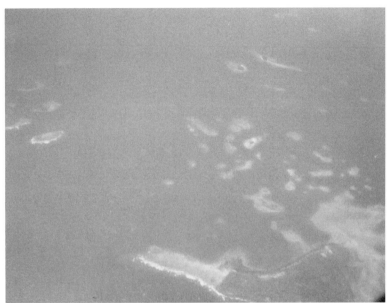

*The coral reefs near Walindi Resort
as seen from Romeo Papa Tango*

sixty-five feet of water, Tufi, off Cape Nelson, and the waters around Salamaua. Outside of P.N.G., we would dive the Great Barrier Reef, off Queensland, Australia, Bali, Indonesia, and the Red Sea, off the coast of Hurgada, Egypt. With the exception of the giant clams on the Great Barrier Reef, we thought the best diving lay definitely under the waters of Papua New Guinea.

I found it tough to get my mind back into the work upon our return from Walindi. My desk, piled high with requests for building estimates and ordering requirements for current projects, along with the flow diagrams on my status board, seemed a poor substitute for holding my lady's hand ten-meters under the ocean's surface as we lazily took in the incredible visions of the undersea life on one of New Guinea's submerged coral reefs. The week in Walindi made up my longest break in the first full year of my contract in P.N.G. No one else did my work while I learned diving. Norbert, Bobby, and Terape did their best while I was gone and kept building supplies heading west to Porgera

and the Top Camp dongas, and east to the Chimbu Mountains to keep the South Chimbu Rural Development Contract moving along. With several smaller projects also going in between, in our own Wahgi Valley, the three new, big delivery trucks belonging to Hailans Homes were stretched to their limit. We had to occasionally ask the lumberyard for the use of one of their big trucks to use, in addition to our own. Having operated for many months without a foul up or accident involving the trucks and building loads, our luck finally ran out in rapid succession.

First, one of Total Hardware's loaner trucks and driver, with a complete house package aboard for Gomgale in the Chimbu Mountains, ran off the gravel road and plunged at least 100 meters (300 feet) down the steep banks of *Wara Chimbu* (Chimbu River). The driver jumped free as he went over the edge and escaped with only minor injuries. The kit house package was trashed and whatever panels survived intact, were quickly confiscated by nearby villagers. I began all the paperwork required by our insurance company for reimbursement and, at the same time, started to build another replacement house package for Gomgale. It put us back a bit on our contract performance schedule, but Bob Eyles, the Chimbu Public Works Manager proved more than understanding as he accepted a letter of explanation to extend the contract deadline, appropriately. In the meantime, George Hook, our General Manager, contracted the winch truck retrieval via that crazy expat aforementioned, and actually got his truck back, reasonably intact.

The second truck incident happened to my

very careful driver, Maike. He headed back from a delivery in the Chimbu Mountains, empty, and slowed down as he passed a stopped P.M.V. (bus) on the side of the road. About the same instant, a five year old national girl broke away from her mother's handhold near the bus and, intent on reaching her friends on the other side of the narrow road, literally ran under the front wheels of Maike's truck as he passed the stationary bus. The little girl died instantly. Several observers assured Maike, who feared for his life and his job that they would tell how the little girl ran in front of his truck. None of the witnesses could help, however, with the long established New Guinea cultural philosophy that there is no such thing as an "accident." Someone always had to pay. In *Tok Pisin*, it is called "*bekim*," or payback, and in some instances, to avenge, or take revenge. Sometimes, if a man is killed in a fight, then someone from the killer's village must die, not necessarily the actual killer. Kind of like, "an eye for an eye." Maike did get pummeled by a few members of the mother's clan at the scene of the accident, but was able to get in his truck and drive away. The mother's tribe saw the writing on the truck and found out who Maike drove for.

A few days later, there arose a commotion at the Hailans Home's security gate. It proved to be a large mob from the grieving mother's clan. They wanted into my office. There appeared no stopping them. They filled the office to overflowing, as I sucked in my breath and tried to appear calm as they encircled my desk. Their "big man" spokesperson stepped to the front and faced me with a fierce look. He was dressed in the traditional regalia of *laplap* in front of his groin, *arse* grass in the rear, numerous shell necklaces and the *moku* insignia of a "big man" hung from his neck, covering his upper chest, and topped with a bird of paradise feathered headdress. I felt a bit overwhelmed, to say the least.

The "big man" started his oratory, some of it in their *Tok Ples,* and parts in *Tok Pisin*, which I could halfway understand as he spoke in "rapid fire." The phrase "*bikpela kampani*" (big company) was laced throughout his delivery many times. As I listened to his "spiel," I knew he had to get it all out without interruption in order to maintain his respect as a "big man" in front of his people. It became increasingly clear to me he talked about "*mani*" (money) in compensation for the child's life, and lots of it. Then he stopped his speech, reached back and pulled the grieving mother to the front to face me. She held up a small jar for me to look at. My stomach did a double flip as I saw it contained an adult finger, bloody at the cut-off end. As I blinked and looked away from the bottle, she held out her left hand for me to see the bloody stump where her little finger had been hacked off as a symbol of grievance for her lost daughter. I looked quickly back to her eyes, as my stomach approached nausea. This spectacle caught me totally unaware. The "big man" started in again with his "*bikpela kampani*" spiel.

My head raced with thoughts. I had to appease them, even though the accident was unavoidable. I knew our insurance covered something of a cash settlement, but I didn't know how much. I didn't want them going after Maike, who we'd sent back to his village to hide out for a while. So in my best *Tok Pisin*, I told them I needed a few days to talk to my big boss man. They should send a representative back to see me in three days. They didn't seem happy with this turn of events. Maybe they thought that at a big company we all had drawers full of money. I don't know, but I offered the grieving mother my sincere condolences, and taking her good hand in mine, looked her in the eyes and repeated, "*tripela de, tasol, plis*," (please, only three days).

Three days later, the whole entourage appeared back at my gate, with the mother holding up her bottled little finger for my consternation. I explained the insurance company's standard settlement of K3,000.00 cash. They could go up to Total Hardware to pick up the cash immediately. They didn't give me a facial clue with regard to their feelings, just moved as a large group out from my gate and headed for Total Hardware to get the cash. I never saw them again and no one came after Maike. The only further issue we had on that incident occurred when the dead child's father, who was divorced from the mother for several years, showed up wanting additional compensation moneys for himself. I sent him packing and told him to settle his "claim" with his ex-wife. Always, always, in New Guinea, if you ran over a dog or a pig in the road, you had to pay, often well beyond the "value" of the animal. There existed no such thing as an accident. A true expression of sorrow never seemed to be asked for or received. The only thing I ever hit, on the road from the mountains to Lae one day, appeared in the form of a daring rooster who'd crossed the road successfully up in front of me, but got spooked and turned back, just as I drove by. All I saw in the rear view mirror was a cloud of rooster feathers as I stepped down on the gas pedal and kept on going. They probably had rooster "road kill" stew in the village that night. I'm not being callous, but with free roaming animals, it happened sometimes.

After all the excitement and sad distractions finally calmed down, I turned my focus back into current and future workloads. In anticipation of the Special Mining Lease (SML) being issued in Porgera and a subsequent contract for some number of relocation houses, I instructed

Some of our first relocation building sites in the mud

my shop foreman, Philip, to build another large level bench for prefabricating the kit house panel frames. Then sure enough, the SML was issued, about the time we finished the additional prefab bench. I soon got called to Porgera to be briefed on the urgency and procedures for the whole relocation project. Even though Hailans Homes helped during the design and negotiating phase with the Porgerans, I was told sixty initial relocation houses would be evenly divided between three companies, Hailans Homes, Coya Construction, and Moku Builders. The division didn't bother me a bit as they accepted my costing submittal for twenty houses without question and I threw in a reasonable contingency to cover the time I'd spent on the design phase of the effort. The mining construction managers didn't tell me what the other two companies negotiated for their housing bids, only that we were all on the same tight schedules to finish our allotted houses. When I reflected on it, with all the work we had going elsewhere, building twenty more houses would push Hailans Homes to its fullest.

When I flew back to Hagen and showed George Hook and Ray the contract for twenty more houses in Porgera, with the promise of more to come, if we performed on this first batch, they both couldn't stop grinning. I felt happy along with them, as it meant big business for all of us, but I knew Hailans Homes had the ultimate responsibility to get it all done. There were several Australian inspectors arriving to oversee the mine construction phase for the parent company, Placer Dome Mining. Those inspectors would be checking our every move. I told my company mates determinedly that day in Ray's office, "Ray, you find the money for the building materials someplace and George, you find a place to get the lumber and hardware we need. Hailans Homes will get the job done, no matter what!"

A month later, October 17, 1988, our first prefabricated relocation house rolled out of the Hailans Homes yard, headed west for Porgera, at least 200 kilometers of twisting dirt roads away. The delivery truck faced the mountains and narrow valleys of the Engan Province on its way through the towns of Wapenamanda, Wabag, Laigam, and finally, Porgera. Four of my foreman, including Norbert and Mondul, each to build five houses, awaited the first delivery. Their work was cut out for them, as our twenty assigned building sites proved to be all located in the mud. The foremen were setting the required steel foundation posts for each house, in their respective concrete pads. Before we could lay the house bearing timbers across the steel posts and fasten them in place on the welded flange brackets, the new mining company inspectors showed up with their building transits and shot the tops of the post brackets for level. They made my guys dig out and reset posts that were out of level by less than one-quarter inch. That seemed ridiculously "picky" under the conditions of the building sites. I tried reasoning with their new inspector, Colin Clemens, but he wouldn't yield.

I told him the bloody sites would move more than a quarter inch, as soon as the next earthquake shook the Porgeran ground. Colin said he applied equal standards to all three builders, so I couldn't argue anymore. I knew down the road he'd have to back off the tight standards, or he wouldn't get anything completed. Then he'd end up on the carpet trying to explain holdups to his superiors. This wasn't Australia. This was in the mud, at 9,000 feet, in the Engan Mountains of Papua New Guinea.

In spite of our building sites being worse than the other two competing companies, we forged ahead of their construction schedules. They hadn't previously built in Porgera as we had. Kivon, along with Benny, my plumber, finished up the last details of the Top Camp bunkhouses and we handed those over to the mining company. They seemed well satisfied with our completed product and promptly paid the final progress payment, which made Ray, our money juggler, extremely happy. After that, when I overnighted in Porgera, which was often enough, the camp manager always arranged my quarters up in our own bunkhouses. I felt right at home up there. With the "dongas" done, our full attention in Porgera then focused on getting the relocation houses done on schedule.

One day, while working in the Porgeran mud in my gumboots to help Norbert catch up, having just gone through another go around with the inspectors, Fritz Robinson showed up to see how we progressed. He was arriving back at his Porgera office after a long and well-deserved holiday in Australia. Fritz looked around our building sites, and after noting our activity, turned to me to say, "It is amazing how much your men have accomplished under these conditions in such a short time."

"Fritz, you are welcome on our job site anytime! Those are the greatest words I've heard in a long time."

Truly, after hearing lots of negative comments on our progress from the inspectors and other administrators, including statements that we would never finish on schedule, Fritz seemed like a fresh, energizing breeze blowing through the Porgeran landscape. I felt lifted by Fritz's observations, making it a point to walk around to each of my crews to share the feeling with them. The foremen obviously took heart from Fritz's words and assured me they would finish on time, as long as I made sure they got the building materials as scheduled. The determination showed in their eyes.

A section of the winding road toward Porgera

One night, soon after, at the Top Camp bar, I ran into the expat manager from Coya Construction who corralled me into talking about the relocation project. Specifically, he pried to find out our bid price for the houses which I didn't feel like telling him, even if he "shouted" (bought) my beer. He finally gave up on that effort, but was drunk enough to explain his costing philosophy – "Go in low, then hit them with lots of extras!" I grimaced as he talked on about what extras would be operative in the Porgeran situation. I finally apologized for being contrary, as he shouted my beer, but told him we were going in straight up, with a bid price per house, which constituted the final and fair price, to be paid on completion – no extras, just as contracted – unless there appeared some extraordinary circumstances later on. He smiled his own shrewd smile and said, "We'll see!" To me the work was tough enough to coordinate as things were, without throwing another wrinkle into the works. There seemed plenty of work to be contracted fair and square. The project wasn't a game. Our bottom line seemed fair to get prompt payment for work accomplished and goods delivered. Extras to me appeared an uncertainty that well could have ended up in litigation. I heard later on, that of a bill submitted for extras from that expat's company for over K300,000, only K30,000 was ever collected. They, in fact, finally packed it in and left the country, unable to compete in Porgera any longer. In addition, they were made to wait a lengthy time for what "extras" they did collect.

The government man in Porgera was an ex-*kiap* named Frank Faulkner. He looked out for the locals' affairs and maintained an office and a home next to the little gravel airstrip. Frank was single and had been in Papua New Guinea for a number of years, working for the new government, after Independence negated his role as an Australian Patrol Officer. Frank talked to me about other Porgeran projects that sat on the burners for government funding outside of the mine site itself. There was a new jail to be built, along with warehouses, and additional administrative staff houses. Frank made it obvious to me that Porgera would be a wealth of work, in and of itself.

Frank became a friendly face in Porgera, when sometimes I ran into less than friendly administrators in the course of a day. One Canadian manager, in jest, but pointedly nonetheless, told me, "You Yanks are like septic tanks. Everyone should have one buried in their yard!"

I laughed him off, while realizing he really didn't care for us Yanks. He would always find a way to give me grief when I needed his approvals. To my knowledge, I was the only Yank then working in those New Guinea Mountains, let alone, subcontracting to the Placer Dome Mining Company at Porgera, so I served as the only vessel at which he could aim his venom. I took his ribbing, but didn't go out of my way to get near him. Then one day he mouthed off to one of his superiors and he found himself placed on the next chopper out of Porgera. Adios, bad mouth. May your future perceptions of life include the warmth of the sunshine and the fragrance of the flowers.

The Hailans Homes factory crew. David is on the left. Terape is on top. My right hand is on Mondul's shoulder.

Village boys from Enga Province near Porgera

257

There had to be cooperation between the mining administrators and us contractors, if the mining construction phase was to stay on any type of schedule. Something unexpected happened continually to try to slow things down. Once a section of the main mountain road into the mine site went down the mountainside in a rumbling landslide. It took several weeks to engineer its repair. In the meantime, to keep things moving along, the mine furnished us with helicopters to get building materials across the slide area. Our trucks would pull up on the Hagen side of the road slide, load the materials off the truck into chopper cargo nets, which in turn would ferry the load to the other side and one of our empty trucks, caught on the Porgera side. With this kind of mining company support, other contractors, and Hailans Homes kept on our construction schedules. The project was complex, in a difficult environmental setting, to coordinate, requiring lots of cooperation by everyone.

It was about that time, I had the occasional feeling, *"I've created a monster!"* I knew I needed help, expat type, to share the burden. Our workload could justify the salary. George Hook told me he had a job position opening approved for a work permit. Which way to go? A couple of days later, David Wissink, my U. S. Peace Corps liaison in Gumine village walked into my office. He visited Hagen to pick up his truck after repair and did I want to go to lunch? I dropped my pa-perwork and said, "You bet, *wontok*! Let's go."

At the time David neared the finish of his two-year tour and seemed unsure of what he would do upon his return to the States. An idea struck me, *"Did he want to stay on in P.N.G. and work for Hailans Homes?"* David knew the people, the language, and was an Iowa farm boy with a fair knowledge of construction. David certainly knew the unexpected ways of Papua New Guinea and that would be a valuable asset. He seemed intrigued with the offer and said he'd talk it over with his wife Melynda and get back to me quickly. For my part, it felt great to think about a coworker to share my load, especially a *wontok*. I'd be able to talk sports and stateside news with David on work breaks. I really felt excited when David got back to me with an acceptance and, a month later, came on board. The men liked him right away. Maybe it was his quiet, but firm, way. Maybe it was his giant size. Maybe it was his total command of their language. Anyway, he snapped right into the system and took some responsibility from my tired shoulders. George found David and Melynda temporary housing and the following month, December, they would move into our place while we took our first six-plus-week holiday and headed for the States. It seemed as if everything was working out. Bring on the workload, we've got another cylinder in our work engine, and things are running smoothly. Shift her up to second gear!

chapter thirty-seven

Explorations in the Islands and Coastal Lowlands

Although my lady and I spent most of our time working and living in the Highlands of Papua New Guinea, we did make time to visit and explore the lowland coastal and some of the island areas. Many of these sojourns became possible due to long weekends, together with the availability of the company airplane, Romeo Papa Tango. That little Cessna 182 always made things easier as far as scheduling departure times to our own individual timing, as well as, a whole lot more exciting.

One such adventure took us into Sepik River country, north of the high Central Range of mountains. Air travel into the Sepik region is a necessity as very few roads exist, with most transport occurring either by water or by air. The Sepik River to P.N.G. is much like the Amazon is to South America. Not only is it wide, but it is deep and navigable for most of its existence. Where it enters the Bismark Sea on the northern coast, the river is said to be six hundred feet deep (200 meters), without a delta. Imagine the tremendous volume of fresh water pouring into the ocean. The Sepik originates in the central mountains, on the northern side of the range,

a willingness to explore, has to be

the prelude, to making discovery

flows briefly along the border with Irian Jaya, then returns eastward to flow over seven hundred, twisting, turning miles (1100 kilometers) before joining the sea. The river only drops about 280 vertical feet (85 meters) from beginning to end—less than six inches per mile—hence the ever changing loops and switch backs. Villagers have fashioned canals across some river loops to shorten travel time required when paddling their dugout canoes. One hundred thirty miles (200 kilometers) inland from the sea, near Pagwi, the Sepik River is reported to still be over one hundred fifty feet deep (50 meters). Bounded on the northern coast by the Bewani, Torricelli, and Prince Alexander Mountains, which reach heights of over 3,000 feet (1,000 meters) and on the south by the Central Range, with altitudes approaching 12,000 feet (4,000 meters), the Sepik River forms a huge flood-plained valley of swamps or grasslands, depending on whether it's the wet or dry season, respectively. A person has to travel large distances, sometimes over thirty miles, from the Sepik River to find stones due to thousands of years of silt deposits. Stones have been carried into river settlements from great distances and hence take on a somewhat valued, or sacred, status. Many end up in the Haus Tambarans, or village spirit houses.

Life along the Sepik is at best described as subsistence living. There exists no industry to speak of, with the exception of the arts, mainly woodcarving. Food that is grown seldom yields a surplus, barely supplying the locals. Crocodiles, heavily hunted in past years, are rarer in numbers these days, but still the occasional *puk puk* can be seen near the riverbanks amongst the *pit pit* (wild sugar cane). There occurs an annual rainfall of 6.5 to 8 feet (2 to 2.5 meters), so the Sepik valley is really wet, with lots of *nat nats* (mosquitos).

Romeo Papa Tango carried Jim, Mary Ann, Sandia, and myself into the Karawari Lodge's airstrip one long weekend. South of the Sepik River, the lodge is in the foothills of the Central Mountain Range, and therefore, a little cooler, less humid, and less mosquito infested. The small lodge settlement is located on the Karawari River, whose waters feed west into the Korosameri River and then on down into the Sepik.

With reservations at the Karawari Lodge, Jim knew to "buzz" the Lodge in Romeo Papa Tango on the way into the small grass airstrip. That signal routine dispatched a riverboat to pick us up at the airstrip's river landing, a bit downstream from the Lodge. Communications in the region required H.F. radios, as telephones did not exist.

Approaching the Karawari Lodge on our river shuttle boat, you could see the traditionally built structures located up on a knoll, maybe two hundred feet above the river. Our local riverboat captain told us the extra height would keep us a bit cooler.

As we stepped from the flat-bottomed river craft onto the landing pier with our luggage, a pickup truck arrived to carry us up to the lodge—a distance of about 100 meters above us

Coming into the Lodge's grass airstrip over the Karawari River

Mary Ann, Jim, myself, and Sandia getting ready to do dinner in the Karawari Lodge lounge

A siesta for Sandia without nat nats for company

(the length of a football field). That was the only road around. Actually it was more like a long driveway. What a luxury to have a truck in that setting. The truck must have been barged in, and likewise, the ongoing fuel requirements to keep it running. Maybe people arrived with lots of luggage, I don't know.

When Sandia and I opened the door to our large room, built of bush materials, the first thing that caught our eyes was the mosquito netting over the big double bed. We looked at each other and promptly broke out our *nat nat* repellent, rubbing it onto exposed skin areas. Satisfied with our insect protection, we walked across the room, beyond the bed, to find the verandah, where the view can best be described as stunning. The peaceful movement of the greenish brown river below flowed through the stillness of the lush humid green expanse of the jungle beyond. We stood quietly studying the scene in front of us for a while, noting the slow, but steady, progress of a passing dugout canoe. The canoe was paddled smoothly by two locals, standing front and rear in their traditional watercraft. An occasional white, river bird glided lazily downstream past the canoe. The whole mental scene exuded tranquillity and restfulness. Perhaps we were the only disturbing element in the whole picture—two expatriates gazing out on the Sepik River valley uttering quiet sounds of amazement at being able to witness and touch that remote paradise.

Our explorations from the Karawari Lodge took us to the Yimas Lakes via a flat-bottomed, petrol powered, riverboat. It's a good thing we hired a knowledgeable guide, otherwise we'd still be on those Lakes somewhere, looking for a way out. After seemingly endless twisting and turning

through vegetation clogged channels, our boat arrived on an expanse of mirror lakes, so placid and smooth. Only the sound of our propulsion, along with the boat's rippled wake, disturbed the surroundings. The waters teemed with bird life, white and soft pink colors stimulating the optical senses. A bird watcher would have thought he'd died and gone to "birder's" heaven. Mountains rose gently to the south of us. The clouds seemed whiter and the sky bluer than usual. Maybe it stemmed from the calmness of it all. Maybe

Bird life along the Karawari Riverbanks

Human life along the Karawari River

it arose from my own slowed mental state. What a contrasting surround when compared to Chicago's Loop or New York City's Grand Central Station, half a world away.

Our river transportation passed small settlements built on the lakeshores. The bush houses were constructed on stilt foundations, probably to compensate for changes in lake levels from the wet to the dry season. I never gleaned the type of fish that were caught in the Yimas Lakes area, but saw evidence of fish netting hanging in several of the settlements we passed through. Our riverboat guide always courteously slowed when we encountered a local canoe. I couldn't relate to the standing-upright paddle style. Sandia and I laughed as we talked about how short a time it would take the two of us to turn over one of those narrow dugout canoes and end up as *puk puk* bait. The locals probably stood and paddled over water before they could walk on *terra firma*.

At the controls, on the plane ride back to Mt. Hagen, my mind became reflective and nostalgic, almost as if emerging from a dream—the river, the lakes, the jungle, the birds, the people, the canoes, but mostly, the undisturbed peace of it all. On the morrow, my telephone would ring a bunch, schedules would be massaged, unexpected problems would have to be solved, but it would be a tad easier, since my heart had slowed a bit. I felt glad to have touched a remote part of the world, known to so very few, and carried away a few small Sepik carvings to remind me of the experience of it all.

Another long weekend trip via Romeo Papa

A local dugout canoe on the placid Yimas Lakes

Tango took Jim, Mary Ann, Sandia, and myself to the extreme southwestern part of Papua New Guinea, to the Bensbach River region, next to the Indonesian border. I'm sure we would have lost our way above the clouds of that vast floodplain were it not for Jim and his previous experience flying into the Bensbach region. Find the settlement of Morehead, north of the Torres

Yours truly at the controls looking for the Bensbach

Strait, on the western side of the Coral Sea, he told me from his temporary copilot's position, then head due west for the Bensbach River and the Bensbach Wildlife Lodge. In the clouds, if you miss the Lodge's short grass airstrip, you could easily end up in another country— Indonesia. A dashed line on the ground does not mark the border between countries, as it does on maps. The other difficulty flying in New Guinea stemmed from the lack of good aeronautical maps. There were no World Aeronautical Charts available for that area of the world. These days, I'm sure, global positioning satellite systems probably serve P.N.G. pilots well.

Anyway, we found the Lodge's little airstrip, in spite of the clouds, and after only one go-around with yours truly at the controls, we were on the ground unloading our luggage. A Lodge pickup truck showed up to carry us to our bush constructed quarters. Of the eleven twin rooms available, we were the only ones scheduled for the weekend, with the exception of a Lodge shareholder, Ian Harris and his guest, John Coleman. We all sacked out in our rooms for a welcome afternoon siesta after a long 450 plus kilometer flight from Mt. Hagen.

Sandia and I awoke to watch wallabies hopping around outside our window. Two or three rusa deer strolled around the Lodge grounds, probably looking for a meal of discarded food from the kitchen. After dinner, we arranged for a boat and several local guides for the morning after. Fishing for barramundi was the plan of action for the following day. Jim kept explaining later, in the lounge beside the dining room, how big the barramundi species became—upwards from 20 to 30 pounds. He also told us the story that when the male barramundi became very large, it changed to a female, giving birth to little barramundi. Skeptical of that story, I'm sure the raising of my eyebrows showed my non-accep-

Landings at remote airstrips were always a novelty for the local people

Rusa deer at home in the Bensbach River region

tance of his facts, which I later learned was the absolute truth. Similarly, the crocodile becomes a male or female depending on the incabation temperature of his, or her, egg. Really! Funny things go on down under that equator.

The four of us aspiring fishermen set off next morning before dawn, with our local male guides and found ourselves motoring down the Bensbach River as the sun rose. Wallabies hopped along the riverbanks. Deer could be seen everywhere, even swimming across huge flooded sections of the river plain. The bird life that greeted our vista proved truly incredible. Great flocks of white and pink birds sometimes lifted into flight startled by our noisy approach on that quiet morning. There appeared flamingos, cranes, and long red legged jabirus—not in flocks of tens, but many hundreds, perhaps thousands.

As if not to be outdone by the other bird life and animal life, the barramundi gave us an excellent day of fishing. Jim must have been using magic bait, as he easily doubled our three catches, all put together. We all caught several large fish, with the biggest returned to the river, as they are female and therefore must live to bear more young.

Over fresh barramundi fish steaks that night, cooked in the Lodge kitchen, Jim told us the deer had been introduced by the Dutch during the early 1900's in the western half of the New Guinea island. Without natural predators, the deer population had flourished. They spread into the eastern floodplains of P.N.G. by the thousands. I wondered later if the crocodiles enjoyed an occasional deer steak, as countless numbers of those deer swam the flooded portions of the Bensbach region.

Upon departure from the Bensbach Wildlife Lodge, Romeo Papa Tango carried an iced down cargo of barramundi fillets for our later con-

Fisherwoman Mary Ann
with a barramundi catch

sumption in the Highlands. Again, the return flight to Mt. Hagen was filled with reflections of joy that there are still remote areas, almost untouched by humans. Hurrah for little Cessnas and their ability to gently touch the remoteness of small grass landing strips.

Way back on Sandia's and my second honeymoon at Ambua Lodge, upon her arrival in Papua New Guinea, we met a *wontok* from Cleveland, who was on a short sojourn with his mom. That meeting occurred shortly after a Denver Bronco victory over the Cleveland Browns in the American Football Conference Championship game in January 1988. We met Gordon and his mom in the Ambua dining area and got to talking, as travelers so often do. When he mentioned he called Cleveland home, I said something like, "Well you probably don't want to associate with us. We're from Denver."

Gordon immediately spoke up, relating that

he was on an around-the-world boat trip and his mother had just flown in to spend a few days with him along the trip. He said, "I don't know what happened in the game. We tried to get news on our boat's radio, but were unsuccessful. Please tell me what happened! The rest of our crew will want to know."

I described as best I could remember, only having seen it in fuzzy black and white at a Port Moresby Hotel, and further, it happened almost simultaneously with Sandia's arrival, so our embraces of love took priority over the embraces by a receiver or running back of the football. I did, however, tell him for sure that the Broncos won the game, along with the score.

Adversarial in football competition initially, we became friends right away. Gordon and his other Cleveland buddies had graduated college together and made plans to sail around the world before becoming committed to family, jobs, and the "normal" social goals, whatever those may be. They bought the sailboat, the Teal, in Florida, sailing the Caribbean through the Panama Canal and on to the Galapagos off the coast of Ecuador. From there, after sailing a twenty-three day Pacific Ocean stretch with the help of an auto-sailor, they reached Tahiti, Samoa, Tonga, Suva, down to the North Island of New Zealand, on to Sydney, up to Brisbane, then the Solomon Islands, and New Guinea. Their boat, a two-masted schooner, was at the time, moored in Madang, on the north coast of P.N.G., at the Jais Aben Resort. Gordon would head back to the Teal and his mom would fly home to Cleveland after their short stay at Ambua.

A few weekends later, Sandia and I flew to Madang, joining Gordon and other crew members for an island sail-around. Besides Gordon, the two other sailors who'd sailed from Fort Lauderdale to New Guinea were the skipper, Terry, and Brian Wood. Then there was George

The Teal

White, who had just recently flown in to join the crew. The only female crew member, Jane, joined up with the Teal at the Sydney Yacht Club, shortly after completing another round-the-world sailing trip. Her experience would help the Teal navigate through the Suez Canal and the Red Sea. George's arrival, with subtle weapons, would give the crew the strength of four stout male sailors to ward off any sea pirates rumored to be lurking in Indonesian waters.

My lady and I sailed for two days, sleeping one night in the Teal's bunk space. Much of the time, we actually spent exploring a few islands off the coast of Madang. One island was named Bagabag, and others that proved small, but well populated. While moored off one island that first evening, an outrigger boatload of maybe half-dozen island kids came out to serenade us in decent English. Probably the songs originated in their mission school. I remember one song they repeated many times, "I can spell coconut, C-O-C-O-N-U-T."

We sang back to them, in questionable harmony, in alternating fashion with ballads and folk tunes that we could remember the words to. Finally, in the darkness, their outrigger disappeared, and they went home. We certainly felt safe and welcome at our mooring. The amazing part of the encounter lay in the shyness of the young kids. In the evening dusk, they were not timid to sing to us from their outrigger canoe pulled alongside the Teal, but the next day when we went ashore, the island kids exhibited ultra shyness, hardly able to talk to us at all. The contrast seemed remarkable. I guess the darkness was their shield.

The spirit of the Teal crew proved contagious. At one point, Sandia and I (mostly me) talked to them about maybe meeting their boat east of Africa, when our New Guinea contracts terminated. We could sail the rest of the way to the States on the Teal. Dreaming is always fun—can't imagine life without it! I'd already been talking to Sandia about investing in our own boat, sailing home, then selling it upon arrival back in the U.S. Sandia, always the practical thinker, asked me if I really wanted to be confined to the small space of a sailboat for long periods of time? The answer, after much thought and reflection, became a "no." I probably could

have done it, with my stubborn nature, but for the two of us, even with a few other crew members, it could only be a dream, not a reality.

The Teal made it around the world in eighteen months. We met some of the crew later on in the U.S. They expressed pleasure regarding their adventure, stating the timing in their respective lives had been perfect for the sea-going venture. Several thought, "I'll never have the chance again!" That is such a true thought for so many of us—when that door of opportunity opens, give it some deep thought, before passing it quickly by to continue doing "business as usual!" You may never get the chance again.

Another long weekend, with air travel again provided by Romeo Papa Tango, Jim as pilot-in-command, me as co-pilot, Sandia and Mary Ann as passengers, saw us fly out to the eastern end of the Island of New Britain and the city of Rabaul. Simpson Harbor, on whose shores Rabaul has been built, is actually the gigantic caldera (crater or mouth) of a huge

Island children. Note the black volcanic soil of the island.

volcano which lets the sea in from the low east rim of the circular harbor. The single Rakunai airstrip was built across the width of a small peninsula protruding out into the harbor, with over water approaches to either runway end. Jim let me do the landing and while I maneuvered RPT into the landing pattern, Sandia and Mary Ann shouted to look down at the large sea turtle swimming in the harbor below. I barely remember giving it a glimpse, only noting its gigantic size, as that runway loomed closer and I was focusing on altitude, not wanting to overshoot on my approach with RPT. That was to be my only landing on an airstrip fronted and backed to seawater. The landing turned out to go smoothly and uneventfully, only my eyeball perspective of the airstrip, while incoming, made it look small—closer up it gained plenty of length and width.

The next morning, Mary Ann, Sandia, and I dove the so-called "submarine base" of Simpson Harbor with rented scuba gear and a certified dive instructor as our guide. It turned out to be a truly amazing dive site. We chose the sub base over the popular deep diving to see Japanese warship wreckage on the bottom of the harbor, approximately three hundred feet down. I didn't know why our dive was called the submarine base, as it seemed an ordinary lava sand beach. No boats were required. You donned your scuba gear on the beach, waddled into the sea water (its not that easy to walk in swim fins!) for maybe six or seven meters, where it suddenly dropped vertically for hundreds of feet—undersea cliffs would be the most apt description.

We worked our way slowly down that seemingly bottomless cliffside, studying the many forms of undersea life. I kept expecting to find submarine tunnels as I'd heard stories of Japanese vessels being pulled into fortress type tunnels during repeated Allied bombings of Rabaul.

Stories placed the myriad of tunnel lengths to total about 360 miles (about 600 kilometers)—some still filled with barges and other war machinery. That was a lot of digging. We never captured Rabaul in WWII; it came to us in the final surrender agreement. None the less, I queried our dive master after we got back to the beach about the name "submarine base." She told us the story she'd heard had the Japanese submarines pulling up to the vertical cliff wall, surfacing, and the sailors would just wade ashore from there. It had been the surface barges and equipment that were run up the tracks out of the water and into the fortified tunnels upon the air raid warning to signal an eminent Allied attack. Only in a few sneak attacks did the Allies send any Japanese shipping to the harbor floor.

The people of Rabaul, and for that matter, most of the Gazelle Peninsula on which Rabaul was built, were Tolais in heritage. Their ancestors invaded the Peninsula from the nearby southern tip of New Ireland several hundred years before. The language of the Tolais is called Kuanua— their *tok ples*. In fact, Rabaul means "mangrove" in Kuanua. The Tolai people as a society are matriarchal, as are many island communities, where clan and property rights pass through the mother's side of the family. The Tolais lost much of their clan lands to German plantation builders after first European contact in the early 1900's. Since then, the struggle to regain their lands has been an uphill battle, which continues even today.

Upon our departure from the Rakunai airstrip by the sea, with Jim at the controls of RPT, he decided to take us on a tour of the volcanoes surrounding Rabaul. There was Kombia (the mother), Tovanumbatir (the North daughter), Turangunan (the South daughter), Tuvurvur, Vulcan, and a few others I don't remember. The "father" stood the tallest, but well down the coast from Rabaul. Jim told us Tuvurvur and Vulcan had last erupted in 1937, my birth year. We flew in close to some of the volcano mouths (calderas), while trying to imagine the force of previous eruptions that leveled Rabaul in the past. We certainly had no premonition at the time that five years later in 1994, Tuvurvur and Vulcan would once again erupt and level Rabaul. I returned to New Guinea and visited Rabaul in mid 1995 to walk amongst the heavy volcanic dust and debris that virtually leveled the city. The wide avenues, the parks were buried under five to ten feet of ash. All but a few buildings had collapsed, after groaning for differing time periods, under the heavy roof loads of volcanic ash. The story on the few remaining buildings, like the Hamamas Hotel, described the owners, or managers, staying on through the eruptions, continually removing the accumulating dust and ash from the rooftops with shovels and brooms. Most inhabitants were driven away by fear at the time when fire and ash suddenly erupted to fill the skies above their normally tranquil Rabaul. A few brave (or maybe crazy) souls stayed on to save their properties. Most of us, thankfully, are never faced with that momentous kind of decision.

Tuvurvur (above) and Vulcan (Below) showing the Rabaul landscape of devastation (July 1995)

As I walked over the thick layer of volcanic ash burying Rabaul, I remembered walking the well lit, wide avenues after dinner, in the evening dusk, laughing with Jim, Mary Ann, and my lady, Sandia. The fresh, salty, sea air, together with the fragrance of tropical plants and flowers, filled one's senses back then. Walking over the ever hardening, black ash deposits, my eyes and nostrils sensed darkness and the pungent smell of Tuvurvur's belching smoke ten months after the eruption. Locals told me that the smoke would last for years. My mind wondered if Rabaul would ever be reconstructed again? Maybe later, when grass and vegetation take root in the rich fertile volcanic soil, and Tuvurvur once again becomes silent. Maybe then the Tolai people will return again. For them, volcanoes must be a part of life. Until then, most businesses and government offices moved about 20 kilometers down the coast to the once sleepy town of Kokopo. The impact of the population burst on that small town is a story in itself. Kokopo, located on Blanche Bay, however, has no harbor. Hence,

I believe later there will be a migration back to Rabaul and Simpson Harbor, starting with the activities supporting the shipping industry, and later, other service businesses. Then Rabaul will rise from the volcanic ash to start the cycle once more.

Yes, and then there was our trip to the Trobriand Islands. Sandia and I used commercial air transport for this island exploration and holiday. The Trobriands (or "Trobs" amongst locals) are a small chain of islands, well east of Lae, located in the Solomon Sea. The largest and main island in the group is Kiriwina. It has some roads and a commercial airport near the small settlement of Losuia.

An exiled Polish anthropologist named Malinowski made the Trobriands famous. He spent his exile, during the First World War, by choice, in the Trobriand Islands. In post WWI times, he published a series of books describing the sexual practices of the islanders, which resulted in a bit of fantasy regarding the "free love" part of the island culture. The Trobriands took on the pseudonym, "The Islands of Love." Supposedly the young island females frequently lured different males into the bush for trysts of love making.

My lady and I arrived on Kiriwina on the 12th of May in '89. I know the date on this particular excursion from the video camera footage. During our four-day island exploration, we based ourselves at the only lodge on the island—the Kiriwina Lodge. We never laid eyes on another expatriate the entire time. Local islanders told us that soon many expats (probably including some curious anthropologists) would be coming as the yam harvest was just beginning along with the famous "love" festivities that marked the harvest occasion.

Our accommodations proved expensive,

adequate, but very basic. Electricity, furnished by petrol generators, was only available for a few hours in the morning and evening. Normally that wouldn't be a big deal for us except for the heat and humidity. That big ceiling fan above our bed spelled "relief" when the power came on. The Lodge, for whatever reason, had been built on the edge of a murky lagoon, so we had to arrange transport to get to distant white sandy beaches for snorkeling and swimming. Several locals told us that another lodge neared completion on one of Kiriwina's beautiful beaches, but couldn't get proper licensing to begin taking in guests. They implied the existing lodge, our lodge, was owned by a member of Parliament, who possessed considerable "clout" when it came to competition. We kind of laughed, as even in this remote island paradise, things remain the same—humans are humans.

As we explored the island further, the one outstanding feature that Kiriwina lacked in comparison to other islands we'd visited, was mountains, or even little hills. The island was basically flat, low-lying, probably coral based in origin. The village houses set up several feet on post foundations for ventilation. Villagers definitely had a pleasant look about them, taller and slenderer than the Highlanders of P.N.G.. Most people we observed, sat about in the shade of overhanging palm thatched house roofs, above walls of woven *pit pit* (young wild, sugarcane stalks). Locals that walked about moved very slowly. The Trobriands seemed laid back in a pleasant, relaxing way.

There appeared to be very little economic activity on the Island. Collections of special Trochus shells were sold abroad to be manufactured into sturdy buttons for the Western World. We saw a small crocodile farm near our lodge that locals told us brought some income for the hides of the reptiles. Beyond these small enterprises, it seemed carving constituted the biggest island industry. The wood looked to be a dark mahogany, or ebony, species of timber. Sandia and I browsed through carved figurines, three-legged stools, and bought a small hand carved table. I am still amazed at the weight of that small table and the intricacy of its eloquent carving. Made from one piece of a log, two human bodies emerge from the round base, topped with animal heads, whose upward stretching arms hold the round carved tabletop. It now quietly, but sturdily, supports our modern cordless telephone/answering machine/caller ID system. What a contrast!

In one village, we came upon the opening celebration of a new mission church. The missionary had given permission for his flock to engage in a yam festival *sing sing*. Locals gathered in kind of a village square, filling the tall yam houses to the top with the newly harvested food staple. The yam houses were actually more like tapered silos, maybe four to five-meters (thirteen to sixteen-feet) tall. Six or seven small diameter tree trunks were strapped together and then dug down into the ground. The trunks tapered open in the upward direction to maybe a meter, or a little better, at the top, with reinforcing strapping every meter or so upwards. These yam houses were filled to the top with yams. This vertical lattice type of enclosure allowed air circulation amongst the stored yams, I assume to prevent rotting in the moist humidity. Around the base of each yam house, the villagers placed what looked like stalks of wild sugar cane. When they finished, retiring to sit under shade trees, there stood one large diameter yam house surrounded by four or five smaller ones.

Sandia and I stood by a tree watching the activities of probably a hundred or so villagers, who sat facing the yam houses. A village "big man" approached me with an invitation to take my video camera out into the center, near the large yam house. When I got out there, I did feel a little conspicuous at first, by myself, the only expatriate in the vicinity, besides Sandia. Then a shrill whistle blew, signaling the beginning of festivities. A group of young females marched toward me uttering a throbbing, repetitive chant. Their only clothing was a white flowered head medallion, held in place with a red cloth bandanna, and a very small grass skirt, dyed bright red. The grass skirt hung from a hoop affair fastened low around the hips. The red color was striking against the glistening light brown of their bodies. As they marched and chanted, the grass skirts would flip from front to back methodically. The female group marched straight at me, parting to pass on either side of me. As I stood, turned to watch their backsides retreat from me, I heard a similar chanting, grunting growing louder—definitely male in origin this time. Turning back, a group of young males, each dressed only in a grayish diaper-like garment approached my camera from the same location the girls had appeared to begin things. The males also marched with that provocative front to back hip thrusting motion. Several marched with their hands placed back on their buttocks, pushing in unison with the chanting, to emphasize the hip thrusting.

The dancing and marching repeated itself several times, finally culminating in a gathering around the yam houses, as other locals rushed forth to add items to the yam structures. Green beetle-nut bundles soon hung from the top and sides of the yam poles. A fairly large live pig, with front and rear feet tied together, was thrust upside down and hung horizontally at the yam house base by means of a long stout pole. Then a bit of Western influence was added to the display of abundance—red and blue cellophane packages of "CheezPops"—an apparent imported local favorite. The colors of the cellophane packets up and down the big yam house gave the whole thing kind of a Christmas tree effect.

Then it ended. The celebration of an abundant yam crop from the fertile island soil was over. Villagers walked slowly toward the shade of their palm thatched roof shelters. A light cooling rain began to fall. The female and male dancers mingled with the other villagers. They all seemed happy with their celebratory effort and then the time had come to lounge quietly in the shade. Such was the island culture.

Later, in conversation with local lodge employees, we learned the culture of the Trobriands was, in fact, very similar to other P.N.G. islands. The island societies proved matrilineal in nature. A wife's family made sure the husband's yam house was amply filled. The village chief's sons belonged to his wife's clan in all property right issues. I believe they told me if a chief dies, he is replaced by one of his oldest sister's sons. In matters of free love, the young female is encouraged to pick a young male for occasional "romps" in the bush. For some secret reason, probably handed down herbal remedies, no children seem to be born from these unions of promiscuity. When a female reaches maybe twenty, she chooses a husband, settles down, and begins to bear children. At yam festival time, they said it was even accepted for wives to seek out another male for a bush tryst. I was clearly led to believe that the "free love" is not extended to expatriates, although one Lodge employee did ask if we wanted dancing girls to come to our room. A polite refusal ended that proposal. Our room already felt hot and steamy enough!

chapter thirty-eight

First Holiday and All Its Aftermath

I was ready, or maybe I should say, was I ever ready. Sandia felt excited to go, also. Time for a holiday. Christmas approached and, with the exception of my short hospital stay in Brisbane, I hadn't been out of Papua New Guinea for the better part of one and a half very intense years. It definitely seemed time to put our "batteries" on a slow easy charge for a little while. The company granted us just short of eight weeks, with round trip airfare to Denver, in return for my long work stint. The normal European standard was five weeks per year and I'd done over sixteen plus months. Lookout Stateside! Sandia and Niugini Bill are coming home!

David knew my system well enough by then to keep things going during my absence and, besides, most of the government and private businesses slowed down over the Christmas Holidays anyway. Many of the Aussies headed south during that same period. For them, it was kind of their summer vacation – a down under summer Christmas Holiday.

lift off, soaring rise, clear blue heaven's sky

leaving earth behind, solo, spirit high

With all our work completed for the South Chimbu Rural Development Program, and the Top Camp Bunkhouses also finished and handed over, all Hailans Homes efforts focused on prefabricating the Porgeran Relocation houses in our little Hagen factory and getting them erected on the specified locations at the Porgera Mine. David had my relocation house inventory parts list, assembly directions, and the foremen's input to help him. It would constitute his "baptism of fire," while I took a much-needed break from the everyday pressures of getting things accomplished in P.N.G.

David's wife, Melynda, would cover Sandia's Total Concept branch store while Sandia took holiday. Melynda seemed anxious to run something and show her female "moxie" after two years in the bush, where it had been truly a man's world. A world in which a woman's opinion didn't carry a lot of weight, even when her skin was "white."

Then the waiting ended, the last minute details were tended to, and it was time to head for the airport. The excitement and anticipation reached an awesome level. David and Melynda drove Sandia and me, with our luggage, to the Kagamuga *ples balus* (airport) to catch our Moresby flight. From Port Moresby it would be on to Guam, Hawaii, and the Stateside mainland.

Ray West showed up at the *ples balus* also. He was flying to Moresby on our flight and then south to Brisbane for a holiday. His wife and kids had already gone ahead of him to their home on the Gold Coast of Australia. Our friend, Rob Jacobsen, who managed the Hagen Bakery next door to Hailans Homes, showed up at Kagamuga while we waited and talked with Ray. He brought a couple of bottles of champagne to toast us a bon voyage and the start of the holiday spirit.

Then I noticed one of my new four-ton Mitsubishi trucks slowly pulling into the airport parking lot. The truck was loaded with a bunch of my workers. It turned out that they commandeered the truck and driver in order to come to the airport to see us off on our holiday. Yaupas (Terape) grinned from ear to ear as he jumped down from the truckbed and signed me for assurance that I would really come back. He put a bear hug on me, with a contented grunt when I signaled him that I would assuredly be back. I couldn't be up tight with them for bringing the truck to the airport, and skipping out on work, as their motivation came straight from the heart. I knew Yaupas must have organized the gesture. Someone poured him a small bit of champagne and he clicked my plastic cup in a toast. Several of my other men handed me small gifts, or keepsakes, to take with me. Our house security man, Yako, handed me a highlands cap and I pulled it on, down over my hair and ears, as they all smiled in appreciation. The hat was a loose knit skullcap consisting of brightly colored

patterns that the highlands men used to keep their body heat from escaping through the head. Another worker, Miok, handed me a *moku*, or big man, necklace made of small horizontal rows of bamboo, which I accepted with thanks, and hung around my neck. Thomas, one of my painters, stepped forward to shyly hand me a red *kina* shell necklace which I also hung around my neck, again much to all of their delight. Then Yaupas signed me that our plane was ready. I started shaking every hand I could reach, while still trying to figure out how Yaupas knew the plane was leaving when he couldn't hear a sound. He was right, however, as a moment later the loudspeakers crackled a garbled message about the Port Moresby flight being in the last stages of its boarding process. Our impromptu tailgate party ended as we ran for the plane waving back at everyone in farewell. As we mounted the platform stairs to the Airniugini flight, I remarked to my lady, "If that's a holiday send-off, I wonder what it will be like when we leave for good?"

The next couple of weeks flew by. After checking on the integrity of our mountain house, hugging friends and neighbors at 9,000 feet in the Colorado Rockies, Sandia and I boarded another flight, this time from Denver to Connecticut, to see my kids, their families, and old New England friends for the Christmas holidays. We gave all the girls gold nugget necklaces and Gary two sizable gold nuggets for pocket conversation pieces. I described to them Mt. Kare-Puge and the gold strike source of the gifts so that they would have some stories to tell about their nugget source. Then we boarded another flight back to Colorado to do some serious personal shopping.

My first shopping priority aimed at finding an 8mm video camera that would easily fit into my ever-present rucksack (backpack/briefcase). My thinking was that videos would describe and explain Papua New Guinea a lot easier and much more vividly than any of my verbal efforts could. I also splurged on a new, "undistressed," leather flight jacket and told Sandia that I could not officially wear it until after my first "solo." Driving around on our shopping quests became an adventure as I had to mentally adjust to the "right" side of the road after the better part of seventeen months learning "wrong (left)" side driving. No accidents occurred, but it took a real focus on my part.

We were at Sandia's mom's house when the call came from New Guinea. Sandia handed me the phone with a quizzical look.

"It's for you. It's David in New Guinea."

I took the phone from Sandia and greeted David.

"Happy Holidays, my man. What's happening in the Land of the Unexpected?"

David's voice sounded weak and far away. He started with an apology for interrupting our holiday and then went on to describe his breakdown, sedation, and the startling fact that I had to return right away as he and Melynda had already scheduled out on an upcoming flight back to the States.

I numbly placed the telephone back into its cradle, while David's sad words ran through my head. He wanted to tell me the bad news himself, and, hence, the call. A quick call to my owner Jim in P.N.G. confirmed the facts, but didn't answer the "why." Evidently the workload and the mining administrators proved a little too much for David to handle. Maybe he was too burnt out from his Peace Corps tour back in the bush of the Chimbu Mountains. I didn't know and would probably never really find out what went wrong. I told Jim I'd have a look around for another mountain builder to fill David's position while I wrapped things up for our early return. Otherwise we could find an Aussie to fill

the new "void" when I got back. I also told Jim I was scheduled for an impending medical fiber optic inspection of my bladder and would follow it up for the peace of mind. Before hanging up, I promised to return as soon as possible and would begin immediately to check out the airline seat availability for an early return to Papua New Guinea.

Sandia and I drove up to the mountains for a New Years Eve party and a farewell to friends. I called ahead to my mountain mate Dick to ask him to think about a builder/carpenter who might consider heading for New Guinea for a six-month "minimum" project. We also found and booked seats back to P.N.G. at the beginning of the second week of January. That trimmed our holiday to just five weeks, but Sandia and I determined to stay upbeat as things always seemed to happen to us with some kind of "purpose."

The New Years Eve party at Vivian's (my "second wife") townhouse was a great time reminiscing with friends and finding out all the latest town gossip. Later, after lots of visiting, Dick cornered me for a drink together. He told me he had mulled over the New Guinea opportunity for a long time. He'd decided he would like to go if it became possible. He hadn't even called anyone else in that regard. Basically, Dick had worked most of his adult life in those Colorado Rockies and wanted the chance to see the outside world to compare how he measured up in a mining camp construction world, especially in the South Pacific. He figured out how to keep his concrete business going from a distance with the fax machine. He could pass his job pricing and estimates through his wife Mary Pat to his reliable foreman, Danny Archer, and keep a scaled down business going.

I felt a bit taken aback and delighted at the same time. I knew Dick's strong points. He

274

could successfully manage a business on his own. He could deal well with people. He was more than sharp enough to negotiate with the expatriate managers at the mining camp, without getting hoodwinked. Dick was physically very fit enabling him to combat the rigors of the Engan Mountains, as well as presenting a strong physical presence during any negotiations with the Porgeran villagers. I felt it necessary, at that time, to describe the hardships and realities of life in the New Guinea Mountains, while Dick listened attentively to me. I told him basically it would not be any picnic and he'd need his wits about him most of the time. Dick seemed undeterred and agreed to take the opportunity at the salary and benefits level I had previously offered – David's package. We shook hands on it. I told him I'd get the paperwork going on the P.N.G. side as soon as I got back and would fax him a punch list of stateside requirements. We went on to finish a grand celebration of the New Year, during which I definitely celebrated a tad too much. The next morning found my head and stomach a bit "*crudo*" (Spanish for raw, or hungover), but it passed by the next day as we headed to Denver to finish up last minute items, along with the scheduled medical checkup, and packing up for our trip back to the South Pacific.

The urologist's voice was saying, "It's not good news. We found two more cancerous tumors. One is inside the tube that connects your right kidney to your bladder. It needs to be removed."

"How do you know they are cancerous?"

"Believe me, I've seen enough of them to know!"

"I've got to leave the country in a few days. How about if I come back next year?"

The doctor looked me straight in the eye with a very serious expression on his face and said, "You could die by then. We need to operate

now!"

"Can you do it right away?"

After consulting with his nurse, I was put on his operating schedule at nearby Lutheran Hospital for two days hence. I promised to take it easy for a week afterward as he instructed. I didn't feel any pain and hadn't shown any traces of blood in my urine, so I went into the operating room on his "say so." I did remember however, that the Australian doctor thought he saw something up that right kidney tube (ureter) also and told me to get this checkup when I was Stateside. Why take any chances? Get it taken care of.

That last week in the States became a blur. I vaguely remember the anesthetic and the morning operation, then much much later, Sandia and Vivian wheeling me from recovery, past the hospital cashier, where I gave them my Visa card to cover the four thousand plus dollars of expenses I had run up with the operation in the outpatient section of the hospital. Without health insurance, there was no way out except pay the cashier in full and then exit to the parking lot. In Australia, the same operation, with two days stay in the hospital, had come to about eight hundred dollars, doctor's fees included. Oh well, I wasn't in Australia and the best medical care in the world just plain costs money.

Later, at Mom's house, the worst pain I'd ever experienced in my life enveloped my abdomen. Deep, sharp, excruciating pain racked my body. My two nursing angels drove away to find an all night pharmacy to fill my "in case of pain" prescription, as I lay writhing on the bed in agony. I remember telling myself not to be a wimp, but it proved a powerful hurt. Twenty minutes after they returned to administer my dosage, the pain began to subside. What blessed relief, to feel the contrast of acute pain, and then, its passing.

The day before our flight connection left

Denver, for Los Angles, we drove to the mountains again, this time to see Elaine Busse, our neighbor at the adjacent "health" ranch. Elaine gladly wrote me out a natural/herbal routine to follow and we purchased six months supply of the recommended vitamin/mineral supplements she suggested from her mail order inventory business. I think the most good, however, came from her comments to me, "Cancer grows in an oxygen starved environment. Stress causes a reduction in your oxygen intake. You've got to remember that stress is self-induced!"

It seemed a simple observation, yet so profound. When we are in a stressful situation, the natural human reaction is shallow breathing, while exactly the opposite is much more healthful. Most of the time, as Elaine noted, we bring stress on ourselves with our perceptions of the world around us. It made so much sense to me and I would conjure that observation up, in various word forms, many times in the future, when "under the gun," so to speak. "Breathe deeply while under fire," would become my motto. Everything can be accomplished, no matter the enormity of it, one step at a time, one foot in front of the other. If we don't control our own lives, who does? Stress is surely and certainly created in one's own mind.

When I finally got up to Porgera and surveyed the problems, it was a shambles. Inventory and tools were missing, our houses were behind schedule, and a whole lot more. One of the Canadian managers had taken great delight in messing with David's head and his responsibilities regarding the relocation project. I sucked in a deep breath, inwardly resolving to get his "number" one-day soon, and listened to his list of "screw-ups" that David supposedly made in my absence. That manager's eyes twinkled as he came down on me with his macho power trip. I responded by scribbling notes in my day timer,

A "filling" station near Porgera. Diesel out of a 55-gallon drum, into a five gallon pail, and then hand pumped into my trusty Hilux

Relocation homes under construction in Mungalip

then stood up in front of his desk.

"No worries. I'm back. I'll get us caught up. I'll work with your inspectors Colin and Alan to get it all corrected. G'day to you!"

Out I walked to get some fresh mountain air. What a task lay in front of me. I took a deep breath and resolved to get on with it, one step at a time! Mount Kajindi seemed like it smiled at my resolve. What a marvelous and beautiful setting I worked in.

It took two months to get back on track in

Porgera, but we did it. We even overcame the setback of a tribal war right in the Mungalip area where our assigned building sites were located. Warriors ran my men off in the middle of the night from their sleeping house. Imagine waking suddenly to screaming warriors brandishing bush knives (machetes), bows and arrows, and spears. As my crews scattered to the bush, they told me they saw the hacked up remains of a fallen enemy warrior on the road outside their shelter. It took me days to talk them back to the job. When you fear for your life, measuring, cutting, and nailing pieces of wood into place is not a high priority, even if the mining managers are trying to keep a schedule. I told my men they were not the enemy and had no tribal feud in the Porgeran vicinity. Most came back, as they needed the work. Others, I never saw again. They probably headed back to the sanctuary of their own home villages. I promised those that stayed on extra food rations and more security guards while they slept. Luckily, the tribal fighting stopped in our area right after that and crews refocused on erecting the housing.

This became one time I went after the mining managers for extra funding and additional time on our completion schedule. They argued against it, but I persisted and finally won some compensation to cover extra expenses. My argument lay in the mining company presence and operations in these remote mountain villages disrupted the normal cultural life of the area, thus causing unrest and the occasional tribal fighting. My men couldn't be expected to work under those conditions without extra pay and additional security measures, at least while they slept.

My men were great. They snapped back into the work and got it done. All the relocation houses I'd left with David were finished, inspected, and handed over to the mining camp. The assigned families were already moving ex-

citedly into their new homes. Each family received a "*tok save*" (verbal instructions) from an Australian lady psychologist, knowledgeable with the New Guinea culture, on how to live in the new house – sort of a list of "how to's," "do's," and "don'ts." For example, how to use the new wood cookstove was explained – no cooking fires to be lit on the varnished plywood kitchen floor, how to work the indoor stainless steel shower stall with water from the cistern roof collector – no use as a toilet allowed – toilet needs served by the outside pit latrine only, etc. Not everyone paid attention to these "*tok saves*" because later, in the ongoing project, the shower stalls would be replaced with outside spigots, for use as bucket showers. It seemed the inside shower stalls routinely clogged up with various kinds of "debris."

Our hard persevering work at Hailans Homes was rewarded by a contract for an additional twenty relocation homes at the Porgeran Gold Mine. With my increased pricing per house, that new contract came to nearly one third of a million *kina* in one chunk. This contract was a big deal for Hailans Homes and Total Hardware. The major portion of the business at Total Hardware now consisted of supplying us for the Porgeran relocation project. One of our competitive builders in Porgera already closed up shop and was getting out, while the other worked far behind schedule. I felt a small twinge of sympathy for them, but how do you say, *"All is fair in love and business in Porgera and good luck to anyone who can hang in there, under those kind of conditions, and get the job done!"*

I learned where the term "wildcatter" came from in those days. That's what it took, a total disregard for all the surrounding havoc, with an intense focus for the job at hand. I liked it, the challenge of it. My men had been chosen well. They could deal. Those that couldn't packed up and went looking for saner, easier work. The crews I was left with consisted of good men, who could get the job done. As previously mentioned, that expatriate Canadian construction manager said the wrong thing to somebody, was relieved of his position, and flown out of the country. His replacement appeared a lot more reasonable to deal with. Best of all, my *wontok*, Dick had been cleared for a New Guinea work permit and was on his way. I knew he'd be able to answer the "bell," no matter how tough the work became. Dick was a mountain man who'd learned to deal with everyday uncertainties and still get the job done.

When Dick arrived, Sandia and I showed him around the Mt. Hagen social scene, small as it was. He liked the Aussie manner right away and made friends quickly with his outgoing easy personality. After a few days in Mt. Hagen looking over our factory operation, I scheduled both Dick and I on a commuter flight to Porgera to walk him through our procedures up there. I took him to all the current job sites and introduced him to each of the foremen, Vau, Vagi, Anua, and Mondul. I told each of them Dick would visit them most days to check on progress and see if they needed any help with anything. He was their new Porgera "*bosman*" and would handle all negotiations with the camp managers. Their efforts needed to be totally directed to the erection of their allotted houses and nothing else. Dick would liaise with the mining officials and me back in Hagen for anything they needed. The foremen seemed happy with the new arrangement, an on-site supervisor. Dick, for his part, seemed amazed at the gigantic effort underway at the mine site. At that point in the development, the mining company spent one million dollars per day and would continue at that rate of expenditure for another year to finish the construction phase of the Porgera Gold Mine. Then the

operational phase would begin and probably last for thirty years. Heavy equipment moved everywhere. Dump trucks, capable of carrying sixty-ton loads rumbled past us shaking the ground we watched from. The tires on those trucks appeared to be twelve-feet in diameter.

Late in the afternoon, I took Dick up to quieter Top Camp to show him where he'd be sleeping at night, while he worked in Porgera, which I had scheduled for Monday through Friday each week. Saturdays and Sundays, I'd get him back to Hagen for factory liaison and recreation. Wednesdays, I'd fly up to Porgera on a chopper in the morning and return on the same day via the last helicopter flight out. Dick's responsibility would be to keep the work going on the relocation houses, make sure building materials/tools didn't disappear from our warehouse, and to coordinate inspections with the mining camp

My mate Dick enjoying a bushwalk with me and Peace Corps friends in Tambul

construction managers. My Wednesdays would coordinate the overall effort, collect progress payments, and make sure everyone remained happy.

After showing Dick the rooms in the dongas, I told him, "Come on, I'll show you where the Top Camp Bar is located up the mountain a little ways – up 250 stairs!" I pointed out the building above us as we headed for the rough-hewn staircase.

We heard a voice from behind us as we started to mount the crude staircase.

"You blokes aren't going up there empty handed are you?"

Dick and I turned to see an expatriate tradesman, an Aussie judging from his dialect, standing beside a pickup truck, motioning us to come over. That's how we met Bill Sherlock, or "*tocayo*" (Spanish for namesake) as I always called him. He was an electrician from Australia, who'd taken a job with an electrical contractor at the Porgera mine. We ended up carrying quite a few fluorescent light fixtures up that winding staircase because Bill Sherlock seemed a likable "Huck Finn" sort of a guy. He and Dick would become close friends in the months ahead. Mining camp workers were, and are, a breed apart from the average tradesman. After we got all his gear carried up to the rambling building of appendages that constituted the mess hall/bar lounge on the mountainside, we downed a few cold ones and I left Dick in Porgera, while I caught the last chopper back to Hagen for the day.

In the ensuing weeks, Dick quickly figured out his job, while I organized and shipped house packages from Hagen. Dick proved resourceful, always figuring out ways around obstacles that somehow tried to slow us down. When he really got stuck, he'd talk his way into using one of the three very busy camp telephones, ringing through to me in "Hagentown." Between us,

we always found a way to solve the immediate problems and factored the solutions into our future operations. At times I had to tell Dick to take "deep breaths" before he described the sometimes unbelievable situations that had occurred. We ran the gamut from his running over a village dog in Mungalip, to someone stealing one of our petrol driven generators and demanding a ransom, before we could get it back. One time we began to dismantle our steel framed warehouse building in order to move it and re-erect it at a location more central to our then present building project. As our men began to remove the exterior steel sheeting, the local villagers told us that the building stood on their land; thus they now owned the building. They told Dick he couldn't take the warehouse down. It took me three months to get that building ordered and shipped in from New Zealand and the locals weren't about to take it over just because they wanted it and were used to it being there. The fact remained, we had erected it originally on church land, with the Catholic priest's permission and in return for the land use, we remodeled a church building for him. *Ayiii*, New Guinea, the "Land of the Unexpected!" Dick finally talked sense to the German priest, who, in turn, quieted the locals down, and we got out of Mungalip with our building. Several months later, at its new location, the building was buried in a huge landslide and we lost it anyway, along with all the materials stored inside. Maybe we should have left it with the people of Mungalip; but then again, they would have learned a bad lesson in appropriating things that didn't belong to them. In the end, the mining company, who'd caused the landslide, compensated us for the building materials and time we lost, by giving us a similar new building, already erected, as a replacement. Such was the nature of their operation. If we didn't get the housing completed, they couldn't move families off the gold laced mountains, and get started on the extraction of that precious yellow metal.

Our Hailans Homes trucks couldn't keep up with the deliveries of the factory-finished, prefabricated, relocation house packages, so I started hiring outside trucking contractors, Hagen Haulers and Traisa Trucking, just to keep up with the required completion schedules set by the mining officials. Dick and I, along with our very able foremen and crews, finished and handed over a group of twenty relocation houses in a record nine weeks time. It made a big difference having a knowledgeable overseer at the mining site, while I pushed to get the right loads out of the Hailans Homes gates and on the road to our Porgera warehouse. What a load off my shoulders, not to have to be in two places at once, especially when the places were hundreds of kilometers apart.

On the weekends, I taught Dick tennis at the Hagen Tennis Club, where we worked up great sweats in the tropical sun. Dick's athleticism allowed him to pick up the game quickly and we played some really competitive matches, usually followed by a few ice-cold S. P. brownies. Those were definitely "earned" beers.

One weekend, Dick won a set from me, the tennis teacher, and he appeared obviously proud of the achievement. When I went up to Porgera, the Wednesday following, one of the Aussie workers made a joking comment as I ran into him while exiting the helipad, "We heard Dick took a set in tennis from you last weekend in Hagen. Is that true, mate?"

I laughed and told him, "Yeah, it's true. He won a set, but I didn't know it would become big news up here!"

Now he laughed with me.

"We don't get a hell-of-a-lot to talk about around this bloody place!"

It gave me something to jive my mate Dick about when he showed up to meet me at the mine's helipad for our regular Wednesday project tour and status checks. He seemed a little embarrassed that it got back to me so quickly, but we had a great laugh about it. *Ayiii*, the machismo and competitiveness of the male species!

Flying lessons had bogged down a bit due to the Hailans Homes monster workload. Sometimes just before taking to the air, I'd get an urgent call at the airport about some factory foul-up in our prefabrication or delivery system. Needless to say, conditions made it difficult to focus on the flying task at hand. Late one morning, however, after making a nice smooth landing, the flight instructor told me to taxi over to the control tower, instead of back to our normal hanger parking spot. My brow wrinkled with curiosity. When I reached the Kagamuga control tower, my instructor opened his passenger side door and jumped to the ground. He stuck his head back inside the Cessna 172 and shouted over the engine noise, "Do two touch and goes and then bring her in for a full stop landing!" He slammed the door securely and walked away.

His words bounced around in my head. He had cleared me to "solo." I sat alone in the aircraft, at the controls, for the first time in my life. No one was beside me to "bail" me out. The excitement rippled through my body, stifling any fears that might have surfaced. I radioed the tower for permission to taxi to the airstrip for take-off and received it.

"Hotel Foxtrot Golf (my Cessna's call letters HFG), taxi and line up behind the Fokker F28. Await take-off instructions."

"Hotel Foxtrot Golf," I acknowledged.

Off I went seeing the F28 passenger jet waiting to enter the runway for take-off. I kept my Cessna a good distance behind him as he pulled onto the runway and began his take-off run. I made all my preflight checks, engine run-ups, and reported to the tower.

"Hotel Foxtrot Golf, ready for take-off."

Then I heard that voice crackle in my headset, "Hotel Foxtrot Golf, cleared for take-off!"

"Hotel Foxtrot Golf."

I was cleared and ready. I glanced to the sky at my right to make sure there was no aircraft coming in for a landing, throttled the Cessna up, and eased to my left out onto the runway, right onto the center of the threshold stripping. A quick glance at all the vital instruments and I eased the throttle out to full power. Down that runway I went and at lift-off, tears of joy ran down my cheeks. The wetness of my eyes caused the sunlight to sparkle and gleam. I was airborne. I felt truly ethereal. I flew by myself – a solo – a spiritual solo in the heavens.

When I reached 1000 feet above the airport elevation, I leveled out and started into my first turn. An audible scream of excitement escaped from my chest. No one heard it except me. I was alone. The green of the bush lay below me. The mountains surrounded me on the horizon. The blue sky glowed above me. I was alone up there. My heart tried to beat its way out of my chest. What a feeling! What an absolute rush of exhilaration! What a spirited natural high! I had wanted to fly all my life and there I was, over the rainforests of Papua New Guinea, 7000 feet above sea level, flying an aircraft by myself – an incredible feeling!

I physically shook off the excitement and concentrated on my two "touch and go" landings and take-offs. They went smoothly. When I brought Hotel Foxtrot Golf in for the final full stop landing, I bounced a little bit, not too bad though. Maybe the bounce stemmed from nerves, I don't know. I taxied HFG for the hanger and her normal parking spot. After

completing the shutdown checklist, I killed the engine and hopped down to the solid concrete that was earth. Several national flying students, who hadn't soloed yet, ran to the plane to congratulate me and pump my hand. I think I said something classic like, "Well, I didn't fall out of the sky!"

They laughed with me, as my instructor approached on foot from the direction of the control tower. He congratulated me on a fine flight and told me he'd been in the control tower all the time I was flying. Never would have thought it, but sure, he ran for the best vantage point and probably wanted to hear my radio conversations, as well. We went as a group inside, where the instructor asked for my flight log book, so he could enter my solo performance and sign it off.

I drove straight for our Hagen duplex, walked right past Sandia and Laurel, our Peace Corps buddy, having lunch on our little verandah without saying a word, opened our bedroom closet, took out my new leather flight jacket, and put it on. When I walked out to the verandah, Sandia took one look at me and shouted out, "You soloed!"

I beamed a grin back at her and said, "Yes I did!"

We ate a great lunch together as they let me excitedly tell them every detail of my newest adventure. I did, however, remove the jacket in the middle of the tale. The noonday sun proved too hot for a full leather jacket, solo or not!

Later I flew a bit more, but the workload limited my concentration of flying. I didn't want to fly without the ability to focus on where I was in the wide blue yonder! I would go around the whole world and back again before I'd get back into the flying again, but that's a later story.

In Porgera, near the gravel airstrip, Hailans Homes obtained the use of a piece of land, through our friendly government liaison Frank Faulkner, owned by a local named Kirabu. I designed a headquarters house with four bedrooms, two baths, a large kitchen, and a living area. The best part was a huge verandah looking straight up at Mt. Kajindi. The location and view were both tremendous. We built a security house nearby the main house and fenced the entire area in with high chainlink mesh. When Headquarters Haus was finished, we installed an H.F. radio to communicate with the Hagen office. The Haus gave us a permanent base to work out of for future projects, especially those outside of the mining camp itself, such as for government and private mine service businesses.

Total Hardware opened a branch store in Porgera to supply the many peripheral businesses that sprang up to serve the mine workers, as well as hardware and lumber products needed at the mine site itself. It turned out that they used Headquarters Haus a lot more than we did at Hailans Homes. Dick seemed happy with his accommodations at Top Camp, especially the chow hall, which cooked all his meals in copious amounts. Let's just say his waistline did not shrink away from starvation in Porgera.

Once, Dick got into a fracas with a good-sized, muscular national who worked for the government electrical company, Elcom. I forget what started it, but the standoff erupted into a display of fists and circling for position to strike the first blow. In that position, unwilling to back down, Dick heard some loud screams behind him and glanced over one shoulder to see three of our crews arriving on the full run – ready to do battle beside him, against the whole Elcom crew of workers. Seeing the reinforcements arrive, the Elcom crew leader and his men decided to back off. They jumped in their utility truck and drove away with fists shaking in both directions.

Our crews expressed pride in Dick for standing up to someone who had a "bully" reputation in the area. When the news got back to me, I had to tell Dick, "Good on ya," but also that expatriates did get kicked out of the country for those kind of incidents, whether the national instigated the incident, or not. His friend, Bill Sherlock was, in fact, told to leave the country for admonishing a national laborer, who decided to get into a bunkhouse "gang" shower, clothes and all, including his mud-caked, rubber boots. As *Tocayo* finished his shower under the adjacent shower nozzle, he didn't appreciate the mud being splashed on his clean, naked body. Of course the drain also quickly clogged, causing more of a mess. Guess *Tocayo* let out some choice cuss words, including racial slurs, at the perpetrator of the incident and that ended it. He was gone – back to Australia. *Ayiii*, the realities of life in a rough and tumble mining camp!

One day I rode in the cab of one of our Hailans Homes delivery trucks from Hagen to Porgera to get a "hands-on" experience of what the drivers were up against. That particular trip was accomplished without any detours or breakdowns. Arriving at the particular building site destination in Porgera to which the load had been designated, I started "humping" building material loads, on my shoulders, along with my crew. We carried the entire load up a muddy hillside to the building area. I wore hiking boots, which were soon covered with mud. Most of my laborers and carpenters walked barefoot, but knew how to dig their toes into the mud to keep from slipping. After the truck was completely unloaded, the foreman Mondul, remarked to me that Hailans Homes now got all the difficult, spread out, building sites, while our competitors got the easier, closely clustered, locations. I told Mondul I'd check it out and had our driver take me over to the locations where our competitors worked.

Mondul proved correct in his observation. It looked to me to be more than the luck of the draw. Both our original competitors, Moku and Coya Construction, had exited Porgera and the country. Building some of the relocation houses now, were two new construction outfits, one of them nationally owned. I didn't care so much about getting more houses to build, as we had all we could handle at that point, but I didn't appreciate getting the hardest sites to build on.

I headed for the engineering building and laid my case before one of the new construction supervisors. I wanted parity in the assigned building locations, or extra compensation for my men who worked in the more difficult terrain. The supervisor more or less laughed at my demands and tried to "sluff" me off.

Sitting there, I glanced down at his brightly polished, tasseled, dress shoes protruding under his worktable. My own mud-caked, hiking boots showed a stark contrast. An idea hit me.

"Let's you and I take a little drive and walk up to a few of the Hailans Homes building sites and then we'll go over to our competitors. Then we'll see what you think!"

I saw him start to squirm as he thought about walking in the mud. Terape taught me body language well. I stood up, as if to go, letting him get a good look at my footwear. Then he told me he had a meeting to go to, but if I'd submit a parity formula for compensation, he'd check into the assignment of the building areas.

My mathematical parity formula, based on distance from existing roads and elevation changes, was later approved. I gave my men a bonus for the more difficult sites. Next go around on housing contracts, Hailans Homes received some nice clustered housing sites to build on. You've

got to fight for that which is right!

The time seemed to be flying by. I stood busy up to my ears. Sandia appeared engrossed in running her business responsibilities. There was not a lot of time left over for having fun.

After Dick wrangled a successful trout fishing trip in the high mountains, where Frank Faulkner had them lifted by helicopter into a great stream location, and then picked up later in the day, I told Sandia we, also, needed a little break. I noticed we were getting a little antsy with each other. The work bogged us both down. There were always so many demands on our time, from different directions. Our spirits were ebbing. Sandia said she couldn't get interested in a holiday.

A few months before, on one of my early morning runs, a couple of local national men shouted at me from their perch in the back of a slowly passing pickup truck.

"We're going to get your *missus*. We know where she is all the time!"

Maybe they pulled my leg, maybe not! I didn't know them. To me, in Papua New Guinea, where "gang" rape happened frequently enough, a woman had to be careful and not naïve. That described my beautiful Sandia, trusting of everyone, and totally naïve when it came to watching her "backside." I kept trying to emphasize to her to be careful. Somehow it seemed to have the opposite effect. She said she could take care of herself and didn't need me telling her what to do! I tried to "back off" my independent lady a little bit, but found that impossible. Maybe I did smother her a little; maybe it stemmed from something else. I'd never taken a Relationships 101 course, but in my nearly two-years in New Guinea, I saw many husband-wife relationships fall apart. Maybe it lay in the nature of the special tension created by the daily uncertainties. I didn't know. One basic fact clearly lay fundamental in my thinking; Sandia was the sky, the mountains, and the oceans to me. She truly represented the world to me. I loved her dearly and wanted us to be together in spirited happiness as we'd always shared.

With my two-year contract nearing its end and the redundant relocation housing running almost on autopilot, notwithstanding the omnipresent unexpected, I began to concentrate on "going finish" and the "around the world trip." Sandia and I had always dreamed about a trip to exotic places when we concluded our work in P.N.G. I started talking to travel agents and collected brochures. Should we head east or west? Which airlines should we use? What primary countries should we stop in? It seemed a big task and it became all mine to accomplish. Sandia wasn't into the trip planning.

"You pick the countries! I'm busy."

Maybe we just needed to get away!

Gary, my son, decided the direction of the travel as we got his wedding announcement for mid-September in Connecticut. The date then was the first of August. I had a month to go on my work contract. So what the heck, we'll go east all the way around the globe. I finally settled into an itinerary like Connecticut, London, down through Europe to Greece, onto India and Nepal, Hong Kong, Thailand, Indonesia, and finally back to Queensland, Australia, where our tickets would have started. We could get to Colorado and home from there easily. Our three allowed airlines would be Qantas, United, and British Airways. The tickets would be "open," meaning we could stay in our primary cities as long as we wanted and just had to book onwards for available seats when we decided it was time to leave.

Sandia commented, "That'll work," and went back to her own labors.

Then Jim called from Lae to ask surprising,

powerful, and profound questions. Would I consider staying on with the company? He held out the possibility of talking about some type of partnership. Barring that, could I stay on four more months until Christmas? He would cover the airline tickets to my son's wedding and return!

They were such moving questions, I told Jim I'd consider them and get back to him the next day. That night seemed like agony. I laid there torn between not letting Jim down and holding onto the most precious thing in my life. I felt, in my heart, that Sandia and I needed to get away from the draining realities of getting things accomplished in those magnificent high mountains of New Guinea.

I talked with my mate, Dick, to ask him if he had any desire to take over the operation of Hailans Homes, if I left the country on schedule? His answer, obviously having been thought about previously, came as a decisive "No." The rigors of it all, the rapid transient nature of friendships, his wife and daughter on their way for a South Pacific vacation, and a lot more he didn't tell me. Dick would not stay if I left.

Sandia seemed to be enjoying the challenge and the newly found independence of her work. She did well at her job. She wouldn't help me much with the decision of staying or leaving. The choice fell entirely to me. The burden of it felt heavy. That night Sandia went to sleep, leaving the decision totally with me.

After sitting on the verandah for a while staring at the night sky of New Guinea, I walked inside to my desk, sat down, took out a sheet of paper, and began to write. I made a pro/con list for staying and leaving. I wrote down notes in both columns. On the staying side of the paper, I soon listed helping out Jim, the challenge of the work, staying with the men that I'd recruited, and the monetary rewards. On the leaving side, I wrote down possibly saving our relationship, the trip around the world, returning ultimately to our home in the Colorado Rockies, the chance to be with family again, and recovering from the "burnout" factor. I then circled the most important, Sandia and me, then helping Jim. I crossed out the low priority stuff like monetary, and the challenge, as I could find them elsewhere. The whole thing really came down to the dilemma of helping Jim against Sandia and our relationship. Maybe Sandia and I were stronger than I even knew, but it was the uncertainty that lay there in my mind. There must surely be someone else who could help Jim. I certainly did not represent the end all in management. By morning, I decided I didn't want to take the chance on staying for what it could do to our future. We would leave as planned. Our round-the-world trip was firmly set. I had only to pick up the tickets. Our backpacks stood packed and ready. The first of September 1989, Sandia and I would leave Papua New Guinea behind us, to head into an uncharted future together.

I rang up Jim right away to tell him my decision. He received it well, said he understood, and asked if I would go with him to Australia before I left, to interview applicants for my manager's position at Hailans Homes. I assured him I would be available for the Australian interviews. He then surprised me by awarding me a large bonus for the work accomplished during my contract. We worked it out that while Sandia and I traveled around the world, we could have our credit card bills sent to the company for payment, with a specified upper limit. It all worked out for the best, I still believe.

Dick's wife, Mary Pat, and his daughter, twelve year old Sarah, arrived to begin tasting the flavor of New Guinea life. I remember putting Sarah and M.P. on a chopper to Porgera so they could stay a few days in the mining camp with Dick. The pilot gave young Sarah the front pas-

senger seat for her first ever ride in a helicopter. She grinned and waved at us from the chopper bubble canopy as they lifted off. What an experience for a youngster! A week later, at the outdoor market in Hagen I felt once again taken by the view of Sarah, a very light-skinned blonde in contrast to her surroundings. The moment provided a startling and beautiful snapshot of the mind. They went on to enjoy a weekend holiday down at the beaches of Madang on the north coast, getting in some diving and snorkeling in the warm, turquoise sea. Then Dick and family left New Guinea a little before us to head for the Australian beaches of Queensland. From there later, they planned a holiday in Fiji and then home to Colorado.

The packing and shipping of a wooden crate with personal stuff, the "go *pinis* (finish) *mumu* put on by our workers, saying goodbye to expatriate friends, the tears of Terape at the airport, my workers rushing forward to give me one last hug, it all seemed a blur of sorts. Arriving in Cairns, Australia, meeting Dick again and spending a few days together on the beach in reflection on the whole thing brought a good perspective on the decision to leave. Sandia and I had the whole world in front of us. We had earned every bit of the joy and excitement that the travel would bring to us. I took in a deep breath of the Australian salt air and told myself, *"You worked damn hard! What you left behind in Papua New Guinea are tremendous efforts. Look only forward. No regrets. No looking back allowed!"*

Sandia looked up at me from her beach towel and smiled one of her beautiful smiles. I felt the spirit! I dove to the warm, bright, sand beside her and wrapped my arms around her. I whispered in my ladies ear, "I adore you. The world awaits the seed of your pollen and the scent of your spirit. Let's go spread it together, my lady of the flowers, wherever we choose!"

285

chapter thirty-nine 39

Around the World in One Hundred and Eighty Days

As I focused on the ceiling high above me, I realized the incredible workmanship that produced the timber framing details of Westminster Abbey centuries earlier. Every piece of timber had been hand chiseled to fit together into the hammer beam truss array before my eyes. A rush passed through me as the splendor of the setting impinged onto my mind. I had only previously seen sketches of this very ceiling and now I stood in the center of Westminster Abbey, one of England's most historic buildings, accompanied by a single security guard. His voice echoed through the otherwise empty chambers as he gave me a personal tour of that hallowed building, which had housed so many of England's historic events.

Westminster Abbey was actually closed for the season, but a pleasant guard helped me obtain an audience with the head of security. After showing them both photos of hammer beam trusses I'd previously designed and built from the ideas of Westminster Abbey, the security chief

backpacks strapped on tight, soul mate at your side

whole world to touch, with strength, spirit supplied

approved my personal tour. Sandia had to wait outside and I had been forbidden to video or photograph the timber work.

There I stood, novice timber framer, staring up at the craftsmanship of the masters. The aura of the scene felt humbling, to say the least. My efforts, which presently stand in the Colorado Mountains, seemed almost primitive in comparison to the chiseled sculptures above me. Tips of the horizontal, truss-beam, extensions had been carved into angels, much as the figureheads on the bow of a ship. The carved figures looked so magnificent; each chiseled uniquely by the hands of an artist.

I heard my security escort telling me he would wait for me back by the entry and I was welcome to stand there gazing at the ceilings for as long as I desired. His departing footsteps echoed through the building, as he briskly marched back toward the entrance, leaving me alone with my excited mental sketching.

The date was late September 1989, and we'd

286

come so far from Papua New Guinea. My son Gary's wedding in Connecticut gave us a chance to be with all the kids and lots of family and friends for a short visit. It always tickled me to get all our offspring, now in their 20's and 30's, in the same place, at the same time, and listen to their expectations and accomplishments in life. They knew my motto well, "Life is a beautiful adventure, but you can only discover, if you are willing to explore." In our conversations, the kids inferred that I always ended up "lucky" at life, which left me to explain that we all make our own "luck" in this world.

Then we'd boarded a flight to Heathrow Airport and now had our feet firmly planted on English soil. This became my first venture to the United Kingdom and I felt like our round-the-world journey had really begun.

"How was it?" Sandia asked as I emerged blinking into the bright sunlight from the darker interiors of Westminster Abbey.

"Sandia, it is more incredible than I'd ever imagined. It would take me months to build one

of those hammer beam timber trusses, even with a model to work from. I am so glad they let me in to see the timber work. Thank you England, and the Westminster Abbey Security People!"

As we walked away, I tried to paint a mental picture of the Abbey ceiling for Sandia using descriptive words for the brushstrokes of the painting that would forever be etched into my mind. What splendid artistic craftsmanship had been completed by timbersmiths of the past. The contrast of what I'd just been privileged to view compared to the quality and blandness of most modern architecture proved indeed striking.

We left Picadilly Circus and the back-packers' lodge behind us and headed west for Whitchurch, a small farming community, to look up old friends. Jill and Mandy Wright who had attended our Rocky Mountain Homesteaders Institute years earlier. During their session, the two traveling sisters stayed with us at *La Casa del Sol* and we came to know them as friends with similar views of a spirited life.

Sandia and I found their family's small organic farm, Wheelbarrow Market Gardens. Jill and Mandy were, as expected, hard at work with other family members, harvesting produce for their market place. We lent, and then bent, our backs to picking a field of onions, trying to beat a forecast of rain. By the next day, when the last onion yielded its grip on the rich, non-chemically fertilized, soil, my lower back burned with pain. My mind mulled over the toughness of our two friends, and their family, for the physical conditioning necessary to run a farm like theirs, basically by hand, with rakes, shovels, hoes, and wheelbarrows. Even

Jill, myself, and Mandy Wright (l to r) at the Witchurch Train Station (photo by Sandia)

though they sold their produce at top dollar (or pound) because it was organically grown, it appeared to me as a tough way to make a living. Part of their harvest sold exclusively to hospitals to be eaten by cancer patients as a possible cure and, at the least, an excellent lifestyle change. Sandia and I, with permission from Jill and Mandy, liberally sampled the produce. Our favorite quickly became the small cherry tomatoes picked right off the vines. The flavor burst of those tomatoes seemed so unlike any delicious taste we'd ever experienced. I think the nourishment of those tomatoes cured what I thought would turn out to be a permanent "onion picking" lower-back disorder.

After several more days of visiting with Jill and Mandy, while sharing a room at Jill's and her young son Billy's little house, we said and waved our good-byes. They watched our departing, backpack laden, figures from positions in their spinach field as we walked off toward the Whitchurch train station. One last look back brought that final picture of the two of them, Jill and Mandy, leaning on their hoe handles with their other arms upraised in a final goodbye. Then we passed over a hill.

Sandia and I rode the trains as far west as Bath, England, there visiting the Roman Solar Baths that gave the city its name. On the return trip to London, we toured the huge cathedral in

Salisbury and stopped in several small villages along the way. Traveling with backpacks, using the railroad system, proved a great way to get around. In those villages, the streets seemed so narrow and the buildings so old, it seemed a different world to us. With the U.S.A. being only a few hundred years old, the surroundings of

Of course we had to visit the famous Stonehenge

A timberframed English village building

288

Sandia at the Eifle Tower

Bridges over the River Seine

an English village gave me a changed sense of time. A few evenings, Sandia and I lifted pints of ale upward in "toasts" to friendship, kinship, and life with the locals. We felt warmed by the hospitality we found in those small villages. The timberframed pubs that they took for granted, gave me a never-ending lesson on the different ways timbers can be joined to form the structural skeleton of a beautiful building. While laughter and singing filled my ears and sips of English Ale stimulated my taste buds, the visible structure of the ancient timbers filled my eyes and exercised my cerebral gray matter.

A hydrofoil journey across the English Channel, followed by a short train ride, brought us to Paris, the city that oozed and seethed with romance. You could feel it in the air. You could see it on the streets. The feeling was visible in the smiles of the people on the streets.

An inquiry at a small, but quaint, row building hotel near the northern train station yielded a reasonably priced room on the top floor. As Sandia and I looked out from our high dormered hotel window, Paris lay before us. The Eiffel Tower was visible in the distance, giving us a landmark signature of where we were in the world. Our room was small and offbeat in a way. The many lines of the dormered ceiling were wall-papered in continuation from the Victorian walls. A small "lift," or elevator, capable of holding maybe three people, carried Sandia and myself up and down from and to the streets of Paris from our tiny penthouse quarters. Yes, we walked along the sidewalks of Paris in the morning holding hands and eating freshly baked croissants, as so many Parisians do. We drank coffee from steaming mugs in sidewalk cafes. We made love to Paris with our eyes and our feet. Sandia and I walked everywhere from the Arc de Triumph, to the Louvre, to the steps of the Eiffel Tower. After climbing what seemed like thousands of stairs, we arrived, a bit tested on lung capacity, at a high observation deck. Leaning on the rail of the observation platform, looking out at the

*Touring the Amsterdam
Canal system*

city before us, we hugged each other in a bit of disbelief. We were indeed in Paris, standing atop the Eiffel Tower, in love with the city and each other. It was a magical time. I felt as if our spirits soared above the tallest buildings. We stayed awhile and played a lot.

Eventually, we moved on, a bit sadly, but at the same time, excited about seeing new places. The train took us, along with our slowly dirtying backpacks, through Belgium to the Netherlands and the picturesque city of Amsterdam. We toured and walked along the network of canals that make the city so distinct. Many of the buildings beside the canals seemed to lean inward and outward slightly from the true vertical. This askewness most certainly resulted from the settling of building foundations over time in a water-based city. The phenomena brought with it again that longer sense of time. Sandia and I even managed to find the small, but famous house, that hid Anne Frank for so long from the searching Gestapo of WWII. The brick row house stood so indistinguishable from the others around it. Only the highly polished brass sign in front, whose lettering included ANNE FRANK in large capitals, set it apart from adjacent structures. A visitor could only imagine the fear that Anne and her family must have felt, while hiding behind the false partitions, when the sirens ap-

proached anywhere close to their building. Then the day came when the sirens stopped outside their home! War is truly hell. The carnage of human politics, greed, religion, and prejudice is so horrible on the one hand, but seems so easily forgotten, and oft repeated, on the other. Wars of choice are so tragic and brutal.

Another train ride took us to Hamburg, Germany, where Sandia had friends from her previous life and work overseas. I met those wonderful friends, Uwe, Elke, Walter, and Renata. They seemed special people indeed, so truly happy to see Sandia again. Uwe and Elke owned and managed a small neighborhood grocery store, which took most of their time and effort. The store was a lifetime labor that they seemed to enjoy and it supported them well. When we stopped in, on our way to Berlin, to say our fare-wells, they both stuffed our packs with munchies and snacks from the shelves of their store. They commented, "Full stomachs travel better, and further!"

On the way to Berlin, we met many student travelers excitedly heading in the same direction. They had electricity about them and seemed to feel things would soon "happen" regarding the Berlin Wall. Their premonitions proved to be correct as the Wall was finally breached later that year. Sandia and I were barely ahead of that part of history in the fall of '89. We walked the Wall, photographed the Wall, and looked over the Wall from the safety of the Reichstag porches next to the Wall. The East German soldiers marched in vigilance on the other side, unblinking as we snapped their pictures and videoed their move-ments. The cold audacity of the Wall stood there. The belief that a line of thick concrete can separate humans into political ideals. Near the Reichstag, on the free side of the Wall, stood many white crosses bearing the names of those who tried to run and climb to freedom, but fell short of that most noble goal, with the bullets of Communism impacting their bodies and taking away their last breaths. Looking at those crosses, names, and dates, I was deeply reminded of just how precious our freedom is.

On one of our journeys through the Berlin train station, while looking at a hotel and lodg-ing bulletin board, Sandia and I heard the fa-miliar sound of Australian English. Two Aussie traveling mates stopped at the bulletin board, also looking for a place to stay. I greeted them with, "G'day mates." Soon we were sharing our life histories over a cup of coffee, as travelers often do when passing in the world. After all, we all were "*wontoks*" of a sort.

One of the two Aussies had even worked four years in Papua New Guinea, demonstrating

Elke, Renata, Uwe, Walter, and Sandia

Some of the crosses in the foreground of the Berlin Wall

Brandenburg Gate with the Wall in the foreground

what a small world it really is. The most notable and, for me, poignant part of the conversation was the ex-P.N.G. worker had been married when he accepted the job in New Guinea and happily took his wife with him to the "Land of the Unexpected." They ended up divorcing during his second two-year contract. The sensitive part of my romantic brain registered his comments and filed them in a decision reinforcement compartment of the gray matter between my ears. I glanced over at Sandia, intently listening to our coffee mates' stories, and smiled inwardly as I reflected on the decision to leave New Guinea. No one can predict the events of the future. You make the choices, after serious and thorough thinking and then go on from there – no looking back and no regrets. Living with regrets will consume the spirit right out of your heart.

Leaving Berlin, we obtained travel visas through East Germany, on the strength of our U.S.A. passports. Our destination lay south in Prague, Czechoslovakia. From East Berlin, we traveled through Leipzig and Dresden to the Czechoslovakian border. During the trip, East German soldiers stationed on the train frequently searched our travel compartment, consisting of two wooden bench seats facing each other. Sandia and I were asked to produce our passports and visas for scrutiny during each search. I think that as they changed soldiers frequently at different railroad stations, each new contingent would begin a new search, all over again, throughout the passenger cars. The soldiers searched under our seats, in our overhead baggage lockers, everywhere. Sandia knew enough German to learn from one Czechoslovakian woman in our sitting compartment that more and more East Germans

were trying and successfully escaping across the border into her country. Watching out our train windows, at various stopping points, we saw the soldiers poking rifles and long poles underneath the carriage of our passenger car looking for potential escapees holding onto the bottom structure of the railroad cars. I watched their futile searches wondering how I would act if I lost my own freedom. It did not make for pleasant thinking.

Before boarding the train in East Berlin, Sandia and I had taken a chance and walked

Czechoslovakian countryside from the train window

away from the railroad station, where we were supposed to remain for several hours waiting for the train to Czechoslovakia. We figured we'd spin a story of looking for travel food utilizing Sandia's best German, if stopped and questioned by East German police. After all, we had our train tickets and visas to back our story. Off to the stores we went.

The few food stores we found visited a bit of culture shock upon us. There was hardly any food at all on the shelves of the stores. The real-

A Prague cathedral

ran out of the compartment and disappeared somewhere. The East German guards filed off the train. A few Czechoslovakian security people climbed aboard. Our Czech lady was nowhere to be seen.

A few minutes later, the train slowly started up and moved away from the border, resuming its travel onward to Prague. That's when the little Czech lady kicked a knock on our compartment door. When I reached out to open the door, she entered with a small steaming cup of black coffee in each hand. She presented the coffee to us and said smilingly in her limited English, "Welcome to Czechoslovakia!"

The tears welled up in my eyes as I took my first sip of her hospitality. She so obviously loved her country and wanted to share it with us. She chattered excitedly much of the way to Prague, with Sandia understanding only parts of her German, but enough to get the gist of our friend's happiness. Her outgoing manner seemed much changed from the more subdued personality we saw while she traveled on the East German side of the border. Her gift, the two little cups of black coffee, represented such an expression of giving that Sandia and I still talk of her today. To reach out like she did, with no expectation in return, taught a true lesson in unselfishness and caring.

After arriving in Prague, we rented a soccer player's little apartment, while he went to stay at his girl friend's place. George was his name. He trusted us with all his "stuff," which included a stereo music system. George kidded us, as he left us in his apartment for a three-day agreement, "Please, you no can rob me!" He worked as a state subsidized soccer player who made some deutschemarks on the side renting his apartment when he could find willing backpackers. Good thing his girl friend cooperated!

Prague proved a treasure chest filled with a

ity appeared as rows of empty shelves, with a few food items here and there. Barrenness, or emptiness, would be the operative description. Only a few customers were visible to us in the three or four stores we walked through. Compared to the abundant supermarkets of the U.S.A., or even the well stocked shelves of Uwe and Elke's grocery in Hamburg, those East Berlin stores proved stark, empty, and dingy. The shopping venture provided first hand visualization regarding the realities of Communism.

My reflections were interrupted when our new friend, the little old Czechoslovakian lady told Sandia we approached the border of her country. She smiled broadly as she pointed ahead out the big smudgy compartment window toward her homeland. Then the train slowed and came to a stop at the border. Our lady friend wealth of art and antique buildings. For whatever reason, the bombs of WWII never fell on Prague. A visa condition during our visit required a traveler to spend the equivalent of ten U.S. dollars per day, or pay the difference upon exiting the country. Sandia and I ate lavishly for several days, consuming expensive foods, along with bottles of wine at our evening meals, and still didn't spend the required amount, even including our hotel bills. A visa-checking official on our train out to Austria made me pay the equivalent of about nine US dollars before he'd stamp our passports

The Yugoslavian countryside

with the necessary exit permit. The money would be available to me for a year through a state bank should we decide to return to Czechoslovakia. The visa-spending requirement seemed much like a great money-gathering scheme by the country; but then again, lots of countries have exit fees considerably higher than nine dollars.

After a few "look around" days in Vienna, we both felt ready and itchy to move on. A long train ride brought us to Budapest, Hungary for a short visit. We found a room with a Hungarian family that had obtained permission to rent out an extra room, sort of a "cottage" industry. The sons of the family took turns canvassing the train station arrivals for travelers with backpacks, who represented potential lodgers.

The Hungarian goulash tasted surprisingly flavorful and fulfilled our pledge to sample the ethnic cuisine of every country we traveled through. At night, the city of Budapest looked remarkably beautiful with the lit-up bridges spanning the Danube River. The famous river divided the city and several bridges carried heavy

traffic from one side to the other.

Sandia lobbied to get out of Budapest quickly, which seemed a bit unusual for her, as she loved exploring new places. Maybe her feelings stemmed from the dirt, dust and indifference of the Eastern Bloc countries, but, in any event, we headed for the train station. There we managed to get seats on a train to Belgrade, Yugoslavia. The tickets represented a great accomplishment as we possessed "zero" language skills in Hungarian and the ticket agent didn't know a word of English.

The train station in Belgrade resembled utter chaos with the clamor and chatter of crowds of waiting passengers and their luggage, much of which consisted of tied up cardboard boxes. We detrained just long enough to get tickets on the same train as it continued on to Athens, Greece. It seemed funny to get thousands of dinar in change for the few deutschemarks I handed the ticket agent as payment for our two seats to

Athens. Then shortly before the train's departure, we boarded our designated car only to find our seats occupied by duplicate ticket holders, who stubbornly refused to look at our tickets.

I told Sandia, "Follow me!" and jumped to the ground walking quickly toward the rear cars. I kept shouting to porters, in English, "We need seats on this train."

I visibly held up a ten-deutschemark note in my hand as I began to trot along. Near the back of the train, a conductor heard me and beckoned us to his car. We ended up with a private sleeper compartment, adjacent to a dining car, for a few additional deutschemarks. Hard currency yielded great results behind the Iron Curtain.

Yugoslavia, as observed from our private train window, appeared as the land before time. Oxen pulled the plows that tilled the soil. Most laborers used their backs and hands to scratch out a living. The old people we observed seemed to have a permanent stoop in their posture. Here we traveled in a Greek sleeping car, served lavishly by Greek waiters and cooks, who know their trade and food preparation so well; looking out at countryside that appeared void of modern machinery and industry. It was truly a time of reflection. I guess we just have to deal with the lot we are born to and go on from there.

Athens was bathed in sunlight. The abundance of white washed building walls added to the brightness of the city. After many weeks behind the Iron Curtain, with its dim, unkempt, and unclean "face of indifference," Athens presented a smiling, bright, and clean looking contrast which lifted our spirits.

After four days of walking the Greek ruins, it seemed time for a little respite – a time away from visiting famous tourist places, a time for "lay-about" by ourselves, a holiday from the holiday. We didn't have to be anywhere by any particular time, so it seemed natural to book two tickets on an Arkadia Lines ferry and head off for a Greek island.

We chose Santorini (also called Thira), whose enclosed circular shaped harbor suggested that an earlier volcanic eruption created the island

Stepping back in time by touching the antiquities of Greece

Power tanning on a Santorini black sand beach

we'd hang out until it got boring. Our spirits soared with the thought of it – just being beach bums for a while.

We hopped on our trusty "Little Lurch," left the beach and backtracked to a nearby small store. There we inquired of the white-haired Greek proprietor if there were any rooms for rent near the beach. He promptly closed the store and walked us to a great little bungalow, with a kitchen, and told us it cost six U.S. dollars per day. Sandia and I looked at each other in acknowledgment and she shook his hand as I searched for some money to seal the deal. Grandpa, as we came to call him, urged us to come back to his store, where he poured out three shots of homemade ouzo. We consummated the rental agreement with a toast to life. Each time thereafter, we'd come into his store for supplies or to pay another day's rent, Grandpa would break out in a big smile, pull out a bottle of ouzo, and pour us all a shot – even if it was seven in the morning. Santorini definitely proved easy living!

Back in Athens about ten days later, tanned and well rested, I stopped by the American Express office to check for any mail they might have been holding for us, and to check out flights to our next stopover, New Delhi, India. Sandia hung out waiting for me outside the offices and got to talking to three Australians, who'd just returned from Egypt, on their way north into Europe. By the time I got my business finished inside, Sandia had heard enough that her heart seemed set on going to Egypt. She told me, "Ever since my third grade Weekly Reader featured the saving of Ramesses II Monuments from the flooding of Lake Nasser, I've wanted to go!"

Living up to her nickname for me,

around a center crater that filled with Mediterranean Sea water to make a sheltered place for our ship to drop us off. The guidebook read, "Santorini has more churches than houses, more donkeys than people, and more wine than water." The description sounded like a marvelous place to "lay-about" for a week or so.

On a 50 cc rented moped, that we dubbed "Little Lurch," we toured the island with our packs, deciding where to stay. In nearly two months we'd seen Stonehenge, cathedrals, the Eiffel Tower, the Berlin Wall, the art treasures of Prague, and the ruins of Greece. Now was the time to see beach sand close up, as in lying on your stomach in the warmth of it, as in letting it sift through your toes very slowly, while the surf gently broke waves near your feet and the sun tanned your body all over.

We found it – a black volcanic sand beach and cove, protected from the open sea by some awesome rock outcroppings. Only a few Europeans occupied the beach. I assumed they were Euros, or maybe Australians, as the women went topless. This would be the beach where

"FlexiBill," I responded, "So let's go!"

Back up the stairs to the Amex office, the two of us went and bought tickets from Athens to Cairo for the very next day. It would be a side trip never to be forgotten. Egypt provided travel nothing short of incredible.

At the Athens airport, passing through the immigration control, Sandia and I made some good travel friends. The short blonde Australian young woman, named Prudence, or Pru as she preferred, in front of us was immediately held up by the soldier checking passports. Evidently Pru had overstayed her visa, not by a day or two, but by half-a-year! They held up the whole line of us, while the soldier and some immigration official chattered about what to do about Pru. The two young women behind us turned out to be Americans, Kelly from Alaska and Carolyn from California. We all started to talk to Pru about her predicament. She had tended bar out on one of the Greek Islands for the better part of a year without paying any attention to visa requirements. Now she'd saved enough money by working (also against visa restrictions) and wanted to move on to see the wonders of Egypt.

The soldier and the official finally started laughing, looked at Pru's determination, and waved her through the line, with a roll of their eyes skyward. "Go to Egypt," the official proclaimed to Pru and reached back for our passports. Sometimes I think it paid to be a young pretty female traveling alone. You could get away with stuff.

Pru did it again upon arrival at the Cairo airport, when she tried to exchange two U.S. fifty dollar travelers checks at the bank currency window. The two wrinkled up checks looked

The streets of Cairo

like they'd been washed a few times in the laundry. It took her a while, but she ended up with Egyptian Pounds for those old travelers' checks. She was a spirit, that Pru.

The first night in Cairo, having just come out of the airport, I found out how nice it would be traveling with the four lovely ladies, Pru, Carolyn, Kelly, and Sandia. Some Egyptian men bought our bus tickets to Cairo and also bought us a round of fruit juices. One of the men said he knew where the Hotel Minerva was located in Cairo and would show us the way. That hotel had been recommended to Pru as a result of talking to other backpackers who'd been to Cairo and passed through her bar in the Greek Islands.

Upon exiting our bus in the middle of Cairo, our volunteer guide led us through those crowded streets and teeming bazaars for many blocks. Then he turned one corner and came to a stop, pointing. There stood the Hotel Minerva, looking quite ancient, but a welcome sight to the five of us, all weary from a long day of travel.

Sandia and I ended up on about the fifth floor in a wonderfully large, high ceilinged room

Obviously, we found the pyramids

And tried camel transport as well

that came right out of British colonial times. The furnishings were classic. Large mirrored dressers and armoires served as closets. A small balcony overlooked the very busy street scene below. Our room contained a large sink for washing, but the common bathroom, with a four-legged tub and toilet, was a short walk down the hall.

Sandia couldn't get to sleep that first night. She kept hugging me and saying, "I can't believe we're in Cairo." That side trip to Egypt obviously meant a lot to her.

The next morning Pru informed us she'd made arrangements during the night, with the

hotel desk clerk, to join a camel caravan traveling out into the Sahara. Pru was truly a "spark plug!" We all waved goodbye to her, knowing she could certainly handle herself. She would be fine. We did wonder out loud to each other how the caravan would fare with her being a part of it. We shared a good-natured laugh.

A few days later, Sandia and I headed by bus to the famous pyramids near Cairo. It seemed appropriate to ride up on the pyramids out of the desert, so we stopped and found a place to rent a couple of sturdy Arabian horses. Along with our horses came a faithful guide named Oman. Sandia still thinks she heard a couple of his young friends call him Michael, but to me Oman of the Desert fit the whole scene much better. Off we went into the shifting desert sands behind Oman, trusting he would lead us to the ancient pyramids of the Pharaohs.

No photographs in National Geographics can prepare you for the vision of the pyramids and the sphinx as you ride up to them on horse-back out of the desert. The pyramids are so enormous. My "onion picking" back flinched as I thought of the slaves, who'd worked maybe their entire lifetimes building a Pharaoh's tomb, block by heavy block. Moses, his people, the Exodus, and the Ten Commandments ran through my mind. Illustrations from the Bible stories of my youth bubbled up from my sub-conscious. Astride my trusty steed, Moonlight, with my lady beside me on her own horse, it all lay in front of us, a true wonder to behold – the pyramids of Cheops, Chephren, and Mycerinus. Cheop's is known as the "Great Pyramid," even though it is only slightly larger than the pyramid built for Chephren. It is estimated that six million tons (twelve billion pounds) of stone went into the construction of the Great Pyramid. That tonnage becomes even more staggering when you think about the fact that no stone was available anywhere near the chosen construction site. All the stone had to be transported over huge distances. The polished limestone facing stones, most of which had been pillaged in the 13th century to help build nearby Cairo, each weighed three tons. These facing stones were placed with such precision that scarcely a gap of one-half a millimeter lay between them.

One guidebook stated Napoleon's claim that the stone from the Great Pyramid was sufficient to build a ten-foot high by one-foot thick wall around the entire border of France. Other estimates of the enormity of the Great Pyramid calculated that within its base would fit the Cathedrals of Florence, Milan, St. Peter's in Rome, and St. Paul's in London, all at once, with enough room left over for Westminster Abbey.

Speaking of the Pyramid's base, I also learned the alignment of the four sides are perfect alignments to the North, South, East and West. Egyptologists figure the stars were used to get the directions so accurate. Such precision seems amazing, considering the pyramids were just giant rock tombs, void of any art work, built to house a small burial chamber somewhere in the midst for one human body and maybe a few supporting servants. The egos of man can take on stupendous proportions at times.

While in Cairo, we met Vico and his friend Magdi – two contrasting characters who were close friends. Vico symbolized a man of the world. He had been married briefly to a French woman and seemed to like foreigners. He served on special assignments with the Egyptian Army using his language skills, which included Hebrew and Yiddish. Magdi, on the other hand, seemed more the true "at home" Egyptian, who carried a picture of his fiancée in a "*chador*," complete with veil to hide most of her face. I remember remarking to Magdi, as he proudly showed us the picture of his betrothed, "She has nice eyes!"

The Sphinx keeping an eye on the pyramids

The skyline of Cairo

The fact is, that's all I could see of her, but her eyes did have a sparkle to them.

I couldn't resist asking about the reason for the cover up of women. Did it represent a religious requirement, or what? Myself, I loved seeing my lady in shorts, or a miniskirt, and halter.

The worldly one, Vico, began to explain in English thusly, "If an Egyptian man looks at a woman who is not covered like Magdi's fiancée, then he loses his breath and gets very tired!"

I looked over at Sandia and she returned my look with equal puzzlement. Then it dawned on me what Vico tried to express. I smiled at the words he had chosen. Losing breath and tired are maybe an interesting way to explain desire, frustration, and testosterone driven male feelings. Topless bathing would never cut it in Egypt!

In the next few days, our new friends, Vico and Magdi, showed us some of the non-touristed spots of interest, in and around Cairo. One of the most memorable and striking visits we made consisted of Cairo's "City of the Dead." Within the Cairo City boundaries, the high walled "City of the Dead" constituted one of the most elaborate cemeteries I'd ever laid eyes on. People built small houses near graves and would come to stay, for varying periods of time, near the graves of loved ones. From the ancient sentry towers placed along the high surrounding walls, the "City of the Dead" lay in marked contrast to the crowded streets of Cairo, outside the walls. Inside, only a few people moved about slowly, obviously in some sort of mourning ritual, while outside, the hustle and bustle of Cairo's everyday business at thousands of bazaars carried on at a rapid pace.

Ultimately, we said goodbye and expressed our gratitude to Vico and Magdi at a farewell dinner, where Sandia and I treated. They had given so much of their time to be with us and share the culture they obviously loved so much. At dinner, they reminded me of my choking attempts, earlier in the day, at a male coffeehouse, while trying to smoke one of their big water pipes. Upon my first exhale, all the men stood to put their hands together in applause for my effort. Vico jokingly said something to the effect

that the present rough tobacco smoked in the water pipes used to be "hashish" in the earlier times, sort of like a water "bong." If what he told us was true, it gave me an inward chuckle because alcohol, even beer, is not permitted in the culture and only available at certain tourist hotels, while the much stronger "stuff" was once openly smoked in coffeehouses. Overall, Sandia and I agreed on the open friendliness of the Egyptian people and felt so fortunate to have met Vico and Magdi.

Following Sandia's memories from her third grade Weekly Reader, we next bought railroad tickets south to Aswan and boarded a late night train. Trying to sleep in a slouchy sitting position proved uncomfortable and not very restful, to say the least. I awoke once to see four or five dark mustachioed faces staring across at us sleeping with our legs draped over backpacks on the train's floor. Ever aware of traveling security, even while not fully awake, I slowly and discretely slipped my small money/passport pouch from a top front accessible pocket, where I always kept it, to a rear pocket behind and underneath me. Satisfied that my effort looked nonchalant and went unnoticed by those faces in the night, I fell back into my tired semi-sleep.

A few hours later, I awoke to a sideways jolt in the train's southward motion and opened my eyes halfway to admit a little of the early morning gray light. The staring faces were gone. The bench seat facing us was empty. I reached up and instinctively patted my usual front vest pocket for money and passports. Startled at the open, empty pocket my tired hand contacted, I came bolt upright, with eyes wide open. Those dark staring faces, along with our money and passports had disappeared into the black night!

"Sandia, Sandia! Wake up! Wake up! We've been robbed!"

My voice filled with alarm as I tried to poke my lady from her sleep. Consciousness slowly replaced my drowsiness. As awareness began to take over, my brain remembered. I slid my hand down to my right back pants pocket to find the slight bulge of our money/credit card/passport pouch. My heart slowed and began to relax. I laughed at my perceived plight. "Go back to sleep, my lady. I'll tell you what happened later."

Soon Sandia breathed deeply and rhythmically in sleep again, but I'd become too hyped to sleep. I sat there feeling badly for any travelers that actually do get robbed, or maybe lose their valuables. At the same time, my mental and physical functions relaxed in that it hadn't really happened to us, but I'd only experienced the anguish of loss in a virtual sense. Relief is a very pleasant emotion.

Aswan, located on the Nile, south towards Sudan, seemed a busy place, paced by its river economy. Eating at riverside restaurants, overlooking busy boat traffic provided us with an interesting education. Most of the boats consisted of feluccas, keeping with the ancient Nile sailing designs, exhibiting four-sided fabric sails, usually white in color. The feluccas came in many sizes, mostly in the ten to thirty meter (thirty to one hundred foot) lengths. Closer inspection showed us that many of those feluccas had navigated the polluted waters of the Nile for a long period of time.

I say polluted in the sense that several of the guidebooks on Egypt described "parasites" that lived in the water of the Nile River. One book stated that mere contact with the river water would allow the absorption of the parasites into a person's skin. The name of the dreaded microorganism doesn't remain in my memory, but the guidebook's stated alarm seemed a little overdone, based on the number of locals we observed doing laundry and bathing in the River's water.

Maybe they had become immune, we decided, and made a pact that we would keep buying bottled water, along with showering only at our backpackers' lodgings.

In our quest of standing amongst the stories from Sandia's third grade Weekly Reader about Abu Simbel, we booked onto what we were led to believe was a comfortable van shuttle for an approximate four hour trip through the stark desert to those famous moved and reconstructed monuments. Our "van" turned out to be a very small taxicab, into which at least seven or so like-minded tourists were crammed. A couple of Aussies, amongst our group, told jokes and added some spirit, in comparison to others who complained and argued with the driver most of the way. The driver and guide, of course, kept telling us the van had only broken down that morning, while the complainers muttered doubts as to the very existence of a larger van.

*The Nile River at Aswan
with a passing felucca*

Finally, after what seemed a lot longer than the actual more or less four hours, our group of cramped travelers arrived at some sort of military checkpoint, cordoned off by a lot of spread out 55 gallon drums, connected by many meters of single stranded rope. This entire scene resided in the middle of a seemingly endless flat landscape of light brown sand. The rifle-toting soldiers checked our driver's and guide's papers, then waved us through the checkpoint toward the nearby Abu Simbel. From our little travel map, I figured we had just crossed into Sudan, making that checkpoint a border crossing.

Suddenly, the four sculptured figures of Ramesses II loomed in front of us. They towered so high above human dimensions (about 50 feet), one had to stand 50 to 100 yards back in order to appreciate the magnificence of the sandstone carved figures. The statues stood as if they represented sentries standing watch over the temple chambers beneath.

The diamond saw marks, or kerfs, made by the modern engineers who moved the whole monument, seemed barely visible. The enormity of the modern cutting, hauling, and reassembling tasks, several hundred feet above its original location down on the banks of the Nile, probably would have impressed the original architects and builders of about 1296 BC. Even the fractured and fallen torso and head of one of the Ramesses II statues had been carefully hauled and placed exactly as it fell centuries ago.

Inside the temple itself, most walls were carved with scenes of great victorious battles from Ramesses's life. However, in the back of the temple sat carved figures of the Gods, with Ramesses, the God – king, sitting among them. I was told that on, and only on, February 23rd and October 23rd, the sun's rays reached back to the statue area, streaming through the front temple doors, to illuminate the statue of Ramesses only.

Careful regard to orientation during temple reassembly kept the sun's choice of Ramesses, over the other Egyptian Gods, intact!

The Queen's Temple stood nearby. It seemed small compared to the Ramesses effort, but the

The entrance to the Ramesses II Temple

The Temple interior as seen from the entrance

statues still towered at 30 feet in height. Again, of the six statues, four depicted Ramesses and the other two, Nefertari, his favorite wife.

One had to squint his eyes to imagine these massive temples sitting down on the banks of the Nile, with the river waters lapping at Ramesses's feet. How overpowering the statues must have been when approached in an ancient river craft!

Sandia felt so elated at our visit to Abu Simbel that the long crowded ride back to Aswan didn't seem to bother her. Witnessing the results of a concerted international effort, costing about 17 million U.K. pounds, and consuming four and one-half years, to save the ancient wonders, made our long taxi ride back to Aswan seem pretty insignificant in comparison.

A couple of days later in Aswan, we met our *wontoks*, Caroline and Kelly. Over a dinner of Egyptian brown beans and rice, the four of us decided to hire a felucca and its captain for a sail down the Nile to Luxor, also called Thebes. The felucca had to be the best way to experience the ancient times, traveling and sleeping on a four-sided sailing craft – four Yanks with an Egyptian skipper to lead the way.

Two mornings later, the four of us carried our back-packs on board a small felucca we'd hired to begin our journey down the Nile River. Our skipper, Achmad, greeted us with a big smile. He dressed in full, pale-blue robes with a white tur-

Our hired felucca on the Nile

(l to r) Caroline, Achmad, Kelly, and me at the tiller (photo by Sandia)

ban on his head. Achmad directed us to a storage space towards the bow for our gear, pushed off, and we soon got underway, leaving only a gentle wake, and Aswan, behind us.

The journey to Thebes took two nights and three days. Achmad manned the rudder, or tiller, almost full time. When he prepared our meals, mostly porridges and Egyptian stews, Achmad let me take the tiller to tack his felucca down the Nile. During those periods, I became aware that he watched me, or just sensed where we were, as I maintained our zigzag course and, even though he stared down at his cooking, would voice a warning if he thought I zigged too close to the riverbank. Achmad's felucca represented his life and livelihood. He didn't want it damaged in any way or run aground. When he wasn't cooking, he remained at the tiller, unless, of course, he lay in sleep when we moored for the night at some convenient spot near the riverbank.

On the second afternoon of our felucca trip, the ladies asked Achmad if there was anyway we could come up with a few beers to celebrate our trip that night. He thought for a minute, then replied that a small village ahead might yield our request.

Shortly thereafter, with the felucca moored near the river's edge and the three ladies remaining as security, Achmad and I set out walking toward the village he had in mind. Two stops in the village, with Achmad chattering with shopkeepers, yielded no beer, but he said they told him in the very next settlement some could be found. Off we walked, through the desert sands, away from the river, for another 20 to 30 minutes, until we came upon a small cluster of low clay-bricked buildings. We were led into the back courtyard of one of the buildings, where a *chador* covered woman reached into an old cardboard box to produce four dusty brown bottles with the standard Egyptian Star beer labels. Achmad bargained and I paid the very reasonable price. The woman seemed happy when I placed the few Egyptian pounds in her hand. I don't think a bustling economy existed back in her small village. Maybe we started something!

Upon returning to the felucca, carrying the four warm "found" beers, we quickly strung them out behind the boat to cool in the waters of the Nile and set off in the approaching dusk down the Nile. Achmad started preparing what he said would be a special stew, while I handled the tiller in what now seemed a familiar tacking routine. At one point, with the sky darkening, while watching some activity on the riverbank, I pushed the tiller to take us back through the river's centerline.

Suddenly Achmad yelled, then ran back to grab the tiller from me. He pointed ahead into the evening twilight at a large dark shape approaching us from downriver. Soon lights and windows became visible. A huge tourist excursion boat headed straight for us! With little wind in evidence, it seemed our sail wouldn't get us out of the way in time, but accepting a little help from the river current, we cleared the big boat by maybe ten to twenty yards.

We all looked up through the large viewing windows of the excursion vessel as it passed so

close we could see the expressions on people's faces as they lifted cocktails, in air conditioned comfort, to toast their comfortable journey up the Nile River. They smiled and laughed, oblivious to the fact that far below them in a small felucca, which rocked in their wake, four backpacking travelers raised their fists in defiance and reflection on the difference in traveling lifestyles. Using our mode of travel, we touched the Nile and villages close to its banks, smelled and tasted its essence, felt the vibrancy of life those waters gave to the surrounding desert, while the big tour boat mode tasted the dulling response of a martini, served in air-conditioned comfort.

As the excursion boat's lights faded upriver, Sandia laughed as I joked that those passengers probably would be flown to Abu Simbel from Aswan, never knowing the fun of a cramped taxi ride through the hot desert for a round trip of 340 miles! Sandia and I hugged, while agreeing we'd rather do it our way, but some day, just for the fun of it, maybe we'd take a first class journey somewhere. The moment seemed fitting to open those four lukewarm beers and raise our own toasts to friends, family, Egypt, our savior captain Achmad, and the star studded night under the Egyptian sky, while sailing down the Nile River towards Thebes. Exploring and sharing with a couple of *wontoks* like Kelly and Caroline felt exciting. We traded life's stories into the wee hours. Later, sleeping on the hard boat deck that night, with Sandia in my arms, seemed just a little bit softer, as our spirits uplifted our physical selves.

The four of us waved goodbye to Achmad the next day from a small boat dock in the Luxor/Thebes area. His felucca sail had become small in the distance when we finally turned and walked toward the city area, feeling the solid ground underfoot, stretching out some leg muscles that hadn't seen a lot of use in the last three days. A long deep rest soon followed lodgings and food, easily found, on a bed with a mattress.

The next morning, leaving our big frame packs with hotel security, the four of us set out on rented bicycles, with small backpacks, to explore the Valley of the Kings. In this valley resided the underground tombs of many of the Pharaohs, the most famous of which was King Tutankhamon, or King Tut. The ride on gravel roads proved hot and demanding. Many tourist buses passed us, leaving one choking in the dust of their billowing exhausts. Our bikes appeared old and well used. The spanner (adjustable) wrench I'd thrown into my backpack turned out to be a blessing along those bumpy dirt roads.

That trusty wrench fixed several bicycle breakdowns and chain throws.

In spite of our early start, by the time we made the center of the tomb area, lots of tourists already lined up at the tomb entrances. The tombs themselves seemed a little too crowded for comfort. We perspired freely climbing hun-

*Life along the
Nile River*

dreds of stairs down into and up out of the deep tombs, through the humid air created by packing so many tourists bodies into small rooms far below the Valley's surface. I remembered my physics and the fact that every average human body put off the same heat as a 100-watt light bulb. Lots of 100-watt light bulbs crawled around the tombs that day!

In the tombs, the paintings on the walls surrounding the coffin bearing sarcophagi really grabbed my attention. The texts of the paintings had names like, "Book of the Underworld, Book of the Gates, etc." The purpose of the Books, implied by tomb guides, lay in the re-education of the pharaoh as he awoke to the afterlife needing to know what to do and how to act. I guess they felt he might forget some things as he visited death for some undetermined length of time while waiting to be ushered into the life hereafter. Many a faithful servant was killed and buried in side rooms of those tombs. Guess the pharaohs didn't figure to know how to take care of themselves or do manual labor in the afterlife either. Coffins of gold were topped with the sculptured facial likeness of their occupants, probably so the Creator could look down and recognize who to "lift up," as if He couldn't see through the gold of the coffin itself.

The Tomb of Tutankhamon, perhaps the most popular, turned out to be the most crowded. The tomb seemed just too famous not to be patient while waiting in line. It consisted of only four small rooms from which a wealth of funerary objects had been moved to the museum in Cairo. King Tut, himself, still laid there to welcome us from inside his gold coffin set into the sarcophagus. Our trusty guidebook told us that the twelve baboons painted on the chamber walls guarded the King through the twelve hours of darkness each night. Evidently, tomb robbers never discovered King Tut's Tomb, as they did most of the others, and hence it yielded some wonderful objects, as well as insight, into the King's life and beliefs.

On the bicycle trip back from the Valley of the Kings, we stopped to walk through the ruins of the

The Valley of Kings

Temple of Ramesses II – also known as Ramesses the Great. I remember standing before the gigantic fallen statue of the king. An Egyptian guide told us of the fallen statue's inspiration to the English poet Shelley, whose poem we looked up:

Two vast and trunkless legs of stone
Stand in the desert…Near them on the sand,
Half sunk, a shattered visage lies, whose frown,
And wrinkled lip, and sneer of cold command,
Tell that its sculptor well those passions read
Which yet survive, stamped on those lifeless things…
And on the pedestal these words appear:
'My name is Ozymandias, king of kings:
Look on my works, ye Mighty, and despair!'
Nothing beside remains. Round the decay
Of that colossal wreck, boundless and bare
The lone and level sands stretch far away.

An apt poem for man's ego etched into a fallen 1,000 ton statue of one's self.

Two days of pedaling rickety bicycles and climbing down stairs and then up from underground tombs left the four of us a little burned out on Egyptian Pharaohs and their Queens. Happy to have visited the ancient cultures of Thebes along the Nile River, all of us felt, however, ready to move on. Kelly and Caroline headed back to Cairo, while Sandia and I decided to travel to the Red Sea to investigate whether the diving justified all the favorable press it had received.

The two of us took a bus for Hurghada, on the coast of the Red Sea, about 250 kilometers northeast of Luxor/Thebes. On the bus trip across the desert, I found myself deep in to Michener's book, Alaska. As many backpackers do, when they are not trading paperbacks, I ripped off sections of the book as I completed them and left them in trash bins along the way, for backpack weight considerations. Anyway, the bush pilot, LeRoy, in Michener's novel, really ignited my appetite for flying again. I vowed to Sandia at the time, that somehow, I'd finish my flying lessons and one-day in the future, the two of us would soar high in the sky and reach our hands toward the face of the sun. In her always-supportive way, Sandia responded with, "I know you'll do it and, besides, you will make a great pilot."

The diving off the coast of Hurghada turned out a bit less than spectacular. Maybe another spot would have been better, I don't know, but the undersea lacked color and much aquatic life at all. Boat guides attributed the conditions to the use of explosives (dynamite) by local fishermen. Seems as if nets and fishhooks didn't yield sufficient catches, so more drastic methods became necessary. Can't see how dynamite fishing would be good for the future of the industry as a whole, but what does a landlubber like me know about it?

Sandia and I left Egypt behind, and I must note, sadly, to head back to Athens, where we caught a flight to England, and from there, flew to New Delhi, India on our round-the-world tickets. Sandia talked most of the way to India about Egypt and how she would have liked to become an Egyptologist. Myself, I just felt lucky and privileged to have visited Egypt the way we did.

chapter forty

The Asian Tour

Arriving in New Delhi, the capital city of India, we set our feet down within the most populated democracy in the world. At nearly a billion people, it appeared to Sandia and me that most of India's population hung out in and around New Delhi. Words like teeming, swarming, and crammed seemed more fitting to use than simply "crowded" to describe the conditions in New Delhi. People slept on beds, outside, near the streets, in front of already crowded buildings. The strong smell of urine permeated one's nostrils as you walked many of the city's sidewalks. For two Colorado Mountain people, the sea of humanity we witnessed stood in stark contrast to anything we had ever experienced before. Our senses peaked to the differences in sights, smells, sounds, tastes,

from mountain tops, above the clouds, to far beaches

kissed by blue-green seas, adventure reaches

The crowded streets of New Delhi

and even touches.

During the ensuing days, as we ventured forth from our backpackers' quarters, named Ringo's, on the roof of a building we found via our ever present Lonely Planet guidebook, Sandia and I encountered another aspect of India for which we felt a bit unprepared. It came by way of the number of people begging on the streets. In other countries, we'd encountered beggars on a smaller scale, usually fairly passive in nature. In New Delhi, however, it required artful skills on our part to dodge the aggressive, reaching hands aimed at and into our pockets and rucksacks. Women, with small children and babies in one arm, would press in on you on the streets, trying to pluck something of value from your pockets or packs. Sandia, ever the kindest of hearts, handed out many, many rupees on those streets, but it eventually got to her – the need to physically dodge those reaching, clutching, hands. Some days, it became a chore to walk to a restaurant and back to our lodgings. Maybe the begging action just manifested from the section of the city we walked in, but I don't think so.

Something I ate in one of those restaurants made me violently ill for several days. The sickness resulted in a nightmare of unending vomit and diarrhea. A fellow backpacker, who'd just returned from trekking in Nepal, gave me some of the medicine (antibiotics and Immodium)

Those antiquities contained such a great history. The mark made by the British cannonball that brought India to its knees in surrender could still be seen inside the Red Fort. The marbled splendor of the Taj looked so magnificent. I got a kick out of having to secretly video a short view of the Taj Mahal (no video cameras allowed), only to find vendors selling high priced videotapes at the exit area, tapes that wouldn't even work in an American VCR. What enormous industry tourism represents in so many countries.

A striking part of India's culture lies in the existence of so many different religious sects. Sandia and I visited Hindu and Sikh Temples

The Taj Mahal at a distance and then closer in

he had carried into the remote Himalayan Mountains. The medicine cured me, but the illness left me in an unbelievably weakened state. Days passed before strength finally ebbed its way back into my depleted body. That would be my only bout with sickness on the entire trip, but it provided lesson enough to make me a believer. We would later acquire similar medicines to add to our first aid pack and carry them religiously into our remote ventures.

One couldn't leave India without visiting the Red Fort in Agra and the nearby Taj Mahal.

asking enough questions to try to understand the fundamental beliefs of those religions. We put the answers to our questions together with a continuing study of Huston Smith's paperback on the world's religions, which had an ever present place in my backpack. Out of respect for the many cultures we passed through, as well as self examination of our own spiritual values, we felt the importance of staying aware of the people around us and what provided meaning in their lives.

Buddha was born a Hindu before he

309

achieved Nirvana, the enlightened state, and went on to establish another approach to knowing God. Gautama Buddha told his followers that he was not the God, but had only reached a state of perfect enlightenment. They too could achieve this state from the inherent suffering of life by mental and moral self-purification. As humans, I think, we find it difficult to believe that each of us does not have some divine purpose or destiny, that our lives don't have significance in the grand scale of it all, that we are somehow different from, let's say, a beautiful flower that grows from seed to blossom, and when its season is over, dies, returning to the very soil, that brought forth its life. I met travelers, who made annual visits to India in order to spend time in contemplation with their gurus. One American psychiatrist carried in his wallet, and excitedly shared with me, a picture of his white haired, white bearded and white turbaned guru. Every six months the psychiatrist looked forward to his pilgrimage to India and the peace he found in the teachings of his guru. He then went back to his stressful job in the States, making it through another six months, before needing that peaceful recharging he found in India.

Sikhism became another religion that found its roots in Hinduism, growing under the influence of Islam. The Sikhs believe in monotheism, rejecting idolatry and caste, or social classes. It seemed remarkable to Sandia and me that the Sikhs produced the mechanics that kept the Indian railway system in such great repair. The trains introduced during British Colonialism, so long ago, still ran smoothly and efficiently, under the careful maintenance program of gifted, and well trained, Sikh mechanics. An Indian railroad executive informed me that, almost without exception, Sikhs accomplished all train repairs. An interesting clique, to say the least.

My lady and I boarded one of those Sikh

maintained steam locomotive driven trains to head east for Gorakhpur and the Nepalese border. The Himalayas beckoned to us that the time for trekking had arrived. We left New Delhi in the late evening enjoying the inexpensive luxury of a well-kept, private, sleeping compartment. Those Brits sure knew how to travel during colonial times. The construction of each main railroad station had included comfortable sleeping rooms that now were made available to tired tourists, journeying through the sizable country, at modest rates.

We awoke from each other's embrace the next morning to gaze out at the Indian countryside. What a stark contrast the landscape presented when compared to the overcrowded cities. I guess there has to be a lot of farmland to feed the massive population. Each small village that we "clickity clacked" through appeared a bit impoverished with tumbling down walls and thatched roofs, in need of repair. It seemed every small home's trash was thrown out their back door onto an ever growing pile of refuse. I clearly remember the thought that surfaced in my consciousness as I gazed out at India's abrupt realities, "*There, but for the Grace of God, go I.*" The happenstance of our birth, the dreams and sacrifices of our ancestors, gave Sandia and me the chance to be backpacking travelers through a distressed, impoverished, and struggling world. We talked of our good fortune, against the backdrop of the Indian countryside, and felt truly thankful to be in a position to touch the world, while appreciating the opportunities we have. It's too easy sometimes to take our lots in life for granted.

After leaving the train in Gorakhpur and taking a short bus ride, we stood gazing at the Nepalese border. The view provided an amazingly simple scene; a small hut manned by Nepalese police, a long tree branch across the road, supported on shoulder high posts either side of the dirt road. Two young dusty boys played badminton back and forth over the horizontal tree branch, serving as the border marker. As the police stamped our passports and waved us through, the laughter of the badminton playing boys resonated in our ears, while their smiles played in our hearts. We found each other's eyes and, without a word, knew Nepal would be a special experience. The spirit of the people had already touched us.

We jumped on a pressingly crowded bus for Kathmandu, only to end up riding on the roof by our own choice, amongst the many pieces of luggage. The clear air and sunshine stroked and warmed our bodies as we rode northeast for Nepal's capital city. What a way to see the country! I also had the thought that if the bus should roll down one of the many embankments it came close to, we could probably jump to safety a lot easier from the roof, rather than the packed interior.

At each stop the bus made, a bevy of vendors descended on us selling all sorts of snacks and fruits. At one such stop, a young girl, maybe six or seven years old, shyly stood back from the older yelling vendors, holding some orange fruits to be sold. Her eyes locked onto mine with an expression of hope. When I reached down from the back of the bus and handed her a Nepalese rupee in exchange for a piece of fruit, her teeth suddenly showed in a most brilliant, but still shy smile. We waved to her as the bus began to move and watched as her hand raised to return our gesture. Her smile lit up the countryside. The shyness of that beautiful smile traveled with us throughout Nepal and onwards.

Kathmandu proved awesome. The accommodations seemed made for backpackers. We spent several days at the Kathmandu Guest House talking and learning from other travelers coming and going from treks into the Himalayas.

View from the top of the Nepalese bus

The smile of our little vendor (center of photo)

Embroidered T-shirts, made exclusively by male sewers, sold at a rapid clip to trekkers looking for souvenirs of their experience in Nepal. I remember seeing the words of a Grateful Dead song, "What a long strange trip it's been!" emblazoned across the chest of a backpacker. My partner in life and I decided to head west for a trek into the Annapurna Range, or Himal, rather than east to the popular Mt. Everest base camp climb. A couple more days of careful shopping and packing completed, we headed west from Kathmandu, by bus, to a village called Pokhara, settled calmly beneath the high peaks of the Annapurna Himal, to make ready for our Himalayan trek.

Pokhara consists of a small picturesque village located beside a large blue-green lake named Phewa Tal. Sandia and I found a comfortable inn that had a roof garden/patio, where we could stare in amazement at the high mountains just north of us. The closest, and most dramatic, peak, called Machhapuchhare, or the "Fish Tail" rose above the others. From Pokhara, it appeared to have only one sharp summit at 22,942 feet (6,993 m), but we would see during our trek west of the peak, that it indeed had a second summit and looked very much like the tail of a fish. With Pokhara's elevation at about 3,000 feet (915 m), the Fish Tail towered approximately 20,000 feet (6,098 m) above us. There exist higher peaks behind Machhapuchhare in the Annapurna Himal, up to 26,545 feet (8,091 m), but they lay further north, thus not so overpowering to Pokhara as the Fish Tail.

The food and desserts in Pokhara seemed surprisingly tasty, as we would find them to be all along the trekking routes. In years past, other trekkers (hippie types) taught the lodges to make everything from apple pie and chocolate cake, to Mexican and Israeli foods. Trekkers needed tasty "munchies" for strength and stamina, as well as pure delight, and had taken the time to instruct local cooks how to make up their favorite foods, or close variations thereof, depending on local supplies. Word always spread along the trails regarding lodges with flavorful food.

At our own lodge, we rented, for a small sum, two light weight goose down sleeping bags that would zip together. They would strap neatly under my big frame pack to keep us warm at higher elevations. The inn also provided a secure storage room for the extra gear we wouldn't need to carry in the high mountains. The rented sleeping bags aired out in the sun on the roof of our lodge before we crammed them into their respective "stuff" bags. Suddenly, we became

The Fish Tail (top center) as seen from Pokhara

very anxious to be on our way – all our maps and trekking gear sat there packed and ready. We would leave early the next morning. Sandia laid down for a nap, anticipating the days of walking and climbing that lay ahead.

Unable to sleep myself, I wandered into the lodge's garden to find a seat on the grass and dreamily reflect on my life, as I gazed up at the mountain peaks in front of me. The innkeeper, seeing my presence in his flower garden, came to sit with me. He asked politely, in decent English, about my origins. Our conversation evolved to God and His meaning in each of our lives. I soon found myself in deep admiration of this "simple" innkeeper from a small village in Nepal. His words remain with me today.

"You see that mountain up there?" he said pointing at Machhapuchhare. "God is on top of that mountain!" speaking metaphorically. "Our purpose in this life is to climb that mountain and to look upon His face and come to know His will. Nothing else matters. You and I will take different paths up that mountainside because I am a Buddhist and you are a Christian. I do not know whose path is easier, or more difficult. We walk the path we are taught. It doesn't matter the difficulty of the climb, only that we make it to the top, and come to know God!"

Tears wet my uplifted cheeks, as my eyes saw a misty Fish Tail through them. My mind thought of so many religions that selfishly preached their doctrines as the only way to God. Here in a flower garden, in a small village, under the mighty Himalayas, an uncomplicated Buddhist innkeeper had given me a truth so profound – it only mattered that we make it to the top of the mountain, regardless of the path, and reach up to touch the face of God. Searching for the "right" path is a waste of energy. Use the one you know, along with the energy you have, and start climbing up the path!

My trekking buddy and I left early the next morning, full of energy and anticipation. Our trail the first day took us past laughing naked children bathing in a public fountain at Pokhara's outskirts, past wonderful waterfalls, cascading down carved out rock formations, through lush green vegetation, up to the settlement of Lumle, at about 5,300 feet (1,613 m). We also passed during that first day, Chinese workers hard at the labor of building a road that led I don't know where, but obviously worked on their project with the Nepalese Government's approval. Maybe the work represented a form of foreign aid?

Our double bed, small room at a Lumle lodge cost us all of five cents U.S. A young Nepalese lady, who couldn't have been more than twelve years old, cooked us a fine, tasty, nourishing meal of *dal baht*, consisting of rice, greens, lentils, and potatoes. It became our meal of choice during the upcoming days. Usually *dal baht* cost twenty-five cents U.S. and your plate would be refilled until you finally signaled "enough." Our young cook, waitress, and lodge keeper also made us a fresh Nepali bread, kind of like a pita bread, in a clay outdoor oven. We snuggled in and slept soundly after the uphill sixteen kilometers we'd trekked our first day

out. My frame pack, which I guessed in the 18 to 22-kilogram (39 to 44-pound) range, took a little getting used to. In maybe four more nights of reading, I would transfer Michener's book, Texas, to some lodge's bookshelf, in exchange for a smaller, less weighty, book. Our prevailing thought that night as we slipped into a tired dreamland resounded as, *"We have started on a trek into the Himalayan Mountains of Nepal."*

The second day out took us to the village named Chandrakot, at 5,125 ft. (1,563 m.) and then down to Birethanti, at 3,400 ft. (1,037 m.). After that, the trail moved us steadily upward through the tiny settlements of Tirkhedhunge to Ulleri, with a stop at Banthanti (meaning rest stop in Nepalese) for a hearty lunch. There we met a Kiwi (New Zealander) named John, a devoted "birder" (bird watcher). We soon left John behind, as his interests focused on the tree

Looks like an excellent place to stay

branches above, while our focus remained on the rock steps ahead, one foot in front of the other.

I should pause to describe to the reader that this was no ordinary trail. Rocks had been placed, probably in time long past, to form crude stairs on the uphill and downhill stretches, all the way to Tibet, and I'm sure, beyond. The trail could only be traversed on foot, or by the many donkeys and yaks that carried supplies to distant and remote villages. A passing donkey train gave the backpacking trekker a chance to sit down for a rest, as the packed animals passed on the narrow trail, one following the other, with a shouting "drover" at the rear. The lead donkey, or two, usually exhibited fine colored, tall, head plumage, which the following pack animals kept in sight. Many of the pack donkeys wore bells around their necks, so a rhythmic chiming of different sounding bells marked their passage. When they passed, it became quiet. You rose to your feet, pulled on your pack, and headed off again, a bit rested.

We soon learned and greeted each approaching traveler, foreigner or Nepalese, with the traditional greeting of the local people. Hands placed together, as if in prayer, with fingers fully extended (to make an upside down "V"), while saying the word, "*Namaste,*" meaning, "I salute the God within you." How beautiful and meaningful, the greeting of Nepal is. What a contrast from the Western world's "hi" or "have a nice day."

According to our trusty Lonely Planet guidebook, <u>Trekking in Nepal</u>, we reached our second day's destination – the village of Ghorapani – at about three in the afternoon. Our legs still felt strong enough to follow other trekkers' advice and went on another few kilometers or so up to the high pass ahead on our trail. There we found several lodges located on the pass summit allowing us to easily find accommodations at an inn

Nilgiri peak towering nearly 13,000 feet above us (at 10,000 feet)

called the Snow View.

The panorama from the pass, located just under 10,000 ft. (3,050 m.) in elevation truly took your breath away. The snowcapped peak of Dhaulagiri I at 26,795 ft. (8,167 m.) marked the westward extreme of our northward view. Sweeping one's eyes eastward (to the right), the peak of Nilgiri at 22,772-ft. (6,940 m.) was followed by the summits of the Annapurna Himal, with Annapurna I, the tallest at 26,545 ft. (8,091 m.). Even gazing from nearly 10,000 ft., the mountains in front of the mesmerized viewer dominated the sky, rising as much as 17,000-ft. above your eye level. The early evening setting sun gave the whole panorama a magnificent glow, almost surreal to one's mind focus. We stood staring at the majesty of the creation, thinking how the moving continent of India rammed into the Asian landmass causing this tremendous uplift. The force of impact that created the Himalayas must have wobbled the planet on its axis. My eight millimeter video camera recorded the whole scene for our memories, as only seeing is believing. The view proved so awesome and humbling at the same time, making the expenditure of precious camera battery power a given. Then darkness brought the panoramic curtain down.

The Snow View Inn had glass windows, a first on the trek, as well as a large wood-fired stove, around which gathered many of the Inn's trekking guests for the night. Many of us washed some clothes in furnished buckets of hot water, hanging them on clotheslines near the big stove to dry. We sipped on cups of hot coffee milk, ate plates of *dal bhat*, and, of course, related stories of our journeys and lives with each other. That's what you do, sitting around a warm woodstove at night on a high pass in the Nepalese Himalayas.

One male trekker's story from that night still sticks curiously in my mind. Seems his trekking party, which included his girl friend, had climbed over Thorung Pass ahead of us (he came from the direction in which we were going), whose summit peaked at 17,700 ft. (5,415 m.). Somehow his girl friend became separated from him, falling behind. Her feet and boots became wet from the snow, but she plodded on, not stopping to dry or take care of her footgear – probably trying to catch up with him at his faster pace. The end result of the story revealed that upon getting over and down from the pass to the mountain village of Muktinath (our destination), his girl friend suffered a severe case of frostbite. She had to be lifted out of Muktinath by helicopter and, after emergency treatment for her blackened feet and several fingers, boarded a flight back to her home in New Zealand. Sandia and I looked at one another in amazement, wondering why he remained there, telling

the story, instead of being on the plane with his lady heading for New Zealand. The story teller made some comment to another listener regarding the importance of the trek to him, how long he'd waited to come to Nepal, as Sandia and I kind of shook our heads in bewilderment. There is nothing more important to me in this world than my lady and our children. Mountains, spectacular as they are, still are only mountains. They won't go away. There are no circumstances under which I would ever have put the injured person of my lady on a plane home, while I continued my mountain trek. In fact, I would not have allowed Sandia to fall behind on that journey over Thorung Pass. I would have taken the shirt off my back to kneel down and dry her feet. I would have carried her on my back. I'm not trying to sound like a hero, but I know I would certainly be on any emergency flight sitting close to her, helping to share and ease her pain. Relationships of love become so deep and lasting when they are important to both the participants. That Kiwi trekker's story left me realizing how contrastingly different people's perspectives on life can be. I remember Sandia and I snuggled even closer that night in our zipped together, toasty, sleeping bags, appreciating the life and love we shared with each other.

The next day, our third day out, we covered only about ten kilometers, but the trail steadily dropped a winding, relentless downhill, giving up almost 6,000 feet of elevation, taking us to the village of Tatopani on the western bank of the Kali Gandaki River. That welcome name Tatopani means "hot springs" in the Nepalese language. My calves felt "hurtin" for certain. Downhill is, often times, tougher to trek than uphill. At a "trail talk" recommended lodge in Tatopani, we found a vacant room on the third floor. Navigating those two flights of stairs tore at my leg muscles. Once in the room, I dropped off the big frame pack (which later weighed in at 25 kilos, or 55 pounds, on an airport scale), to lie on our bed, stretching out my rebellious leg muscles. Sandia showed up a little while later with a monster piece of rich, dark, chocolate cake to lift my spirits. I liked Tatopani from that first bite of delicious cake. Its nourishment went straight to the aching muscles.

Later that night, we ate "hybrid" Mexican food, washed down with a cold Nepalese beer. The two beers seemed slightly overpriced, but considering they'd come in on a porter's back, or in a donkey's pack, they tasted well worth their cost. Over dinner, Sandia and I declared the next day a "Hot Springs" holiday – no trekking allowed! Sleep came easily to our tired bodies, as visions of spectacular mountains played on a wide mind screen in our dreams.

The layout of the Hot Springs couldn't have been better. Natural pools in the rocks provided hot, very hot, and really, really hot alternatives, along with a separate warm soapy pool for doing laundry by hand. Immediately adjacent to the hot pools flowed the icy cold, powerful waters of the Kali Gandaki River. A cold plunge following the really hot pool sent my sore leg muscles into ecstatic vibrations.

Later, after several hot/cold plunges, with our laundry done and laid out on the rocks to dry in the brilliant sun, we got to chatting with other travelers resting by the edge of the hot pools. One of the trekkers we met neared the end of his journey (traveling opposite to us), as well as his vacation, and was due back soon to his job at Boeing in Seattle. Sandia came up with another great fun idea, when she heard him mention Boeing Aircraft. Our friend, Geoffrey worked at Boeing as one of their lawyers in the Labor Relations Department. Once I'd mailed a letter to Geoffrey from our old P. O. Box 1, Mount Hagen, Western Highlands Province, Papua New

View down to Tatopani (far center left in the river gorge)

Guinea address, which he seemed sure constituted either a fake, or that I'd talked some missionary into mailing it for me. He wrote back, and being the comic that he is, challenged me if I was really in the mountains of New Guinea, to address a coconut and send it to him. I never accepted the challenge, although tempted, because the local P.N.G. post office guy told me it wouldn't make it to Seattle due to their laws regarding germs, parasites, or something like that. Now though, Sandia saw our new Boeing acquaintance as a chance to get a letter from the Himalayan village of Tatopani in Nepal to Geoffrey via Boeing's interoffice mail system. He'd surely wonder how we managed to accomplish this one. There on the rocks, beside the hot pools, we composed a letter to Geoffrey and family then handed it over to our special courier, while assuring him that no recourse would come to him. We'd take responsibility. He laughed, saying it appeared a fun plot and he would happily get the letter into the Boeing internal mail system on his first day back.

I have to pause to tell the reader why our special Boeing courier showed a little reluctance at first to deliver our letter. In short, our friend Geoffrey's dad, Malcom, at the time was the "head honcho" (CEO) of Boeing, and our courier knew the connection well. Whether he believed our friendly relationship with Geoffrey or not, he knew in the internal mail system, the sender of an interoffice envelope could remain anonymous. If he knew Malcom, he wouldn't have worried.

The first time I'd met Geoffrey's mom and dad, and, in fact, grandmother was at a Christmas Eve family dinner at their home on Puget Sound. We made a short visit to see Geoffrey, his wife Mollie, and their three boys at the time. Knowing only that Geoff's dad worked as some kind of a Boeing boss, as per Sandia's passing remarks (her ex attended law school with Geoffrey), I baked two of my special pumpkin pies so as to contribute to the family dinner. When the time came to leave for his dad's house, I dressed in my usual, sort of decent, blue jeans,

My lady getting used to hot springwater

then jumped into the back seat of Geoffrey's car, to sit next to Sandia, while carefully balancing a pie on each knee during the car ride. I remember going through a security gate, then pulling up to a large, estate type, house. Already becoming self-conscious about my jeans, not to mention the homemade pies I balanced in my two palms, we walked into the entryway. Staring up at me from a small entry table were a few Christmas cards. One in particular caught my eye. Queen Elizabeth and Prince Philip signed it below their picture. Now I really became self-conscious, standing there in my jeans and carrying pies.

To make a long story short, I felt so welcome that night it seemed awesome. After dinner, Geoffrey's dad walked me out on their lawn, next to Puget Sound, to ask my advice on a lap pool that he'd contracted to be built as a Christmas present for his wife. He had heard of my "inflated" building talents from Geoffrey's dinner story of my unsolicited reconstruction work to shore up the foundation of the back porch at his house. (Hey, Sandia and I always work for our keep!). Anyway, I gave Malcom my humble opinions on his project and our conversations went on. He told me, the pie baker, that he baked all of his wife's bread as she had an allergy to certain grains. I also remember his mentioning that he made peanut brittle, from scratch, which he gave each of his vice presidents for Christmas cheer. I felt totally disarmed and at ease in his presence. There occurred also the expression of agony he felt because of impending layoffs of thousands of Boeing workers following the holiday season. For those of you that think all CEO's are cold and heartless when it comes to the business of running a large company, I can vouch otherwise, surely for one past

Boeing honcho. His family received top priority. He took care of them and made their friends feel warm and welcome in his home.

Back to Nepal, the next morning when we hit the trail out of Tatopani, two things happened. First, I couldn't believe how great my body felt, especially my legs. Their spring and strength came back, raring to go. Secondly, a trail dog adopted us. We called him "Tato," short for the village where he'd found us. It felt uplifting to have a tail wagging, black haired, short legged, trekking companion with us. Obviously, Tato knew the trail well. Also, we saw that he didn't like the pack burros passing us on the trail. Tato gave them plenty of clearance when they got anywhere close to us.

The lodging signs in Marpha were good for a chuckle

Tato fought his way through the array of various settlement dogs appearing along our up-hill route beside the Kali Gandaki River. On his first encounter with other dogs challenging Tato's right of passage, I ran to stand with him against three good sized, snarling, dogs trying to back him down. Before I could reach him, however, Tato lit into the three of them, sending them all scurrying back into their village, tails between their legs. From then on, we knew our newly found trekking buddy could hold his own, letting him lead the way proudly up the trail ahead. We learned, a couple of days later, that Tato lived on the trail, adopting trekkers who fed him, traveling back and forth along the same trail he knew so well. Obviously, he'd backed off the same village dogs any number of times.

*Himalayan village children on
"The roof of the World"*

Sandia taking a photo of me near the Tibetan border
(The women didn't want their photos taken)

In Tatopani, we decided that I'd continue to carry our big frame pack. I felt the workout and the conditioning of the trekking rigor seemed well worth the effort. Some other trekkers used porters, available all along the route, to carry frame packs, children, or whatever. They charged about one U.S. dollar per day plus lodgings, in addition to picking up their gambling debts, which could amount to who knows what. Always the independent ones, with area map in hand, we would find the way towards Tibet on our own. Sandia carried some of her essentials in a small backpack and I carried the rest. That way, we remained self-contained and could move at whatever pace we decided, stopping whenever we had the notion – the only way to go!

The next few days we covered the upsloping trail at better than fifteen kilometers per day, stopping at some remote, but comfortable little lodges, always on the recommendations of trekkers passing us, coming down the trail. Sleeping in the villages of Ghasa and Marpha, each morning we found faithful Tato waiting outside for us, or truer probably, the remnants of the breakfast we brought him. At the lodge we

chose in Marpha, a village located in the Lo Montang (the mustang) near the Tibetan border, two other couples also stayed the night at our lodge. One young couple hailed from Germany and the other, Finland.

The table setting at the lodge bears description. The tablecloth was actually a blanket; large enough that the portion hanging down from the table's edge provided ample material to tuck around one's waist, letting all our legs and fannies be enclosed within a table topped tent enclosure. Under the center of the table sat a large urn, into which lodge workers periodically added hot glowing coals. The setup provided a pleasant, warm place to linger over food and hot drinks. Both the couple from Germany and Finland spoke reasonable English, allowing us to swap life stories. Both couples expressed envy for our American spirit, as they called it. They'd all recently completed University studies and were now expected to get on with careers, not travel. The German couple, I remember, both worked in the medical field – one in medicine and the other in psychiatry. They'd recently married, and chose Nepal for a long honeymoon, explaining there would never be another chance to travel for them again, as it went against cultural beliefs and parental teachings. The young Finnish couple described similar demands on their "debt" to Finnish family and society. "You Americans seem so free to do whatever you want. Look at the two of you, traveling around the world for however long you want! You're not even on a honeymoon."

We defended our position only mildly, admitting that the freedom of the American culture is one of its greatest attributes, where a person could be, and do, whatever they wanted, as long as they worked to support the goals that appeared important to them. So many nations we'd traveled through professed the stereotype that all Americans chased the almighty "dollar." Many in the developing nations, such as New Guinea, thought all citizens of the U.S.A. possessed super wealth, probably based on the travelers they'd seen, or maybe served in some capacity. We assured our German and Finnish lodge companions that most Americans were, like them, devoted to their work, families, and the "American Dream." Only a small percentage of us Yanks gave high priority to lengthy world travel or overseas employment. Our lodge mates went on to ask many questions regarding our years of work in Papua New Guinea. They seemed particularly interested in the living conditions of an expatriate, even though they felt they'd never have the opportunity, or maybe wouldn't want it anyway. Sandia and I always welcomed the chance to glean insights into the perspectives of other cultures, as it helped to shape and hone our own views on life. At that warm lodge table, one evening in Marpha, a mountain village high in the Nepalese Himalayas, it felt wonderful to be an American – "let freedom and spirit ring" – especially for this couple of hippie backpacking Yanks!

The next morning, our sixth out of Pokhara, the mountains greeted us sporting a fresh coat of snow. Warm bulky knit sweaters, along with lined pants, purchased in Kathmandu, kept us comfortable while trekking along at near freezing temperatures. We'd both opted for the lighter weight, ankle high, cross-trainers, leaving our heavier hiking boots behind. Not planning to climb over Thorung Pass, the cross-trainers proved their worth on the long uphill stretches of trail. Warm socks and the motion of walking provided our feet with plenty of generated heat. Brightly knitted mittens and skull pullovers,

complete with earflaps, kept our hands and heads pleasantly warm. Bright sunlight during the day also took the chill off the crispy morning temperature.

On we climbed, the Kali Gandaki River trail leading us through the fairly large settlement of Jomsom, where the famous Gurkha soldiers trained. We noted a couple of things about Jomsom, while passing through. There existed an airstrip there, served by STOL (short takeoff and landing) capable Twin Otter aircraft, as well as electrical power at the lodges. However, I'd left my video camera battery charging apparatus behind in Pokhara, for weight considerations, and would continue to ration my carried battery power for notable footage. We had understood, obviously incorrectly, that no electrical power existed in villages along our Annapurna route. The airstrip presented an alternative to retracing our route on foot back to Pokhara. Afterall, we'd done the tough part, the uphill direction. Some trekkers flew to Jomsom and trekked down from there. We left it to discuss on the trail ahead.

Leaving Jomsom and the disappearing Tato behind us, Sandia and I trekked on toward our goal for the day, a place called Chyanche (pronounced chan-cha) on our map. The landscape quickly became stark and barren beyond Jomsom, void of trees and vegetation. Not one building did we pass. At one point, nearing late afternoon, we lost the poorly marked trail, following instead an incorrect draw that led to nowhere. Using precious time, with the approach of colder darkness, we retraced our steps, finally regaining the correct trail. In the darkness, with the temperature falling rapidly, a dim light became visible on the trail ahead. It turned out to be candlelight from the single small, low building that made up Chyanche. In the dark of night, the lodge provided a welcome sight, but turned out to be a little on the suspect side of

The mountain terrain beyond Jomsom

any accommodations we'd seen to date.

The sign over the door said Chyanche Lumbe, meaning "lonely hotel" in the local language. As we stepped through the door into the dimly lit, smoky, interior, our joy at finding lodgings for the night became tempered with a bit of fear due to the surroundings. A dried out animal, like a weasel, was nailed (impaled) intact with two spikes to the overhead beam under which we ducked to step into a room with two tables – the dining room. As we sat, the obviously unwashed and unkempt proprietress appeared to ask us if we'd like something to eat. Our eyes found each other. With a look, we knew our stomachs felt too hungry not to eat and ordered two plates of *dal bhat*. There seemed to be no other guests staying at Chyanche Lumbe, which

added to our feeling of discomfort.

A little later, the main door opened, as Sandia and I tiredly, but hungrily ate a fairly bland rendition of our trekking staple, *dal bhat*. From the blackness outside, in walked two male backpackers looking for food and lodgings. As they inquired of the proprietress for available rooms, we knew they hailed from Australia, and as it would turn out, the city of Newcastle. Their presence immediately took the edge off our discomfort, having other travelers staying the night at the lonely hotel, especially Aussies!

In conversation later, we learned that along the different route the Aussies traveled to arrive at Chyanche, this would be considered a decent hotel. Since we had come from the direction they headed, we gave them names of lodges that they'd find really "posh" in comparison. They seemed excited about prospects on the trail ahead for them. They had been on the trail for several weeks and our description of the Hot Springs at Tatopani came as exhilarating news for them. We shouted our mates a beer and exchanged travel stories for a couple of hours. Sandia and I finally told them, "Good on you mates – time for us to sleep!"

After putting the lodge furnished bedding into a room corner, we covered the lodge bed with two sheets we'd packed in. Then pulling our two down sleeping bags over us for warmth, we snuggled in for much needed sleep, still a tiny bit wary of what might live in the mattress below us.

Leaving the next morning, the eighth day on the trail, our set goal focused on a village named Muktinath about fifteen kilometers distant, but roughly 3,000 feet higher in elevation. In fact, Muktinath, our final destination, sat at the base of the western approach to Thorung Pass. From there, we would turn around and head back to Pokhara. We weren't equipped for, nor had we ever planned to climb over Thorung Pass and its nearby permanent glaciers. Muktinath would be plenty fine for us.

We climbed steadily away from Chyanche Lumbe and as the trail took an abrupt eastward turn from our northerly route, I turned back to look down on the lonely hotel. Standing thus, I heard Sandia's voice say, jokingly from behind me, "I'm always going to call that place – Caca Lumbe!" A good laugh always helps the spirit, especially on the uphill sections!

Sandia had been trekking along on a worsening sore foot, aggravated by the up slope that day. I took her pack, strapping it onto my chest, to ease the weight on her throbbing foot. She kept on like a trooper, one foot in front of the other, seldom complaining. After lunch in a small village, which included delicious yak

On the trail, looking toward the final destination of Muktinath

cheese, I mistakenly thought Muktinath was the settlement just ahead, only to reach it and see a sign telling us its name—Jharkot. Muktinath still lay five kilometers up ahead. It's a hard pill to swallow, when you tiredly think you've made your destination, only to find, instead, you've got a rigorous uphill five kilometers yet to trek.

Doubting my strength reserve, moving forward more out of stubbornness and resolve, I trudged through Jharkot, on up the trail beyond. On the trail ahead of me, I saw the familiar orange robes of a Buddhist monk. He walked alone, with shaved head bowed, obviously on his way to the Buddhist Shrine in Muktinath. Instead of the traditional sandals for footwear, his feet were clad in leather hiking boots, probably left behind, or given to him, by some foreign trekker.

The monk's pace seemed peaceful and steady. I fell in behind him a few meters, with Sandia right on my tail. I took up his pace. I thought I heard him humming, not a tune, but what you would call a mantra, over and over. My eyes focused on and followed those hiking boots, which sometimes remained at my eye level as the monk climbed the steep trail ahead. He never turned to look back at us, although he must have heard us behind him, in procession. We never talked, only walked. The monk provided a steady pace. I took strength from the peace and sound of his gait. There we went, right up to Muktinath, single file, steady, and the day's trek ended. The monk turned a corner in the village and silently disappeared. We never even saw his face, that monk who pulled us, led us, and drew us up the trail.

At our lodge later in Muktinath, we listened to travelers who'd come west over Thorung Pass, and were asked, and tempted, to join a group leaving early the next morning to head east over the Pass, but decided against it. We'd done our trek as planned. Our cross-trainers and clothing seemed inadequate for the climb over. Sandia's foot still felt buggered. We agreed to trek back down to Jomsom, catch a Twin Otter for Pokhara, and head back to Kathmandu, just in time for Christmas. Our friends, Jim and Mary Ann had their names on a standby list for a Christmas flight to Kathmandu from New Guinea, via Australia, to meet us. We didn't need to prove anything more by climbing over Thorung Pass, certainly not to each other. Muktinath had been our goal and we sat exhilaratingly there, high in the Nepalese Himalayas – trekking mission accomplished! I reached out my tall brown beer bottle to clink Sandia's, as our eyes locked in a deep smile.

Learning a bit from the village carpenters along the trail

On the way back to Jomsom, we fell in behind some yaks and their drovers, while talking over plans for the next phase of our trip. Did we want to go into Mainland China, or not? Planning provides half the fun. Next thing we knew, the drovers hopped on to the backs of their yaks, fording a river we'd come to. No big deal for them, as we watched them move away from the other shore. It became apparent, upon researching our map, that if we didn't cross there, we'd have to retrace several kilometers to get around. I slipped off my shoes, tying them around my neck, and stepped into the strong, incredibly icy current. The river rocks proved round and slippery. I almost went down, packs and all. Retreating to the bank, I pulled on a pair of flip-flops for traction. All of this action, I took just to ensure not having to walk the rest of the way with cold wet shoes and feet. I headed across again, with a little better traction this time. Sandia stood watching from my embarkation point, thinking about her own modus operandi. About mid-stream the current became so strong it ripped one of the flip-flops right off my foot in mid-step. Almost crotch deep, I slipped and plowed my way ahead, finally making the other bank in bare feet, the second flip-flop bobbing its way downstream. As I sat to pull on my dry socks and cross-trainers, I looked up to see Sandia, walking across the river, shoes and all, saying, "So what if my feet are wet. It feels good on my sore foot!" She was probably right. We turned, laughing, to follow the yak team, which, by now, had grown small in the distance.

My lady and I celebrated Christmas in Kathmandu on our own. Our friends, Jim and Mary Ann from New Guinea, never made it to Nepal to join us, due to heavy holiday flight traffic. Our Christmas Eve dinner, with a few trekking mates from Canada, turned out to be really memorable. The Abu Rami Restaurant posted a sign in their window advertising a Holiday "Torkey" dinner. We knew the spirited proprietor, Pancha, from our previous stay at the nearby Kathmandu Guest House. He loved joking with the foreign visitors, who frequented the Abu Rami. Pancha's staff laid out a great buffet dinner topped off with apple pie and homemade rice wine. The main course consisted of "torkey," as Pancha pronounced it, along with mashed potatoes, gravy, stuffing, and lots of vegetables. Pancha even walked up to our table, during the meal, to show us an ancient, slightly rusty, can of cranberry sauce, which he never opened! He just wanted to show it off. The can probably did the circuit of the half-dozen small tables in his restaurant every holiday season, when foreign customers dined there. The shared meal provided a great farewell to an awesome Nepal Himalayan trek.

Before leaving the wonderful city of Kathmandu, it proved necessary to visit two embassies, the American and the Indian. At the Embassy of the United States, they sewed twenty new pages into our passports, as all existing pages overflowed with rubber stamp marks and visas. The procedure didn't take long, only the waiting and paperwork. It had to be done only with their official machine. At the Indian Embassy, we applied for a new visa to enter their country. Our old one had expired, since we spent a long while in Nepal. We found it necessary to fly on from Delhi with our tickets. Trying to reroute from Kathmandu had proved impossible. Anyway, the Aussie in front of us at the visa window applied for another Indian entry visa, on top of the six months worth of visas he'd already used up. The Indian clerk/official told the Aussie, in a very pompous tone, "You have already been in India for six months. Why should I issue you another visa?"

To which, the Aussie, with a big smile, re-marked, "Well, India is a big country!"

The response, along with the smile, caused the clerk to laugh out loud. He forthwith reached for his official visa stamp and entered another entry permit into the Aussie's passport. The clerk shoved the passport back toward the owner and, still smiling, beckoned to us with, "Next in line!" I guess it pays to be friendly, as opposed to high and mighty, everywhere in the world. A joke and a smile can maybe disarm even a rigid bureaucrat.

A week later at midnight on New Year's Eve, Sandia and I, arm in arm, strolled along the streets of Hong Kong watching people shop. Horns tooted among the many cars on the busy streets, but basically people went on with their shopping. That's what they do in Hong Kong – buy things!

With a visa for Mainland China stamped into our new passport pages, we next headed north for Guangzhou (previously called Canton) to touch the interior of China and its people.

There existed very few foreigners in Guangzhou. In fact, the only foreigners we ran into consisted of a small group at the Sun Yat Sen Museum. One lady from that group, an American, walked up to us inquiring what tour group we traveled with. When we answered that we traveled on our own, she seemed dumbfounded, then turned to gesture others in her group to come over to meet us. Sandia reached into my backpack to pull out a copy of our Lonely Planet Guide to China and went onto to politely explain how one could do it on their own, with a little planning, seasoned with some good old common sense. Judging from the looks on their faces during Sandia's question and answer session, I'm not sure she convinced them to travel on their own. Later though, she confided to me that it had been fun chatting with *wontoks*.

The other consequence of so few foreigners

became apparent to us the next day as we walked to the outskirts of Guangzhou to find a small zoo, which exhibited panda bears. Walking briskly along the city streets, it seemed amazing to see the extent of bicycle traffic. I mean, we're talking thousands of

*A future Chinese
military man?*

Guangzhou bicycle traffic lane

locals riding bicycles. The bike lanes measured equal to, or greater than, the automobile travel lanes, existing side by side on the pavement. The bike traffic proved so tightly packed, those bicyclists, staring over at the two of us walking along, bumped into other bicycles, causing many to stop in a bicycling "jam." It happened frequently enough that as we strode along toward the zoo, we knew foreigners, especially out walking, must be a rare sight for the locals. We waved in greeting at the bikers several times noting the looks of amazement on their faces.

A waitress at one little Guangzhou restaurant spoke decent English. I remember she told us her name was Kitty and she'd learned our language from the radio! Can you imagine learning a language from the radio? Amongst other guidance, Kitty told us about a park where students hung out. She said many of the students also spoke English, which upon visiting, we found to be true. Talking with students, on the steps of a monument dedicated to workers, surrounded by a large treed park area, provided much enlightenment. They asked many questions regarding stories they'd heard about our country. We gave

them detailed, truthful answers from the perspective of the average American on the street. No, we didn't have criminals controlling our streets... Yes, the family was really important in the States... Yes, education was free and available for everyone that wanted it, excepting, of course, higher education, but there existed state universities with reasonable tuition and plenty of student loan programs... Assuredly, any student who desired a university education in the States could achieve his, or her, goal... Yes, likewise there were jobs for almost everyone... Yes, our quality of life remained excellent...

The students, in turn, answered our queries, while noticeably glancing around to see if anyone paid us too much attention. They seemed to talk freely. No sort of police or government officials challenged our conversations. I clearly remember, as one student finished up his dialogue regarding China's internal problems, he concluded that China was far too large to run like the U.S.A., but things would get better for his people, "When the old man dies!" We assumed he talked about Ding Zhou Ping from his assertion. So often young thinking differs radically from "the old guard" – in China's case, rulers are usually in their eighties or more. Chinese elders are looked up to in their society, where our own seniors, in general, seem tucked away someplace, out of the way. Oh, the wisdom of the ages is so often overlooked.

My lady and I left Guangzhou, and China, in the stateroom of a riverboat bound for Macao (or Macau), the Portuguese colony, famous for its gambling casinos. Our cruise down the Zhu Jiang (Pearl) River turned out to be a bit more spirited than expected, as several Europeans and an American couple had booked passage on our little excursion riverboat as well. I have to remark the cost of a private stateroom, with a television (that didn't show anything), proved remarkably cheap – about twelve dollars U.S. for each of us! They served cold Chinese beer, Tsing Tao, aboard, so our small group partied down the better part of the overnight trip, arriving in the port of Macao much in the need of sleep.

At a backpackers' lodge near the wharf in Macao, sadness struck me as I hung my freshly hand-scrubbed clothes on some lines in our quarters. My T-shirts, looked no longer white, but more of a dull gray. Everything in my pack looked pretty dingy. I reflected on how far we'd come and how many weeks, months, we'd been "on the road." Hard to explain, but the gray of my clothes affected my spirit. I knew part of it stemmed from our room having only one small high window, but that didn't change the clothing color, only the contrasts. Sandia, as always, came to the rescue. We changed the very next day to another lodge with sunny rooftop accommoda-

tions, several blocks away. On the way, Sandia stopped in a store to buy a bottle of Chinese bleach. Soon my rewashed laundry hung on lines outside on the roof, in the sun and the ocean breeze. It sparkled with brightness and freshness, renewing my spirit as well. The words of a female backpacker in England came back to me, "You two haven't been traveling long. Your clothes are too clean!"

Macao consisted of a tiny peninsula connected to two small islands, Taipa and Coloane. The total area of the colony measured just over 6.5 square miles, with the islands making up two-thirds of the total. It once had been a Portuguese trading post aimed at commerce with China and neighboring Asian countries, but without a fighting force, that the rival British used in the Boxer Rebellion around 1850, the trading turned out to be much less than expected. With about 400,000 residents situated in such a tiny land area, the population density was huge and still growing. The people consisted mainly of migrant Chinese and Macanese, or Portuguese – Chinese mixed race. Main languages seemed to be Cantonese and Portuguese, with many shop owners speaking English also. I heard that Portugal and China had recently made an agreement that Macao would return to China in December of 1999 under some special rule to allow it to stay a capitalistic economy for some long period of time. Guess China needs the hard currency flowing into the main tourist industry of Macao – gambling!

Besides studying Macao's colorful history, we watched the Hong Kong dollars move across the gaming tables. The Colony offered pure straight gambling, without any amenities, like musical shows, or other fancy food and entertainment – just gambling. A forty-five plus minute hydrofoil ride got a gambler from Hong Kong to Macao. It was interesting to watch the faces of gamblers as

Wooden boat building industry in Macao

intersection, six lanes of vehicles, many of them three wheelers, came to a screeching halt. Then the mopeds and motorcycles edged to the front between lanes. When the light turned green, the quicker accelerating motorcycles would peel away, while the slower starting cars would finally overtake and pass them before the next red light and it would all start over again. The sounds of the screeching tires and the automobile horns filled the city air of Bangkok. Upon entering a building, after the exterior door closed, it seemed so quiet and peaceful compared to the outdoors. Cairo had been noisy, but Bangkok topped them on the decibel scale. It seemed in so many crowded cities; people drove with one hand on the horn.

We spent several days getting acquainted to the diverse cultures of Bangkok, which ranged from ornate Buddhist Temples to the sex shows of the Pat Pong area. The latter came into being during the "rest and recreation" (R&R) tours of our GIs from nearby Viet Nam. The "girlie" bars competed with each other for customers, so to say the live shows seemed innovative and different would be a colossal understatement. Wild would be a better choice of words. Hotels appeared plentiful and inexpensive; as were Indian tailors ready to measure you up for a custom made suit, costing fifty to seventy dollars U.S. After the final fitting it proved easy to make arrangements to ship the suit home, rather than trying to stuff it into a backpack. My custom pinstriped suit still wears great.

they pursued their passion, experiencing joy and anguish, with lots in between.

From Macao, we backtracked on our round-the-world tickets, going west from the Hong Kong area to Bangkok, Thailand, the land of the smile. So many of the places we visited had been former colonies of the European Nations, but not Thailand, formerly Siam. Bangkok seemed a beehive of activity, with street traffic like no other place we'd seen. Six lane streets, in one direction, amazed us as we watched from overhead sidewalks. When the traffic light turned red at an

Bangkok temples and statues

Following a great urge to get out of the city and its pollution, both air and noise, along with a common need to lie on a sunny beach, Sandia and I headed south, by train, down the Thai Peninsula. Our goal focused on the island of Ko Samui, off the East Coast. A British acquaintance in New Guinea recommended the island as a "must visit" in Thailand. With the distance down to the island ferry demarcation point in excess of 600 kilometers, we'd purchased train tickets for a sleeping berth. Our railroad car as-

signment placed us among many other foreigners heading for island paradises off the East and West coasts of the skinny Thai peninsula. Ko Phuket seemed the preferred destination off the West Coast, while Ko Samui and Ko Phangan attracted tourists off the East side of the peninsula. With the islands to look forward to, and the availability of iced down buckets of tasty Thai beer from the train's porters, the train car soon took on a party atmosphere. We got acquainted with several groups around us, with the usual swapping of stories and travel ambitions. The most notable friend we made that night on the train was a very relaxed Canadian, who took a short holiday from teaching in China. Charlie LaPointe sported a white ponytail and a white beard similar to Colonel Sanders of Kentucky Fried Chicken fame. He'd once built his own home back in Canada, using the geodesic dome design. After raising several children as a single parent, Charlie volunteered to teach English in China. I thought it seemed hilarious when he described the mountain village school he taught at, only to later answer our query regarding the village population with, "Somewhere near ten million." Guess villages in China are large! Charlie went on in conversations to express perplexity at the lack of freethinking amongst his high school students. He said he often challenged them to write a thesis with alternative thinking, or solutions to problems, differing from the mainstream accepted ideas. Charlie expressed dismay at the results of his efforts. It appeared as if his students were afraid to step out of line to think differently. Conformity proved easier. Charlie also said he had to be careful along those lines, as his responsibility lay in just teaching English, not how to think for one's self. This trip represented his first time out of China in a year, with another year left on his contract. In some ways, he looked a bit shell shocked, reminding me of my first time out of Papua New Guinea after sixteen plus months. Meeting people, speaking English in conversation, moving and looking freely around, truly seemed a surreal awakening.

Short on sleep, but long on desire, Sandia and I groped our way from the train the next morning to an island ferry shuttle bus, and finally to the Ko Samui ferry, sleeping in between embarkation and debarkation.

Soon we sat on our packs, feet in the white sand, near the ferry dock, on the tropical island of Ko Samui (Ko means island in the Thai language). The smells tantalized one's nostrils with the scents of tropical flowers like the hibiscus, coupled with the smells of mango fruit trees and banana palms. Bright colors of the tropical flowers highlighted the predominately lush green backdrop of the island. The sounds of many birds sweetened the rhythmic gentle splash of waves on the beach. I could feel my internal motor slow down to a lower gear. Lay back time was upon us.

Hiring an almost new motorcycle near the beach, for only six dollars U.S. per day, we toured the island in search of our guidebook's lodging recommendations. With Sandia's arms wrapped tightly around my waist, our two packs strapped on behind her, we let the island breeze buffet our faces and hair as we circled the island feeling a great sense of freedom.

Our base in that island paradise became a small cottage at the Family Bungalows, located on Big Buddha Beach. I didn't see any families staying there, but a family, who seemed to have many gorgeous daughters, managed the beach hotel. Other guests consisted of a few more couples, and three single tugboat captains, all from the Vancouver area of Canada. The funny part

The sun setting over the Ko Samui fishing and shrimping fleet

of this story came from the happenstance that the tugboat captains only met while traveling in Thailand. They hadn't known each other back in Vancouver – small world, eh? Actually, only one of them used the Canadian punctuation, eh.

The cottage had a private bath, a huge bed, desk area, and a great verandah facing the beach – all for six dollars U.S. per day. The host family provided their own restaurant for guests serving some unbelievable dishes under a covered patio. Our favorite offering usually for dinner, some-times for lunch, consisted of fresh prawns cooked in butter and garlic. One night I remember we ate a smaller order for dessert, after consuming a large order of the freshly caught prawns for the main course. The island fishermen kept the lodge restaurants supplied with fresh seafood on a daily basis. For breakfast, I mostly ate a fresh bowl of mixed tropical fruit, along with freshly baked bread and jam. Sandia and I ran along the beach-es most mornings, barefoot in the sand, beside the blue-green waters of the Gulf of Thailand. The daughters that served the restaurant always approached me as I finished my beach run with, "What would you like for breakfast today, sexy boy?" I'm sure it originated from their standard phraseology, but the smile they put with it made it all the more uplifting.

Beautiful Thai girls walked the beaches, selling the art of their talented hands for mas-sages on the beach, or back at your cottage, if you preferred. Baggies of "killer weed" would be delivered to your room upon request. One of the tug boat captains, Randy, told me he loved the "magic" mushroom omelets served at the restaurant next door, except that he wasn't able to sleep much. When I asked him what he did at night, he told me he rode his motorcycle round and round the island, putting hundreds upon hundreds of miles on the cycle's odometer. That made for amazing mileage on a pretty small is-

Our friend Charles LaPointe
on the Ko Samui beach

Our island transport and water buffalo spectator

land.

Ever exploring, Sandia and I discovered a fresh water stream falling into a large crystal clear pool, surrounded by palm and banyan trees. The water felt cool and nice on our naked bodies as we swam lazily around the pool's surface. There existed no waves, only the ripples we created, as well as those near the waterfall. Holding each other on the rocks afterwards as the sun warmed our bodies provided such bliss. Truly, we felt the rapture of yet another paradise.

The days peacefully slipped by on Ko Samui until they merged into several weeks. My lady and I found ourselves ready to move on, eager to trek the northwest part of Thailand we'd heard so much about from other travelers – the so called Golden Triangle formed by the intersection of Thailand, Burma (Myanmar), and Laos.

Arriving in Chiang Mai by train, we easily found backpackers' accommodations. There it proved easy to get advice regarding the best trekking guides to hire, as many of the other guests had recently returned from treks toward Chiang Rai, north of us.

Leaving our non-essential gear behind us in safekeeping at the backpackers' lodge, we left Chiang Mai with two other couples, one from Switzerland, the other from Sweden. The Swiss couple seemed very high spirited, while the Swedes, quieter and a bit more reserved. In addition to our soon to be trusted guide was a carrier, kind of a Thai "Sherpa." He carried much of our food that wouldn't be supplied at our village stopover points.

The highlights of those walking days included a subterranean cave, complete with stalactites and stalagmites. The cave oozed humidity, which shut down my omnipresent eight millimeter video camera. Several of us carried crude torches – sticks with rags wrapped around and around the top, dipped in kerosene, and then ignited.

The light from the torches provided eerie shadowing of all the cave protrusions as we followed our guide and carrier under a mountain, through the cave. Several very narrow points in the cave required a little squeezing through, while testing your claustrophobic mentality. The damp atmosphere of the cave was laced with the strong stench of mineral deposits to go along with the smell emanating from our own kerosene torches.

Then we saw natural light ahead. It almost seemed blinding upon emerging into the daylight of the Thai jungle, even with a full green canopy of tree leaves overhead. We stood around blinking our eyes at each other after the better part of two hours traversing that cave in the near darkness of three shadowy kerosene torches.

Later in the trek, as promised, we rode elephants for an afternoon. What an experience! Elephants are such huge animals. I got to ride the neck of an elephant with my bare legs tucked in behind those humongous ears. The initial excitement of riding behind the elephant's head soon became tempered, however, first, by his bristly hairs which rubbed my bare legs like steel wool and, secondly, every time the elephant saw some tender green leaves, he would reach head, and trunk, out to grab them, even over the edges of ravines. At one point, our guide yelled back at me from the lead elephant, "Do not be afraid. They are very sure footed animals!" At that instant, I looked down a long way to a river below, as my elephant reached far out for some tender young leaves. Our guide proved correct as the elephant's feet stayed firmly on the mountainside trail, even as his head and trunk reached out for choice morsels. Whacking him on the head usually got him moving again after his tasty dalliances.

At night, we slept in bamboo village huts prearranged by our trekking guide. Certainly trekkers represented a bit of a cottage industry

*Elephant transport near
the Golden Triangle*

Sandia with Thai village ladies

for the remote villages. Fires, stoked up at night, dried our soggy boots and clothing. We came to know our trekking partners pretty well. The Swedish guy had just completed his Ph.D. in Physics and his wife boasted a new M.D. degree. The animated Swiss couple were trades people, the husband an electrician and the wife a waitress. Nights around the fires, we traded stories, aspirations, and promises to keep in touch.

Finally, someplace south of the small city of Chiang Rai, we boarded bamboo rafts to head back toward Chiang Mai. The river graciously accepted us as novice polers and navigators. We soon found out why our rafts had been built only about one meter wide by five meters long. Sometimes the distances between protruding river rock formations weren't much more than the width of our raft, allowing us to just squeeze through on the swift river currents. It seemed obvious they'd done this trip many times before and knew their river dimensions well.

Those river nights, we'd pull our bamboo rafts ashore at the designated sleeping villages to stretch our bodies and feel terra firma below our feet. It felt good to sit down after standing most of the day, poling our raft between river rocks.

Three days on the river brought us to the end of our trek. You could tell up ahead on the riverbanks that the end was near, as hundreds of used rafts sat there, piled up in sort of a river cove. They need to figure a way to recycle those wonderful rafts.

Several other raftloads of trekkers, including some we'd had friendly, river water fights with along the voyage, disembarked with us to await the scheduled shuttle bus for Chiang Mai. The men sipped at bottles of Thai beer, while we watched our ladies shop for jewelry among several Thai lady vendors. Sandia bought a pretty silver necklace as a trek souvenir.

An amazing part of the beautiful, colorful

city of Chiang Mai manifested in the beauty of the local women. Sandia seemed to always be poking me to look upon yet another exotic face passing us nearby. She expressed amazement, as did I. Whatever combination of genetics brought it about, I don't know, but we certainly felt immersed in a center of remarkable human female beauty.

Chiang Mai also taught us how small the world really is. A Peace Corps friend from New Guinea appeared in Chiang Mai the same time we visited. Then we ran into another Euro, who we'd met in Mt. Hagen.

From Thailand, we flew to Singapore, and from there to Indonesia and the island of Bali. Singapore seemed a bit sterile to us after Thailand. We did find a passable Mexican food restaurant, which seemed exciting, but for the most part, Singapore proved all business. I noticed that unlike so many cities we'd passed through, no drivers on the Singaporian streets honked their horns. A quietly efficient traffic moved down those avenues. A cabbie answered my question regarding the absence of horns with the retort, "If you drive properly, no horn is needed!"

Sandia also pointed out a sign to me at the entrance to a public restroom at the dock where we boarded a ferry for the nearby Indonesian Island of Bintan. The sign stated that the fine for failing to flush a toilet after use was 150 Singaporian dollars! Mr. Lee ran an efficient, businesslike country. All the toilets were certainly clean and flushed, and there didn't occur any noise pollution from those dreadful car horns in that densely populated country.

Bali turned out to be a lively island in the Indonesian archipelago. Sandia and I loved the beaches and the mountains of Bali. A rental Susuki beach convertible enabled us to tour most of the island for the better part of a week.

A Buddhist stronghold, in a primarily Muslim country, Bali felt peaceful and calm, maybe with the exception of some pushy beach vendors.

Our Thailand trekking buddies and faithful guide

Village bathing in the Monkey Forest

However, most of the local people epitomized pleasantness. We dove the blue-green sea one day, then drove to a high volcanic lake the next. Several pleasant days at an inn near the Monkey Forest refreshed our spirits. Without electrical power, we used only furnished candles, bedding down early, and waking with the sun. Our adjoining bathroom had been purposely left without a roof. Flowering vines clung to the walls of the bathroom. A warm bath, looking up at the blue sky, with the strong scent of flowers in one's nostrils felt euphoric. With great mental difficulty, we left the Monkey Forest Inn, but we did it – booking a flight from Bali to Brisbane – to end our round-the-world tickets – Australia to Australia. We'd get back to the States some way from there.

Staying at a quaint lodge in Brisbane, we rang up Jim and Mary Ann in P.N.G. to say hello, only to find they were about to catch a flight to Brisbane for a day of interviewing applicants for my old position. Their most recent hire had just been fired. Jim asked could we meet them at the Brisbane Sheraton two days hence, Saturday, and help with the interviewing process. Answering certainly in the affirmative, we felt excited to see our friends after our many months of traveling.

Jim, George Hook, and I put our heads together that Saturday, interviewing nine Australian applicants for the advertised position, Manager of Hailans Homes. Sandia and Mary Ann went shopping. By late afternoon, the last applicant left us with no clear standout for the job. Sandia and Mary Ann returned from their fun day, while George took off to check on his Brisbane home. For my part, I felt exhausted from the mental pressure of the interviewing process. I heard Jim's voice say, "Well we owe you guys a dinner for the effort today. Let's go down to the restaurant here in the hotel. I hear it's a great buffet."

Waiting in the food service line a little later, with Jim just in front of me, and the ladies gabbing away up ahead of us, Jim turned to quietly say, "Bill, I've got a question to ask you." Then he paused, and said, "Ah, no worries, you wouldn't!"

Jim did this unfinished question thing several times, finally prompting me to respond, "Ask me. Ask me. What's the question?"

"Well, I wondered if you'd come up to New Guinea for a little bit to bid a contract up at the Porgera mine. You know Porgera well. If you don't do it, I'll have to and I don't have the time!"

I asked him how much time is a little bit, to which he estimated less than a month.

"Let me go up ahead and ask Sandia her feelings. I'll be back in a minute."

Sandia's answer came as a quick, "Okay with me."

I turned to give Jim a thumbs-up sign. Mary Ann's voice came to my ears as I looked at Jim. "Great. We already bought your tickets on the chance you'd say yes. You leave for New Guinea tomorrow morning at ten o'clock!"

The dinner proved exciting as Jim explained the contract included the first fifteen buildings of the Suyan Township, the hub of the permanent infrastructure for the operating gold mine – an estimated twenty-year precious metal extraction project. They would arrange for a car to pick us up at our lodge in the morning to get us to the Brisbane Airport. The contract bid specifications awaited me at the Total Hardware offices in Mt. Hagen. Use whomever I needed to put it all together. The company would cover all expenses. We could live at their furnished flat above Total Hardware. The project would be a welcome challenge after six-plus months of traveling with backpacks.

chapter forty-one

Back to Papua New Guinea

Arriving in Mt. Hagen, I found the contract specifications and accompanying blueprints. Along with a current hardware and lumber price list, I began figuring the material estimates. In the meantime, Sandia arranged helicopter transport to the Porgera and the Suyan Township construction site. It turned out to be soft and boggy soil, not what you'd want to construct twenty-year buildings on. We took a few photographs; one with my boot sunk in the wet clay rich soil. The pictures would demonstrate the point of questionable soil conditions.

It turned out that I had four-weeks until the contract submittal deadline. At the beginning, four-weeks seemed plenty of time, but I soon learned otherwise. Everyone at Total Hardware, the purchasing manager, sales manager, and the temporary guy at Hailans Homes indicated they were buried up to their ears in work, always behind schedule. Without a lot of help, along with old friends stopping in to say hello, two weeks went by much too quickly, leaving me with lots more than two additional weeks work to go for

sometimes, one has to go back, in order

to know, which way he needs to go forward

the final submittal price. I began to get a little nervous.

Then it hit me! Let's go to Australia and rent a hotel room next to the Placer Dome Mining Offices. I'll work around the clock until it's done. I can call back for any special equipment pricing and, after all, we've done the important thing. We've walked the lousy soil they want to build this first phase of Suyan on top of. We didn't need to stay in Hagen at all. Again, Sandia made all the arrangements while I continued compiling the material and labor estimates.

The next evening, we looked out from our fourth-floor suite at the Harborside Hotel in Cairns, Australia. I could see the mining offices two blocks south of us on the other side of the street. The date was the 2nd of March 1990. I had until the 15th at 5 P.M., to get the bid submitted. We had rented a living room, bedroom, kitchen suite, so the unit provided plenty of space to spread all the paperwork out. I wore nothing but a sarong for the next thirteen days. We called for room service, or Sandia went out to get carryout and brought it back. She supported me with the food, running for copies, back massages, and diverted me periodically with lots of love.

The room maid asked Sandia one day, "Does he ever put on clothes?"

Sandia politely answered her, "He's working on a big project with a tight deadline."

Friday, the 15th of March, arrived in what seemed like only a moment, but by mid-afternoon I had the almighty number, the bid price. I checked it, rechecked it, and added another few percent for any other contingencies I might have missed. I wrote up the submittal sheets. Sandia ran for the required copies while I showered and pulled on real clothes.

We walked into the Placer Dome Mining Offices at four-thirty, one- half hour before the deadline. A receptionist pointed out the contract supervisor's office. I walked over to knock on David Harley's door. He turned from his desk with an expression of surprise on his face when he noticed the contract documents in my hand. I introduced myself as he joked that all the other bids were still coming through their fax machine. I commented that the bid submittal constituted a big deal to our company and I also wanted to tell him in person that the ground they asked the contract winner to build the first phase of the Suyan Township on was a mess— totally inadequate for the long term structures. I held out a few photographs to demonstrate the point. As he studied the photos, David said he was familiar with a lot of the work we'd done at the mine site. He further said he appreciated the input on soil conditions and would pass the comments on to the site engineers in Porgera. Then it came down to thank you very much for stopping in, upon which I turned to leave on his cue.

My lady and I walked out of the mining offices as the clock signaled five o'clock, the deadline, and found the nearest pub to lift a pint in celebration. The contract figuring had ended.

The bid price of nearly two million Kina had been submitted on time. I needed a break, big time. We both needed a break. Several hours later, and many V.B.'s (Victoria Bitters) later, Sandia got me back to our hotel bed. As I held her in my arms, she told me there would be a great adventure waiting for us on the weekend.

"Just leave it with me. You'll love it!"

I knew I would.

By the time I woke up the next morning, Sandia had made all the necessary arrangements. We were scheduled to scuba dive the Great Barrier Reef off the Australian coast.

That weekend I came about as close as I have ever come to becoming one with the sea. The colors of the fragile coral defy description – soft blues and pale striking pinks. The undersea life centered on the reef seemed so abundant from the orange and black clown fish hiding in their sea anemone to black tipped reef sharks. The giant clams occupied my favorite part of the dives. We'd never seen them in the waters of New Guinea. After much inspection, I finally slipped my fist past the soft lipped shell edges into the clam's interior. Visions of old Johnny Wiesmuller (Tarzan) movies, where the clam squeezed down on his foot, holding him to near drowning, until he pried the powerful jaws apart with his superior strength, passed through my mind. That would have been a trip, clamped by a giant clam on the Great Barrier Reef. Actually, the soft edging, or lips as I'm calling them, prevented the full closure of the shells, allowing tiny sea creatures to be filtered in for nourishing consumption by the clam. I found I could easily reach inside and pull my hand out of those colorful soft edged shells. We did four dives that weekend, each time finding new aspects of the Great Barrier Reef. What an opportunity to see one of the very fragile wonders of our oceans.

The following week, we took several days

driving around and ended up north at the beach town of Port Douglas. We totally fell in love with the place – the old Victorian architecture, the shops, the restaurants, and the splendid sandy beaches. There existed only one industry in Port Douglas and we were it, the tourist. Everything there supplied the vacationers' pleasure.

I checked in with George Hook in P.N.G. the following Friday to see if there had occurred any word on the contract. He told me the news – all bids had been put on hold until the engineers found a different, more suitable, site for the Suyan Township. Could I please give him the telephone number of our lodgings in Port Douglas as Jim wanted to call me later to chat me up regarding the contract hold.

The essence of Jim's call later that night dealt with could we hang out until the bloody engineers got the ground thing worked out for the contract. Thinking out loud, I mumbled something to the effect that that could take a while and maybe we'd head back for the States. We both suffered a bit of homesickness at that point. After all, I hadn't been really home for the better part of three years. Then Jim hit me with an offer I couldn't refuse. Go south in the rental car to Maroochydore, just north of Brisbane on the Sunshine Coast, find a flat (apartment), enroll in a flying school, and finish my pilot's license. The company would cover our expenses.

"Good on you, mate. It's a bloody deal!"

Sandia looked at me as I hung up.

"What's happening?"

Excellent wheels for the Queensland beach country

"Tomorrow we start driving south for Maroochydore! I'm going to enroll at Fogarty's Flying School as soon as we get there. What a chance! What an awesome chance! Jim wants us around when the Suyan Contract has to be re-submitted."

The trip south to Maroochydore took three days. The pavement seemed punctuated by kangaroos hopping across and along the two-lane road, especially around dusk. We stopped one night in Rockhampton, home of the beef cattle industry in Australia. The hotel pub served big juicy steaks at the bar, to be washed down with pints of tasty Aussie beer. Two thirsty Australian Army blokes, on some kind of daytime maneuvers in the area, adopted us at the bar. I think they liked Sandia and Yanks in general. They spent the night teaching us "Strine" as they called it, Australian slang. We practiced and learned expressions like fair dinkum (genuine or true), tucker (food), piss (beer), boomers and joeys (big and small kangaroos), tinnie (can of beer), crook (sick), dunny (toilet), chook (chicken), fair go (a chance), nick (to steal), to get nicked (to be caught), and on and on. The language lesson provided lots of spirited fun. They shouted (bought) us quite a few beers. Wow, can the Aussies drink piss! We finally excused ourselves, drained the last of our glasses, so as not to be disrespectful, and staggered up to our room above, holding on to each other for support. My stomach felt bloated from all the beer I drank, while my face hurt from all the laughter we had enjoyed. Australians love their humor.

Fogarty's Flying School turned out to only hold formal classes and the schedule required twelve weeks to complete the classroom studies and hands-on flying. The next session wouldn't start for another month. I wanted a self-paced schedule that I could start right away. We ultimately found another school at the Maroochydore Airport, called Sun Coast Flying, where you made your own schedule. Ten kilometers from the airport, after a bit of searching, we found a small flat at the Trafalger Towers on the thirteenth floor. The view from the sun deck looked down on the Maroochydore River as it joined the Pacific Ocean. I would spend a lot of study time on that breezy viewing deck.

We turned in the rental car, and bought two used ten-speed bicycles that came with a buy back promise. The bikes would be our exercise along the Sunshine Coast. No sense wasting money on a rental car that would sit most of the time.

Sandia got up early everyday to get my breakfast and pack me a lunch. She said it would be her contribution to the flying effort. I'd head off on my bike, waving up to my lady until I couldn't see her anymore. Sandia usually spent the day exploring the Maroochydore – Mooloolaba beach areas, returning to our rental flat to meet me at dusk. The ten-kilometer ride to the airport in the morning really got me

pumping by the time I reached the Sun Coast facility. Days there varied busily between getting flying time in one of their Cessna 152 trainers and taking the required series of exams. When I pedaled home at dusk, Sandia would have a super meal waiting, after which I'd study till I fell asleep. On weekends, Sandia showed me around the beach places she'd explored during the week. Following this routine, I earned my restricted license, good to fly within a five- mile radius around the airport, in three weeks time. I next dove into navigational training and soon flew solo navigational exercises inland toward the "outback" of Australia. The seacoast of Australia is certainly more remarkably featured than the inland stretches of open sandy spaces. You had to fly to predetermined checkpoints within plus or minus two minutes of your estimated arrival times given on a previously submitted and approved flight plan. I remember landing at remote places in Queensland with names like Kingaroy, where a control tower, with air traffic controllers, did not even exist.

Exactly six weeks from the time I started, I waited for the big test. The C.A.A. (Civil Aeronautics Authority) Inspector was up flying for his second test of the day. He'd failed the first student for misidentifying towns along the test flight route. Nervously staring out of the window while pacing in the testing area, I noted the buildup of clouds. My "scaredy cat" self considered calling off the test, as pilot-in-command, due to the weather moving in. Then I heard my name called. My testing time had arrived. My flight plan had already been submitted and approved. Another student whispered that the second test had ended in a failure also. My knees trembled as I walked toward my trusty aircraft. Then I thought, "Oh hell, let's get this sucker done and over!"

The C.A.A. Inspector stood by my little

Cessna 152 awaiting my instructions, as if he constituted an ordinary passenger. I was pilot-in-command. I did my walk around inspections of the aircraft, then made sure he was properly harnessed into the copilot's seat and off we went. He never said anything, just made notes in his notebook, as I taxied and took off according to my radioed clearances.

At one point later, I thought I flew above a town required on my flight plan, except that I was a few minutes early. The town looked identical to that which showed on the map in my lap, except for the railroad tracks. The town I wanted had one set of dead end tracks which did not appear below me. Lo and behold, three minutes beyond, another town appeared down in front of me. The railroad tracks matched perfectly. The time figured within my arrival limits. I radioed my position to search and rescue at the checkpoint. The inspector wrote something in his notebook. I'd came close to blowing it on the previous town, but saved it by precise times and those wonderful railroad tracks.

Now I heard the inspector's voice in my headset telling me to change my flight plan, requiring me to land at Brisbane – Archerfield, Australia's busiest airport. Putting the air traffic controllers on standby, I recalculated my routes and times, radioing in the changes. I made it into and out of the Brisbane – Archerfield Airport with soggy armpits, but otherwise okay. Next thing I knew, the inspector reached over and killed my throttle, forcing me through emergency landing procedures. Moments later, not one hundred feet off the ground, satisfied that I could put the plane down on the empty field I'd selected, he told me to pull out of my approach. Over the ocean, a little later, after pulling out of a forced spiral dive in less than two hundred feet, I finally heard his voice say into my headset, "Take her home!"

Parking the Cessna 152 at our hanger, the inspector's only comment instructed me to tie the aircraft down properly. He headed for the Sun Coast offices. I fastened that faithful 152 to the tie-down eyes in the concrete and stood to stretch my aching muscles. Then I heard a voice and looked toward the hanger. Tony, my flight instructor, ran toward me. He yelled, "You passed. You passed. Bill, you are an Australian Pilot!" Truly, I'll never forget those words. Dreams of my youth now became reality. I didn't hold back the tears of joy.

After all the handshakes of the Sun Coast Flying staff and the presentation of my wings, I jumped on my ten-speed bike to excitedly head

My faithful Cessna two-seater aircraft

for Trafalger Towers and my Sandia. I don't think those bicycle tires touched the pavement all the way home. It seemed like a dream. Something I'd longed for so many years ago became real now.

I was a pilot!

I quietly, gently turned my key in the dead bolt of our flat. I could hear Sandia moving around inside. Then I kicked the door open with great gusto to announce, "The Red Baron requests your presence at dinner this evening!"

Sandia flew into my arms. "You passed. You did it!" she kept saying over and over with the greatest, excited smile on her face.

I showered my tired, but vibrating body and waited for Sandia to finish getting ready. The phone rang. George Hook called from Papua New Guinea.

"They just took the bloody contract off hold. They want resubmittals within three weeks. How soon can you get up here?"

"George, you have the most incredible sense of timing. We'll leave day after tomorrow. Tomorrow, come hell or high water, I'm taking my lady for a plane ride around here. I am an official Australian pilot as of about two hours ago!"

"Congratulations, Bill. I'm proud of you. Your tickets will be waiting for you at the Brisbane Airport. Tell Sun Coast Flying to send me the final bill. See you the day after, *Masta Pilot Bill.*"

I gave Sandia my wings at dinner that night, at a Mexican food place we liked. We always got a kick out of the fact that a neat Canadian guy managed the Mexican restaurant, in Australia. My two flight instructors, Tony and Brad, joined us for the celebration. They told us that the previous licensing record at Sun Coast had taken seven weeks, start to finish. I had broken that by a full week. I smiled and said, "Thanks for the compliment, but my boss used to give me a lot of flying time in the cloudy skies of Papua New

Guinea, so I had a little head start on this thing."

The next day, Sandia and I flew the areas above and around the Maroochydore – Mooloolaba area, getting a look at beaches we'd pedaled our bikes to on weekends. Flying brought an interesting change to our normal mode of transport. From the air, the earth's surface is a whole different perspective. Sandia amazed me with her total trust of my newly licensed flying skills. She did put her foot down, though, when I wanted to show her stall maneuvers and spiral dive recoveries. So we kept it mostly straight and level, excitedly seeing the familiar landmarks fifteen hundred feet below. Sandia loved studying the maps and correlating the features with the terrain below us. I kidded her, "Need that map. Up here, you can't pull into a gas station for directions!"

The next afternoon, we arrived in New Guinea, deciding to stay this time in the Lae company offices on the Eastern Shore of the Huon Gulf. Jim and Mary Ann traveled in the States at the time, but had left word for me to use the company plane, the Cessna 182, Romeo Papa Tango (RPT), if I needed it. What a trusting boss Jim was. The two of them would return about the time the new bid had to be submitted for the Suyan Contract.

I flew, with Sandia as my copilot in charge of maps, Romeo Papa Tango to Porgera to get a look at the Suyan Township building area and check on any particulars that might have changed regarding the contract specifications. Satisfied, we took off from that crazy, one-way, ten percent graded, gravel airstrip, in the down hill direction. As we circled the future gold mining area, I pointed down to the Porgera River, remarking to Sandia, "Into that river, they intend to dump the residuals of the potassium cyanide gold leaching process. They have convinced the

Environmental Minister that it will be sufficiently neutralized for discharge into the river water. I pity the villages downstream in years to come. Their lives will certainly change as a result of this mining operation!"

Back in Lae, the work on the contract numbers seemed easier this time. I only triple checked my previous estimates and inserted updated material and labor prices. My final numbers bumped the previously submitted bid price by about K300,000 to approximately 2.1 million kina (near two million U.S.)

Jim arrived from the States in time to put his "John Hancock" on the submittal sheets. I asked him as he signed the first copy, "Aren't you going to look at the price inside?"

"I trust your numbers. It's okay."

"Jim, look at the numbers, please. Tell me what you think!"

He flipped to the tally page, stared for a moment, then let out a whistle.

"We'll never get this contract. These numbers are too high for fifteen dongas!"

"Hey Jim, six of them have private baths for the big managers, and besides, nothing is easy in Porgera. There is enough contingency to get you through this one, if we win it!"

"Why don't you stay and build it?"

"Jim, I need to go to our Colorado Mountains and soon. It's been near three years now. We're missing those hills big time!"

"Okay mate, just thought I'd ask."

We walked together to the fax machine and sent the bid through to Cairns, Australia and the Placer Dome Mining Offices. I felt a certain finality in getting the transmission sent off. Now it would only be the waiting for the selection process.

Sandia and I flew Romeo Papa Tango to Mt. Hagen to wait out the Placer Dome selection. We played some tennis at our old club,

but mostly helped out at our old jobs. The men in the Hailans Homes shop/factory expressed their hopes about the new contract. I told them not to count on it, until we heard one way or the other. My heart hoped for them and the job security the contract would provide. The date came and went at the middle of May for the contract award. No messages from Placer Dome. Then I heard about the cutting of the telephone trunklines down the mountain from us. A Highlands tribe had leased some of their land to sit the cable tower bases on. Now they wanted higher lease fees! To punctuate their claim, they had climbed one tower to cut cables containing most of the Highlands telephone lines. Only a few emergency line patches worked, while the lease negotiations went on. No one at the mine site or Mt. Hagen had talked to Australia for days.

I sat at the Hailans Homes office telephone, totally driven by curiosity, and started dialing David Harley's (the Contract Officer) office number in Cairns. Without a modern re-dial button on the phone, I had to re-dial the whole number thing each time, country codes and all. I sat there dialing, making a mark on a paper each time I dialed his number. By some miracle, on the 53rd try, I must have linked up through an emergency patch, as David answered his phone way south in Cairns.

"Bill, what's happening up there? We haven't been able to get through to anyone."

I told him the cable-cutting story very briefly, as I busted to know about the contract award.

"David, did Placer Dome select a contractor yet?"

"Yes they did. You got it! Hailans Homes will build Phase I of Suyan! We've been trying to call you for the last three days. The signed contract award is in the mail to your company today."

"David, thank you for the work opportunity. I'd better get off this bloody phone and get things rolling at this end. We've got a lot of things to get into motion here."

Before letting either Jim or George in on the news, I walked into the shop to call the men together. There is no greater sound in this world than the laughter and *ayiiis* of New Guinea men happy to get work, happy to be able to provide for their families into the future. In between hugs, I told them they must do good hard work on this project. Their heads shook in the affirmative as I saw many tearful eyes. As I walked away, Yaupas (Terapi) lectured them with his hand signs, beckoning towards my retreating person. I knew between Yaupas and Norbert, things would go well in that shop. You could cut the eagerness in the air with a knife!

Late afternoon had arrived when I caught George at the golf course clubhouse ready to get in nine holes before dark. George seemed beside himself when he heard the news. He said he'd head back to the office to start thinking about the material ordering. I told him to go hit the ball, morning would happen quickly enough.

"Have you called Jim yet?"

"Not yet, you were closer. I'll try to call as soon as I hang up. George, the amount of materials and manpower on this thing, with the deadlines is scary. I'll meet you in your office first thing tomorrow. We can get started then. Go hit them straight for now!"

When I finally got through to Jim in Lae, after another dialing sequence, he seemed even more excited than George did. This constituted the biggest contract Jim had ever had in New Guinea. Success on Phase I would surely lead to more contracts. Everyone seemed happy. I graciously refused once more to stay and build it. Sandia and I felt happy because we focused on home, leaving Papua New Guinea, my men, our friends and coworkers, on excellent terms—a definite win-win situation. The Colorado Rocky Mountains awaited our touch. My lady and I were really going home! Tears and smiles filled our beings with an unbelievable bitter sweetness. We were heading home!

Goodbye to Papua New Guinea for now, all its people, and wonderful mysteries!

chapter forty-two

Our Third "Going" to New Guinea

Sandia and I left Papua New Guinea by way of the northern coast town of Vanimo, and from there, hopped a short flight to Jayapura, Irian Jaya, on the western half of the New Guinea Island. We traveled west from Jayapura to the Island of Bali, in Indonesia. Sandia had set her sights on doing an imported whole-sale silver jewelry business from our Colorado Mountains. She wanted to take a closer look at the silver factories in that part of the world. Costs were based on the weight of the silver, at the going world price, with the workmanship of the jewelry basically free. Sandia shopped, selected, and purchased various samples ranging from rings to ornate necklaces. Several calls to U.S. Customs in Hong Kong told us to just keep receipts and declare the silver upon entry to the United States. How naïve we felt in the import-ing business. At Customs, later in Los Angeles, when I mentioned we had silver jewelry, with receipts, and wanted to know how much duty we owed, several "very less than friendly" agents descended on us, confiscated the jewelry, along with receipts, and sealed it all in boxes. They told us we'd have to hire an Import Agent in order to

time passes, life can be shorter than it seems

it is okay to be driven by dreams

get our silver out of their grasp!

To make a long story short, we hired an Agent in Denver for the sum of bet-ter than four hundred dol-lars to get back the jewelry worth less than three times that value. Sandia ended up giving away lots of it as gifts and still wears different favorite pieces today. Needless to say, she didn't end up going into the jewelry import business. Her decision stemmed not so much from the administration that the business required, or her lack of love for silver jewelry, but, at least in part, from that initial impression (impact) we were left with after dealing with U.S. Customs and its airport representatives.

Unloading our luggage in our Colorado Mountain cabin and hideaway, we headed for Pensacola, Florida and my son's graduation from Troy State University. Our chosen mode of trans-port became the old reliable "drive away," where responsible car moving companies gave you the first tank of gas and sent you on your way to a specific destination turn-in point. We had to post a bond for the car, of course, which would be refunded to us upon turning the car over in the same shape we had received it in. Mostly they are nice cars that wealthier people have shipped, rather than driving, like us poor folks.

The graduation went superbly. Gary took his Bachelor's Degree in Business, already working on his Master's, while still serving Uncle Sam's Navy. Later he would be selected to officer training and work his way up to his latest commission as Lieutenant Commander. All this after eight years as a "white hat" (enlisted man), made Gary what the Navy calls a "Mustang." I, of course, tried to talk him out of staying in the military, maybe because I'm what the military would call a "Maverick!" But to each, his own. We are all unique individuals. I never listened to everything my father tried to tell me either. Gary made an excellent decision for himself and his family.

From Pensacola, we caught a bus to Jacksonville, where a repossessed red Miata awaited our expert guidance and driving skills up to a Newark, N. J. bank. We drove that little sports car on a lot of back roads going north. I had to pry Sandia from behind the wheel, so I could get a chance to drive it once in a while. How she loved that little red car! It proved a sad time to leave it in the bank parking lot, where some administrator had already spoken for it, but we had to leave it. We made the short hop from there to Connecticut on the train. There we hugged and visited with all the girls, Sandia's Kirsten, and my three, Sherrie, Andrea, and Deborah—my fourth, Lynne still lived back in Colorado at that point. I always felt that not all of the kids really understood Sandia and me, but sort of tolerated our spirits and optimistic philosophies. They, caught up in their day to day routines, couldn't relate totally to our "life is such a magnificent opportunity" outlook. Perspective remains an individual choice to make, sort of like "the cup is half-full, or half-empty" classic analogy. Perspective cannot be administered with a "hypodermic needle," but only from a dose of

life itself. You've met those in life that chose the misery side of the coin. They're not a whole lot of fun to be around. Life is too short as it is. I'll take the other side of the coin—let the sun shine in and let it shine out at the same time! Sunshine provides a lot easier perspective for the heart. After all, life is such a chance—have fun at it. There exist many millions of human beings that fare much worse in this world, trust me, than we do here Stateside. This country represents the flagship on the oceans of the world.

Returning to the quiet peace of our Colorado mountains, Sandia and I walked the forest behind *La Casita* one day, naked I might add, leaving our clothes at the base of a big old spruce tree by the cabin. We sat on a log near a small mountain meadow watching a few deer graze on the lush green grass in front of us. The animals hardly gave us a sideways glance. We talked of the future and what it might be and what it might hold for us. As we sat there, remarking that we truly lived in paradise, we realized that our surroundings manifested but one of many kinds of paradise in this world. We both acknowledged a strong desire to head back out into the world, not just to remain and exist in our own little created blissful abode. Life, for us, has to have meaning. Sandia and I decided, on the log that day, to volunteer for the U.S. Peace Corps, specifically to a Spanish speaking assignment somewhere. I already worked on my doctoral dissertation, having found a university to accept me on a nonresidential status. I'd completed all required course work earlier, about thirty credits beyond the Master's, and had only to put about four years of research into an acceptable dissertation format, along with passing oral exams. This I eventually accomplished, as well as finishing a timber-framed barn, which proved bigger than our home. In the meanwhile, we applied to the Peace Corps and waited for an assignment, and waited, and waited. I learned free style cross-country skiing late that winter, February and March of 1992. You can free style over the snowy landscape faster than a person can run. In the springtime, morning skiing over the frozen crust of the meadows is the greatest feeling of exhilaration and freedom. Sandia worked that winter at the nearby Grand Lake Cross-Country Ski Touring Center, which made learning to free style ski on thirty- kilometers of groomed trails a lot easier.

An earlier construction shot of the timber-framed barn. Must have been 4th of July!

Finally we got a Peace Corps assignment to Northern Guatemala, near the Mexican Border, to help with the repatriation of those Guatemalans' who had fled the notorious regime that Nobel prize winner Rigoberta Menchu so vigorously fought against and wrote about, on behalf of her indigenous countrymen. To say we felt excited would have been an apt description. Soon after, however, we got a phone call from Washington, D.C. Some health official red flagged us because of the low-grade bladder cancer I'd truthfully marked on the application submittals. After much discussion regarding resolution of the setback, I headed for Denver to undergo a physical examination and obtain a letter from the doctor stating that I was totally in remission.

Another month or two passed, after the doctor submitted the "asked for" paper work stating my physical well being looked more than excellent. In the beginning of September, we got another phone call from Washington, telling

us that Cancer Society guidelines required five years of remission before I could be accepted to the Peace Corps. Not having the full five years, they gave our assignment to another couple. The Peace Corps aircraft would leave two weeks later for Guatemala, without us. We felt devastated. Then we looked at each other, sucked it all back in, and started working on a plan "B." We decided to head into Mexico to find our own project. You have to be flexible in this life. Rigidity can get you knocked around a bit.

After some traveling in Mexico, and lots of reflection, we ended up enrolling at *Universidad de Guadalajara's Centro de Estudios para Los Extranjeros* (University of Guadalajara's Foreign Student Study Center). Studying there totally immersed us in the language and the culture. Our teachers only spoke Spanish and many of the foreign students couldn't speak English. We conversed with Japanese, Swedish, German, and students of other nationalities, only in Spanish— our common language of interest. Sandia, with her ethnic background, studied several levels ahead of me, so we would meet for coffee between classes. Living with a family near the University further improved our language skills. After a full day in class, then conversing with our host family at night, I sometimes begged my lady to speak to me in good old English, to give my brain a rest. In all, we did three five-week enrollment sessions, or one "all day, every day" semester of the Spanish language, while attending some lectures in other fields, delivered also in *Español.*

During the last five-week session, one day we met, at the student coffee shop, another student from Colorado. He was enrolled at the University of Colorado in Denver (U.C.D.), doing language credits abroad. The light bulbs in our heads blinked on brightly. If U.C.D. would accept Sandia's 18 credit hours in Spanish from *U de G,* along with about 30 credits she'd completed years earlier at a Community College in Virginia, she could be on her way to a Bachelor's Degree. We researched U.C.D. at the American Ben Franklin Library in Guadalajara and Sandia decided to apply. They ultimately accepted her, with full credit for all previous course work, and we headed for Denver, of course, by way of Palenque, Tulum, and other fabulous ruins from past civilizations, so prevalent in Mexico and Guatemala.

I found jobs teaching physics at various colleges, in and around Denver, on an adjunct basis. Schools always seem to look for physics instructors and I love teaching the basic core course of all the sciences—no bias here! We lived in a small rented flat in the inner city and loved it. Sandia studied like a woman possessed. She loved her field of study, Latin American Studies. We spent one Christmas/New Years semester break climbing in the Andes Mountains of Ecuador. When we weren't climbing volcanic mountains like Tungaraua, near Cotapaxi, we bicycled down

into the Amazon rainforest (taking a bus back up) and hung out in the hot springs of a mountain town named Baños—an utterly wonderous place for flavorful food and great relaxation. Then we headed back to our respective schools again and buckled down to studying and teaching. The next Christmas break found us trucking food supplies into the Tarahumara Indians near Creel, Mexico. Their corn crops had been decimated by three years of drought and we made one village our own little "peace corps" project. Lots of great Stateside people, and one mountain newspaper, Sky Hi News, helped us out in purchasing the hundreds of kilograms of rice, beans, and fresh fruit. We are not heroes, but there were kids in that village dying of malnutrition. One infant girl who died, as reported in an Associated Press article, proved to be my Spanish namesake, Guillermina. I'm sure we helped some of those families through the rest of winter. For us, it

A high mountain village in the Andes

made a superb Christmas present to be in the Copper Canyon area of Mexico, pushing our old Isuzu Trooper, loaded to the top, over some of those rugged dirt and rocky roads. We met some wonderful, sharing, proud, indigenous people while on the project. Their fertile ancestral lands have been taken from them, leaving them to fend for their families on high barren lands, but they never seem to complain. They make up a proud people. Again, it's all about perspective.

As Sandia neared the completion of her degree, in the spring of '95, we again reflected on the future. And again we applied to the Peace Corps—surely this time they would find a spot for two willing volunteers who could teach physics, math, or whatever they named, someplace in the Spanish speaking world. At the same time, Jim and Mary Ann wanted us to return to Papua New Guinea to help them. Graduation grew closer, without a Peace Corps assignment. I think we got lost some place in a big bureaucratic pile of paper.

Suddenly, the celebration of Sandia's stud-

Tarahumara Family at a
mountain village mission school

ies and graduation brightly exploded on us. To make it even sweeter, Kirsten had transferred from Hunter College in New York after her sophomore year, to complete her studies also at U.C.D. She would graduate the same day with her mom, on, would you believe, Mothers' Day. The press found out from the University and they ate it up. Videotaped interviews, taken in our little inner city flat, showed up on the local news and there were articles in both Denver newspapers. Sandia's grades (straight A's) had earned her finalist as Outstanding Graduating Senior and also Honor Society Graduate. I felt so proud of my lady, and Kirsten, that day. News reporters with video cameras stood on stage to photograph her degree presentation. Sandia earned, and truly deserved, the honors she was accorded. I experienced first hand, the tremendous effort she put forth to earn her letters. From simple, beautiful, and humble beginnings, Sandia stood proud on that auditorium stage. My heart almost burst from my chest with pride for her.

Yes, we staged a celebration party at an adjoining city park and lots of special friends and family came a long way to get together after the graduation. The "get together" provided a well-earned kick back time! The hugs and smiles flowed that day, along with tasty Mexican food and a keg of cold beer.

Having sold our precious mountain retreat the summer before, after much reflection and the decision to move on in life, we were now free to go wherever seemed appropriate to the two of us. All our kids certainly had entered adulthood and lived on their own. Without a nod from the Peace Corps, we decided to head back to Papua New Guinea once more to help out Jim and Mary Ann in their businesses. So we stored away our "stuff" in a small rental single car garage and headed off to Sydney, Australia to meet Jim and

M. A. This effort would be our third "going to P.N.G."

As a prelude to Papua New Guinea, Jim and M.A. proposed a trip around Australia in their Beach Baron, Tango Charlie Hotel (TCH call letters), a twin engine aircraft. Sandia and I kidded Jim if the fly around composed some kind of a bribe for what awaited us in New Guinea! "Of course not," came his smiling response. The trip represented something he'd always wanted to do and the then present timing seemed right. We voted to sign on and share in the trip!

My lady and I flew to Brisbane to spend a few days visiting our old friend Ray West and his family, which included a bit of tennis, before catching a flight up to Cairns, in Queensland, where Tango Charlie Hotel underwent a scheduled flight maintenance inspection. It would be several days in the overhaul facility at least, we were told. Sandia and I looked at each other and said "Port Douglas" at the same time. Back at our Cairns backpackers' lodgings, we found out our favorite Port Douglas accommodations, Port O'Call, ran a shuttle bus from Cairns. Believe me, we found seats on the next bus north. The next few days, Sandia and I went through "*mucho*" suntan lotion, while doing beach towel reflections on recent college study loads and how awesome life could be.

Tanned, rested, and well fed, we headed back down the thirty miles, or so, to Cairns, only to find another short delay for our around-Australia trip, while Tango Charlie Hotel had a new rubber fuel bladder (lining) installed on one side. No reason to get up tight, so we caught a dive boat out to Green Island to get in some "fish looking" time in those Great Barrier Reef waters. Returning from a splendid morning in the sea, we found Jim and M.A. had arrived from Sydney, and the work on Tango Charlie Hotel ended. TCH was ready for the Australian skyways.

We headed about due west out of Cairns, passed over Normanton, finally putting down in Burketown for fuel. Jim told me the right engine fuel pump had quit. The right engine would start then, as it remained hot, but wouldn't start cold the next morning if we continued on to our destination of Gregory Downs, near the Queensland border with Northern Territory. It appeared as if we had to spend at least the night, maybe longer, in Burketown looking for a flight mechanic with a fuel pump. Then Jim got into a conversation regarding our problem with the pilot of a small commercial aircraft. The other pilot suggested starting the left engine first, then using cross fuel feed and the left engine fuel pump to prime the right engine. Jim excitedly said, "that'll work," and we climbed aboard TCH and took off for Gregory Downs.

Gregory Downs is a true Outback Australian town (or "road stop" in Austspeak), in the middle of nowhere, consisting of only a few buildings. I couldn't even spot the airstrip in the surroundings of the town, until Jim pointed it out, right in the middle of town, between buildings. What a hair-raising landing it became. The short strip looked only about twelve feet wide with high grass on both sides. I thought sure we'd clip our right wing tip on the steel barn at the threshold of the strip and hook our wheels on the high wire fence marking the strip's boundary, but we did neither and made a smooth pinpoint landing, followed by a taxi into the tall grass for a parking spot. There waiting to meet us stood the motel-restaurant-pub owner to give us, and our luggage, a short ride across the street to his establishment.

The Pub grub proved tasty, but the air felt cold. June is winter in the Outback, Down Under. We all appeared anxious for a snuggle under some warm blankets. The surprise back in our room came from the frogs in the loo (toilet). The frogs find the only place to hang out where water is available, but it sure looks funny to see them crowding up in the toilet! I guess you could say, "Only in the Outback!"

Mid-morning the next day, Jim and I walked over to Tango Charlie Hotel to get her started and the right engine warmed up. Heavy in my pocket lay the collapsible hunting knife Sandia had found earlier on a morning hike along the dry Gregory River with Mary Ann. The left engine started easily, but no amount of fuel feed valve switching could start that buggered right engine. I told Jim I'd hop out of the cockpit to have a look at the right fuel pump. "Give me a couple of minutes, then hit the right fuel pump switch," I told him as I jumped down to the ground.

Crawling up into the nacelle (casing) of the right engine, I found the fuel pump electrical wiring to be intact. Then I heard a click which must have been Jim flipping the switch to the "on" position. Reaching into my pocket, I pulled out the heavy hunting knife and began to tap on the fuel pump body. In an instant, I heard the fuel pump start whirring. I jumped down from the engine nacelle to climb back into the cockpit.

"It's working," I shouted over the left engine noise to Jim.

"I saw it," Jim yelled back, pointing at the right-engine fuel-pressure gauge, which was now indicating proper fuel pump pressure.

The right engine then started like a champ, and we let it warm up for a bit. Later, upon shut down, Jim tried the fuel pump again and it worked fine. Oh, the exact science of a hunting knife "hammer."

A little later, with luggage and ladies on board, we took off for the 850 kilometer (527 mile) trip to Kakadu National Park, just east of Darwin in Northern Territory. Arriving over Kakadu, we landed at a small airstrip in Cooinda, dropped off Mary Ann and Sandia, with our gear, and flew to a bigger airstrip in Jabiru, about 54 kilometers north. There Jim parked the plane and we rented a 4WD Suzuki jeep for touring. By the time we got back to Cooinda in the jeep, the ladies had all the gear stowed in our rooms. It had been a long day. How great that first cold Aussie beer tasted!

Kakadu National Park adjoined the Arnhem Land Aboriginal Reserve, the largest aboriginal reservation in Australia. Kakadu is loaded with Aboriginal Art sites which consist of rock art paintings. My only comment, "awesome art!" A lot of Aboriginal history is depicted in the priorities of the rock paintings. The art showed fishing, especially the Baramundi, the turtles, the hunting, and the people themselves, including drawings of what the experts perceive are the illustrations of the first European encounters, that is a "stick" figure with a pipe in his mouth. Usually the rock art appeared under overhangs, where it was semi-protected from washout and direct sunlight to prevent ultraviolet fading. Also notable, the artwork is never found in dead end gorges, where Aborigines feared superstitiously that they could be trapped by their enemies and killed while working on rock paintings. They always seemed to work under rock overhangs that had several escape routes.

While in Kakadu, we all did a 3.6-kilometer walk through a rainforest area in the Park near the South Alligator River. As we walked, we read from a pamphlet that identified about 24 species of trees, explaining what the Aborigines used each of them for by way of healing and other cultural applications. The walk finished in a billabong area (a backwater forming a stagnant pool) which teemed with wildlife, ranging from fresh water crocodiles, to an abundance of bird life, including egrets and jabirus. Beyond the rainforest area, we encountered some wallabies bounding for their lives from a very fast dingo (wild dog).

The next day we did a jeep trip to Jim-Jim Falls which took the better part of the day. To get there, we had to navigate 50 kilometers of graveled "corduroy" road traveled best at high speed 2WD, followed by an eight-kilometer stretch of road which included some very deep standing water. The water lay so deep, in fact, that we learned to pick our way off road through the trees to get around several of the wet areas. One particular "puddle" we came upon had a big Land Rover Discovery stuck right smack in the middle of the deepest part. Our little rental Suzuki hooked up to his nylon tow rope and on the third try, the Suzuki pulled him out, much to the happiness of the driver's wife, who still sat in the car with her arms crossed, looking a little up tight. We had pulled over to let him speed past us only a short time before he got stuck!

A good half-hour hike from the car park and we stood gazing at the amazing Jim-Jim Falls. The water fell about 215 meters (705 feet) and splashed down into a huge deep dark pool. Nearby, to our amazement, lay a beautiful beach. Remembering our vow to swim to the falls, Jim and I plunged into the deep pool for about a 150-meter swim to the base of the falls. Jim immediately came back out of the water, leaving me to only make it half-way before returning to the warmth of the shore. The water was freezing! It felt so good to dry off, put warm clothes back on, sit in the sun, and eat some food.

Upon returning from Jim-Jim Falls, we all took a previously scheduled river cruise. The life along the river proved abundant. Egrets, jabirus, geese, kingfishers, jehovas, and many other bird species could be seen. We also saw at least three crocodiles; the last big "saltie" (salt-water species of crocodile) just laid there on the riverbank staring at us with only an occasional blink of the eye. He (or she) probably measured fourteen feet in length. What a specimen! I sure didn't want to tangle with him in the water or anywhere else for that matter!

From Kakadu National Park, we aimed Tango Charlie Hotel west into Western Australia for a visit to Purnalulu (the Aboriginal name meaning crumbling sandstone) dubbed Bungle Bungles by the Australians. The Bungles consist of hundreds of strangely rounded rock towers (beehives) probably carved out by ancient sea waves when the oceans stood hundreds of feet higher than modern levels. The towers are horizontally striped in alternate bands of orange and black, due to layers of silica and lichen, respectively. The sandstone formations are so fragile, no form of climbing is allowed.

We landed TCH on a small gravel airstrip in the Bungles National Park and by prior arrangement rented canvas accommodations in a tented campsite, where meals and solar showers were included. Mick and his wife, Marva, ran the camp and guided us on some incredible treks through the strange land formations. We awoke there each morning to the accordion strains of "Morning has broken, like the first morning, Blackbirds are singing, …" and we knew breakfast would soon be ready, along with a different hiking direction.

Leaving the Bungles, we flew over the famous Argyle Diamond Mine, then south over Hall's Creek, and finally down to Uluru, or Ayers Rock, as the Aussies call the sacred Aboriginal site. The best part of Australia's pet rock came from the aerobic workout of a brisk 45 minute walk/climb to the top and then, after a short rest, a 22 minute sprint to the bottom. I believe the vertical rise of Uluru is about 335 meters (1,100 feet), an excellent workout, none the less. Coming down, I wondered what the Aboriginal tribes thought of us tourists climbing all over their sacred site? Obviously, the Australian Government has their permission.

From Uluru, we flew to Alice Springs, to spend an enjoyable evening in Australia's geographic center, before heading off for Coober Pedy in South Australia. Coober Pedy (the Aboriginal name meaning "white fellow's hole in the ground"), the famous opal mining location, is located in the Andamooka Fields, where most life occurs underground. From the air it looked like a moonscape. Most buildings are located underground in the soil conditions which are very susceptible to large augers. I believe they made one of the Mad Max (Mel Gibson) movies in Coober Pedy. We stayed at an underground hotel, ate at underground restaurants, shopped at an underground bookstore, and, in general, explored the underground mining aspects of Coober Pedy. Coming out of the men's room in one restaurant, I curiously asked the owner where the flush of the loo went? He described a deep augured shaft, that if it ever filled up, they'd switch the plumbing to another deep empty shaft. An amazing place, Coober Pedy, with its extremes in temperature, ranging from 122 degrees Fahrenheit in the summer, to very cold in the winter. No wonder everyone took to auguring holes to make earth sheltered living quarters. We

The two of us standing atop Uluru

*The Coober Pedy augured "moonscape"
from a few hundred feet up*

visited in June and it was cold.

Leaving Coober Pedy behind us, we flew the last leg of our trip to Sydney, where Sandia and I caught a commercial flight north to Papua New Guinea. The "mind blowing" Australian Tour had ended. It had again been the opportunity of a lifetime. Now the 4th of July had arrived and we headed for assignments in P.N.G. Time to

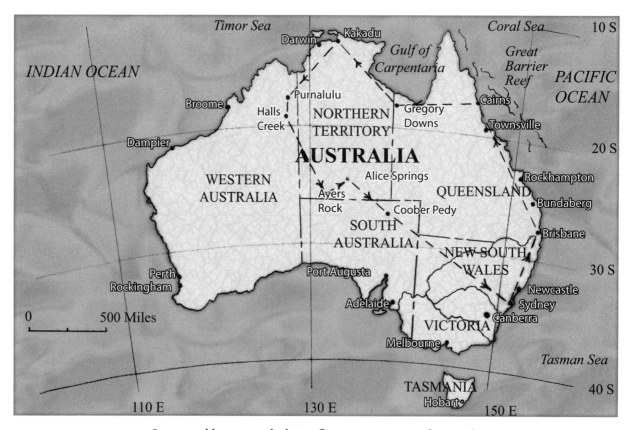

Our monthlong anti-clockwise flying circuit around Australia

buckle down to the challenge of work in that developing nation where the unexpected proved commonplace. Within a few days of our arrival, I stood literally buried in work, this time in the coastal city of Lae, on the Huon Gulf.

My work assignment consisted of, as quickly as possible, setting up a kit house factory, marketing the units, and getting the houses into production as I'd done previously in the mountains of New Guinea.

I borrowed my man, Norbert, from the Total Hardware, Mount Hagen factory, with permission from Steve Hui, the manager, and began work in a vacated steel mechanics' building George Hook found for me on the corner of their Lae lumber/hardware operation. We started by building several large assembly work benches, then bought and had shipped in from

Port Moresby, a big Wadkins 450mm radial arm saw, a 400mm table saw, another smaller radial arm cut-off saw, a large drill press, and brought in three-phase electrical power to run all the equipment. I then, reluctantly, let Norbert head back to the Hagen operation and his family. By that time, I'd recruited seven men to work our new coastal factory, Philip (a previous foreman from Mt. Hagen who traveled all the way from the Porgera Gold Mine to work with me), Doge, Kopi, Dingo, Golo, Ben, and Kambaya (also from Hagen). Soon we had signed orders for four G 42 (three-bedroom units) houses and thirteen more in the final stages of contracting negotiations. We focused in on the prefabrication of the first four kit houses.

I marketed the coastal kit house design as Niugini Haus Kits, "helping to build Papua New

Guinea, one house at a time," obviously a fundamental analogy to a Stateside investor slogan. Total Homes as we dubbed our operation, in short order, had the thirteen G 22 (two-bedroom units) houses under contract, along with another small office building, for a total value of about K300,000 in work. We were on the map. I even taught myself TurboCad (Computer Assisted Design) at night and on weekends from a Xerox copy of Steve Hui's instruction manual and a borrowed back up copy of his software. We could design and build pretty much anything. Total Homes became a real viable business in just short of three months elapsed time. The men and I celebrated the final loading of those four G 42's onto flatbed trucks for delivery to the nearby wharf. From there they would be delivered by ocean transport to Alotau. The Haus Kits would be barged to the distant Milne Bay Province in about four days, where a Total Homes crew, headed by Doge, would receive them and begin assembly. The first house packages completed and shipped from Total Homes made cause for jubilation. My factory men reflected pride in their work and deserved the Friday afternoon reward party we threw in our "new" factory setting.

The Sunday morning following, Jim and M. A. invited us over to their flat for breakfast. Jim said he wanted to talk to us about the business. The gist of the conversation that morning centered on Jim's desire to sell the businesses, for reasons

that shall remain his own. He wondered how long it would take Total Homes to complete the kit houses then under contract and how much financial support I'd need to do it. I explained to Jim that the only uncertain supply I faced lay in the steel bracketing and tie rods required for each house to render them cyclone resistant, basically tying the roof structure all the way down to the foundation beams. The design had been approved and stamped by a P.N.G. Civil Engineer as required. The oil palm plantation, on which the Niugini Haus Kits would be assembled, stood just below 10 degrees South latitude and could experience occasional cyclones. The reader should note that within plus or minus 10 degrees either side of the equator is known as the Equatorial Trough, in which no major storms occur, but beyond, all hell can break loose in the form of gales, cyclones, and hurricanes. I told Jim I'd get onto pushing the fabrication of the required steel cyclone hardware first thing in the morning at the local steel company I had contracted the parts with. Sandia and I told them

One of our Niugini Haus Kits being assembled

we'd help with whatever else they needed to enhance their business sale opportunity. I volunteered to type up a Total Homes proforma, the contracted and realistic projected revenues for the next six months, for use as a sales tool.

Leaving Jim and Mary Ann at their flat, Sandia and I spent the balance of that Sunday, discussing what this new direction meant in our lives. She would help sell down the Total Concept business. I would push the Total Homes schedule; not accepting any new projects to be delivered before the Alotau contract was finished. If Jim successfully sold the companies, we decided to leave the country, not staying on with the new ownership.

A week or so later, an explanation point underscored our decision to leave. Sandia, at the Total Concept showroom/warehouse, only a block away from the Total Hardware/Total Homes facility, sent over one of her girls, Teresa, to pick up a small payroll of about K700, along with the mail. Walking back to Total Concept, carrying the payroll/mail in a bigger manila inter-office mail envelope, she fell under attack by two robbers with bush knives, who hacked away at her until she released her grip on the packet they wanted. This happened so quickly at ten in the morning, in broad daylight. Teresa limped and crawled her way to Sandia's office, wailing at the top of her lung power. Her right arm appeared nearly severed at the elbow (probably from trying to hang onto the package to which she'd been entrusted) and her left knee was chopped up badly. The rest looked to be superficial wounds that would heal. It had to be an inside job, set up by someone in the pay-

*Two of my main men in Lae,
Philip on my right and Wilson on my left*

roll loop. Sandia, understandably freaked out, composed herself and drove Teresa to emergency aid at the Lae Hospital. I didn't hear about the incident until it was over and Sandia came back to Total Concept from the Hospital. She looked pretty shook up. I took her home to our flat for a quiet time, which ended in a realistic discussion of the then present conditions existing in Papua New Guinea. To us, things seemed to be going downhill. The Kina had recently been devalued to about 75 percent of its prior value. In other words, the Total Hardware inventory, which had been valued at four million Kina, now was worth only three million. Expatriate salaries linked to the Kina had likewise been devalued. Landowners downstream of the Porgera Gold Mining effort complained of river pollution and the decrease in their previous quality of life. They hired legal representation from abroad to fight for their rights, but had only limited success to that time. Many New Guineans expressed to me, twenty years after independence, that their oil and mineral rich resources were being depleted to the interests of foreign companies and their own politicians. They felt fear for their country's future, describing similarities to the "rape" of Africa. I heard stories that the millions of tons of tailings and waste rock discharged annually by mining operations into the Fly River System affected life along the river and even began to impact the coral beds far out in the Great Barrier Reef. All of this, and more, served to fortify our recent decision to leave Papua New Guinea behind us. During our initial contract, in the mountains of P.N.G., we'd felt a comfort in being part of a developing nation—teaching skills, creating jobs, and making a small mark on the majestic landscape and its people. This time there just wasn't the same comfort. In fact, beyond those people we worked around and with, Sandia and I felt a real discomfort with the day to day realities of life in P.N.G. I would have stayed with it, in my own stubborn way, but when Jim decided to sell the lot, we knew in our hearts that it had to be "mission accomplished"—time to move on. We'd created a new factory operation, along with quite a few jobs, met more people, taught more skills, and helped our friends, Jim and M. A. It would again turn out a win-win situation.

The date showed the middle of October. I figured that all contracted houses could be delivered in eight to nine weeks, putting us out of P.N.G. by mid-December. Steve Hui had a similar number of houses contracted out of the Mt. Hagen Hailans Homes factory, bringing total kit house projected revenues to the K600,000 plus figure. Jim had begun preliminary discussions with interested buyers. Things were moving!

Sandia took great excitement in planning our trip home this time. She thought about going west through Jayapura into Southeast Asia, specifically Viet Nam, then onto Turkey and finally to the East Coast of the U.S.A. It's always great

to dream. I didn't care, as I focused in on the kit house prefabrication and delivery schedule from our new Lae factory. We couldn't leave until I got it done—a promise is a promise. I felt up to my "eyeballs," to use a phrase, in the coordination of it all.

We managed to get seven houses prefabricated and shipped to Alotau in one lot the first week of November. The days flew by! Suddenly it seemed we could probably leave a bit earlier than previously anticipated. The Total Homes factory system appeared better oiled than I thought. Saturday overtime for my men helped the schedule a bunch. The office building lay near completion. We would ship it separately, leaving just a final lot of six houses to finish the contract with the Alotau oil palm plantation for their staff housing.

Sandia finally figured out that Turkey would be too cold in the winter, so we figured on just heading south to Port Douglas, our favorite beach community, for a bit of beach bumming, then onto the States and Colorado.

My men seemed a little nervous with the uncertainty of the rumor of our departure and the possible sale of the company. I'm sure it shook up the job security they'd felt earlier on, but they kept their assignments moving along.

Then Jim found potential buyers and I flew with him in Romeo Papa Tango up to Goroka in the mountains to work out the details. After two days of negotiations, the deal was signed and Jim had his contract copies and deposit checks tucked away in his briefcase. Reaching the Goroka Airport, we found one small setback in the form of a dead battery in our dependable aircraft, along with a driving rainstorm, but it couldn't quench the excitement of the moment. I got drenched while doing my first propeller pull-through by hand, but RPT faithfully kicked over and I climbed aboard, with both hands still in-

355

tact, searching for a towel. We lifted off through the rainstorm, climbing above the clouds to find much sunnier weather. Everything was falling into place now.

In typical fashion, as the number of days grew shorter, the workload got heavier. In addition to the Milne Bay/Alotau project houses, refurbishing some of the handover properties fell under my umbrella. To accomplish this, I absconded with some of the lumberyard employees and put them to work as painters and carpenters, fixing up six staff flats to be included in the business purchase agreement. I kept my own factory guys hard at the prefabrication of those last houses to Alotau. All of it, along with the necessities of leaving as well, sure made time pass quickly. I commissioned two of my factory guys to build Sandia and I a strong shipping crate, into which we put personal things, along with a few P.N.G. artifacts, for a long ocean voyage to the States. We'd be left with carrying only our ever-dependable frame packs out of Papua New Guinea.

It seemed only a moment passed, before we found ourselves in Port Douglas, Australia. The date was the 3rd of December '95. My head whirled with reflections of New Guinea-declining a last minute offer from the new ownership to stay on at Total Homes, Norbert's voice on the telephone wishing us warm farewells, my man Philip's brave smiles, Dingo's tears, all the Hardware guys responding to my "thank you's,"

our friend Wilson and I doing one last Wahgi War Call together, waiting at the Lae Airport with Frank Faulkner during a not so unusual flight departure delay, a XXXX beer on the flight to Cairns, then six hours of deep sleep in a Cairns backpackers' lodge. Awaking, we caught the Port O'Call shuttle to Port Douglas, where we skidded out for several days. The local life remained a "hoot." My lady and I shared a "pot of piss" in a local pub when a "pub crawl" came through, mostly women. The object of the crawl was to drink a pint in each pub in Port Douglas. All I could say from that observation, "Some of those Aussie women represent a tough breed!" Maybe it comes from the "Sheila" mentality some of the Aussie men put on the women, sort of a "chicken/egg" thing. Those women could certainly drink us under the table.

When the "pub crawl" left us, my lady and I started making some comments about getting back into shape, then the waitress came over with two more "pots"—the shape thing could wait one more day!

A well deserved "pot of piss" in Port Douglas and, perhaps, our final farewell salute to P.N.G.

Epilogue

Life back in the States settled into the purchase of a townhouse northwest of Denver, from which we could come and go at our pleasure. Sandia trained and took a job with a major airline as a flight attendant. I guess traveling gets into one's blood. Myself, I began teaching freshman and sophomore physics at a local college until a sweetheart of a little granddaughter needed us. Bad decisions and choices by her parents (my daughter), and others entrusted with her care, regarding drugs and alcohol, left the little one traumatized in foster care. She is with us now and every day, my lady and I fight with passion, to give our little one a chance at life. She deserves nothing less than the best opportunity. All the adult issues can go straight to hell, as far as we are concerned. The interests of the children have to come first. I don't know what it says about the society around us, but many more than five million kids are now being raised by their grandparents—and that's only the one's of record. We've joined a grandparents' support group. The situations described at those meetings almost always involve the abuse of drugs and alcohol, leaving the little ones in a tragic wake of neglect and abuse. Some of the stories seem downright scary. Dealing with the trauma and neglect of our own little now seventh grader

the choices we make,
can cause them such strife

God help the children,
and their chance at life

is the toughest thing I've ever done, but truly the most meaningful. Perhaps everything we've done and experienced has just been an apprenticeship to bring to this little one's chance at life. She improves day by day—singing songs, painting happy pictures, and smiling have slowly replaced the grim negativism. My shins don't ache anymore from being kicked. Her perspective, although fragile at best, has brightened. She teaches us about the joys of childhood. She definitely now chooses to see a world lit up by sunshine. We all have that choice. Each morning, upon awakening, we alone choose how to view that, which is served up on our "plate," to feed us that day. Savor the taste of life. Let it nourish your spirit. The "meal" of life is the greatest opportunity we'll ever have to share in. Sure, sometimes things happen that appear difficult to deal with, but they'll just make the happy times seem even happier. It's part of the balance in life. Just enjoy and breathe deeply. Set reasonable goals, but be willing to take a risk. The awesome voyage on the sea of life is too short to waste time dropping anchor in murky waters. Keep the fresh breath of free winds full into your sails. Study your charts and circle some out of the way harbor. Be ready to explore someplace new. You can only discover, if you're willing to explore. That next port-of-call will be a fabulous experience! It doesn't have to be halfway around the world. It could be close to your home port. Just make sure to share it with someone you love. Make some great memories. They will surely nourish your spirit later in life.

Thanks for reading and sharing our humble journeys.

The Devine Weaver

My life is but a weaving
    Between my God and me;
I cannot choose the colors
    He worketh steadily.
Oft times He weaveth sorrow
    And I in foolish pride,
Forget that He seeth the upper,
    And I the underside.
Not till the loom is silent
    And the shuttles cease to fly,
Shall God unroll the canvas
    And explain the reason why.
The dark threads are as needful
    In the Weaver's skillful hand,
As the threads of gold and silver
    In the pattern He has planned.

Author Unknown

*A visit with our little feisty one at four years
of age back while she was in foster care*

*Backcountry camping in the
Colorado Mountains at five years*

*Our young lady, a few years later,
while traveling in Mexico*

FOR ADDITIONAL COPIES OF THIS BOOK, VISIT
www.wokabautpublishing.com

OR EMAIL
sales@wokabautpublishing.com